汪兆銘政権人名録 OSS（米諜報機関）1944 年作成
BIOGRAPHIES OF PUPPET CHINA（OSS, 1944）

編集・解題　三輪宗弘

クロスカルチャー出版

凡　　例

1．本書は、米国国立公文書館Ⅱの「BIOGRAPHIES OF PUPPET CHINA」（RG226, Entry: A1-154, Box: 85）を底本とした。タイトルは『汪兆銘政権人名録― OSS（米諜報機関）1944 年作成』とし、英文タイトルは「BIOGRAPHIES OF PUPPET CHINA（OSS, 1944）」と表記した。

2．DECLASSIFIED のスタンプは最初と最後だけ示した。他は削除した。

3．解題に使用した OSS 作成「STRUCTURE AND PERSONNEL OF THE NANKING PUPPET GOVERNMENT（AND HONG KONG）」は英国国立公文書館で編者が撮影したものを使った。請求番号は WO208/2886 である。英国国立公文書館所蔵の資料は手書きで漢字名が加筆されている。

4．解題は編者三輪宗弘と Tai Wei LIM（英文）が執筆し、LIM 氏には海外の英語文献の紹介をお願いした。

5．曽支農氏の学位論文『汪政権による「淪陥区」社会秩序の再建過程に関する研究―『汪偽政府行政院会議録』の分析を中心として―』（国立国会図書館関西館所蔵、東京大学）から組織図や人事異動一覧などを解題で紹介した。

6．復刻に際し適宜縮小して収めた。

汪兆銘政権人名録 OSS（米諜報機関）1944年作成
BIOGRAPHIES OF PUPPET CHINA（OSS, 1944）

目　　　次

解題……………………………………………………………… 1～42

BIOGRAPHIES OF PUPPET CHINA ……………………………… 45～304

汪兆銘政権人名録 OSS（米諜報機関）1944年作成
BIOGRAPHIES OF PUPPET CHINA（OSS, 1944）

解　　題

三　輪　宗　弘
（九州大学記録資料館教授）

Tai Wei LIM
（Senior Lecturer Singapore University of
Social Sciences and National University
of Singapore Research Fellow Adjunct）

『汪兆銘政権人名録』解題　　　　　　　　　　　　　　三輪宗弘

　米国国立公文書館Ⅱの RG226（Entry#: A1-154、Box#: 85）の中に OSS（Office of Strategic Service）の作成した『汪兆銘政権人名録』（*BIOGRAPHIES OF PUPPET CHINA*）があったので、これは貴重な資料だと思い、コピーを取った。OSS が日本のラジオ放送を傍受し、その記録と公刊物から汪兆銘政権に関係ある人物を網羅しようとしたものである。**表1「汪兆銘政権漢字表記、英語表記対照表」**には主要な人物の中国語簡体字表記、漢字日本語表記、英語での二通り表記（ウェード式ローマ字表記とピンイン）の対照表を示した。この対照表を大いに活用していただきたい。中国人に関しては公刊物の情報も加えられているため、充実した内容であるが、日本人に関してはラジオ放送の傍受の記録を付け足した簡単なもので、残念ながら役には立たない。文芸評論家の小林秀雄が登場するのには驚いた。宣伝部長林柏生と大学時代から親交のあった詩人草野心平の名前はなかった。ドイツ、イタリアなどの外交官やカトリック教会の宣教師の名前も出てくるが、どのような人たちが中国にいたのかわかる程度である。中国人に関しては、年鑑などの情報も取り入れられたことは言うまでもない。OSS の Research and Analysis Branch が 1945 年 1 月 12 日付けで刊行した「STRUCTURE AND PERSONNEL OF THE NANKING PUPPET GOVERNMENT（AND HONG KONG）」の情報も加味されている。英国国立公文書館（TNA）にも所蔵されており、請求番号は WO208/2886 である。TNA 所蔵の冊子の中には手書きの漢字が書き込まれた「アルファベット順の人名リスト」があったので、**表2「WO208/2886 氏名リスト」**という名前を付けて掲げた。『汪兆銘政権人名録（OSS 作成）』の利用に活用され、氏名の漢字と英文綴りの照合に役立ち、効率よく調べることができるだろう。「*」印は『汪兆銘政権人名録（OSS 作成）』にリストアップされていない人物である。

　今回世に出した『汪兆銘政権人名録』は、すでにマイクロフィルム（O.S.S./ State Department Intelligence and Research Reports, Part I Japan and Its Occupied Territories During World War II Part 1 Reel 3）として公刊されているとは気づかず、これは資料集として公刊したら多くの研究者に有用だろうと思い、猪の如く猛進した。国立国会図書館憲政資料室で閲覧できる。当時筆者が関心を持っていたのは、汪兆銘政権の中に重慶の国民党と八路軍（共産党）のスパイが送り込まれ、それに OSS がどのように関与していたのか、していなかったのかという点にあった。華北労工協会などを通して、昭和 19 年（1944）に組織的に密偵（特務工作員）が日本に労務者として送り込まれたのではないかというのが筆者の仮説であり、裏付けを取る資料が OSS の資料群の中にあるのではないかという仮説で資料を探し回っていた。また日本に昭和 19 年に来た労務者の 1000 人当たりの死亡率が 200 という通常考えられない高い数字であり、日本人労働者と戦時動員された朝鮮人労働者の死亡率が 5/1000 と比較すると異常な値である。筆者はなぜこのように高いのか、何らかの原因があるはずだと考え、裁判記録や裁判の報告書を読んだが、来日した直後に死亡していることがこの異常な数値 200 の原因であることがわかってきた。筆者は衰弱した労務者が故意に送り込まれ、その

中に共産党と国民党の健康なスパイも紛れ込まされていたという見通しを立てた。かかる問題意識の中で、米国国立公文書館や英国国立公文書館で資料捜索の最中に、この『汪兆銘政権人名録（OSS 作成）』に遭遇し、工作員を送り込んだ人物を特定できるかもしれないと欣喜雀躍したのである。

　汪兆銘政権は、日本では「傀儡」と揶揄され、中国では「汪偽（「汪兆銘偽国民政府」の略称）政権」と烙印を押され、今回刊行する英文には「PUPPET CHINA」と書かれている。筆者はたまたま 2018 年 11 月に中国国営テレビの「汪偽政権」の TV 番組（王暁華氏の授業形式）の文字を見ながら、日本に協力した裏切り者を丹念に放映する番組を凝視した。呉佩孚が日本に条件を突き付け、参加しなかった点を高く評価され、潔癖な人格者であったと評価され、一方で汪偽政権の軍隊や警察を組織した人物として王克敏や葉蓬は唾棄すべき悪玉であった。特務工作関係の胡蘭成は張愛玲の元夫と紹介されていた。この番組を眺めながら、軍閥の取り込みに失敗した点が汪兆銘政権の致命的な弱点になったと納得した。視点には教えられることが多く、私にはいい勉強になった。中国人の自分の意志で日本と「和平」を結ぼうとした人たちがいたが故に、「汪偽」と今でも断罪されているのだと閃き、これは研究するに値すると直截的に思った。蒋介石はアメリカの傀儡と呼ばれないのは何故なのだろうか。米国の財政援助に頼らなければならなかったのではないのか。なぜ蒋介石は対日戦に勝利したにもかかわらず、手に入れかかった中国の統一に失敗して、大陸から台湾に逃げ出さなくてはならなかったのだろうか。日本の敗戦後、汪兆銘政権を傘下に収め、日本軍に示したように汪兆銘政権幹部にたいしても復讐せずに徳を持って対処できなかったのだろうか。日本人にできても、中国人にできなかったのはなぜなのだろうか。ニューヨーク郊外のハイドパークにある F. D. ローズベルト大統領図書館に所蔵されている財務省モーゲンソー関係文書には国民党への財政支援、法幣への膨大な資金援助が記録されている。通貨の信用力という点で、日本が行った汪兆銘政権への財政援助と米国が蒋介石国民党政権に行った財政援助の比較は行わなければならないだろう。F. D. ローズベルト大統領図書館所蔵の資料はネットで公開されており、また現物も同図書館で閲覧することができる。

　曽支農氏の学位論文『汪政権による「淪陥区」社会秩序の再建過程に関する研究─『汪偽政府行政院会議録』の分析を中心として─』（国立国会図書館関西館所蔵、東京大学）で 31 巻からなる中国第二歴史档案館編『汪偽政権政府行政院会議録・国内版』の資料を主に駆使して組織の変遷を丁寧に追っているが、「はじめに」で問題点として「学術的かつ客観的な史料分析・検証が乏しく、政治先行的な論断による推測的なものが多かったことである。特に中国・台湾側における研究は、殆ど汪政権＝「傀儡政権」の断罪の裏付け・指摘・批判に力点を置く傾向が顕著である。」と指摘している。鋭い指摘でこの点にこそ今後の研究課題があるだろう。同氏の学位論文の別冊には人事や組織の変遷の図表があり、「汪政権各方面代表人物の経歴」「汪兆銘南京政府研究参考文献目録」も、解題を書くに際して参照させていただいた。公開されている文献を丁寧に読み込んだ、素晴らしい学術的な貢献である。同氏の作成した図表を後段に**表 A** から**表 E** として一括して掲げた。さらに関心を持た

れた方は国立国会図書館関西館で曽支農氏の学位論文を閲覧請求されたい。

　筆者は2018年11月に中国第二歴史档案館を訪問したが、汪兆銘政権に関する資料は相当残っていた。資料の大海の中で、戦時中日本へ行った労務者に関する、華北政務委員会の労働者関係の資料を13件開示請求したが、許可されたのは4件だけであった。今後資料の公開がすすみ、通説が二転三転するだろうと資料を眺めながら思いを巡らした。日本軍や日本人顧問の意で動く、傀儡政権ならばここまで資料が残るのだろうか、と思った。様々な研究テーマで、すでに公刊された資料も丁寧に読めば新しい見方を提示できるだろう。「傀儡」「敗北主義者」「偽政権」という評価を貶めるレッテルは張られ過ぎた。この流れに疑義を呈している研究もある。日本では先駆的に高橋久志、土屋光芳、柴田哲雄、新地比呂志などによって、資料や回想録に基づいた学術的な研究論文が世に問われていることを付記しておく。若い研究者が手に取るべき研究業績であろう。

　南京市にある中国国立公文書館である「第二歴史档案館」の所蔵資料は、『第二歴史档案館利用指南』を紐解くのがよい。「第四章　日偽档案」には22の「全宗号」からなっている。全宗号は米国国立公文書館のRecord GroupとEntryの中間の分量の資料群であろう。一斑を挙げよう。「汪偽国民党中央政治委員会」(1940－1945)の全宗号の番号は「2006」であり、「汪偽国民政府」(1940－1945)は「2002」で、「汪偽外交部」(1940－1945)は「2061」で、「偽臨時政府行政委員会」(1937－1940)は「2014」で、「偽中華民国維新政府」(1938－1940)は「2001」である。

　南京市档案館編『審訊汪偽漢奸筆録』(江蘇古籍出版社　上・下　王春南責任編輯)には以下の22名の漢奸裁判に関する資料が記録されている。目次に欠落があったが、ネットで簡単にダウンロードできる。登場人物は以下の通りである。

1 陳公博　2 周仏海　3 褚民誼　4 温宗亮　5 江亢虎　6 陳璧君　7 梅思平　8 林柏生　9 李聖五　10 丁黙邨　11 陳春団　12 羅君強　13 王蔭泰　14 蔡培　15 袁愈佺　16 鄧祖禹　17 伍澄宇　18 楊惺華　19 殷汝耕　20 劉玉書　21 汪時璟　22 周作人

　益井康一『漢奸裁判史　1946－1948』(みすず書房、1977年)の巻末に「主要人物の経歴」があり有用である。特に「十八　特務工作隊「七十六号」」(196～219頁)には、蒋介石政府のCC団と藍衣社という特務工作機関と丁黙鄭と李士群の「七十六号」について紙幅を割いている。同書によれば、丁と李の集めた特務工作員は「三〇〇人余、これを行動隊に一五〇人、市党部、新聞関係に二〇人、情報関係に二〇人、通信暗号解読班に四〇人」(201頁)を配置したと記述されている。周仏海は特務工作機関「七十六号」と密接にかかわっていたことは押さえておかねばならない。周仏海と国民党の特務機関のトップ戴笠との関係、共産党の諜報機関との関係は調べなければならない。米国のOSS、英国のSOE、国民党のCC団と藍衣社、共産党の特務機関、「七十六号」の地下活動も解明していくべき課題であろう。また劉傑『漢奸裁判　対日協力者を襲った運命』(中央新書、2000年)の参考文

献一覧もよくまとまっているので、参照されたい。同書には、周仏海と国民政府軍事委員会調査統計局（軍統局）との関係についても言及されている（219～221頁）。呈蔡徳金編『周仏海日記』（みすず書房、村田忠禧他訳、1992年）は基本的な文献である。安藤徳器編訳『汪精衛自叙傳』（昭和16年）も基本文献である。汪兆銘から捉えた中国の問題点が鋭く指摘され、日本との関係でどのような克服すべき問題点があったのか、よくわかる。

　以下引用する資料は、蒋介石と汪兆銘の対立が「和平」をめぐり妥協できなくなり、反蒋介石への動きになったことを伝えている。その間に、後段で触れる、ハノイへの脱出そして暗殺未遂事件が起きる。二人の対立は修復不可能になった。

　「汪ハ重慶政権内部ノ和平派ヲ獲得スル為蒋ニ和平ヲ勧告セントシ最後迄努力シ現ニ重慶脱出直前ニ於テハ長時間ニ亘リ蒋ト未曾有ノ激論ヲ闘ハシ物別レトナリタリ」（矢野領事「渡邊工作現地報告」41頁、「竹内工作一件　上海ニ於ケル工作」、外務省外交史料館所蔵『支那事変ニ際シ支那新政府樹立関係一件　矢野記録　第三巻』請求番号「Ａ－6－1－1、8－5」）

　「現ニ存在スル北支、中支等ノ諸政権ハ必スシモ解消スルコトヲ要求スル次第ニハ非ス既存ノモノハ能フ限リ其ノ儘トスル考ナリ」（同上、54頁）

　「北支ノ王克敏ヨリハ懇篤丁重ナル書簡ニ接シ居リ維新側ノ陳群及任援道ヨリハ汪ノ出馬ノ際ハ之ニ合流スル旨ノ書簡ニ接シ居レリ」（同上、54頁）

　「日本政府ハ汪精衛ヲ中心トシテ中央政府樹立工作ニ専念スルモノナリヤ又呉佩孚其他ノ利用ヲ考慮スルモノナリヤ」（「梁、陳、任、三氏トノ会見記録」（昭和十四年五月二十六日）、興亜院華中連絡部、同上、13号）

　「「汪」「呉」工作指導腹案」（同上、16号別紙）では「汪ヲシテ呉及既成政権等ト協力シ文武ノ実力ヲ具備セル強力ナル政府ヲ樹立」とあるように、「呉汪先ツ合作」、「既存政権等ト協力」「重慶政府諸勢力就中其ノ要人ヲ獲得」によって「基盤地盤ヲ確立」することで「文武ノ実権ヲ具備セル強力ナル政府ヲ樹立セシム」意向であった。昭和14年6月6日の「五相会議決定」の「新中央政府樹立方針」の中で「一、新中央政府ハ、汪、呉、既存政権、翻意改善ノ重慶政府等ヲ以テ其ノ構成分子トナシ支那側ノ問題トシテ此等ノ適宜協力ニ依リ之ヲ樹立スヘキモノナリ」とされたが、呉佩孚の協力が得られなかった。

　上の点に関連して、『太平洋戦争の道　別巻　資料編』（朝日新聞社、昭和38年）に掲載された「五相応酬要領」（285～86頁）の「「呉」工作指導腹案」の中で「2　呉ノ名義ヲ以テ実施スル重慶政府ノ軍権切崩シ工作ハ之ヲ益々強化ス右工作ハ同時ニ新中央政府ノ軍隊建設工作ノ意義ヲ有スル如ク指導スルモノトス」とあるが、呉佩孚の合作に期待したものは軍備の充実という狙いであったことが読み取れる。日本の陸軍は汪兆銘の弱点が軍事力にあったことを見抜き、その弱点を補うのが呉の取り込みであった。汪兆銘からすれば、呉工作の失敗は軍事力の点で、日本軍に頼るしかなくなったことを意味した。

　陳昌祖『陳昌祖回顧録　汪精衛との日々』（下田貴美子訳、羊亭社、2014年）は一読すべき

文献である。陳昌祖は、汪兆銘の妻陳璧君の弟であり、事実上の母親代わりであり、家族関係を伝え、汪兆銘と陳璧君への愛情ある記述で溢れている。陳璧君の父親は錫の鉱脈の発見で財をなした華僑であった。フランスで一緒に過ごした、曽仲鳴と結婚した方君璧のことも回想している。ハノイで藍衣社（蒋介石の組織したスパイグループ）に襲撃され、亡くなった曽仲鳴と重傷を負った方君璧の「ハノイの悲劇」（1939 年 3 月 21 日）に関して、同じ家に住み、惨劇を目撃した陳昌祖の記述には迫力があり、汪兆銘が殺害されなかったのがまったくの幸運であったことがわかる。この暗殺未遂は蒋介石と汪兆銘の決裂につながったことは明白であろう。

　「蒋介石が、一方では和解をちらつかせながら、一方では自分を殺すような指令を出していたことで、四哥・汪精衛は蒋介石をもはや信用できなくなったのである。」（179 頁）

　陳昌祖の兄の陳耀祖が 1940 年（昭和 15）に広東省の省長に指名され、1943 年に藍衣社によって暗殺され、陳春圃が継ぎ、汪兆銘の死後、個人的な理由で職を辞めたと記されている。姉の陳璧君は陳昌祖に「広東に行って省長の地位を引き受けてくれないかと私に切り出した」（210 頁）とある。陳昌祖が断ったため、褚民誼に頼むことになったと回顧している（211 頁）。褚民誼はフランス留学中に接点ができ、汪兆名と親交があった（41 頁参照）。陳璧君の弟でなければ知り得ない人事の裏側や人間関係を明らかにしている。
　日本の 1945 年 8 月 15 日の敗戦とともに、事態は一変した。陳昌祖の回想は生々しい。
　8 月 16 日に陳公博は南京政府の解散を宣告し、「一握りの重慶の官吏たちが政府機関を接収するために飛行機で南京に到着した。日本の占領下で長いこと潜んでいた蒋介石の秘密警察はその隠れ家から出て、街をうろつき、好きなように略奪、強姦、殺人を行った。」「蒋介石から送られた官吏が、占領下に潜んでいた秘密警察よりましというわけではなかった。…中略…彼らの傲慢さは限りがなく、そして威張ることといったら信じられないくらいだった。」（213 頁）と綴っている。陳昌祖は軍の「空軍の長」という理由で 9 月 25 日に逮捕され（216 頁）、1 年間拘束されたが「私は死刑判決を受ける代わりに、十二年間収監の判決を受けた。理由は簡単だった。私のかつての先生だった呉稚暉氏が私のために蒋介石に話してくれたのだ。」（223 頁）このように軍関係者の判決は恣意的であったのだろう。
　蒋介石と共産党との内戦に関して、「重慶から戻ってきた官僚たちが日本占領期間の間の税金をさかのぼって集めようとしたことである。」（227 頁）と指摘して、「住民たちを怒らせ、共産党の側に追いやった」と述べ、共産党政権の下でも自分たちの境遇はこれ以上悪くなりようがない」と感じて、「二つの選択肢のなかから共産党を選んだのである。」（228 頁）との洞察を披露している。軍事的な装備などで圧倒的に有利であった国民党が台湾に逃げ出すに至った原因を鮮やかに鋭く抉っている。
　四姐陳璧君は蘇州監獄から上海監獄に移された。共産党政権下でも救出の動きはあり、孫文夫人・宋慶齢と何香凝の尽力で「汪兆銘とその和平運動の理念や主義とは関係ないと公式に認めれば監獄から出す」（236 頁）ということになったが、「四姐・陳璧君は、そうす

ることを拒絶し」、1959 年 6 月 17 日に 68 歳の生涯を上海監獄で閉じたと書かれている。

　事実上の親代わりであった汪兆銘と陳璧君に対して「彼らを歴史のページのなかの正しい場所に置くだろう。私は二人のことを、二人の為したことを、二人の勇気と謙虚さを、二人が不正と止むことなく戦ったことを、二人が逆境に対したときの冷静さを誇りに思う。」（237 頁）と述べている。

　陳璧君の人脈を確認しておこう。いわゆる「公館派」と呼ばれているグループである。汪兆銘夫人陳璧君、妹婿褚民誼、弟陳耀祖、甥陳春圃、林柏生、李士群、周隆庠である（劉傑『漢奸裁判』135 頁参照）。殺された曽仲鳴と結婚した方君璧や女性闘士の曽醒も入れてよいであろう。

　脱線するが、邵毓麟『抗日戦勝利の前後―中国からみた終戦秘話―』（本郷賀一訳、時事通信社、昭和 43 年）によれば、国民党の参謀本部次長劉斐、作戦部長郭汝瑰は、国民党に放たれていた共産党スパイであったと書かれている（135 頁）。国民党の特務の元締め戴笠の事故死が特務機関に与えたマイナスを記述している。邵毓麟は蒋介石を高く評価する一方で、汪兆銘への評価が対照的に低いのは当然である。邵が同書で師と仰ぐ王芃生は、TNAの資料によればイギリスの SOE が資金を提供していた。国民党が台湾へ逃げなければならなかった考察は陳昌祖回想録と読み比べられたい。また読者諸賢には、汪兆銘のライバルであった蒋介石の日記もぜひ紐解いていただきたい。

　汪兆銘の考え方を拾っておこう。汪兆銘が 1939 年（昭和 14）6 月 12 日に米内光政海軍大臣との会談で以下の骨子の考え方を披露している（「米内海相、汪会談要領」、『極東国際軍事裁判記録 88』、国立公文書館所蔵、法務省－平成 11 年度－4B－22－2126）。

「汪、自分ハ今次ノ事変ニ関スル貴国政府ノ声明ヲ読ミ、日本ノ真意ハ要スルニ（一）蘇連ノ支那ニ対スル赤化即チ東洋ニ対スル蘇連ノ脅威ヲ防止スルタメ支那ヲ援ケテ其ノ発展ヲ図リ反共ノ共同目標ノ下ニ新東亜ヲ建設セントスルニアリ、（二）決シテ彼ノ英国ガ印度ニ対シ臨ミタルガ如キ態度ヲ採ルモノニ非ザルコトヲ諒解セリ、事変以来支那国民一般ハ此ノ機会ニ支那ガ日本ノタメ侵略セラレ支配セラルヽニ至ルニ非ズヤト疑ヒ不安ニ駆ラレツヽアリ、若シ日本ノ真意ガ果シテ自分ノ諒解シ居ル如キモノナリトセバ右国民ノ不安ハ総テ解消スベシ共産党ノ問題ハ一層重大ナリ支那ハ一九二四年ヨリ一九二六年迄共産党ヲ容レ所謂容共政策ヲ取リタルガ当時自分ハ政府部内ニ在リ種々ノ困難ニ遭遇セル経験アリ一九二六年共産党ヲ排斥シテ、以後ハ倒共ノタメ、約十年ニ亘リ多大ノ犠牲ヲ払ヒ来レルコト御承知ノ通リナルガ今次ノ事変発生ト共ニ蒋介石ハ再ヒ容共政策ヲ採ルニ至レリ自分ハ之ニ対シテハ絶対反対ノ態度ヲ持シ屢々其ノ不可ナルヲ進言セルモ容ルヽ所トナラス、爾来二年間、共産党ハ益々猖獗ヲ極メ東洋ノ事態愈々危険トナルニ至レリ依ツテ自分ハ日本ト提携シテ反共ノ事ニ従ハント決意シタル次第ニテ其ノ第一歩ノ工作トシテハ先ヅ国民党ヲシテ日本ノ要望スル二点即チ共同防共ト日支提携ヲ接受セシメ所謂東亜新秩序ノ建設ニ努力シタキ考ヘナリ、今回ノ訪日モ此ノ工作ノタメ貴国政府当局ノ意見ヲ徴スルニアリ

タル次第ナルガ幸一昨日米総理大臣、陸軍大臣ニ会見シ今日ハ親シク閣下ト会談スルコト
ヲ得タルハ光栄ノ至リナリ」（傍点　引用者）

　汪兆銘が共産党や共産主義に対して批判的な態度を取ったことがわかる。英国国立公文
書館に残されている汪兆銘関係資料の中には、汪兆銘を「反共主義者」として捉えている
資料が残されている。米国の資料が「傀儡」としている資料が多いのとは違っていると筆
者は思った。上の米内海軍大臣との会談で、汪兆銘は蒋介石と決裂に至った背景には共産
主義に対する姿勢「容共政策」にあったことを明確に述べている。

　汪兆銘と日本側との交渉記録を読んでいて面白いと思う点は、日本側が蒋介石には妥協
できなくても、汪兆銘ならどこまで妥協できると考えたのか、実際に妥協したのかという
点である。この点がはっきり表れたのは満洲の帰属問題、満洲からの日本軍の撤兵問題で
あった。この点への理解は、日中間の「歴史認識」を考えるうえで示唆に富んでいる。今
日でも生きた歴史の教材だろう。妥協できなくとも突っ込んで話せた点は何であったのだ
ろうか。筆者には知的好奇心が湧き上がるテーマである。

　以下引用しよう。1934 年の汪兆銘の見解である。昭和 9 年 4 月 2 日に南京の須磨弥吉郎
総領事から廣田外務大臣に送られた電文第 368 号である（『極東国際軍事裁判弁護関係資料
494』、国立公文書館所蔵、法務省－平成 11 年－4B－22－3063）。

　「（一）両国ハ共存共栄スヘキモノタルコト併モ其ノ共存共栄ハ国家百年ノ計（タル？）
ヘキモノニシテ一時的ノモノニ非ズ更ニ例言スレハ若シ日本カ支部ヲ持ツニ英国ノ印度ニ
対スルト同様ニ遇スルコトナク恰モ独、墺両国ノ如キ関係ヲ結フニ於テハ両国ノ共栄ハ容
易ニ実現セラルヘク又日本トシテモ之ニ依リ英国ノ印度ニ対スルヨリヨリ以上ノ利益ヲ収
メ得ルモノト考ヘ居ル次第ナリ、（二）次ニ現在両国ノ隔離セル原因ハ満洲問題ニシテ之ニ
対シ両国ノ主義ハ根本的ニ相違シ居ル処此ノ原因問題ニ触ルルシテ到底事態ノ改善困難ナ
ル現状ニ鑑ミ茲ニ両国ハ満洲問題ヲ将来誠意且ツ和平ノ方法ヲ以テ解決ストノ原則ヲ定メ
度シ即チ換言スレハ今後日本モ武力ヲ以テセス又支那モ亦義務軍等（ノ？）力ヲ以テ対抗
セス双方和平的方法ニテ解決ストノ趣旨ヲ定ムル次第ナリ右二原則ノ設定ニ対スル貴見如
何ト申出タリ。
三、依テ本使ハ御話ノ中（一）ニ付テハ本使就任当時貴下ノ御意見モアリ本使ニ於テ全然
同感ノ旨、答ヘ置キタル通ニテ何レノ点ヨリ見ルモ両国カ共存共栄ス可キモノタルコトハ
何等異議アル可キ筋合ノモノニ非ザル処（二）ノ点ハ果シテ如何ナルコトヲ意味スルモノ
ナリヤト不審シタル上抑々満洲国ノ存在ハ既成ノ事実ニシテ之ヲ如何トモ変更スル余地ナ
キコトハ既ニ累次本使ヨリ言明シタル通ナリ従ツテ此ノ事実ニ触ルルモノナルニ於テハ全
然考慮ノ余地無シトシテ一応釘ヲ刺シ置キタルニ汪ハ支那側ノ立場ヨリ云ヘハ満洲問題解決
セサル限リ国民ノ感情ハ止マス例ヘハ親善モ困難ナル事態ニテ而モ国民ハ満洲ノ回復ヲ前

提トシ居ル次第ニ付此ノ点ニ鑑ミ前□（二）ノ原則ニ依リ国民ニ対シ拠リ所ヲ示ス必要ア
ル次第ナリトテ尚種々迂遠ナル論ヲ試ミ居リタルガ

四、本使ヨリ満洲事件発生ノ原因ハ貴下モ充分承知シ居ラルル筈ナルカトテ簡単ニ日露戦
後ノ経緯既往ニ於ケル独立的事実張家ノ不法等ニ関シ一言シタル上此ノ際寧ロ支那カ東亜
ノ大局ニ着眼シ釈然トシテ既往ノ感情ヲ捨テ一歩ヲ進メテ日清支三国共存共栄ノ方針ニ出
ヅル事、我方ノ希望スル処ナリトノ趣旨ヲ述ヘタルニ

五、汪ニ右既往ノ経緯ニ付テハ充分ニ了解シ居レリ自分ハ犬養内閣当時満洲問題解決ノ機
会有リシニ拘ラズ、遂ニ其ノ機ヲ失シタルモノト考ヘ居ルカ、現在トナリテハ支那国民ト
シテハ此ノ儘ニテ日本ト親善セヨト言フモ到底了解出来ザル次第ナルカ例ヘハ満洲問題ハ
両国間ニ於ケル海上ノ暗礁ト等シク之ヲ取去必要有ル処今直ニ取リ去ル事ハ困難ナルニ付
該当暗礁ヲ一時其ノ儘保留シ置キタル儘船ヲ通航セシメントスル次第ナリ即チ右ノ如キ原
則ヲ定メ置ケハ国民モ拠リ所カ出来ル次第ナリト述ヘタルニ付本使ハ更ニ右汪ノ例言ヲ一
応繰返シテ念ヲ押シ即チ満洲問題ハ解決困難ナルニ付其ノ儘保留シ置クモ、右ノ如キ原則
設定ニ依リ国民指導ノ拠リ所ヲ得テ親善ノ途ヲ開カントスルモノト解釈？スル旨ヲ述ヘ右
委細了解セルニ付貴意ノ次第篤ト外相ニ報告シ考慮ヲ求ムヘキ旨答ヘタルニ尚□□右□意
見ハ自分ニ於テ早クヨリ考ヘ居タルモ実行ノ見込立タスシテ発表スルハ徒ニ反対ヲ招キ成
功スル所以ニアラスト認メ今日迄言出スコトヲ差控ヘ居タル次第ナルカ若シ日本側ニテ右
原則決定ニ同意セラルルナラハ自分ノ方ニテ必ス之ヲ実行シ得ル自信アリト言明シ得？、
右御含ニテ実現方努力ヲ請フト述ヘ尚本使帰任後早目ニ会議シ度ト希望セリ」（傍点　引用
者）

　満洲を巡る日本の国民感情と中国の国民感情の相違は政治決着するような生易しい問題
ではなかったことがよく理解できる。汪兆銘はこの問題の難しさを理解し「右既往の経緯」
の了解、つまり日本の立場である、日露戦争の結果としての満洲と、中国の立脚する立場
である、中国の固有の領土としての満洲が屹立し、「満洲問題ハ解決困難」であったことを
踏まえ、その火中の栗を拾うが如く、汪兆銘は解決の道を模索したことがわかる。

　汪兆銘政権の誕生に際して、上述したように軍閥呉佩孚との合作に失敗したが、臨時政
府と維新政府などの主要メンバーで基盤を固めようとしたことがわかる。外務省外交史料
館所蔵の『支那事変ニ際シ支那新政府樹立関係一件　汪精衛関係　第一巻』では「三巨頭
会談」で汪兆銘政権の人事を摩擦なく固めようとしたことがよくわかる。「三巨頭会議決定
事項」（九月二十一日　於聚星倶楽部）では「中央政治委員会ハ汪精衛ノ準備セル条例を原案
トシ王克敏、梁鴻志ハ中央政治会議ニ於テ其ノ無修正通過ニ努ム」とあり、「三、中央政治
会議員配当ハ其ノ 1/3 ヲ国民党ニ 1/3 ヲ臨時及維新政府ニ残余ノ 1/3 ヲ満蒙政府其他ノ各党
各派無党無派ニ分ツ」と書かれている。強力なる中央政府を目指した汪兆銘政権がこの微
妙なバランスの上に樹立されたことは知っておかなければならないであろう。汪兆銘政権
の最初の「議員配当」は『汪精衛自叙伝』（263～264 頁）によれば以下の通りであった。

10

汪精衛	主席
陳公博	国民党
周佛海	国民党
褚民誼	国民党
梅思平	国民党
林柏生	国民党
丁黙邨	国民党
曾醒	国民党
劉郁芬	国民党
李聖五	国民党
葉蓬	国民党
王克敏	臨時政府
王揖唐	臨時政府
齋燮元	臨時政府
朱深	臨時政府
殷同	臨時政府
梁鴻志	維新政府
温宗堯	維新政府
陳羣	維新政府
任援道	維新政府
高冠吾	維新政府
諸青来	国家社会党
李祖虞	国家社会党
趙毓松	中国青年党
張英華	中国青年党
趙正平	無党無派
楊毓珣	無党無派
岑徳廣	無党無派
趙尊嶽	無党無派
卓特巴札布	蒙古連合自治政府
陳玉銘	蒙古連合自治政府

『汪精衛自叙伝』（263〜264 頁）より作成。

中央政治会議で決定をみた国民政府の陣容は下記の通りである。

林森	国民政府主席
汪精衛	国民政府主席代理
汪精衛	行政院長
褚民誼	行政副院長
陳公博	立法院長
未定	立法副院長
温宗堯	司法院長
朱履龢	司法副院長
梁鴻志	監察院長
顧忠琛	監察副院長
王揖唐	考試院長
江亢虎	考試副院長
陳羣	内政部長
褚民誼	外交部長（兼任）
周佛海	財政部長
鮑文樾	軍政部長（部長代理）
汪精衛	海軍部長（暫時兼任）
趙正平	教育部長
李聖五	司法行政部長
梅思平	工商部長
趙毓松	農鉱部長
傳式説	鉄道部長
諸青来	交通部長
丁黙邨	社会部長
林柏生	宣伝部長
周佛海	警政部長（兼任）
岑徳廣	振務委員長
陳濟成	僑務委員長
羅君強	邊疆委員長
楊壽楣	水利委員長
陳春圃	行政院秘書長
張韜	最高法院長
林彪	行政法院長
（未定）	考選委員長
江亢虎	銓鈂部長（兼任）
夏奇峯	審計部長
参謀本部長	楊揆一（部長代理）
（未定）	軍事参議院長
任援道	軍事参議副院長（院長代理）
蕭叔萱（部長代理）	軍事訓練部長
陳公博	政治訓練部長（兼任）
劉郁芬	開封綏靖主任

葉蓬	武漢綏靖主任
齊燮元	華北綏靖総司令
任援道	蘇浙皖三省綏靖総司令（兼任）
王克敏	華北政務委員会委員長
王克敏	△常務委員兼内政総署督辦（兼任）
汪時璟	△常務委員兼財政総署督辦
齊燮元	△常務委員兼綏靖総署督辦
湯爾和	△常務委員兼教育総署督辦
王蔭泰	△常務委員兼実業総署督辦
殷同	△常務委員兼建設総署督辦
朱深	△常務委員兼政務廳長
董康	△委員

『汪精衛自叙伝』（266～270 頁）より作成。

　九州大学に来られた縁で知り合った、シンガポール大学の Tai Wei LIM 氏に英文で解説をお願いしたところ、陳璧君がマレイ華僑であり、LIM 氏は汪兆銘に与えた陳璧君の影響の大きさを指摘され、汪兆銘が混乱回避や秩序維持に果たした役割もそれなりに評価すべきであるという見方を示され、最近の英文の研究を同氏の解題の中で紹介いただいた。また華北政務委員会については特にお願いして紙幅を割いていただいた。英語圏の研究者にも参考になるだろう。英語の読者にもガイド（指南）となるであろう。

　汪兆銘政権が歴史の中に位置づけられることで、日中相互理解につながり、多様な見方が享受されることを願いながら、また「偽」とか「傀儡」という枠に囚われない研究が行われることを願いながら解題を締め括りたい。

付記
　この解題を書くにあたって、九州大学統合新領域学府ライブラリーサイエンス専攻の大学院生に協力いただいた。特に私のゼミに所属する周緯哲氏には文献情報や人名リスト作成、さらには南京にある中国第二歴史档案館の指南役までお願いした。諸原真樹氏と戴栩楊氏にデータ入力で助けていただいた。早稲田大学の島崎尚子教授にはシンガポール大学の Tai Wei LIM 氏と小生を引き合わせていただいたことを記しておきたい。

謝辞
　クロスカルチャー出版の川角功成社長には『米国司法省戦時経済局対日調査資料集（第 1 巻～第 5 巻)』（2008 年）を一緒に刊行したが、どこの出版社も引き受けていただけなかったのを思い出した。今回の『汪兆銘政権人名録』（OSS 作成、1944 年）もご一緒に仕事をさせていただいた。解題が遅れたにもかかわらず、我慢強くお待ちいただいた。リスクを厭わずに引き受けていただき、販売で恩返しができることを願うばかりである。

＊本書は JSPS 科研費の課題番号「16K03779」による成果の一部である。

表 1：汪兆銘政権漢字表記、英語表記対照表

	名前（中国）	名前（日本）	現代中国語での英文表記	人名録の英文表記	人名録の頁
1	周佛海	周佛海	Zhou fo hai	Chou Fwo-hai	47
2	梅思平	梅思平	Mei si ping	Mei, Ssu-ping	133
3	马良	馬良	Ma liang	Ma, Liang	131
4	潘毓桂	潘毓桂	Pan yu gui	Pan Yu-kuei	138
5	赵毓松	趙毓松	Zhao yu song	Chao Yu-sung	16
6	赵琪	趙琪	Zhao qi	Chao Chi	14
7	赵叔雍	趙叔雍	Zhao shu yong	Chao Shu-yung	16
8	赵正平	趙正平	Zhao zheng ping	Chao Cheng-ping	13
9	褚民谊	褚民誼	Chu min yi	Chu Min-yi	54
10	张英华	張英華	Zhang ying hua	Chang Ying-hua	12
11	张永福	張永福	Zhang yong fu	Chang Yung-fu	13
12	张韬	張韜	Zhang tao	Chang-Tao	10
13	陈维远	陳維遠	Chen wei yuan	Chen Wei-yuan	28
14	陈公博	陳公博	Chen gong bo	Chen Kung-po	24
15	陈群	陳群	Chen qun	Chen Chun	19
16	陈济成	陳濟成	Chen ji cheng	Chen Chi-cheng	18
17	陈壁君	陳壁君	Chen bi jun	Chen Pi-chun	25
18	陈春圃	陳春圃	Chen chun pu	Chen Chun-pu	20
19	陈之硕	陳之碩	Chen zhi shuo	Chen Chih-shih	18
20	沈尔乔	沈爾喬	Shen er qiao	Chen En-chin	21
21	溥侗	溥侗	Pu tong	Fu-Tung	63
22	傅式说	傅式說	Fu shi shuo	Fu Shih-Shuo	63
23	富双英	富雙英	Fu shuang ying	Fu Shuang-Ying	63
24	严家炽	嚴家熾	Yan jia chi	Yen Chia-chih	197
25	樊仲云	樊仲雲	Fan zhong yun	Fan Chung-Yun	59
26	鲍文樾	鮑文樾	Bao wen yue	Pao Wen-yueh	139
27	彭年	彭年	Peng nian	Peng Nien	140
28	殷同	殷同	Yin tong	Yin Tung	200
29	徐良	徐良	Xu liang	Hsu Liang	77
30	徐苏中	徐蘇中	Xu su zhong	Hsun Su-chung	80
31	夏奇峯	夏奇峯	Xia qi feng	Hsia Chi-feng	69
32	何庭流	何庭流	He ting liu	Ho Ting-liu	68
33	何佩瑢	何佩瑢	He pei rong	Ho Pei-yung	67
34	许继祥	許繼祥	Xu ji xiang	Hsu Chi-hsiang	74
35	江朝宗	江朝宗	Jiang chao zong	Chiang Chao-Tsung	36
36	江亢虎	江亢虎	Jiang kang hu	Chiang Kang-hu	37
37	江履谦	江履謙	Jiang lv qian	Chiang Lu-chien	38
38	顾忠琛	顧忠琛	Gu zhong li	Ku Chung-chen	95
39	顾继武	顧繼武	Gu ji wu	Ku Chi-wu	95
40	孔宪鉴	孔憲鑑	Kong xian jian	Kung Hsien-chien	98
41	黄香谷	黄香谷	Huang xiang gu	Huang Hsiang-ku	84
42	胡兰成	胡蘭成	Hu lan cheng	Hu Lan-cheng	81
43	任援道	任援道	Ren yuan dao	Jen Yuan-tao	89
44	汪时璟	汪時璟	Wang shi jing	Wang Shin-ching	178
45	汪翰章	汪翰章	Wang han zhang	Wang Han-Chang	173
46	汪曼云	汪曼雲	Wang man yun	Wang Man-yun	177
47	王荫泰	王蔭泰	Wang yin tai	Wang Yin-Tai	181
48	王克敏	王克敏	Wang ke min	Wang Ke-min	176
49	王修	王修	Wang xiu	Wang Hsiu	174
50	王楫唐	王楫唐	Wang yi tang	Wang I-tang	175

51	温宗尧	温宗堯	Wen zong yao	Wen Tsung-yao	184
52	罗君强	羅君強	Luo jun qiang	Lo Chun-chiang	126
53	李文滨	李文濱	Li wen bin	Li Wen-pin	113
54	李士群	李士群	Li shi qun	Li Shi-chun	109
55	李讴一	李謳一	Li ou yi	Li Ou-yi	108
56	李圣五	李聖五	Li sheng wu	Li Sheng-wu	109
57	李租虞	李租虞	Li zu yu	Li Tsu-yu	112
58	林彪	林彪	Lin biao	Lin Piao	118
59	林柏生	林柏生	Lin bo sheng	Lin Po-sheng	118
60	梁鸿志	梁鴻志	Liang hong zhi	Liang Hung-chih	115
61	刘培绪	劉培緒	Liu pei xu	Liu Pei-hsu	123
62	刘郁芬	劉郁芬	Liu yu fen	Liu Yu-fen	125
63	凌霄	凌霄	Ling xiao	Ling Hsiao	119
64	蔡培	蔡培	Cai pei	Tsai Pei	163
65	齐燮元	齊燮元	Qi xie yuan	Chi Hsien-yuan	34
66	石星川	石星川	Shi xing chuan	Shin Hsing-Chuan	147
67	朱扑	朱撲	Zhu pu	Chu Pu	56
68	朱深	朱深	Zhu shen	Chu Shen	56
69	苏体仁	蘇体仁	Su ti ren	Su Ti-jen	150
70	周化人	周化人	Zhou hua ren	Chou Hua-jen	48
71	周隆庠	周隆庠	Zhou long xiang	Chou Lung-yang	49
72	岑德广	岑德廣	Cen de guang	Tsen Te-kuang	なし
73	诸青来	諸青來	Zhu qing lai	Chu Ching-lai	52
74	萧叔宣	蕭叔宣	Xiao shu xuan	Hsiao Shu-hsuan	71
75	载英夫	載英夫	Zai ying fu	Tai ying-Fu	155
76	郑大章	鄭大章	Zheng da zhang	Cheng Tai-chang	33
77	丁默邨	丁默邨	Ding mo cun	Ting Mo-tsun	161
78	汤尔和	湯爾和	Tang er he	Tang Erh-ho	156
79	汤澄波	湯澄波	Tang cheng bo	Tang Cheng-po	156
80	董康	董康	Dong kang	Tung Kang	169
81	邓租禹	鄧租禹	Deng zu yu	Teng Tsu-yu	160
82	唐蟒	唐蟒	Tang mang	Tang Mang	157
83	杨揆一	楊揆一	Yang kui yi	Yang Kuei-i	193
84	杨寿楣	楊壽楣	Yang shou mei	Yang Shou-mei	194
85	叶蓬	葉蓬	Ye peng	Yeh Peng	196
86	余幼耕	余幼耕	Yu you geng	Yu Chin-ho	201
87	陈耀祖	陳耀祖	Chen yao zu	Chen Yao-tsu	29
88	周迪平	周迪平	Zhou di ping	Chou Ti-ping	なし
89	许修直	許修直	Xu xiu zhi	Hsu Hsiu-chih	なし
90	周学昌	周學昌	Zhou xue chang	Chou hsueh chang	48
91	张北生	張北生	Zhang bei sheng	Chang Pei sheng	9
92	徐天深	徐天深	Xu tian shen	Hsu Tien shen	79
93	蔡洪田	蔡洪田	Cai hong tian	Tsai Hung tien	162
94	缪斌	繆斌	Miao bin	Miao Pin	133
95	乔万选	喬萬選	Qiao wan xuan	Chiao Wan hsuan	40
96	焦莹	焦莹	Jiao ying	Chiao Ying	40
97	吴颂皋	吳頌皋	Wu song gao	Wu Sung kao	189
98	陈福民	陳福民	Chen fu min	Chen Fu ming	21
99	汤良礼	湯良禮	Tang liang li	Tang Liang li	157

注：『新国民政府人名鑑』『最新支那要人伝』『民國人物大辞典』『中国抗日战争大辞典』などを
参照して作成。周緯哲氏の協力を得た。

表2：「WO208/2886 氏名リスト」

1.	Aw Boon-haw	胡文虎*	48.	Chao Ju-heng	趙如珩
2.	Chan Lim-pek	陳廉伯*	49.	Chao Kuei-chang	招桂章
3.	Chan Pai-li*		50.	Chao Kung-wei	
4.	Chan Pok		51.	Chao Mu-ju	趙墓儒*
5.	Chang Chao	張超	52.	Chao Pao-chin	趙寶芝
6.	Chang Chao-chi		53.	Chao Shu-yung	趙叔雍
7.	Chang Che-tieh		54.	Chao Tsun-yueh	趙尊嶽
8.	Chang Chi	張奇	55.	Chao Yu-sung	趙毓松
9.	Chang Chi-liu	張企留	56.	Chen Chang-tsu	陳昌祖
10.	Chang Chia-yun		57.	Chen Cheng-lun	陳承綸
11.	Chang Chien-chu		58.	Chen Chi-cheng	陳濟成
12.	Chang Chun	章駿	59.	Chen Chien-yuan	陳見園
13.	Chang Chuo-kun	張焯堃	60.	Chen Chih-shih	陳之碩
14.	Chang En-lin	張恩麟	61.	Chen Ching-hsuan	陳青選
15.	Chang Er-chang		62.	Chen Chun	陳群
16.	Chang Feng-liang	張仿良	63.	Chen Chun-hui	陳君慧
17.	Chang Heng	張衡	64.	Chen Chun-pu	陳春圃
18.	Chang Hsien-chin	張顯之	65.	Chen Chung	陳中
19.	Chang Hsueh-ming	張學銘	66.	Chen Chung-fu	陳中孚
20.	Chang Jen-li	張仁蠡	67.	Chen En-pu	陳恩普
21.	Chang Ko-min		68.	Chen Fu-mu	陳孚木
22.	Chang ku-shan	張孤山*	69.	Chen Hao-ming	潘鶴鳴*
23.	Chang Kuang-yen*		70.	Chen Jih-ping	陳日平*
24.	Chang Kuo-yuan	張國元	71.	Chen Kuang-chung	陳光中
25.	Chang Lan-feng	張嵐峯	72.	Chen Kung-po	陳公博
26.	Chang Pei-sheng	張北生	73.	Chen Kuo-cheng	
27.	Chang Peng-sheng	張鵬聲	74.	Chen Kuo-feng	陳國豐
28.	Chang Ping-chuan	張秉權	75.	Chen Li-min	陳利民
29.	Chang Po-yin		76.	Chen Liang-chao	潘諒昭*
30.	Chang Shu-chin	章樹欽	77.	Chen Pi-chun	陳壁君
31.	Chang Shu-chun	章叔淳*	78.	Chen Pin-ho	陳彬龢
32.	Chang Su-min	張素民	79.	Chen Po-fan	陳伯蕃
33.	Chang Tao	張韜	80.	Chen Pu	
34.	Chang Te (h) -chin	張德欽	81.	Chen Sheng-neng	
35.	Chang Ting-chin	張廷金	82.	Chen Te (h) -kuang	岑德廣
36.	Chang Tse-hstn	張策勳	83.	Chen Tiao-chin	陳挑琴*
37.	Chang Wei-ju	張慰如	84.	Chen Tzu-yi	陳子彝*
38.	Chang Wen-huan	張文煥*	85.	Chen Wei-cheng	陳維政
39.	Chang Yen-ching		86.	Chen Wei-yuan	陳維遠
40.	Chang Yi-chou		87.	Chen Wen-chao	陳文釗
41.	Chang Yi-nien	章頤年	88.	Chen Wen-yun	陳文運
42.	Chang Ying-hua	張英華	89.	Chen Weng-yu	
43.	Chang Yu-ching	常玉清	90.	Chen Yien-tan	
44.	Chang Yu-yun	張幼雲	91.	Chen Yu-san	陳有三
45.	Chang Yuan-chen	張元振	92.	Chen Yun-wen	陳允文
46.	Chang Yung-fu	張永福	93.	Cheng Chih	
47.	Chao Cheng-ping	趙正平	94.	Cheng Hsi-chang	

95.	Cheng Hung-nien	鄭洪年
96.	Cheng Keng-hsin	
97.	Cheng Kuang-hsun	奠洸薰
98.	Cheng Liang-pin	鄭良斌
99.	Cheng Nien-peng	程年彭
100.	Cheng Pao-yuan	
101.	Cheng Sheng-tien	程勝天
102.	Cheng Ta-chang	鄭大章
103.	Cheng Yi-kuei	
104.	Cheung Koo-shan*	
105.	Cheung Suk-shun*	
106.	Chi Hsieh-yuan	齊燮元
107.	Chia No-fu	
108.	Chia Shih-yi	賈士毅
109.	Chiang Chia-chou	
110.	Chiang Kang-hu	江亢虎
111.	Chiang Nan-chun	江南椿
112.	Chiang Shang-ta	江上達
113.	Chiang Shui-yi	蔣水沂
114.	Chiang Tso-hsuan	姜佐宣*
115.	Chiang Wei-tsung*	
116.	Chiang Yung-kun	江榮坤
117.	Chiao Jung	焦瑩
118.	Chiao Wan-hsuan	喬萬選
119.	Chien Sen	
120.	Chien Ta-huai	錢大槐
121.	Chien Wei-t sung	錢慰宗
122.	Chien Wen	簡文
123.	Chin Chia-feng	金家鳳
124.	Chin Chih-hsun	
125.	Chin Fu-sehng	金馥生
126.	Chin Mo-shen	秦墨哂
127.	Chin Shao-fu	金少甫
128.	Chin Shou-liang	金壽良
129.	Chin Ya-hsiu	秦亞修
130.	Chiu Yun-to	邱韻鐸
131.	Chou Ching-fang	鄒敬芳
132.	Chou Chuan-sun	鄒泉蓀
133.	Chou Chung-ching	周仲慶
134.	Chou Fu-hai	周佛海*
135.	Chou Hsueh-chang	周學章*
136.	Chou Hua-jen	周化人*
137.	Chou Kuan-hung	周貫虹*
138.	Chou Li-ke	周禮恪*
139.	Chou Lung-hsiang	周隆癢
140.	Chou Lung-kuang	周龍光
141.	Chou Nai-wen	
142.	Chou Tso-jen	周作人
143.	Chou Tso-min	周作民
144.	Chou Yao-nien	周耀年*
145.	Chou Ying-hsiang	週應湘
146.	Chou Yueh-jan	周越然
147.	Chow Sir Shouson	周壽臣*
148.	Chu Ching-lai	諸青來
149.	Chu Li-ho	朱履龢
150.	Chu Min-yi	褚民誼
151.	Chu Pao-heng	諸保橫
152.	Chu Po-chuan	朱博泉
153.	Chu Pu	朱樸
154.	Chu Sen*	
155.	Chu Tung-chueh	褚通爵
156.	Chu Yi	朱毅
157.	Chu Yu-chen	朱玉軫
158.	Chung Hung-sheng	鐘洪聲
159.	Chung Jen-shou	鐘任壽
160.	Chung Po-chuan	
161.	En Ke Pa Tu	恩克巴圖
162.	Fan Chung-yun	樊仲雲
163.	Fan Ko-kung	
164.	Fan Yung-tseng	范永增
165.	Fang Huan-ju	方煥如
166.	Fen Chu-pai	翁初白
167.	Feng Chieh	馮節
168.	Feng Chin	馮翔
169.	Feng Hao	馮浩*
170.	Feng Ping-shao	
171.	Feng Pi-nan	
172.	Fu Chun-shih	傅君寶
173.	Fu Shih-shuo	傅式說
174.	Fu Shuang-ying	富雙英
175.	Han Ching-chien	韓清健
176.	Han Wen-ping	
177.	Hao Peng-chu	郝鵬舉
178.	Heng Shan-chang	橫山長
179.	Ho Chin-hang	何志杭
180.	Ho Ching-hsiang*	
181.	Ho Chuo-hsien	何焯賢*
182.	Ho Han-lan	何瀚瀾
183.	Ho Hsing-chang	
184.	Ho Jih-ju	何日泖*
185.	Ho Kom-tong*	
186.	Ho Ping-hsien	何炳賢
187.	Ho Shih-chen	何世楨
188.	Ho Ta-yung	
189.	Ho Tao-yun	何道澐
190.	Ho Te (h) -kuang	何德光*
191.	Ho Tung, Sir Robert	何東*
192.	Hou Hsisng-chuan*	

193.	Hou Wen-an	
194.	Hsi Chin-chou	冼錦洲
195.	Hsi Tse-wen	奚則文
196.	Hsi Wei-t ing	冼維挺
197.	Hsia Chi-feng	夏奇峯
198.	Hsiang Chih-chuang	項致莊
199.	Hsiang Hsun	項峋
200.	Hsiang Kang-yuan	項康元
201.	Hsiao Shu-hsuan	蕭叔萱
202.	Hsieh Ko	謝恪
203.	Hsieh Pao-sheng	謝葆生
204.	Hsien Ping-hsi*	
205.	Hsiung Chien-tung	能劍東
206.	Hsiung Chuang-tung	
207.	Hsu Chi-tun	徐季敦
208.	Hsu Chiang	許江
209.	Hsu Chien-ping	許建屏
210.	Hsu Chien-ting	許建廷
211.	Hsu Chin-yuan	許金源
212.	Hsu Chung-jen	徐中仁
213.	Hsu Hsi-ching	許錫慶
214.	Hsu Hsiang-sheng	徐租生
215.	Hsu, Jabin (courtesy name, Hsu Chien-ping)	
216.	Hsu Li-chiu	許力求
217.	Hsu Liang	徐良
218.	Hsu Nai	
219.	Hsu Nien-li	徐念劼
220.	Hsu Shao-jung	許少榮
221.	Hsu Su-chung	徐蘇中
222.	Hsu Tien-shen	徐天深
223.	Hsu Tsun-kung	
224.	Hsu Yang-chih	
225.	Hsu Yi-tsung	徐義宗
226.	Hsueh Feng-yuan	薛逢元
227.	Hu Chuang-ta	
228.	Hu Fang-chun	
229.	Hu Kuo-hua	
230.	Hu Lan-cheng	胡蘭成
231.	Hu Shan	
232.	Hu Shan-cheng	胡善俪
233.	Hu Tse-wu	胡澤吾
234.	Hu Ying-chou	胡瀛洲
235.	Hu Yu-kun	胡毓坤
236.	Huang Chiang-chuan	黃江泉
237.	Huang Chi-hsing	黃其興
238.	Huang Chung*	
239.	Huang Ko-ming	黃克明
240.	Huang Min-chung	黃敏中
241.	Huang Pao-shu*	
242.	Huang Ping-chen	黃秉真
243.	Huang Po-chin	黃伯芹*
244.	Huang Ta-chung	黃大中
245.	Huang Tzu-chiang	黃自強
246.	Hung Chou	洪鑄
247.	Jen Hsi-ping	任西萍
248.	Jen Yuan-tao	任援道
249.	Jung Chen	榮臻
250.	Jung Tzu-heng	
251.	Kao Cheng	高政
252.	Kao Han	高漢
253.	Kao Kuan-wu	高冠吾
254.	Kao Shu-ying	
255.	Kiu Kuk*	
256.	Ko Ting-yuan	戈定遠
257.	Kong Kai-tung*	
258.	Kong Po-tin*	
259.	Ku Chi-wu	顧繼武
260.	Ku Chung-shen	顧忠琛
261.	Ku Hai-chiu*	
262.	Ku Huan-chang	顧煥章
263.	Ku Pao-heng	顧寶衡
264.	Kuan Cheng-pin	關承斌
265.	Kuan Hsin-yen	關心馬*
266.	Kuang Chi-tung	廣啟東*
267.	Kuang Yi-hsien	
268.	Kung Hsien-keng	孔憲鏗
269.	Kung Ping-chuan	公秉權
270.	Kuo Chien-yuan	郭謙元
271.	Kuo Hsien-hung	郭顯宏*
272.	Kuo Hsiu-feng	郭秀峯
273.	Kuo Tsan	郭贊*
274.	Kuo Wei-min	郭衛民
275.	Kwok Chuen*	
276.	Lai Chun-kuei	賴春貴
277.	Lai Kong-sun*	
278.	Lau	
279.	Lau Tit-sing*	
280.	Lee Jee-chor*	
281.	Lei Yu-chun	
282.	Li Chang-chiang	李長江
283.	Li Chi-fen*	
284.	Li Chi-hsin	李啟新*
285.	Li Chia-kan	
286.	Li Chien-nan	李建南
287.	Li Chih-wen	李志文
288.	Li Ching-wu	李景武
289.	Li Chiu	李就*
290.	Li Chuan-shih	李權時

291.	Li Chung-chao		
292.	Li Chung-fu	李忠甫*	
293.	Li Fei		
294.	Li Hao-chu	李浩駒*	
295.	Li Suan-tiao	李宣調	
296.	Li Hua	李譁	
297.	Li Ju-ching		
298.	Li Kan-huang	李乾璜	
299.	Li King-hong*		
300.	Li Kuan-chun	李冠春*	
301.	Li Kuang-wo		
302.	Li Li-wen	李勵文	
303.	Li Ou-yi	李謳一	
304.	Li Pei-chiu	李霈秋	
305.	Li Sheng-po	李升（生）伯	
306.	Li Sheng-wu	李聖五	
307.	Li Shih	離石	
308.	Li Shih-fu		
309.	Li Shou-shen	李壽山*	
310.	Li Ssu-hao	李思浩	
311.	Li Ssu-hsien	李思賢	
312.	Li Su-yu		
313.	Li Sung-chieh	李松俠	
314.	Li Sung-ching	李頌清*	
315.	Li Tai-fang	李泰芳	
316.	Li Tsu-fan	李祖範	
317.	Li Tsu-yu	李祖虞	
318.	Li Tung-hsia		
319.	Li Tzu-fang	李子芳*	
320.	Li Tzu-yung	李紫東	
321.	Li Wen-pin	李文濱	
322.	LiYu-lin		
323.	Lia Kia-fan*		
324.	Liang Chi	梁繼*	
325.	Liang Hsiu-yu	梁秀予	
326.	Liang Hung-chih	梁鴻志	
327.	Liang Shih	梁式	
328.	Liao Chia-nan	廖家楠	
329.	Liao En-tao	廖恩燾	
330.	Lien Yu	廉隅	
331.	Lin Chi	林其	
332.	Lin Chia-min	林珈珉	
333.	Lim Chien-chih	林廉之	
334.	Lin Chien-yin	林建寅*	
335.	Lin Chih-yen	林知淵	
336.	Lin Chiung-an	林炯庵	
337.	Lin Ju-heng	林汝衡（王行）	
338.	Lin Kang-hou	林康候	
339.	Lin Piao	林彪	

340.	Lin Po-sheng	林伯生	
341.	Lin Ta-chung	林大中	
342.	Lin Yin		
343.	Lin Yu-ken	林佑根	
344.	Ling Hong-fat*		
345.	Ling Hsiao	凌霄	
346.	Ling Hsien-wen	凌憲文	
347.	Ling Kang-fa	凌康發	
348.	Liu Ching-chen		
349.	Liu Chun-yang		
350.	Liu Chuo-pak*		
351.	Liu Hsieh-tang	劉燮堂*	
352.	Liu Hsing-chen		
353.	Liu Pei-hsu	劉培緒	
354.	Liu Po	劉渤*	
355.	Liu Shu		
356.	Liu Tieh-cheng	劉鐵誠*	
357.	Liu Tsu-wang		
358.	Liu Tsun-pu	劉存樸	
359.	Liu Wei-chun	劉煒俊	
360.	Liu Yang-shan	劉仰山	
361.	Liu Yu-fen	劉郁芬	
362.	Liu Yu-sheng	柳雨生	
363.	Lo Chai-sing*		
364.	Lo Ching-kwang*		
365.	Lo Chun-chiang	羅君強	
366.	Lo Hsu-ho	羅旭和*	
367.	Lo Kuk-wo*		
368.	Lo, M. K.*		
369.	Lo Wen-chin	羅文錦*	
370.	Lo Yung-ku	駱用弧*	
371.	Lu Ai-yun	陸藹雲*	
372.	Lu Chih-hsueh	盧志學	
373.	Lu Feng	魯風	
374.	Lu Jun-chih	陸潤之	
375.	Lu Jung-chien	陸榮錢（？）	
376.	Lu Meng-shu	盧夢殊*	
377.	Lu Shan-chih	陸善熾	
378.	Lu Yi-jan	陸怡然	
379.	Lu Ying	盧英	
380.	Lu Yung-chuan	盧用川	
381.	Luk Tan-lan*		
382.	Luke Oi-wan*		
383.	Ma Chi-tsai	馬驥材	
384.	Ma Hsiao-tien	馬嘯天	
385.	Ma Kian*		
386.	Ma Tien-ju	馬典如	
387.	Ma Ying*		
388.	Ma Yun-teng		

389.	Mai Cheng-ming	麥靜銘	
390.	Mai Tao-chu	麥兆（桃？）初	
391.	Mao Ching-fan		
392.	Mao Tsu-ming	茅子明	
393.	Mei Lan-fang	梅蘭芳	
394.	Mei Sau-ping	梅思平	
395.	Men Chih-chung	門制中	
396.	Meng Hsiu-chuang	孟琇椿	
397.	Miao Pin	繆斌	
398.	Moy, Herbert Erasmus		
399.	Ni Tao-lang	倪道烺	
400.	Nieh Lu-sheng	聶潞生	
401.	Ou Ta-ching	區大慶	
402.	Ou Tao-kung		
403.	Pai Kung-chen		
404.	Pan, C. C.*		
405.	Pan, S. H.*		
406.	Pan Tzu-chun	潘子鈞	
407.	Pang Ping-hsun	龐炳勳	
408.	Pao Wen-yueh	鮑文樾	
409.	Pei Fu-heng	裴復恆	
410.	Peng*		
411.	Peng Chih-te (h)		
412.	Peng Nien	彭年	
413.	Peng Yi-ming	彭義明	
414.	Pi Shu-chih	畢書之	
415.	Pi Tse-yu	畢澤宇	
416.	Pih, H. C.*		
417.	Poon Shunt-um*		
418.	Pu Li-fu	卜立夫	
419.	Pu Tung	溥侗	
420.	Pu Yu	卜愈	
421.	Shao Hsi-lien	邵希廉	
422.	Shao Shih-chun	邵式軍	
423.	Shao Wei-ming	邵蔚明*	
424.	Shen Chen-kang	申振綱	
425.	Shen Er-chiao	沈爾喬	
426.	Shen Ting-shan	申聽禪	
427.	Shen Tung	沈同	
428.	Shih Hsing-chuan	石星川	
429.	Shih Shao-ching	石少卿*	
430.	Su Cheng-te (h)	蘇成德	
431.	Su Ko-min		
432.	Su Ko-nien		
433.	Sun Chih-chieh	孫志傑	
434.	Sun Chung-li	孫仲立	
435.	Sun Hsiang-fu	孫祥夫	
436.	Sun Kuang-chuan	孫廣權	
437.	Sun Kuei-yuan	孫魁元	

438.	Sun Li-fu		
439.	Sun Liang-cheng	孫良誠	
440.	Sun Ming chi	孫鳴岐	
441.	Sun Tien-ying	孫殿英	
442.	Sun Tsu-chi	孫祖基	
443.	Sun Yun-chang	孫雲章	
444.	Sung Shao-hsiung	宋紹雄	
445.	Tai Jo-lan	戴若瀾*	
446.	Tai Tse	戴策	
447.	Tai Ying-fu	戴英夫	
448.	Tam, William N. Thomas*		
449.	Tan Ya-shih	譚雅士*	
450.	Tan Yuchung	譚友仲	
451.	Tang Cheng-po	湯澄波	
452.	Tang Hui-min	唐惠明	
453.	Tang Liang-li		
454.	Tang Mang	唐蟒	
455.	Tang Sheng-ming	唐生明	
456.	Tang Shou-min	唐壽民	
457.	Tang Yat-yan*		
458.	Tang Ying-huang		
459.	Tao Hsiao-chieh	陶孝潔	
460.	Tao Kang-te (h)	陶亢德	
461.	Teng Chao-chien	登肇堅	
462.	Teng Chi-tung		
463.	Teng Shih-chang	鄧士章	
464.	Teng Tsan-hsiang	鄧贊鄉	
465.	Tieng Hsi		
466.	Ting Chao	丁超	
467.	Ting Mo-tsun	丁默村（邨）	
468.	Tong Ching-kan*		
469.	Tong Ping-tat*		
470.	Tsai Hung-tien	蔡洪田	
471.	Tsai Kan-shun		
472.	Tsai Ko-chien		
473.	Tsai Pei	蔡培	
474.	Tsai Sheng-pai	蔡聲白	
475.	Tsai Wen-shih	蔡文石	
476.	Tsai Yun-shih	蔡運實	
477.	Tsang Cho	臧卓	
478.	Tsao Miao-sheng		
479.	Tsao Pang-yeh		
480.	Tsen Hsi-yung*		
481.	Tseng Jung	曾榕*	
482.	Tseng Kwong-kung*		
483.	Tseng Shou-chao	曾壽超*	
484.	Tso Ju-liang		
485.	Tsung Chih-chiang	宗志強	
486.	Tu yi-Chien	杜益謙	

487.	Tung Chung-wei	董仲偉*
488.	Tung Kang	董康
489.	Wan Ta-hua	
490.	Wang Chi	汪屺
491.	Wang Chi-min	
492.	Wang Chia-chun	王家俊
493.	Wang Chin-hsia	王錦霞
494.	Wang Han-chang	汪翰章
495.	Wang Hsi-wen	汪希文
496.	Wang Hsiao-shui*	
497.	Wang Hsiu	王修
498.	Wang Huai-ling	
499.	Wang Jen-chih	
500.	Wang Ke-min	王克敏
501.	Wang Man-yun	汪曼雲*
502.	Wnag Min-chung	王敏中
503.	Wang Ping	王平
504.	Wang Shih-ching	汪時璟
505.	Wang Shu-chun	王樹春
506.	Wang Tai	王泰*
507.	Wang Te(h)-feng*	
508.	Wang Te-kuang	王德光*
509.	Wang Tsung-chun	汪宗準
510.	Wang Tung-ming	王通明*
511.	Wang Wei-fan	王維藩
512.	Wang Yi-fang	王一方
513.	Wang Yi-tang	王揖唐
514.	Wang Yin-tai	王蔭泰
515.	Wang Ying-kuo	
516.	Wang Yu-chia	王遇甲*
517.	Wang Yu-chin	
518.	Wang Yung-nien*	
519.	Wei Fan	尾坂
520.	Wei Kuo-lun*	
521.	Wei, Peter*	
522.	Wei Tu-tung	魏睹東
523.	Wen Lan-ting	
524.	Wen Tsung-yao	溫宗堯
525.	Wong, Peter M.*	
526.	Wong Yat-chung*	
527.	Wu Chen-hsiu	吳震修
528.	Wu Hua	伍華*
529.	Wu Hua-wen	吳化文
530.	Wu Kai-hsien	吳開先

531.	Wu Kai-sheng	吳凱聲
532.	Wu Lan-hsi	巫蘭溪
533.	Wu Pei-yuan*	
534.	Wu Peng-fei	
535.	Wu Sung-kao	吳頌皋
536.	Wu Wen-tse	吳文澤*
537.	Yang Cheng-yu	楊正宇
538.	Yang Chieh	楊傑
539.	Yang Chih-ching	楊志清
540.	Yang Hsing-hua	楊惺華
541.	Yang Hung-lieh	楊鴻烈
542.	Yang Kuei-yi	楊揆一
543.	Yang Pao-yi	
544.	Yang Shou-mei	楊壽楣
545.	Yao Hsi-chiu	姚錫九
546.	Yao Shun-po	姚順伯
547.	Yeh Fu-hsiao	葉扶霄
548.	Yeh Hsueh-sung	葉雪松*
549.	Yeh Lan-chuan	葉蘭泉*
550.	Yeh Peng	葉篷
551.	Yeh Shou-peng	
552.	Yeh Yu-tsai	葉友才
553.	Yen Cheng-kun	顏成坤*
554.	Yen Chi-hsuan	燕琦瑄
555.	Yen Hui-ching	顏惠慶
556.	Yen Te(h)-kuei	顏德桂
557.	Yen. Dr. W. W. (courtesy name, Yen Hui-ching)	
558.	Yeung Tsin-lei*	
559.	Yeung Yun-tak*	
560.	Yin Tsai-wei	殷再緯
561.	Yin Tso-chien	尹祚乾
562.	Yip Kui-ying*	
563.	Yu Chin-ho	余晉龢*
564.	Yu Chueh-yun	余覺雲*
565.	Yu Po-lu	余百魯*
566.	Yu Shih	與市
567.	Yuan Chu-fan	
568.	Yuan Hou-chih	袁厚之
569.	Yuan Li-tun	袁禮敦
570.	Yuan Shu	袁殊
571.	Yuan Yu-chi	阮毓麒（？）
572.	Yuan Yu-chuan	袁愈佺
573.	Yung Ngai-sung*	

注：合計 573 名。（*）は『汪兆銘政権人名録（OSS 作成）』に掲載されていない（合計 122 名）。
英国国立公文書館（TNA）所蔵 "STRUCTURE AND PERSONNEL OF THE NANKING PUPPET GOVERNMENT (AND HONG KONG)" の「III. ALPHABETICAL LIST OF NANKING PUPPET OFFICIALS」（pp.56〜84）より作成、請求番号 WO208/2886

表 A：汪兆銘中央政治委員会委員移動一覧表

委員分類	第一期 （40・3・24 汪兆銘による公布）	第二期 （41・4・5 第 42 回中政会決議）	第三期 （42・3・26 第 87 回中政会決議）
当然委員	汪兆銘、陳公博、温宗堯、梁鴻志、王揖唐、王克敏	汪兆銘、陳公博、温宗堯、梁鴻志、王揖唐	汪兆銘、陳公博、温宗堯、梁鴻志、王揖唐
列席委員	褚民誼、朱履和、江亢虎、顧忠琛	徐良、朱履和、江亢虎、顧忠琛	
指定委員	周佛海、褚民誼、陳璧君、梅思平、陳群、林柏生、劉郁芬、任援道、焦塋、陳君慧、陳耀祖、李聖五、葉蓬、丁黙邨、傅式説、楊揆一、鮑文越、蕭叔萱、李士群	周佛海、褚民誼、陳璧君、梅思平、陳群、林柏生、劉郁芬、任援道、焦塋、陳君慧、陳耀祖、李聖五、葉蓬、丁黙邨、傅式説、楊揆一、鮑文越、蕭叔萱、李士群	周佛海、褚民誼、陳璧君、梅思平、陳群、林柏生、劉郁芬、任援道、焦塋、陳君慧、陳耀祖、李聖五、葉蓬、丁黙邨、傅式説、楊揆一、鮑文越、蕭叔萱、李士群
延聘委員	斉燮元、朱深、殷同、高冠五、卓特巴扎布、趙正平、繆斌、趙毓松、諸青来、趙尊岳、岑徳広	王克敏、斉燮元、朱深、殷同、高冠五、趙正平、繆斌、趙毓松、諸青来、趙尊岳、岑徳広	王克敏、王揖唐、斉燮元、朱深、殷同、高冠五、趙正平、繆斌、趙毓松、諸青来、趙尊岳、岑徳広
合計	40 名	39 名	36 名

委員分類	第四期 （43・4・1 第 122 回中政会決議）	第五期 （44・3・29 第 133 回中政会決議）	第六期 （45・4・5 第 146 回中政会決議）
当然委員	汪兆銘、陳公博、温宗堯、梁鴻志、江亢虎	汪兆銘、陳公博、温宗堯、梁鴻志、陳群、顧忠琛	陳公博、温宗堯、梁鴻志、陳群、顧忠琛
列席委員			
指定委員	周佛海、褚民誼、陳璧君、梅思平、陳群、林柏生、劉郁芬、任援道、焦塋、陳君慧、陳耀祖、李聖五、葉蓬、丁黙邨、傅式説、楊揆一、鮑文越、蕭叔萱、李士群、高冠五、繆斌、陳春圃、羅君強	周佛海、褚民誼、陳璧君、梅思平、陳群、林柏生、任援道、焦塋、陳君慧、陳耀祖、李聖五、葉蓬、丁黙邨、傅式説、楊揆一、鮑文越、蕭叔萱、高冠五、繆斌、陳春圃、羅君強	周佛海、褚民誼、陳璧君、梅思平、陳群、林柏生、任援道、焦塋、陳君慧、李聖五、葉蓬、丁黙邨、傅式説、楊揆一、鮑文越、蕭叔萱、高冠五、繆斌、陳春圃、羅君強
延聘委員	王揖唐、王克敏、斉燮元、朱深、汪時璟、趙正平、諸青来、趙毓松、岑徳広、王陰秦	王揖唐、王克敏、斉燮元、汪時璟、趙正平、諸青来、趙毓松、岑徳広、王陰秦	王揖唐、王克敏、斉燮元、汪時璟、趙正平、諸青来、趙毓松、岑徳広、王陰秦
合計	38 名	35 名（汪精衛 11 月病死）	34 名

出所：曽支農『汪政権による「淪陥区」社会秩序の再建過程に関する研究―『汪偽政府行政院会議録』の分析を中心として―』（学位論文、東京大学）別冊 3 頁。

表 B：人事異動一覧表（1940・3・30～1941・8・16）

院長	汪精衛 （40・3・30～41・8・16）	海軍部長	汪精衛（兼） （40・3・30～40・5・30） 任援道（兼・代） （40・5・30～41・8・16）
副院長	褚民誼 （40・3・30～40・12・12） 周佛海 （40・12・12～41・8・16）	教育部長	趙正平 （40・3・30～41・8・16）
内政部長	陳群 （40・3・30～41・8・16）	司法行政部長	李聖五 （40・3・30～41・8・16）
外交部長	褚民誼（兼） （40・3・30～40・12・12） 徐良 （40・12・12～41・8・16）	工商部長	梅思平 （40・3・30～41・8・16）
財政部長	周佛海（任、兼） （40・3・30～41・8・16）	農鉱部長	趙毓松 （40・3・30～41・8・16）
軍政部長	鮑文越（代） （40・3・30～41・3・24） 鮑文越 （41・3・24～41・8・16）	鉄道部長	傅式説 （40・3・30～41・8・16）
交通部長	諸青来 （40・3・30～41・8・16）	僑務委員会 委員長	陳済成 （40・3・30～41・8・16）
社会部長	丁黙邨 （40・3・30～41・8・16）	辺境委員会 委員長	羅君強 （40・3・30～41・8・16）
宣伝部長	林柏生 （40・3・30～41・8・16）		
警政部長	周佛海（兼） （40・3・30～40・12・19） 李士群 （40・12・19～41・8・16）	糧食管理委員会 主任委員	梅思平（兼） （40・7・9～41・8・16）
水利委員会 委員長	楊寿楣 （40・3・30～41・8・16）	全国経済委員会 委員長	汪精衛（兼） （40・12・19～41・8・16）
賑務委員会 委員長	岑徳広 （40・3・30～41・8・16）	文物保管委員会 委員長	徐良（兼） （41・3・24～41・10・27）

出所：同上、曽支農学位論文別冊 9 頁。

表C：人事異動一覧表（1941・8・16～1943・1・13）

院長	汪兆銘 （41・8・16～43・1・13）	教育部長	李聖五 （41・8・16～43・1・13）
副院長	周佛海 （41・8・16～43・1・13）	司法行政部長	趙毓松 （41・8・16～42・3・11） 羅君強 （42・3・11～43・12・30）
内政部長	陳群 （40・3・30～41・8・16）	実業部長	梅思平 （41・8・16～43・9・10）
外交部長	徐良 （41・8・16～41・10・27） 褚民誼 （41・10・27～43・1・13）	交通部長	丁黙邨 （41・8・16～43・1・13）
財政部長	周佛海（兼） （41・8・16～43・1・13）	宣伝部長	林柏生 （41・8・16～43・1・13）
軍政部長	鮑文越 （41・8・16～42・8・20）	水利委員会 委員長	諸青来 （41・8・16～43・1・13）
海軍部長	任援道（兼・代） （40・5・30～42・8・20）	賑務委員会 委員長	岑徳広 （41・8・16～43・1・13）
僑務委員会 委員長	陳済成 （41・8・16～41・12・31） 陳君慧 （41・12・31～42・8・20）	首都警察総監署 総監	蘇成徳 （42・6・2～43・1・13） 鄧祖禹 （42・6・30～43・1・13）
辺境委員会 委員長	羅君強 （41・8・16～42・3・11） 陳済成 （42・3・11～43・1・13）	新国民運動促進 委員会委員長	汪兆銘（兼） （42・6・2～43・1・13）
糧食管理委員会 主任委員	蔡培 （41・12・31～43・1・13） 顧宝衡 （42・2・28～43・1・13）	中央物価対策委 員会委員長	梅思平（兼） （42・9・3～43・1・13）
全国経済委員会 委員長	汪兆銘（兼） （41・8・16～43・1・13）	政務委員	陳君慧（41・12・31 免） 趙尊岳（42・3・11 免） 陳済成（42・3・11 免） 李士群（42・6・5 免） 傅式説（42・6・30 免） 蔡培（42・2・28 任） 汪曼雲（42・6・4 任） 蘇成徳 42・6・30 任 戴英夫（42・8・27 任） 顧継武（42・8・27 任）
文物保管委員会 委員長	徐良（兼） （41・8・16～41・10・27） 褚民誼（兼） （41・10・27～43・1・13）		
社会運動指導委 員会委員長	周佛海（兼） （41・8・16～43・1・13）		
中央物資統制委 員会主任委員	梅思平（兼） （41・9・4～42・9・3）		

注：「社運指」は社会運動指導委員会、「新国促」は新国民運動促進委員会の略称である。
出所：同上、曽支農学位論文本文 12 頁。

表 D：中央政府実力者らの地方への異動一覧表

省別	任職者／任職機関	中央での役職
江蘇省長	李士群（43・1・13〜43・9・9） 陳群（43・9・10〜44・11・2） 任援道（44・11・2〜45・8・16）	清郷委員会秘書長 行政院内政部長 軍事委員会海軍部長
浙江省長	傳式悦（43・1・20〜44・9・14） 項致荘（44・9・14〜45・5・2） 丁黙邨（45・5・2〜45・8・16）	行政院鉄道部長、政務委員 「軍事委」駐杭州綏靖主任公署主任 行政院社会福利部長
安徽省長	高冠吾（43・1・20〜43・12・30） 羅君強（43・12・30〜44・12・26） 林柏生（44・12・26〜45・8・16）	（江蘇政府主席から転任） 行政院司法行政部長 行政院宣伝部長
湖北省長	楊揆一（43・1・20〜45・3・3） 葉蓬（45・3・3〜45・8・16）	軍事委員会常務委員、弁公庁長 軍事委員会常務委員、陸軍部長
広東省長	陳耀祖（43・1・20〜44・4・6） 陳春圃（44・4・14〜45・4・26） 褚民詮（45・4・26〜45・8・16）	（省政府主席から転任） 行政院建設部長 行政院外交部長
江西省長	鄧祖禹（43・5・6〜43・12・30） 高冠吾（43・12・30〜45・3・3） 黄自強（45・3・3〜45・8・16）	行政院首都警察総監署総監 （安徽省長から転任） 軍事委員会政治部長
淮海省長	郝鵬挙（44・1・13〜45・8・16）	（蘇淮特別区行政公署行政長官から転任）

出所：同上、付録 42 頁。

表 E：汪政権管轄地域一覧

地方政権別	存在期間	官署駐在	トップ（最終在任）	所属
蒙彊地域各盟・省・市				蒙古自治政府
河北省政府	40・3・30〜45・8・16	清苑	栄臻	華北政務委員会
山東省政府	40・3・30〜45・8・16	済南	楊毓珣	同上
山西省政府	40・3・30〜45・8・16	大原	王驤	同上
河南省政府	40・3・30〜45・8・16	開封	鮑文越	同上
北京特別市政府	40・3・30〜45・8・16	北京	許修直	同上
天津特別市政府	40・3・30〜45・8・16	天津	周迪平	同上
青島特別市政府	40・3・30〜45・8・16	青島	姚作賓	同上
蘇北行政専員公署	39・7・12〜40・3・30	徐州	李海春	同上
威海衛行政専員公署	38・3・25〜40・5・21	威海衛	（不明）	行政院
江蘇省政府	40・3・30〜45・8・16	蘇州	任援道	同上
浙江省政府	40・3・30〜45・8・16	杭州	丁黙邨	同上
安徽省政府	40・3・30〜45・8・16	蚌埠	林柏生	同上
広東省政府	40・4・20〜45・8・16	広州	褚民詮	同上
湖北省政府	40・10・3〜45・8・16	武昌	葉蓬	同上
江西省政府	43・5・6〜45・8・16	九江	黄自強	同上
淮海省政府	44・1・3〜45・8・16	徐州	郝鵬挙	同上
南京特別市政府	40・3・30〜45・8・16	南京	周学昌	同上
上海特別市政府	40・3・30〜45・8・16	上海	周佛海	同上
漢口特別市政府	40・10・3〜43・10・19	漢口	張仁蠡	同上
廈門特別市政府	43・3・26〜45・8・16	廈門	李思賢	同上
蘇淮特別区行政公署	42・1・15〜44・1・13	徐州	郝鵬挙	同上
浙東特別区行政公署	42・5・26〜43・3・31	寧波	沈爾喬	同上
委員長駐蘇北行営	41・9・15〜43・5・27	泰県	臧卓	軍事委員会
駐蘇北綏靖主任公署	43・5・27〜45・8・16	揚州	孫良誠	同上

出所：同上、曽支農学位論文本文 30 頁。

25

The Wang Jingwei (Wang Ching-Wei) Government: A survey of archival and secondary sources by Tai Wei LIM (Senior Lecturer Singapore University of Social Sciences and National University of Singapore Research Fellow Adjunct). Work in progress, no circulation, embargo until delivery.

Introduction. This writing is a survey of secondary sources related to Wang Jingwei 汪精卫 (1883–1944) and his pro-Japanese administration supported by the Japanese government. It is an attempt to first curate digital information about the topic of Chinese collaborationism during the Sino-Japanese War (1937 to 1945) and also the Pacific War (1941-1945). It focuses on the Wang Jingwei regime in particular as this regime was recognized as the major backbone of pro-Japanese factions within the Chinese political elite circles in the duration of the two wars. Yun Xia argued that the primary purpose for setting up the pro-Japanese regimes was the pragmatic reason of control over a large territory:

> In order to effectively control the occupied territory with limited manpower...Japan supported... the Reformed Government (Weixin zhengfu, 1938-1940) in Nanjing, led by Liang Hongzhi, and the Provisional Government (Linshi zhengfu) in Beijing, headed by Wang Kemin (that controlled occupied regions in North China.) In March1940, Japan sponsored a Nanjing National Government (Nanjing guomin zhengfu) headed by Wang Jingwei. This central China regime replaced the Reformed Government and the Provisional Government, and absorbed their important bureaucrats.[1]

The administration in Nanjing 南京 operated from March 1940 to August 1945 within the Sino-Japanese war and later Pacific war period of 1937-1945. The origins of Wang's government is traceable back to the "Peace Movement" (*Heping yundong* 和平运动) established in January 1938. On 26 October 1938, Chen Bijun, Chen Gongbo, Zhou Fohai, Mei Siping, and Tao Xisheng (陶希聖) gathered in Chongqing to discuss collaboration with the Japanese under the cover of peace and Chen Bijun overcame Chen Gongbo's resistance to this decision within the group.[2] On 30 October 1938, **Gao Zongwu (高宗武)** and **Mei Siping** approached members of the Japanese government in Shanghai to set up what would eventually be the Wang Jingwei pro-Japanese government.[3] The Wang Jingwei defection from Chongqing happened in December 1939.

The thesis statement in this writing argues that (1) perceptions of collaborationism have gone

---

[1] Yun, Xia, "Traitors to the Chinese race (Hanjian)': Political and Cultural Campaigns against Collaborators during the Sino-Japanese War of 1937-1945 (Oregon: Department of History and the Graduate School of the University of Oregon), 2010, p.15.

[2] Yick, Joseph K.S., ""Pre-Collaboration": The Political Activity and Influence of Chen Bijun in Wartime China, January 1938–May 1940" dated 2014 in (SERAS) Southeast Review of Asian Studies Volume 36 (2014), available at http://www.uky.edu/Centers/Asia/SECAAS/Seras/2014/4Yick.pdf, pp.63-64.

[3] Yick, Joseph K.S., ""Pre-Collaboration": The Political Activity and Influence of Chen Bijun in Wartime China, January 1938–May 1940" dated 2014 in (SERAS) Southeast Review of Asian Studies Volume 36 (2014), available at http://www.uky.edu/Centers/Asia/SECAAS/Seras/2014/4Yick.pdf, p.64.

digital as pro-Japanese regimes, groups and individuals are now subjected to the multiplicity of interpretations in the digital medium. The democratization of information afforded by the internet allows members of the public to add their comments and interpretations of collaborationism, puppet regimes and thereafter shape memories of the Sino-Japanese war that morphed into the Pacific War when the Americans entered the fray after Pearl Harbour; (2) the pro-Japanese collaborators are not a homogenous group and there is surprising heterogeneity in their affiliation, association and closeness to Japan. Amongst them, there is also rivalry and competition, e.g. Wang Jingwei's administration and the North China Political Council; (3) the lines between being opportunistic, collaborationist, heroically undercover behind enemy lines are at best ambiguous and unclear. The net result of all three items is a proliferation of perceptions about individual actors active in the Sino-Japanese War when viewed through different degrees of loyalties to various regimes, ambiguity in the shadowy world of collaborationism, with such perceptions now magnified by the democratization of information so that the public can scrutinize the bits of online information about these characters.

Methodology. One of the most comprehensive list of Wang Jingwei regime collaborators with the Japanese found on record in the English language is the "Biographies of Puppet China" published by the Research and Analysis Branch Office of Strategic Services (OSS, forerunner of the Central Intelligence Agency or CIA) in Honolulu on 25 August 1945 with the conclusion of the Pacific War that month. Using this important document as a guide, the author then looked through secondary digital sources to curate information about this list of collaborators, their allies and associates. In addition to narrating the histories of the listed individuals, the objective of this writing is not to prove or disprove the authenticity of any document but to survey the available information and record perceptions of collaborationism in the contemporary context. In other words, the writing is more interested in the narratives than corroborating evidence, which is equally important and the subject of a later study in a series of collaborationism research.

Literature review. In terms of literature review, this writing is indebted to John Hunter Boyle's seminal work *China and Japan at War 1937-1945* published in 1972. Boyle makes the elegant and eloquent argument that Japanese scholarship's interests in collaborationism lies in the fact that they are still groping for identity affirmation of whether they belong to the East or the West or an intermediary between the two in the early 1970s, at the time of Boyle's writing.[4] The search for identity meant that the Japanese may have been wondering if they were the introducers of modernity to their Chinese counterparts, making them collaborating teachers of modernity. Boyle points out that some Japanese may even believe that Wang may have been a collaborator/learner of Japanese modernity but Chiang Kai-shek was also a puppet of Western imperialists (Japan's militarists believed that Chiang may even have fallen into puppetry collaboration with his masters

---

4 Boyle, John Hunter, China and Japan at War, 1937-1945: The Politics of Collaboration (Pal Alto: Stanford University Press), 1972, p.viii.

Soviet Union and Chinese Communist Party after the Xian Incident).[5] Chiang and Wang were merely student collaborators of two different set of imperialists according to this reading and they served different teachers.

But, if the Japanese were the West and distancing themselves from the East (as what Fukuzawa Yukichi advocated), then they were not collaborators but late imperialists. For this group, they conceptualized themselves as pragmatists who were able to further advance Japanese power if they set up puppet regimes and divide Northern Chinese power elites. If they were an intermediate bridge between the two, the grey ambiguous area that the Japanese were playing in China becomes even more pronounced, it may be possible that the Japanese were acting as both in the prewar and wartime eras. Thus, collaborationism is shaped not only by the Chinese collaborators but also the people and organizations they sought collaboration with. The decisive turn away from collaborating with willing, semi-willing or reluctant Chinese collaborators appears to be less pronounced or motivated between July 1937 to January 1938 when the advocates of accommodation ebbed in strength and power.[6]

Boyle's interest in studying Wang and other collaborators is to highlight the complexity of this character and not simply label him as a traitor or a hero. Wang is currently conceptualized as the villain of the Sino-Japanese war stories by many stakeholders in the Chinese-speaking world. It is popular perceptions and narratives that this writing is interested in studying. With electronic resources, such narratives and perceptions are transmitted even faster to a global audiences. Thus, some website resources with recorded perceptions of alleged collaborators are also included in this writing. It must be emphasized these are popular perceptions and should not be conflated with reality or evidence to support those assertions, perceptions or narratives. This somewhat parallels with Boyle's writing who firmly argued that he is not out to make Wang Jingwei a hero or villain or to provide evidence or supporting statements either way.[7] In reality, Wang was powerless from the start as he lacked military backing and went opposite of hardening trends and calls for resistance amongst the Chinese populace; in fact, Wang was only part of a loose federation of puppet regimes that included: those in Inner Mongolia, Peiping, Reformed Government of Republic of China based in Central China, Henry Aisingoruo Puyi, etc.[8] However, as we shall see later, Wang Jingwei and other Chinese collaborators had leverages that they can pull over their regime supporters from Japan.

---

[5] Boyle, John Hunter, China and Japan at War, 1937-1945: The Politics of Collaboration (Pal Alto: Stanford University Press), 1972, pp.9 and 10.

[6] Boyle, John Hunter, China and Japan at War, 1937-1945: The Politics of Collaboration (Pal Alto: Stanford University Press), 1972, p.3.

[7] Boyle, John Hunter, China and Japan at War, 1937-1945: The Politics of Collaboration (Pal Alto: Stanford University Press), 1972, p.2,

[8] Boyle, John Hunter, China and Japan at War, 1937-1945: The Politics of Collaboration (Pal Alto: Stanford University Press), 1972, p.4.

Then, there is a comparative perspective. Not all collaborating regimes or individuals had the same intensity of collaborative pliability. According to Boyle, **Henry Puyi** was one of the most pliable collaborators and he became infected with joy and thought of getting a new set of dragon robes when he was supported by the Japanese Commander of the Kwantung army.[9] However, at the war crimes trial with the end of WWII, he would reveal that he was a mere instrument of the Japanese with no real power and did his Japanese masters' bidding. Some collaborative puppet regimes even played Japanese political and military factions against each other. This then goes against the grain that the puppet regimes were powerless. In fact, Boyle indicated that some of them even deployed traditional Chinese strategies to play different factions against each other to maintain survival of the regime, e.g. **Wang K'o-min** leader of the Provisional Government in North China played Major General Kita Seiichi, Lt General Terauchi Hisaichi of North China Army and General Doihara Kenji of Army General Staff against each other.[10] In terms of the degrees of collaborative pliability, the Japanese military leaders also had to be careful not to create organizations that are too close in nature and characteristics to Japanese organizations. When that happens, there is no resonance between the organization they have created and the Northern Chinese populace they wish to subjugate. An example in this sense was the Hsin-min Hui which Boyle noted became ideologically too pliant such that they were not able to convince the populace of their autonomy and thus easily demonized by Communist Party informational campaigns.[11]

Kita Seiichi and Wang Jingwei were aligned against Wang K'o-min whom they considered obstinate but they needed K'o-min and his asset ownership of North China Railways to hedge against their mutual mortal enemy General Doihara Kenji.[12] Such leverage over the Chinese was even more pronounced as the Chinese collaborators were fully aware of the greatest asset they represented. It would be overly resource draining if Japan had to commit its own staff and military officers to make the Chinese comply with their rule, and manpower as well as human resource was something they could not spare at a time of national wartime emergency and crisis-coping conditions --- ultimately, both the Japanese and Chinese were aware of the fact that the Japanese were foreigners and thus Chinese collaborators made sense as Chinese faces of Japanese regimes.[13] The Japanese military establishment and colonial autocrats could not simply co-opt any Chinese elites. Boyle noted this in his publication when he highlighted the fact that many of the collaborators with the

---

9 Boyle, John Hunter, China and Japan at War, 1937-1945: The Politics of Collaboration (Pal Alto: Stanford University Press), 1972, p.11.

10 Boyle, John Hunter, China and Japan at War, 1937-1945: The Politics of Collaboration (Pal Alto: Stanford University Press), 1972, p.11.

11 Boyle, John Hunter, China and Japan at War, 1937-1945: The Politics of Collaboration (Pal Alto: Stanford University Press), 1972, p.95.

12 Boyle, John Hunter, China and Japan at War, 1937-1945: The Politics of Collaboration (Pal Alto: Stanford University Press), 1972, pp.11-12.

13 Boyle, John Hunter, China and Japan at War, 1937-1945: The Politics of Collaboration (Pal Alto: Stanford University Press), 1972, p.12.

Japanese were dis-spirited remnants of the *ancien regime* or corrupt band-wagoning individuals without abilities or integrity who were rejected by both the Nationalists and the Communists.[14]

The amorphous nature of collaborationism and puppet regime is seen by the fact that these labels are constantly evolving. For example, Wang Jingwei was not perennially the Japanese-leaning Han traitor. In fact, there was a point of time after 1927 (until it was clear he had defected to Japan in 1939) when he was known as the Stalinist puppet, leader of the left-wing factions of the Nationalist Party, believer of Stalin's idea/worldview of the need for reliance on a foreign power.[15] Even when his actions appeared pro-Japanese appeasement before 1939, it was usually a consequence of complex manoeuvrings by Generalissimo Chiang Kai-shek and the military commanders and leaders. For example, Wang took the flak for what was perceived as the diplomatic appeasement of the Japanese when the secret Chiang-engineered Ho-Umezu Agreement was signed was made public and inflamed students and activists alike. In fact, Wang became the target of an assassination attempt by a newspaper reporter-assassin on 1 November 1935. The Ho-Umezu Agreement had consequences. Because Hopei (Hebei in Hanyu Pinyin) was separated from Nanjing Nationalist Party Kuomintang control and cleansed of anti-Japanese elements, a new regime the East Hopei Autonomous Anti-Communist Council/Government armed with a Japanese-trained Peace Preservation Corps (Pao-an Tui) under the leadership of Yin Ju-keng was formed to eventually absorb 5 Chinese northern provinces into a single government.[16] The collaborationist government soon transformed into a centre for smuggling activities (in silver, opium, narcotics) and poppy cultivation operated by Japanese and Korean gangs, undermining the Nationalist government's financial stabilization drive and anti-narcotics efforts.[17]

Limitations. The names on the OSS list of collaborators in the Wang Jingwei regime are written in traditional Chinese but secondary sources used both Wades Giles as well as Hanyu Pinyin systems of Romanization to discuss events related to this subject matter. This complicated the search for relevant materials in secondary sources of information. Some of the digital secondary sources are ideologically-driven, drawing from state media, private investigators, independent researchers, online encyclopaedias and academic sources for an eclectic portrayal of diverse sources of information as well as popular perceptions of collaborators.

---

[14] Boyle, John Hunter, China and Japan at War, 1937-1945: The Politics of Collaboration (Pal Alto: Stanford University Press), 1972, p.97.

[15] Boyle, John Hunter, China and Japan at War, 1937-1945: The Politics of Collaboration (Pal Alto: Stanford University Press), 1972, p.25.

[16] Boyle, John Hunter, China and Japan at War, 1937-1945: The Politics of Collaboration (Pal Alto: Stanford University Press), 1972, pp.39-40.

[17] Boyle, John Hunter, China and Japan at War, 1937-1945: The Politics of Collaboration (Pal Alto: Stanford University Press), 1972, p.40.

Background of collaboration leading up to the Wang Jingwei government.

In 1935, the *Chicago Tribune* reported that the Japanese government had an inherent fear of communism in North China. The *Tribune* reported that Colonel Seiichi Kita head of the Japanese military general staff's China branch based in Tokyo was worried about Soviet Union's infiltration and support for Chinese communists in northwestern China; and argued that the military strongmen in that region are leaning towards Japan to realize the unification of China, Japan and Manchuria.[18] However, these warlords mostly had their own agendas and they were a varied lot with vastly different political ambitions. Therefore, Japan had challenges selecting a head for the North China Provisional pro-Japanese Government in Peiping that was set up on 14 December 1937; and the first pro-Japanese head of the administration, **Wang K'o-min**, made way for **Wang I-t'ang** in June 1940, who was in turn replaced by **Chu Shen** on 9 February 1943 before he passed away shortly after a couple of months after that; thereafter, Wang I-t'ang came back to head the administration before he became sick and passed on the position to **Wang Yin-t'ai**.[19] As for the legislative branch, **Liang Hongzhi** held the ceremonial roles of nominal governor of Jiangsu and chairperson of Legislative Yuan when the Reformed Government (chaired by Liang) merged into Wang Jingwei's Nanjing Nationalist Government on 30 March 1950.[20] Liang was sentenced to death for treason in Suzhou and executed by gunfire in Shanghai on 6 November 1946.[21]

When Japan established a second pro-Japanese government, the Reformed Government, at Nanking on 28 March 1938, they faced challenges but eventually attracted **Liang Hung-chih (Liang Hongzhi in Hanyu Pinyin)** to operate the pro-Japanese government regime from Nanjing, and it was relocated to the New Asia Hotel at Shanghai (becoming the "Hotel Government") before it was eventually integrated into Wang Jingwei pro-Japanese national government of in March 1940.[22] Wang Jingwei's government represented the greatest existential threat to the Nationalist Party:

> ...before Wang Jingwei, two accomplished politicians, Wang Kemin and Liang Hongzhi, had established regional puppet regimes with the sponsorship of the Japanese. However, the political significance of such regimes were incomparable to Wang Jingwei's National Government. This was not just because the Wang Jingwei regime declared itself to be a

---

18 Powell, John, "Japanese Chief Tells Fears if Reds in N. China" dated 22 December 1935 in the Chicago Tribune [downloaded on 1 Jan 2017], available at http://archives.chicagotribune.com/1935/12/22/page/19/article/japanese-chief-tells-fears-of-reds-in-n-china, p.19 (Part I)

19 Budge, Kent G., "Collaborationist Governments" dated 2015 in The Pacific War Online Encyclopedia website [downloaded on 1 April 2017], available at http://pwencycl.kgbudge.com/C/o/Collaborationist_Governments.htm

20 Wikiwand, "Liang Hongzhi" in the Wikiwand website [downloaded on 1 April 2017], available at http://www.wikiwand.com/en/Liang_Hongzhi

21 Wikiwand, "Liang Hongzhi" in the Wikiwand website [downloaded on 1 April 2017], available at http://www.wikiwand.com/en/Liang_Hongzhi

22 Budge, Kent G., "Collaborationist Governments" dated 2015 in The Pacific War Online Encyclopedia website [downloaded on 1 April 2017], available at http://pwencycl.kgbudge.com/C/o/Collaborationist_Governments.htm

national regime, in direct competition with Chiang Kai-shek's government in Chongqing. Different from the heads of other puppet regimes, Wang claimed that he represented orthodoxy (zhengtong) of both the Chinese government and Nationalist party ideology. This claim was not ungrounded given Wang Jingwei's important role in the early history of the Nationalist Party and his close relation to Sun Yat-sen, who was respected as the founding father of the Republic of China and the Nationalist Party.[23]

Wang Jingwei quickly embraced the narrative of Pan-Asianism in order to justify his collaborationism with a pro-Japanese government.

Throughout the course of Wang's regime, he had to justify to the Chinese living under his Reorganized National Government the reasons for collaboration…Wang often pointed to the concept of "Dr. Sun Yat-sen's Pan Asianism"…[and] In a radio address of June 1941, Wang criticised the nationalists for not staying true to Sun's legacy and having "failed to make united efforts for the attainment of that ideal [Pan-Asianism]" …buying into the Japanese idea of a 'New Order' in East Asia by collaborating and associating his prestige with it.[24]

Things did not go well for the Wang Jingwei regime as they were not able to displace the influence of the Nationalists, whether in running the region economy or in the hearts and minds of some elites. For example, the Nanjing Government was rocked by the realignment of **Kao Tsung-wu (Gao Zongwu)** and **T'ao Hsi-sheng (Tao Xisheng)** back into Kuomintang in January 1940 when they surfaced in Hong Kong and accused Japan's government for exerting pressures (taxes and customs) on the Nanking Government, and simultaneously, along with these defections, **Chou Fo-pei (Zhou Fobei)**, worked as a spy for Chiang Kai-shek in the Nanking Government.

Wang Jingwei's inner circle.

Wang Jingwei's political confidante was none other than his own wife, Chen Bijun, well known to be a strong and dominant personality in his life. **Chen Bijun 陈璧君**（1891–1959）was married to Wang and started her official collaboration with Japan in May 1940 when the administrations in Guangdong 广东 province and its capital Guangzhou 广州（Canton）were founded, becoming her sphere of influence from May 1940 to August 1945 or what the Nationalists and Communists termed as her "small dynasty"（*xiao wangchao* 小王朝）.[25] Chen's role in the formation of the pro-

---

23 Yun, Xia, "Traitors to the Chinese race (Hanjian)': Political and Cultural Campaigns against Collaborators during the Sino-Japanese War of 1937-1945 (Oregon: Department of History and the Graduate School of the University of Oregon), 2010, p.33.

24 Lowe, George, "Can Wang Jingwei's Decision to Collaborate with the Japanese During Wartime be Justified?" undated in the Duke East Asia Nexus website [downloaded on 1 April 2017], available at http://www.dukenex.us/can-wang-jingweirsquos-decision-to-collaborate-with-the-japanese-during-wartime-be-justified.html

25 Yick, Joseph K.S., ""Pre-Collaboration": The Political Activity and Influence of Chen Bijun in Wartime China, January 1938–May 1940" dated 2014 in (SERAS) Southeast Review of Asian Studies Volume 36 (2014), available at http://www.uky.edu/Centers/Asia/SECAAS/Seras/2014/4Yick.pdf, p.58

Japanese regime was prominent right from the start, beginning with the escape of Wang from Chiang Kai-shek's surveillance. Wang Jingwei and his wife Chen Bijun travelled to Hanoi through Kunming 昆明 Yunnan facilitated by the regional warlord in that area, **Long Yun 龙云** who was personally dissatisfied with Kuomintang's presence in his province diluting his control over local affairs and Chiang Kai-shek's recruitment of manpower from his sphere of influence.[26]

Chen also communicated with the French Hanoi government to provide protection and accommodations for them facilitating Wang Jingwei's escape to Hanoi in December 1938. Japanese Colonel Nakano Hidemitsu 中野英光 of Special Services Agency of the 21st Army guarding Guangdong formed the Guangdong Public Security Maintenance Committee in Guangzhou in December 1938 supported the pro-Japanese regime of **Peng Dongyuan 彭东原** (previously a high-ranking Cantonese Guangdong-based naval personnel) and **Lü Chunrong 吕春荣** from Guangxi who were resisted by many elites within the same region.[27] Wang Jingwei's presence turned things around in favour of the collaborationist regime when his pro-Japanese rule started in May 1940.[28] Even Wang's personal assistant **Hu Lancheng 胡兰成** observed Chen Bijun's dominant role in Wang's pro-Japanese regime, for example, on 26 May 1939, Chen sat and intervened in an important "top-level cadre meeting" in Shanghai for deciding the official name of the government, flag and other associated matters despite not having any appointments in the government, earning her the unofficial title of "anonymous but responsible prime minister".[29]

Legislative elites in the Wang Jingwei government.

Chen Gongbo was the head of Legislative Yuan of the Wang Jingwei government when it was formed and became head of the Nanjing Kuomintang Nationalist government after the death of Wang in 1944 and, after the war, he escaped to Japan but was extradited by the US-led SCAP (Supreme Commander of Allied Powers) forces and then executed in Suzhou in 1946.[30] According to China state-media China Central Television (CCTV), Chen tried to buy off a well-known Colonel (later posthumous Major-General) Xie Jinyuan, a figure respected by both the Kuomintang and the

---

26 Yick, Joseph K.S., ""Pre-Collaboration": The Political Activity and Influence of Chen Bijun in Wartime China, January 1938–May 1940" dated 2014 in (SERAS) Southeast Review of Asian Studies Volume 36 (2014), available at http://www.uky.edu/Centers/Asia/SECAAS/Seras/2014/4Yick.pdf, p.65.

27 Yick, Joseph K.S., ""Pre-Collaboration": The Political Activity and Influence of Chen Bijun in Wartime China, January 1938–May 1940" dated 2014 in (SERAS) Southeast Review of Asian Studies Volume 36 (2014), available at http://www.uky.edu/Centers/Asia/SECAAS/Seras/2014/4Yick.pdf, p.65.

28 Yick, Joseph K.S., ""Pre-Collaboration": The Political Activity and Influence of Chen Bijun in Wartime China, January 1938–May 1940" dated 2014 in (SERAS) Southeast Review of Asian Studies Volume 36 (2014), available at http://www.uky.edu/Centers/Asia/SECAAS/Seras/2014/4Yick.pdf, p.65.

29 Yick, Joseph K.S., ""Pre-Collaboration": The Political Activity and Influence of Chen Bijun in Wartime China, January 1938–May 1940" dated 2014 in (SERAS) Southeast Review of Asian Studies Volume 36 (2014), available at http://www.uky.edu/Centers/Asia/SECAAS/Seras/2014/4Yick.pdf, p.66.

30 Wikiwand, "Chen Gongbo" in the Wikiwand website [downloaded on 1 April 2017], available at http://www.wikiwand.com/en/Chen_Gongbo

Chinese Communist Party:

> After the establishment of the government of Wang Jingwei, Chen Gongbo became the first puppet mayor of Shanghai. He induced Xie Jinyuan to capitulate many times and invited Xie Jinyuan to be the chief of the staff of the No. 1 puppet army. Xie Jinyuan tore the warrant into pieces and shouted at the traitors. He said, "my parents are Chinese and their son also is a Chinese. Chinese are never flunkies." On April 24, 1941, when they were doing morning training at 5 that morning, **Hao Dingcheng** and three other soldiers brought out daggers an iron pickaxe and some other weapons hidden in clothes and ganged up and attacked Xie Jinyuan, stabbing his head and breast. Because of the serious wounds and the blood loss too much, Xie Jinyuan passed away at 6 o'clock at the age of 37. The four murderers were caught on the spot. According to them, they were bought off by the puppet government of Wang Jingwei. As the news spread, more than 100 thousand people came to express their condolences. On May 8, the Chinese government decreed Xie Jinyuan the major general of the infantry posthumously.[31]

Zhou Fohai was one of the most versatile operatives of the regime and was appointed to be the Minister of Finance, Treasury, Foreign Affairs consecutively and maintained command over a section of the Wang Jingwei army while taking over the portfolios of police minister, treasurer and mayor of Shanghai after Chen Gongbo.[32] Zhou Fohai reversed his earlier affiliation and went back to the Nationalists when he anticipated Wang and the Japanese would lose the war, sending info to Chiang's regime, assassinating Li Shiqun and strengthening his hold over the Wang regime.[33] After the Pacific, Zhou was held in Chongqing and then shipped to Nanjing Jiangsu Province where he was charged for treason and received the death penalty that was lightened to life imprisonment by Chiang Kai-shek and eventually passed away in prison on 28 February 1948 due to stomach and heart ailments.[34] Zhou was a good example of constantly shifting and evolving alliances between Chinese collaborators and their Japanese partners. Very often, pragmatic self-preservation would emerge as a priority reason for switching sides and changing partners. After Zhou who was second in command in the Wang regime was **Li Shiqun**, head of the No.76 Secret Service. When the Wang regime was set up, Wang Jingwei needed to consolidate his power within his regime and depended on his head of secret service Li Shiqun, who was connected with both the Communists and the Nationalists in the past, used his expertise to smash the Nationalist security networks in Shanghai

---

[31] China Central Television (CCTV), "Xie Jinyuan" undated in the CCTV website [downloaded on 1 April 2017], avialable at http://www.cctv.com/lm/176/71/88857.html

[32] Wikiwand, "Zhou Fohai" in the Wikiwand website [downloaded on 1 April 2017], available at http://www.wikiwand.com/en/Zhou_Fohai

[33] J. van de Ven, Hans, War and Nationalism in China 1925-1945, (London and NY: RoutledgeCurzon), 2003, pp.285-286

[34] Wikiwand, "Zhou Fohai" in the Wikiwand website [downloaded on 1 April 2017], available at http://www.wikiwand.com/en/Zhou_Fohai

and rose quickly through the regime to become the Jiangsu Governor and went around to unite and pacify other pro-Japanese forces.[35]

Gangster/Assassin/Fascist collaborators.

Collaborationism laid in a grey area of ambiguity, and the Chinese collaborators themselves have access to informal sources of power. One of the areas in which Chinese collaborators accumulate power is through the underworld which operates outside the law and away from governmental scrutiny. Three well-known Shanghainese underworld racketeers/gangsters became pro-Japanese operatives: **Gu Zhuxuan** (nicknamed "The Emperor of Subei", his brother **Gu Sungmao** (previously a rickshaw puller who became a supervisor in the Star Rickshaw Company and Subei dialect theatre owner) and **Wei Zhongxiu** (previously head detective of the Public Safety Bureau and follower of Green Gang boss Du Yuesheng).[36] Dai Li, the rising star who would become the chief (and ranking General) of Juntong (translated as Military Statistics but it was really a secret police organization) operated the fascist Blue Shirts' espionage and underground activities.[37] Under Dai Li's command to attack domestic traitors, undercover operative Zheng Jiemin organized the killing of Hunanese military warlord **Zhang Jingyao** who was seeking Japanese support and protection and it successfully intimidated other would-be *hanjian*s ('Chinese traitors') like **Wang Kemin, Wang Jitang**, and **Gao Wenyue** who went underground while Duan Qirui and Wu Peifu declared loyalty and feelings of patriotism to the Nationalists.[38]

The assassins also targeted pro-Japanese theorists. On 5 December 1937, **Su Xiwen**, a philosopher who received his education in Waseda University theorized "the Great Way" (the *Dadao*) and set up a pro-Japanese municipal government in Shanghai that used a combination of Chinese lunar calendar and Showa-reign Japanese calendar for official dating purpose.[39] The

---

35 J. van de Ven, Hans, War and Nationalism in China 1925-1945, (London and NY: RoutledgeCurzon), 2003, p.285.

36 Wakeman, Frederic Wakeman Jr., "Hanjian (Traitor)! Collaboration and Retribution in Wartime Shanghai" in Becoming Chinese: Passages to Modernity and Beyond, ed. Wen-hsin Yeh, [downloaded on 1 Jan 2017], (California: University of California Press), 2000, available at http://publishing.cdlib.org/ucpressebooks/view?docId=kt5j49q621&chunk.id=ch09&brand=ucpress, p.303.

37 Wakeman, Frederic Wakeman Jr., "Hanjian (Traitor)! Collaboration and Retribution in Wartime Shanghai" in Becoming Chinese: Passages to Modernity and Beyond, ed. Wen-hsin Yeh, [downloaded on 1 Jan 2017], (California: University of California Press), 2000, available at http://publishing.cdlib.org/ucpressebooks/view?docId=kt5j49q621&chunk.id=ch09&brand=ucpress, p.303.

38 Wakeman, Frederic Wakeman Jr., "Hanjian (Traitor)! Collaboration and Retribution in Wartime Shanghai" in Becoming Chinese: Passages to Modernity and Beyond, ed. Wen-hsin Yeh, [downloaded on 1 Jan 2017], (California: University of California Press), 2000, available at http://publishing.cdlib.org/ucpressebooks/view?docId=kt5j49q621&chunk.id=ch09&brand=ucpress, pp.303-4.

39 Wakeman, Frederic Wakeman Jr., "Hanjian (Traitor)! Collaboration and Retribution in Wartime Shanghai" in Becoming Chinese: Passages to Modernity and Beyond, ed. Wen-hsin Yeh, [downloaded on 1 Jan 2017], (California: University of California Press), 2000, available at http://publishing.cdlib.org/ucpressebooks/view?docId=kt5j49q621&chunk.id=ch09&brand=ucpress, pp.306-307.

Japanese authorities running the show in Shanghai did not respect Su and his philosophy and its Secret Service brought in a tough pro-Japanese enforcer **Wang Zihui** to operate Japan's Shanghai activities while poet **Liang Hongzhi**, previously a Beiyang civil servant became a Japanese supporter.[40] Further up north, the Japanese started unifying all pro-Japanese regimes into a centralized North China government(provisional government or Linshi zhengfu, Rinji seifu) in January 1938 headed by **Wang Kemin** in Beiping south China while a reform government (Weixin zhengf u, Ishin seifu) was established in March 1938 in Nanjing headed by Liang Hongzhi.[41] On April 28, 1938, the reform government set up a Supervisory Yamen (duban gongshu) to manage the municipal administration of the Dadao government and, in compliance, Su Xiwen formally endorsed the reform government by using its flag on 3 May 1938 and assumed the head of the Supervisory Yamen until October 15, 1938, when **Fu Xiaoan** took over the Shanghai Special Municipality (Shanghai tebie shi) while Su became the pro-Japanese Hankou mayor (Su eventually went to Tokyo to possibly avoid being killed).[42]

Collaborators with nexus to the Communists.

Some scholars argue that apparently, during the 1st KMT-CPC Cooperation (1924–1927), Mao Zedong supposedly enjoyed good relationships with Sun Yat-sen and Wang Jingwei, and according to this narrative especially when Wang was the President of the Nationalist government and Mao worked as Director of the National Government's Propaganda Department.[43] This school of thought indicated that Communist regime asked **Pan Hannian** to become acquainted with the Wang Jingwei administration that split with Chiang Kai-shek and formed the pro-Japanese Nanjing National Government.[44] Unbeknownst to the Nationalists and its secret alliance with Zhou as well as pro-Japanese elements of the Wang regime, Li Shiqun was already in contact with Pan Hannian the Communist spy who was passing information to the Chinese Communist Party (CCP)

---

[40] Wakeman, Frederic Wakeman Jr., "Hanjian (Traitor)! Collaboration and Retribution in Wartime Shanghai" in Becoming Chinese: Passages to Modernity and Beyond, ed. Wen-hsin Yeh, [downloaded on 1 Jan 2017], (California: University of California Press), 2000, available at http://publishing.cdlib.org/ucpressbooks/view?docId=kt5j49q621&chunk.id=ch09&brand=ucpress, p.307.

[41] Wakeman, Frederic Wakeman Jr., "Hanjian (Traitor)! Collaboration and Retribution in Wartime Shanghai" in Becoming Chinese: Passages to Modernity and Beyond, ed. Wen-hsin Yeh, [downloaded on 1 Jan 2017], (California: University of California Press), 2000, available at http://publishing.cdlib.org/ucpressbooks/view?docId=kt5j49q621&chunk.id=ch09&brand=ucpress, p.307.

[42] Wakeman, Frederic Wakeman Jr., "Hanjian (Traitor)! Collaboration and Retribution in Wartime Shanghai" in Becoming Chinese: Passages to Modernity and Beyond, ed. Wen-hsin Yeh, [downloaded on 1 Jan 2017], (California: University of California Press), 2000, available at http://publishing.cdlib.org/ucpressbooks/view?docId=kt5j49q621&chunk.id=ch09&brand=ucpress, pp.307-8

[43] Modern Chinese Literature and Culture (MCLC) Resource Center, "Truth of Mao Zedong's Collusion with the Japanese Army (1)" dated 2 July 2016 in The Ohio State University (OSU) MCLC Resource Center website [downloaded on 1 April 2017], available at https://u.osu.edu/mclc/2016/07/02/truth-of-mao-zedongs-collusion-with-the-japanese-army-1/

intelligence agencies and even met with Wang Jingwei offering protection to him.[45]

Pan Hannian allegedly contacted Wang Jingwei, Li Shiqun and Zhou Fohai in the Wang government, a development recorded in Zhou Fohai's diary and the writings of Zhou Fohai's son but, in 1955, Mao caught and incarcerated approximately 1000 individuals accused of spying (Mao critics say under his alleged secret command), including Pan Hannian who died in jail in 1955 (some analysts speculated that perhaps he had excessive information about the elites, particularly their strategy of "conspiring with the Japanese army").[46] In 1982, Pan Hannian's name was reinstated after support from his allies who gathered evidence to indicated that he faithfully worked for the communists under command from the elite leadership (Refer to books like *Pan Hannian the Intelligence Career* [Author: Qi Yin, People's Publishing House, 1996] and *Biography of Pan Hannian* [Author: Qi Yin, Chinese People's Public Security University Press, 1997]).[47] In the reinstated narrative, Pan Hannian apparently spied and extracted useful ideas about the Japanese military from Japanese sources for the Communists' war against Japan, contributing to eventual victory.[48]

Institutions: North China Political Council (華北政務委員会 in traditional Chinese character, Hua-pei Cheng-wu Wei-yuan-hui in Wades Giles romanization and Kahoku Seimu Iinkai in Japanese).

The Chinese embassy in Lithuania claimed that the pro-Japanese North China Political Council was set up by Japanese diplomat Koki Hirota who later became Prime Minister and Foreign Minister simultaneously between March 1936 and January 1937 when his country signed the Anti-Comintern Pact with Germany and Italy and then set up the Political Council before buttressing Wang Jingwei's regime.[49] By early 1938, Ma Zhao noted that Japanese-controlled northern China had Beijing and Tianjin urban centers as its core and emanated outwards to envelop Manchuria,

---

44 Modern Chinese Literature and Culture (MCLC) Resource Center, "Truth of Mao Zedong's Collusion with the Japanese Army (1)" dated 2 July 2016 in The Ohio State University (OSU) MCLC Resource Center website [downloaded on 1 April 2017], available at https://u.osu.edu/mclc/2016/07/02/truth-of-mao-zedongs-collusion-with-the-japanese-army-1/

45 J. van de Ven, Hans, War and Nationalism in China 1925-1945, (London and NY: RoutledgeCurzon), 2003, p.286

46 Modern Chinese Literature and Culture (MCLC) Resource Center, "Truth of Mao Zedong's Collusion with the Japanese Army (1)" dated 2 July 2016 in The Ohio State University (OSU) MCLC Resource Center website [downloaded on 1 April 2017], available at https://u.osu.edu/mclc/2016/07/02/truth-of-mao-zedongs-collusion-with-the-japanese-army-1/

47 Modern Chinese Literature and Culture (MCLC) Resource Center, "Truth of Mao Zedong's Collusion with the Japanese Army (1)" dated 2 July 2016 in The Ohio State University (OSU) MCLC Resource Center website [downloaded on 1 April 2017], available at https://u.osu.edu/mclc/2016/07/02/truth-of-mao-zedongs-collusion-with-the-japanese-army-1/

48 Modern Chinese Literature and Culture (MCLC) Resource Center, "Truth of Mao Zedong's Collusion with the Japanese Army (1)" dated 2 July 2016 in The Ohio State University (OSU) MCLC Resource Center website [downloaded on 1 April 2017], available at https://u.osu.edu/mclc/2016/07/02/truth-of-mao-zedongs-collusion-with-the-japanese-army-1/

Mongolia Shanxi Province and Shandong Province while the occupation areas of control was split into Rehe Province (came under Manchukuo); Suiyuan and Chahar (administered by the United Autonomous Government of the Mongolian Frontier or Mengjiang lianhe zizhi zhengfu 蒙疆聯合自治政府); and Hebei, Henan, Shanxi, and Shandong Provinces, as well as Beijing and Tianjin under the North China Political Council (Huabei zhengwu weiyuanhui 華北政務委員會) which amalgamated with Wang Jingwei's government in Nanjing in 1940.[50]

John Hunter Boyle argues that the purpose of establishing the pro-Japanese North China Political Council was to shore up the financial autonomy of North China through the power to receive a majority percentage of China's customs fees, salt revenue and excise taxes and eventually drive it towards independence from the rest of China through this funding.[51] In the negotiations, Wang tried to increase the percentage of collection with Japan and managed to make some headway but was not entirely please when Japan worked with the Council to facilitate bonds issuance while the pro-Japanese Peiping's Federal Bank of China managed financial activities including currency issuing for China --- all activities that Wang and his administration supposed were under the purview of his government.[52] Japan directly communicated with the North China Political Council, bypassing Wang's government, prompting Wang to advocate for the power to appoint Council membership, vet its initiatives and control monetary decisions for North China but all were denied.[53]

The North China Political Council obtained more than just financial autonomy but also obtained defense and security powers related to combating communism, North China public security, the stationing of Japanese troops in the region, access points to buried mineral and other resources, appropriation, logistics and transportation of strategic or necessary materiel to Japan, Manchuria, Mengchiang and North China, transportation and communication systems as well as mobilize an independent military force, the Pacification Army (Suiching-chun).[54] The importance of this Council is supported by the fact that when its members (even former members) visited

---

[49] Embassy of the People's Republic of China in the Republic of Lithuania, "History of Japanese Militarism and Circumstances Concerning the Issue of Yasukuni Shrine" dated 16 Jan 2014 in the Embassy of the People's Republic of China in the Republic of Lithuania website [downloaded on 1 Jan 2017], available at http://www.chinaembassy.lt/eng/sr/t1119633.htm

[50] Ma, Zhao, Runaway Wives, Urban Crimes, and Survival Tactics in Wartime Beijing, 1937–1949 ("Introduction") dated 20 July 2015 in the Harvard University Asia Center Publications Program website [downloaded on 1 Jan 2017], 2015, available at http://publications.asiacenter.harvard.edu/files/asia_center_publications_program/files/ma_intro.pdf, p.6.

[51] Boyle, John Hunter, China and Japan at War, 1937-1945: The Politics of Collaboration (Pal Alto: Stanford University Press), 1972, p.271.

[52] Boyle, John Hunter, China and Japan at War, 1937-1945: The Politics of Collaboration (Pal Alto: Stanford University Press), 1972, p.271.

[53] Boyle, John Hunter, China and Japan at War, 1937-1945: The Politics of Collaboration (Pal Alto: Stanford University Press), 1972, p.271.

[54] Boyle, John Hunter, China and Japan at War, 1937-1945: The Politics of Collaboration (Pal Alto: Stanford University Press), 1972, p.271.

Tokyo, the news was disseminated empire-wide. For example, Singapore's *Syonan Shimbun* reported that the Japanese Emperor and Premiere Tojo met with **Wang I-tang** (former chair of the North China Political Council) of the Central Political Council of the National Government of China in the Tokyo Imperial Palace.[55] A material evidence of the importance and existence of the pro-Japanese Council were the stamps that the regime issued. Amongst the stamp-collecting communities in the world, the stamps issued by North China Political Council are classified under the "Japanese Occupation of China Stamps North China", and the 4th founding year of the pro-Japanese North China Political Council was commemorated in 1944 with the series known as "1944 4th Anniversary of North China Political Council with T 7".[56]

Background. The North China Political Council was initially a separate creation from the pro-Japanese Wang Jingwei government. An early member of the original Council was Chang Hsiao-liang (Chang Hsueh-liang) born at Hai-chen, Liaoning in 1898 was the eldest son of the late Chang Tso-lin and a professional military man who was trained at the Military Training Academy of the Three Eastern Provinces and fought at the Anfu-Chihli War, overcoming the Anfu forces at Hsiao-Chan, Chihli.[57] Roy K. McCall argued that Zhang Swyeliang (also spelt Zhang Xueliang in Hanyu Pinyin and Chang Hsueh-liang in Wades Giles romanization)'s father (**Chang Tso-lin**) was a Japanese collaborator who was killed by Japanese troops for not going against Chiang Kaishek.[58] He was promoted to a brigadier-general by the Peking Government in November 1920, dispatched by his father to Japan study military strategies in 1921 and was militarily involved in Northern China's balance of power, becoming a major figure who led to the downfall of the Northern Military Coalition Government of Feng Yu-hsiang, Yen Hsi-shan and Wang Ching-wei at Peiping in 1930; and, in November 1930, he was appointed to serve on the Standing Committee of North China Political Council in 1931.[59]

Because of this history, after the war ended, when the Allies began to identify Japanese collaborators during the Tokyo International Military Tribunal, the defense lawyers for the North

---

55 Domei, "Tenno Heika Receives Wang I-Tang in Palace" dated 15 May 1943 in Syonan Shimbun [downloaded on 1 Jan 2017], available at http://eresources.nlb.gov.sg/newspapers/Digitised/Article/syonantimes19430515-1.2.2, p.1.

56 International Education Media Trinity House, "Japanese Occupation of China Stamps North China" in the World Stamp Catalogue website [downloaded on 1 Jan 2017], available at http://www.worldstampcatalogue.org/japan/1944_4th%20anniversary%20of%20north%20china%20political%20council.html

57 The China Weekly Review, Who's who in China; biographies of Chinese leaders 5th Edition (Shanghai China: Shanghai China Weekly Review), 1936, available at https://archive.org/stream/5edwhoswhoinchina00shanuoft/5edwhoswhoinchina00shanuoft_djvu.txt

58 McCall, Roy K., China's Greatest Statesman: Zhou Enlai's Revolution and the One He Left Behind in his Birthplace of Huai'an (Indiana Bloomington: iUniverse), 2015, unpaginated online version

59 The China Weekly Review, Who's who in China; biographies of Chinese leaders 5th Edition (Shanghai China: Shanghai China Weekly Review), 1936, available at https://archive.org/stream/5edwhoswhoinchina00shanuoft/5edwhoswhoinchina00shanuoft_djvu.txt

China Political Council regime argued that the campaign towards autonomy started in North China even before the occurrence of the Marco Polo Bridge Incident.[60] After the Tangku Agreement was inked in May 1933, the legitimate national government at the time founded the North China Political Committee which controlled the locations of Hopei, Chahar, Suntung, Shanshi, Suiyuan, Peiping and Tientsin on 17 June 1933.[61] The Council appointed Huangfu (also Huang Fu) to be the chief Committee member. Besides identifying collaborators and listening to their defence, the pro-Japanese collaborators' properties were also quickly confiscated and resold:

> ...**Miu Bin**, the deputy principal of the Wang Jingwei government's Judicial Yuan, was sentenced to death, and his "grand mansion with garden" (huayuan yangfang) on Shaoxing Road, Shanghai, was confiscated. After its confiscation, several parties fought over it, including the American embassy, Chiang Wei-kuo, Zou Haibin (a committee member of the Control Yuan) and Xia Qin (chief justice of the Supreme Court).[62]

Concluding remarks.

Retaliatory measures against collaborators were understandable in the context of the victor parties seeking justice and accountability for the war. Thus, punishments meted out to collaborators are likely to be harsh to demonstrate the consequence of band-wagoning with the enemy. However, as indicated eloquently by Boyle, collaborationism was complex and ambiguous. There are tensions between self-preservation and lofty ideas when collaborators make their decisions in throwing their lot with the Japanese elites. There are also ambiguity in power distribution between the collaborators/puppets and their puppet masters because, sometimes, the Japanese elites needed Chinese collaborators more than the collaborators needed them when it comes to pacification of local populations. In some cases, the collaborators were willing, pliant and nursed imagined fantasies of autonomy, accumulation of power and independence of thought but only to discover reality was far from what they imagined. For others, the attraction of power is so strong that they only earned to wear dragon robes (Aisingoro Henry Puyi) and relive the imperial dynastic dream.

Other than local elites and former elites of *ancien regimes*, other collaborators with real sources of autonomous power acquire them through informal means without state participation. The state steps in when it becomes convenient to use such informal sources of power to resolve their problems or to keep the order without deploying state forces. Thus, underworld-state collaboration is another feature of Chinese collaborationism with the Japanese authorities. These informal sources of power emerge even stronger in the vacuum of state power, for e.g. when the Kuomintang

---

[60] Cryer, Robert and Neil Boiste (Editors), Documents on the Tokyo International Military Tribunal: Charter, Indictment and Judgements, Volume 1 (UK: Oxford University Press), 2008, p.1056.

[61] Cryer, Robert and Neil Boiste (Editors), Documents on the Tokyo International Military Tribunal: Charter, Indictment and Judgements, Volume 1 (UK: Oxford University Press), 2008, p.1056.

[62] Yun, Xia, "Traitors to the Chinese race (Hanjian)': Political and Cultural Campaigns against Collaborators during the Sino-Japanese War of 1937-1945 (Oregon: Department of History and the Graduate School of the University of Oregon), 2010, p.57.

was compelled to leave Northern Chinese areas like Hopei (Hebei) under Japanese pressure. Equally non-helpless are the skilful collaborators who are accurate and precise in analysing power equilibrium and strategically play one elite faction against another, e.g. Japanese rival factions and rival power centres amongst the military leaders and bureaucrats. Both informal sources of power and elite collaborators are able to leverage their association with one faction against another for self-preservation and even expansion of power base. The most capable of the elites know that they are in a favourable position when it comes to courtship by Japanese elites to pacify local populations. To that end, collaborators can keep their power and status within Chinese societies. Of course, some of these elites collaborators eventually turned out to be embedded spies or/and free agents that switch sides in accordance with where the power pendulum swings.

Bibliography:

Boyle, John Hunter, China and Japan at War, 1937-1945: The Politics of Collaboration (Pal Alto: Stanford University Press), 1972

Budge, Kent G., "Collaborationist Governments" dated 2015 in The Pacific War Online Encyclopedia website [downloaded on 1 April 2017], available at http://pwencycl.kgbudge.com/C/o/Collaborationist_Governments.htm

China Central Television (CCTV), "Xie Jinyuan" undated in the CCTV website [downloaded on 1 April 2017], avialable at http://www.cctv.com/lm/176/71/88857.html

Cryer, Robert and Neil Boiste (Editors), Documents on the Tokyo International Military Tribunal: Charter, Indictment and Judgements, Volume 1 (UK: Oxford University Press), 2008

Domei, "Tenno Heika Receives Wang I-Tang in Palace" dated 15 May 1943 in Syonan Shimbun [downloaded on 1 Jan 2017], available at http://eresources.nlb.gov.sg/newspapers/Digitised/Article/syonantimes19430515-1.2.2, p.1.

Embassy of the People's Republic of China in the Republic of Lithuania, "History of Japanese Militarism and Circumstances Concerning the Issue of Yasukuni Shrine" dated 16 Jan 2014 in the Embassy of the People's Republic of China in the Republic of Lithuania website [downloaded on 1 Jan 2017], available at http://www.chinaembassy.lt/eng/sr/t1119633.htm

International Education Media Trinity House, "Japanese Occupation of China Stamps North China" in the World Stamp Catalogue website [downloaded on 1 Jan 2017], available at http://www.worldstampcatalogue.org/japan/1944_4th%20anniversary%20of%20north%20china%20political%20council.html

J. van de Ven, Hans, War and Nationalism in China 1925-1945, (London and NY: RoutledgeCurzon), 2003

Lowe, George, "Can Wang Jingwei's Decision to Collaborate with the Japanese During Wartime be Justified?" undated in the Duke East Asia Nexus website [downloaded on 1 April 2017], available at http://www.dukenex.us/can-wang-jingweirsquos-decision-to-collaborate-with-the-japanese-during-wartime-be-justified.html

Ma, Zhao, Runaway Wives, Urban Crimes, and Survival Tactics in Wartime Beijing, 1937–1949 ("Introduction") dated 20 July 2015 in the Harvard University Asia Center Publications Program website [downloaded on 1 Jan 2017], 2015, available at http://publications.asiacenter.harvard.edu/files/asia_center_publications_program/files/ma_intro.pdf

McCall, Roy K., China's Greatest Statesman: Zhou Enlai's Revolution and the One He Left Behind in his Birthplace of Huai'an (Indiana Bloomington: iUniverse), 2015, unpaginated online version

Modern Chinese Literature and Culture (MCLC) Resource Center, "Truth of Mao Zedong's Collusion with the Japanese Army (1)" dated 2 July 2016 in The Ohio State University (OSU) MCLC Resource Center website [downloaded on 1 April 2017], available at https://u.osu.edu/mclc/2016/07/02/truth-of-mao-zedongs-collusion-with-the-japanese-army-1/

Powell, John, "Japanese Chief Tells Fears if Reds in N. China" dated 22 December 1935 in the Chicago Tribune [downloaded on 1 Jan 2017], available at http://archives.chicagotribune.com/1935/12/22/page/19/article/japanese-chief-tells-fears-of-reds-in-n-china, p.19 (Part I)

Research and Analysis Branch Office of Strategic Services (OSS) Honolulu, Biographies of Puppet China Assemblage #57 (Honolulu: OSS), 25 August 1945.

The China Weekly Review, Who's who in China; biographies of Chinese leaders 5th Edition (Shanghai China: Shanghai China Weekly Review), 1936, available at https://archive.org/stream/5edwhoswhoinchina00shanuoft/5edwhoswhoinchina00shanuoft_djvu.txt

Wakeman, Frederic Wakeman Jr., "Hanjian (Traitor)! Collaboration and Retribution in Wartime Shanghai" in Becoming Chinese: Passages to Modernity and Beyond, ed. Wen-hsin Yeh, [downloaded on 1 Jan 2017], (California: University of California Press), 2000, available at http://publishing.cdlib.org/ucpressebooks/view?docId=kt5j49q621&chunk.id=ch09&brand=ucpress

Wikiwand, "Chen Gongbo" in the Wikiwand website [downloaded on 1 April 2017], available at http://www.wikiwand.com/en/Chen_Gongbo

Wikiwand, "Liang Hongzhi" in the Wikiwand website [downloaded on 1 April 2017], available at http://www.wikiwand.com/en/Liang_Hongzhi

Wikiwand, "Zhou Fohai" in the Wikiwand website [downloaded on 1 April 2017], available at http://www.wikiwand.com/en/Zhou_Fohai

Yick, Joseph K.S., ""Pre-Collaboration": The Political Activity and Influence of Chen Bijun in Wartime China, January 1938–May 1940" dated 2014 in (SERAS) Southeast Review of Asian Studies Volume 36 (2014), available at http://www.uky.edu/Centers/Asia/SECAAS/Seras/2014/4Yick.pdf, pp.58-74

Yun, Xia, "Traitors to the Chinese race (Hanjian)': Political and Cultural Campaigns against Collaborators during the Sino-Japanese War of 1937-1945 (Oregon: Department of History and the Graduate School of the University of Oregon), 2010.

BIOGRAPHIES OF PUPPET CHINA

ASSEMBLAGE # 57

(Second Edition of Assemblage #17)

Research and Analysis Branch
OFFICE OF STRATEGIC SERVICES
HONOLULU, T. H.
August 25, 1945

B I O G R A P H I E S   I N   P U P P E T   C H I N A

A S S E M B L A G E   #57

Second Edition of #17

This list is taken from FCC short-wave
Intercepts of Radio Tokyo and
affiliated stations, dating from
December, 1941, to March 14, 1945
and from other sources.
Complied by
Research and Analysis Branch
OFFICE OF STRATEGIC SERVICES
Honolulu, T.H.
August 25, 1945

BIOGRAPHIES OF PUPPET CHINA

TABLE OF CONTENTS

Chinese.	1
Chinese Addenda.	206
Japanese	207
Burmese	255
Filipino.	255
Thailander.	255
Indian	255
French	256
German	257
Italian.	259
Portuguese.	260
Russian.	261
Other European	261

NOTE

This list of names is made up primarily from those already published in the following:
ASSEMBLAGE #49: PROGRAMS OF JAPAN IN CHINA
     Part I: Central Coastal Provinces
ASSEMBLAGE #51: PROGRAMS OF JAPAN IN CHINA
     Part II: Southern Coast
ASSEMBLAGE #52: PROGRAMS OF JAPAN IN CHINA
     Part III: Northern Coast
References to page numbers in these assemblages follow many of the names. To this original list have been added other names taken from various sources. The most important of these is a manuscript list of biographies prepared by M.O. Branch of OSS. These are referred to as "OSS-Ms." Another prolific source has been various reports prepared by the Inter-Departmental Committee for the Acquisition of Foreign Publications. Many of these are lists of names taken from the so-called Nanking Year Book -- 1943. In every case these are referred to as "IDC". Another source is R&A Publication STRUCTURE AND PERSONNEL OF THE NANKING PUPPET GOVERNMENT (AND HONGKONG ADMINISTRATION), January 12, 1945, referred to as "R&A 2565." R&A 2565.1 reached this office too late for it to be used as a check on the names included here. Reference should be made to this publication as it may contain supplementary information.

BIOGRAPHIES OF PUPPET CHINA

CHINESE

Ai Lu-chan -- Legislative member, Legislative Yuan, Nanking (1943)

Lu-chien -- Inspector, China Office, East Asia League (1943)

An Fu-tsao -- Executive Director, Sino-Japanese Cultural Association, Wu-ch'ang and Hankow Branches (1943)

Ao Ta-ching -- Born, 1896, Chungshan, Kwangtung; American educated; parents living in Chicago; joined Japanese in 1937; Director, Ping-Sui Railway (OSS-Ms.)

Aw Boon-haw (Aw Bang-ho, Aw Bung-law, Aw Bung-maw, Hu Wan-hu, Wu Wen-hu) -- Chinese financier cooperating with Japan; called "Tiger Balm King"; originally resided in Singapore and in Hongkong; outstanding Chinese merchant; organized company to transport rice, etc. from neighboring countries; elected President, Civilian Food Assistance Association (1943), contributing half million dollars as capital; made donations to clergy, nuns, etc.; Proprietor, HSIANG TAO JIH PAO (51:231)

Ba Unyei -- Vice-Commander, Tsingtao Special Municipality Peace Preservation Corps; resigned (8/15/44)

Bang How (Hsia P'eng) -- Once Head, Criterion Trading Company, a munitions company (7/15/44) (49:162)

Bun Ritsu -- Governor, Kiangsu Province; Commissioner, Suchow

Ch'a Li-ch'iu -- Inspector, Citizens' Savings Movement Committee, Shanghai (1943) (49:162)

Shih-chi -- Executive member, China Journalists Association (1943)

Ch'ai Hsieh-yuan -- Member, Invited Committee, Central Political Council (12/38); Commander-in-Chief, Pacification Corps, North China (12/38) (52:230)

Tsung -- Judge, Supreme Court, Nanking (1943)

Chan -- Made economic report on price of rice (5/15/44)

Min-pat -- Educator; Education Section, Chinese Council; Officer, Chinese Representative Association; Chairman, Hongkong General Relief Association (51:231)

Pai-li -- Hongkong Representative, Chinese Language Society (51:231)

Pok -- Staff member, CHUNG SHAN JIH PAO, Canton (OSS-Ms.) (51:231)

-1-

CHINESE

Chan R. -- Puppet working for Japanese, Hongkong;
        Superintendent, British Internment Camp,
        Stanley, Hongkong (OSS-Ms.)

    Shan-k'un -- Director, Citizens' Savings Movement
        Committee, Shanghai (49:162)

    Sin-ho -- Former Editor-in-Chief, SHANGHAI HSIN
        PAO; turned from Chungking to Nanking govern-
        ment; outstanding critic (9/5/42) (49:162)

    Tsu-chi -- Vice-Treasurer, National Government of
        China (7/18/44)

    Wu-ping -- Member, ... Committee of Municipal
        Council, Shanghai (5/13/44) (49:162)

    Yueh-ling -- Member, Finance Committee, Municipal
        Council, Shanghai (5/13/44) (49:162)

Chang -- Chief, Peace Preservation Army; attended con-
        ference re world situation and importance
        of exterminating communist forces (9/12/43)

Chang -- Chief, Department of Reconstruction, Kwangtung
        Provincial Government, Canton; Executive
        member, Commodity Investigation Committee
        (51:231)

    Ch'ao -- Secretary, National Government, Nanking
        (1943); Head, National Athletic Association;
        Ministry of Social Welfare, Nanking; Can-
        didate Director, Sino-Japanese Cultural
        Association; member, China-Japan Returned
        Students Club; member, All-China Athletic
        Association; Minister, residing in Ministry
        of Foreign Affairs (R & A 2565)

    Chao-ch'ang -- Executive Director, China Educa-
        tional Reconstruction Association, Chekiang
        Branch (1943) (49:162)

    Chao-chi -- Chief Judge, Chekiang High Court
        (R & A 2565)

    Chao-li -- Outstanding Chinese Moslem leader; mem-
        ber, Chinese Moslem Near East Goodwill
        Mission (1938) (OSS-Ms.)

    Chao-ming -- Executive member, China Journalists
        Association (1943)

    Che-tieh -- Magistrate, Hua-hsien, Kwangtung
        (OSS-Ms.)

    Chen, Lt. Gen. -- Assistant Chief-of-Staff,
        National Government Military Council
        (10/5/44)

    Chen-ch'un -- Publisher, SHIH YEN PAO, Peiping
        (1943) (52:230)

    Chen-fu -- President, Examination Yuan; Director,
        Sino-Japanese Buddhist Research Society, Nan-
        king (8/3/44); made inspection tour, Japan
        (10/13/44)

CHINESE

Chang Chen-fu -- President, Examination Yuan; Director, Sino-Japanese Buddhist Research Society, Nanking (8/3/44); made inspection tour of Japan (10/13/44)

Cheng-tzu -- Candidate Inspector, Education Committee, Shanghai (1943) (49:162)

Ch'i -- Director, Peace Preservation; Head, Bureau of Public Safety, Huaihai Province (R & A 2565)

Ch'i-huang -- Commander, 12th Division, Nanking Army (IDC - 3/30/42)

Ch'i-ko -- Secretary, Kuomingtang Third District Party Headquarters, Canton (IDC - 12/43)

Ch'i-liu -- Member, Committee of Political Councillors, Nanking (1943); member, Social Welfare Committee, China Office, East Asia League

Chi-ying -- Publisher, HU CHOU HSIN PAO, Hu-chou, Chekiang (1943) (IDC-H 2562)

Chia-hsiang -- Chairman, Directors, Metal Wires Association, Shanghai (IDC 7264)

Chia-hsun -- Vice-Secretary, Chinghsiang Administration, Hangchou Sector (6/8/43)

Chia-ngau -- Minister of Communications (DIO - 1/1/42)

Chia-yun -- Head, Reconstruction Bureau, Canton (OSS-Ms.) (51:231)

Chiang-sheng -- Chairman, Directors, Liquor Factories, Shanghai; Alcohol Extract Factories (IDC 7264)

Chiang-to'ai -- Secretary, Control Yuan, Nanking (1943)

Ch'ien -- Judge and Chief of Court, North China Branch, Supreme Court (1/17/43) (52:230)

Chien-an -- Publisher, HOPEH JIH PAO, Pao-ting, Hopeh (1943) (IDC-H 2562)

Chien-chih -- Inspecting member, China Journalists Association (1943); Publishers Committee, China Writers Club

Chien-fei -- With Japanese Huang Hsieh Chun, Tung-cheng and vicinity, commanding 3,000 men (6/39;OSS-Ms.)

Chien-heng -- Counsellor, National Government, Nanking (1943)

Ch'ien-li -- Publishers Committee, China Writers Club (1943)

CHINESE

Chang Chieng-ch'u (Chang Li-ch'u; Chou Wang-hsien;
　　　Sun Chien-ch'u) -- Director, European-
　　　American Bureau; Minister, Foreign Affairs,
　　　Nanking; Officer, 8th District, Shanghai
　　　(1943)

Chih-hsueh -- Inspector, Citizens' Savings Move-
　　　ment Committee, Shanghai (1943) (49:162)

Chih-p'ei -- Secretary General, Hankow (12/2/43)
　　　(IDC)

Chin-hsai -- Legislative member, Legislative Yuan,
　　　Nanking (1943)

Chin-wu -- Publisher, TANG TU JIH PAO, Tai-ping,
　　　Chekiang (1943) (IDC-H 2562)

Ching-hsi -- Head, General Affairs Section,
　　　Kuomintang Headquarters, Kwangtung Prov-
　　　ince; graduate, Pennsylvania Normal School;
　　　formerly worked for Provincial and City
　　　Party Headquarters, for Provincial Social
　　　Movement Committee (IDC - 12/43) (51:231)

Ching-hsien -- Chairman, Directors, Industrial
　　　Fat and Oil Company, Shanghai (1943)

Ch'ing-hung -- Executive Inspector, China Edu-
　　　cation Reconstruction Association, Shanghai
　　　Branch (1943) (49:162)

Ching-ken -- Head, China Deaf and Dumb Education
　　　Association, Shanghai (1943) (IDC 7265)

Ch'ing-liang -- Director, China-Japan Returned
　　　Students Club (1943)

Ching-lu -- Manager, Kuo Hsin Bank, Shanghai
　　　(IDC 7270 - 1943)

Ching-shan -- Commander, pro-Japanese troops;
　　　with Japanese Huang Hsieh Chun in Honan
　　　(6/39;OSS-Ms.)

Ch'ing-yu -- Former police officer, Pao An Tui,
　　　in demilitarized zone; commanding 4,000
　　　soldiers of East Hopeh Peace Preservation
　　　Corps in and around T'ungchow; with
　　　Japanese in North Hopeh (since 7/37)(OSS-Ms.)

Ch'ing-yueh -- Judge, Administrative Court,
　　　Nanking (1943)

Cho-k'un -- Mayor, Canton; gave press interview
　　　re education and teachers' salaries in
　　　Canton (IDC 11/15/43) (51:231)

Cho-sheng -- Manager, Central Reserve Bank,
　　　Hankow Branch, Hupeh (IDC 7270 - 1943)

Ch'uan -- Inspector, China-Japan Returned Stu-
　　　dents Club (1943)

Chun -- See Chang Tsun

CHINESE

Chang Chung -- Ex-Head, 3rd Section, Canton Police
(51:231)

Chung-chih -- Chief, Political Affairs, North
China Political Council (2/8/43)

Chung-chin -- Vice-Chief, General Affairs Board,
North China Political Affairs Commission
(6/28/44) (52:230)

Chung-huan -- Member, Kiangsu Provincial Government; member, Pao-chia Promotion Committee
(IDC 3/30/43); Director, China Office,
East Asia League (1943); Assistant Chairman and Chairman, Literary Movement Committee, China Educational Reconstruction Association

Chung-kang -- Director, Shanghai Education Committee (1943) (49:162)

Chung-neng -- Director, China Office, East Asia
League (1943)

Chung-sho -- Manager, Ta Kang Bank, Shanghai
(IDC 7270 1943)

Chu'o-k'un -- Mayor, Canton; succeeded by Lau in
September, 1944 (R & A 2565) (51:231)

En-ling -- Chief, Office of Engineering, Shanghai
(1943) (49:162)

Er-chang -- Acting Director, Printing Press,
Ministry of Finance, Nanking (3/44) (R & A
2565)

Erh-k'ang -- Technical Supervisor, Directorate-
General of Industry, North China Political
Commission (7/40;OSS-Ms.)

Fang-hiang -- Chief, Office of Land Affairs,
Nanking (1943) (IDC-V-I)

Feng-ping -- See Chiang Feng-mei

Feng-yuan -- Chief Secretary, North China Branch,
Supreme Court, North China Political Commission (7/40;1/17/43) (52-230)

Fu-hsing -- Head, 4th Section, Canton Bureau of
Police (IDC 1/6/44) (51:231)

Fu-tseng -- Legislative member, Legislative Yuan,
Nanking (1943)

Han-kuang -- Chief, Broadcasting, Radio Station
Administration, Nanking (1943)

Hao-ju -- Chairman, Directors, Iron and Steel
Stores, Shanghai (IDC 7264)

Heng, Lt. Gen. -- Chief of Staff, Department of
Military Education (O-57); Vice-Chief of
Staff, National Military Council Nanking
(R & A 2565)

-5-

CHINESE

Chang Ho-wei -- Publisher, SHIH MEN HSIN PAO, Shih-men, North China (1943) (IDC-H 2562) (52:230)

Hsi-ju -- Editor-in-Chief, HSIN T'IEN TSIN PAO, Tientsin (1943) (IDC-H 2562) (52:230)

Hsiao-i (yi) -- Chief of Court, North China Branch, Supreme Court, North China Political Commission (1943) (52:230)

Hsien-chih -- Chief, Bureau of Grains, Shanghai (1943) (49:162) Inspector, China Office, East Asia League

Hsin -- Head, Electrical Communications Corporation, Swatow (1943) (49:162)

Hsin-min -- Trustee, Lu-ta Mining Industrial Company (over half of capital of this company owned by Shantung Mining Industrial Company (8/5/43) (52:230)

Hsin-pei -- Commissioner, Directorate-General of Education, North China Political Commission (7/40;OSS-Ms.)

Hsing-t'i -- Editor, HSIN SHAO NIEN, a magazine, Peiping (1943) (52:230)

Hsiu-k'ung -- Editor, SHIH YEN PAO, Peiping (1943) (52:230)

Hsiu-ming -- Member, Propaganda Committee, China Office, East Asia League (1943)

Hsueh-hai -- Assistant, Investigation Section, China Educational Reconstruction Association (1943)

Hsueh-ming -- Born, 1908, Haich'eng, Siaoning; second son of Marshal Chang Tso-lin; Mayor, Tientsin (1932-33); went to London to study (1934); went to Princeton (1938); left for China (11/41); caught by Japanese, Hongkong (12/26/41); member, National Military Council, Nanking (1943) (OSS-Ms; R&A 2565)

Hsun -- Commissioner, Directorate-General of Industry, North China Political Commission (7/40;OSS-Ms.)

Huang-chuan -- Inspector, North China Aluminite Mining Industrial Company, Ltd. (8/5/43) (52:230)

Hung-ching -- Director, China Educational Reconstruction Association, Hankow Branch (1943)

Hwei-yung -- Ousted Warlord; older brother, Shan Swei-ming

I-fei -- Manager, China Mao Hsing Bank, Shanghai (IDC 7270 1943)

CHINESE

Chang Jen-li (Jen-mu; Wen-li) -- Mayor, Hankow, under
        Japanese domination (OSS-Ms.-4/20/39);
        Director, Sino-Japanese Cultural Associa-
        tion, Wu-ch'ang and Hankow Branches (IDC-
        1943); Honorary Chairman, Directors,
        China Educational Reconstruction Association,
        Hankow Branch; member, Central Executive
        Committee, Nanking, North China Executive
        Council; North China Representative, New
        Citizens Movement Promotion Committee
        (IDC 1943); Chairman, Tientsin Fourth
        Inter-city Athletic Meet (6/9/44); Mayor,
        Tientsin Special Municipality; present at
        transfer of Italian Concession (8/17/44)
        member, National Economic Committee
        (52:230)

Jen-mu -- See Chang Jen-li

Jen-shou -- Director, China Movie Association
        (1943)

Jui-ching -- Commander, 7th Brigade, Independent
        Nanking Army (IDC 3/30/42); Military Ad-
        visor, National Government, Nanking (1943)

K'e -- Advisory member, Ministry of Information,
        Nanking (1943)

Ke-ch'ang -- Executive Director, East Asia League,
        Nanking Branch

Ko-min -- Appointed Vice-Minister, Propaganda
        and Publicity (6/27/44); Chairman, Prepara-
        tory Committee, Third Greater East Asia
        Literary Conference, Nanking (8/31/44)

Ku-shan -- President, East Asia Cultural Associa-
        tion, Asiatic Affairs Bureau, Hongkong
        (R&A 2565) (51:231)

Kuang-ta -- Member, Propaganda Committee, China
        Office, East Asia League (1943)

Kuang-yen -- Journalist, Hongkong (51:231)

Kuei-ching -- Assistant Chief, Ministry of the
        Army, Nanking (1943)

K'un -- Assistant Chairman, China Educational
        Reconstruction Association, Chekiang Branch
        (1943) (49:162)

Kuo-chen (cheng) -- President, Chinese Islam
        Federation, North China (52:230) (3/19/43)

Kuo-hui -- Minister, residing in Ministry of
        Foreign Affairs, Nanking (1943); member,
        Committee on Application of Constitution

Kuo-jen -- Secretary, Legislative Yuan, Nanking
        (1943); Inspector, China Writers Club

Kuo-yuan -- State Councillor, Nanking (1943)

-7-

CHINESE

Chang Kwang-tung -- Director, Reconstruction Department, Kiangsu Provincial Government (7/22/44)

Lan-feng (fong?) -- Member, National Military Council (1943); Commander, 2nd Group Army, North China (1/21/44); promoted to post of Commander-in-Chief, 4th District Army (10/10/44); attended conference at Kaifeng (DIO) (52:230)

Li-ch'u -- See Chang Chieng-chu

Li-p'ing -- Assistant Chairman, China Educational Reconstruction Association, Chekiang Branch (1943) (49:162)

Liang-chi -- Candidate Director, China Educational Reconstruction Association, Hankow Branch (1943)

Lieh -- Member, Committee on Culture, China Office, East Asia League (1943)

Lien-fang -- Director, Citizens Savings Movement Committee, Shanghai (1943) (49:162); Chairman, Directors, Metals Association (IDC 7264)

Liu -- Leader, Chinese Secret Society, Hankow; mobilized junks for Japanese (6/24/44)

Lu-shan -- Inspecting member, China Journalists Association (1943)

Lung, Dr. -- Archaeological work at Moulinkwan, Tsinnien, Hsien (12/25/43)

Meng-hsiung -- Inspector, Shanghai Special Municipality Journalist Association (1943) (49:162)

Meng-pai -- Head, Central Electrical Communications Corporation, Tai-chou Branch (1943) (IDC-H 2562)

Ming -- Mayor, Amoy (0-58)

Mu-min -- Counsellor, National Government, Nanking (1943); member, Directing Committee, China Office, East Asia League

Nai-ch'ien -- Inspector, China Educational Reconstruction Association, Chekiang Branch (1943) (49:162)

Nan-p'u -- Chairman, Secretariat, Ministry of the Navy, Nanking (1943)

Ngo -- Executive Director, China Educational Reconstruction Association, Anhwei Branch (1943)

Dr. P. H. -- Councillor, Executive Yuan (DIO 10/29/43)

CHINESE

Chang Pai-yin -- Secretary, Kuomintang Tenth District Party Headquarters, Canton (IDC 12/43)

Pao-fan -- Editor, TAI YUAN JIH PAO, T'ai-yuan, North China (1943) (52:230)

Pei-sheng (Chang Peh-sheng?) -- Special Administration Supervisor, 1st District, Kiangsu Province; Special Village Pacification Supervisor (1943) (49:162); member, Pao-chia Promotion Committee (3/30/43)

Peh-sheng -- See Chang Pei-sheng

Pen -- Candidate Director, China Educational Reconstruction Association, Hankow Branch (1943)

Pen-cheng -- President, Chefoo Electric Corporation, Chefoo (IDC 6699 1943)

P'eng-sheng -- Social Affairs Commissioner, Chekiang (R&A 2565)

Pi -- Director, North China Electrical Industry Company, Peiping (IDC 8/5/43) (52:230)

Ping-ch'uan -- Member, National Economic Committee (1943); Director, General Affairs Department, Ministry of Industry, Nanking

Po-chieh -- Head, MIN HSING Communications Company (1943) (IDC-H 2562)

Po-yin -- Managing Editor, CHUN SHAN JIH PAO, Canton; Executive Inspector, Social Welfare Committee, East Asia League, Canton Branch (IDC 1943) (51:231)

Shan-k'un -- Director, Sino-Japanese Cultural Association, Shanghai Branch (1943) (49:163)

Shen-ho -- President, Chiao-ao Electric Corporation, Tsingtao (IDC 6699 1943)

Shih-ch'uan -- Director, Sino-Japanese Cultural Association, Shanghai Branch (49:163)

Shih-shieh(?) -- Legislative member, Legislative Yuan, Nanking (1943)

Shih-yen -- Member, North China Hsin Min Society; Envoy to Tokyo (1/7/44)

Shin-chi -- Member, North China Political Council (2/8/43) (52:231)

Shou-p'eng -- Editor, CHIA HSING HSIN PAO, Chia-hsing, Chekiang (1943) (IDC-H 2562)

Shu-ch'ing (chin) -- Chief, Office of Social Welfare, Anhwei (1943) (IDC)

Shu-ch'un -- Member, Chinese Representatives' Association, Hongkong (51:232)

-9-

CHINESE

Chang Shu-shen -- Member, Committee for Punishment of Central Officials, Nanking (1943)

Shu-wei -- Director, Shantung Coal Production and Marketing Industrial Company (IDC 8/5/43) (52:231)

Si-ho -- Finance Minister, Nanking (7/31/42)

Sse-wen -- Editor, HSIN WAN JIH PAO, Ho-fei, Anhwei (1943) (IDC-H 2562)

Su-min (Chiang Su) -- Chief, Shanghai Office of Enemy Properties transferred to National Government of China (6/30/44) (49:163); Director of Taxation; Chairman, Land Tax Administration; Chief, Customs Office, Nanking; Director, China Educational Reconstruction Association; Vice-President, Central Reserve Bank, Nanking

Sung-tao -- Chairman, Directors, Hotel Association, Shanghai (IDC 7264 1943)

Szu-ling -- Adviser, Citizens Savings Movement Committee, Shanghai; Chief, Bureau of Public Health (49:163)

Ta-cheng -- Judge, Administrative Court, Nanking (1943)

Tai-king -- Secretary, Roman Catholic Church Charity Relief Workers' Association (2/22/44) (46:163)

T'ao -- President, Supreme Court, Executive Yuan, Nanking (1943); Inspector, China Office, East Asia League

Te(h)-ch'in -- One of leaders, Green Circle Society, Ch'ing Pang (1940) Shanghai (R&A 2565)

Teh-piao -- Vice-minister, Propaganda, Chekiang(?) resigned (1/3/45)

T'ieh-sheng -- Editor, CHUNG KUO WEN YI, a magazine, Peiping (1943) (52:231)

Ting -- Leader, Chinese Secret Society, Hankow; mobilized junks for Japanese (6/24/44)

Ting-chih -- Commander, 4th Regiment, Nanking Army (3/30/42); Propaganda Head, 4th District Party Headquarters, Kuomingtang Headquarters, Canton (12/43)

T'ing-chin -- Honorary Director, Sino-Japanese Cultural Association, Shanghai Branch (1943) (49:163); Head, Chao-tung University, Ministry of Education, Nanking; President, National Communication (R&A 2565)

Tsai-po -- Inspecting member, Control Yuan, Nanking (1943)

CHINESE

Chang Ts'ao -- Legislative member, Legislative Yuan, Nanking (1943)

T'se-hsun -- Magistrate, Wuhu Hsien, Anhwei (R&A 2565)

Tsi-chun -- High official, Hsin Min Hui; to supervise joint local meetings of Hsin Min Hui (6/7/44)

Tso-wen -- President, GEA Culture Deliberative Association, Peking; again chosen president (11/43) (52:231)

Tsun (Chang Chun?) -- Chief, Narcotic Prohibition Headquarters, Shanghai (4/5/44) (49:163); Chief, Police, Ministry of Justice, Nanking; Chief, Sales Administration of Special Merchandise, Ministry of Interior, Shanghai

Tsung-chou -- Head, Hua-pei Communication Company, North China (1943) (IDC-H 2563)

Tsung-yu -- Director, China Educational Reconstruction Association, Chekiang Branch (1943) (49:163)

Tun-fu -- Secretary, Ministry of Auditing, Nanking (1943)

T'ung -- Judge and Chief, North China Supreme Court (1/17/43) (52:231); Legislative member, Legislative Yuan

Tz'u-ch'i -- Executive Inspector, China Writers Club (1943)

Tzu-p'ing -- Candidate Director, Sino-Japanese Cultural Association (1943) (52:231); Director, China Japan Returned Students Club

Dr. Walter -- Friend of K. P. Fong; participated with him in Japanese propaganda broadcasts to U. S. (DIO 11/13/43)

Wan-lu -- Secretary General, Directorate-General of Industry, North China Political Commission (OSS-Ms. 7/40)

Wang-sen -- Privy Councillor, Manchukuo; in Nanking (12/1/42) (52:231)

Wei -- Candidate Director, China Educational Reconstruction Association, Hankow Branch (1943)

Wei-ju -- Chief, Directors, Chinese Stock Exchange, Shanghai (1943) (49:163); Manager, Kuo Hsin Bank, Shanghai

Wei-yi -- Executive Director, China Educational Reconstruction Association, Anhwei Branch (1943)

-11-

CHINESE

Chang Wen-huan -- Chairman, Board of Directors, National Commercial Bank, Nanking (52:231); Secretary, Ministry of Interior, Nanking (1943)

Wen-li -- See Chang Jen-li

Ya -- Director, China Educational Reconstruction Association, Chekiang Branch (1943) (49:163)

Ya-tung -- Counsellor, Directorate-General of the Interior, North China Political Commission (7/40;OSS-Ms.)

Yang-chi -- Prize winner, North China Labor Association (5/31/43) (52:231)

Yen-ching -- Commander, "Chang Yen-ching" Division, Armed Forces, Nanking (1943)

Yen-t'ien, Gen. -- Commander, 2nd Division, East Hopeh Army (since 1/1/36); also member, East Hopeh Government (11/25/35); former police officer; with Japanese (since 7/37) (OSS-Ms.)

Yi-ch'en -- Division Chief, Relief, Shanghai Municipality Social Welfare Bureau (1943) (49:163); Inspector, China Educational Reconstruction Association

Yi-chou -- Commander, Puppet Forces, Fukien (1943) (R&A 2565)

Yi-hien -- Chief, Office of Village Pacification, Chekiang (1943) (49:163)

Yi-nien -- Councillor, Chinghsiang Administration, Hangchow Sector (IDC 6/8/43); Commissioner, Pacification and Suppresion of Subversive Elements Department, Chekiang (R&A 2565)

Yi-p'eng -- Managing Director, Chairman of Directors, and Chairman of Counselling Committee, Shanghai Citizens Savings Movement Committee (1943); Candidate Inspector, China Educational Reconstruction Association, Chekiang Branch (1943) (49:163)

Yi-peng -- Minister of Justice, National Government (1944); visited Shanghai (5/3/44)

Ying-hua (Chang Yu-ching?) -- Member, State Council, National Government (12/38); one of leaders, Green Circle Society, Ch'ing Pang, Shanghai (1940)

Ying-tseng -- Member, Social Welfare Committee, China Office, East Asia League (1943)

Yu-ch'ing -- Chairman, Huang Tao Hui (Yellow Way Society), established by Col. Doihara, (1/38) Doihara gave Chang $100,000 to organize the society; Huang Tao Hui headquarters, rooms 623-25, New Asia Hotel, Tiendong Road, Shanghai (OSS-Ms.)

-12-

CHINESE

Chang Yu-ch'uan -- Born, 1880, Canton; studied, Anglo-Chinese College, Foochow, Quuen's College, Hongkong, Peiyang University, Tientsin, Imperial University of Japan, University of California, Yale University from which he received L.L.B. degree (1903) and L.L.M. (1904); appointed inspector of schools, Shansi, Chihli, Shantung, and Honan (1906-07); Secretary to President of China; concurrently, Counsellor, Ministry of Foreign Affairs for Kiangsu (1913); Chief, Investigation Bureau, Ministry of Foreign Affairs (1920); Chief, Legislative Board, North China Political Commission (7/40; OSS-Ms.)

Yu-fang -- Publisher, TA CHU PAO, Hankow, Hupeh (1943); Executive Director, Sino-Japan Cultural Association, Wu-ch'ang and Hankow Branches

Yu-yun -- Chief, Bureau of Construction; Chief, Office of Economics, Kwangtung (51:232); Member, National Economic Committee (1943)

Yuan-chen -- Chief, Legal Department, Police Bureau, Anking, Anhwei (R&A 2565)

Yun-fang -- Director, Chamber of Commerce, Shanghai (1943) (49:163)

Yung -- Deputy Chief, Water Police Patrol, Canton Police Patrol (IDC 1/6/44)

Yung-fu -- Member, State Council, National Government (12/38); Trade Commissioner, Commercial Attache for French Indo-China (1/21/43); member, Standing Committee, Central Supervisory Committee, Nanking (R&A 2565)

Yung-ting -- Adviser, Citizens Savings Movement Committee, Shanghai (1943) (49:163)

Chao -- Inaugurated, Minister of Propaganda, Nanking (1/17/45)

An -- Magistrate, Ch'en Hsien-yu, under control of Government of Kwangtung (IDC 5/42) (51:232)

Cheng -- Judge and Chief, Supreme Court, Nanking (1943)

Cheng-k'ai -- Publisher, TAI YUAN JIH PAO, Taiyuan, North China (1943) (52:231)

Cheng-p'ing -- Minister of Education; member, Central Political Council (12/38); Director, Sino-Japanese Cultural Association, Shanghai Branch (1943); State Councillor; Director, China Office, East Asia League; Honorary Chairman, Directors, China Educational Reconstruction Association; Head, Shanghai University; President, National Shanghai College; Director, China-Japan Returned Students Club (49:163)

-13-

CHINESE

Chao Ch'i -- Born, 1882, Yeh Hsien, Shantung; educated in Germany; returned to China (1913); Mayor, Tsingtao (1925-29); organized Tsingtao Peace Maintenance Commission 7 days after Japanese occupation of port (1/17/38); Governor, Shantung, replacing T'ang Yang-tu (3/30/39); concurrently, member, North China Political Commission (3/30/40) (OSS-Ms.) (52:231)

Chi-wu -- Chief, Police Bureau, Peiping (O-62; 52:231); Chief, Political Bureau, Hsin Min Hui (1/20/43;OSS-Ms.); member, Committee on Culture, China Office, East Asia League

Chih-ch'eng -- Commissioner, Directorate-General of the Interior, North China Political Commission (7/40;OSS-Ms.)

Chien-tzu -- Publisher, SU PEI JIH PAO, T'ai-hsien, Kiangsu (1943) (IDC-H 2562)

Chien-yao -- Training head, 5th District Party Headquarters, Kuomintang, Swatow

Chih-chia -- Assistant Chief, Second Police Office, West Shanghai (1943) (49:163)

Chin-ch'ing -- Assistant Chairman and member, Education Committee, Citizens Welfare Association, Shanghai (1943) (49:163)

Chin-p'ing -- Executive Director, Sino-Japanese Cultural Association, Shanghai Branch (1943) (49:163)

Ching-ting -- Member, Committee of Territories and Borders, Municipal Council, Shanghai (5/13/44) (49:164)

Chu-ch'eng -- Candidate Director, China Educational Reconstruction Association, Shanghai Branch; Director, Education Committee, Shanghai (1943)

Chu-kuang -- Publisher, CHIEN LI MEI, a bi-monthly, Shanghai (1943) (49:164)

Chun-hao -- Editor-in-Chief, SHUN PAO, Shanghai (11/15/43) (49:164)

Hsien-cheng -- Commissioner, Directorate-General of Industry, North China Political Commission (7/40;OSS-Ms.)

Hsin-che -- Director, North China Communications Corporation (1944)

Huan-yun -- Editor, SHIH MEN HSIN PAO, Shih-men, North China (1943) (52:231)

I-chen -- Director, Central China Electrical Communications Stock Company, Shanghai (1943)

CHINESE

Chao Ju-hang -- (See also Wang Yi-fang) Chief, Social
   Education, Ministry of Education, Nanking
   (1943); Assistant, Research Section, China
   Educational Reconstruction Association

  Ju-heng -- See Wang Yi-fang

  Ju-tiao -- Chairman, Directors, Medicine Factories,
   Shanghai (IDC 7264)

  Jun-feng -- Secretary, Ministry of Education,
   Nanking (1943)

  Kuan-sheng -- Head, Central Electrical Communications Corporation, Wu-hsi Branch (1943)
   (IDC-H 2562)

  Kuei-chang -- See Chao Kwei-chang

  Kung-wei, Maj. Gen. -- Chairman, Peace Preservation Committee, Tsingyun, Kwangtun (51:232)

  Kwei-chang, Vice-Admiral (Chao Kuei-chang; Chiu
   Kwai-cheung) -- Commander-in-Chief,
   Kwangtung River Defense Headquarters, a
   fleet of one gunboat (5/10/40); Chao's
   fleet consisted of 5 armed launches (8/41);
   Vice-Minister of Navy, Head of Naval Mis-
   sion to Tokyo (10/10/43); member, National
   Military Council, Nanking (1943) (R&A 2565;
   OSS-Ms.)

  Liang-kung -- Secretary, National Government,
   Nanking (1943)

  Mu-ju (Chao Mo-ju) -- Legislative member, Legislative Yuan, Nanking (1943); Executive Director, Central Electrical Communications
   Corporation; Chairman, Board of Directors,
   Central Telegraph Bureau, Nanking; Inspecting member, China Journalists Association

  Pao-chih -- Chief, Bureau of Education, Kiangsi
   (1943); Executive Inspector, China Educational Reconstruction Association

  P'eng-ti -- Vice-Minister, Civil Affairs (Interior)
   while Lu Yung-huan was Minister (2/37)

  Ping, Miss -- "Friend" of K. P. Fong; allegedly
   alumna, Mills College (DIO 11/13/43)

  Pu-chiu -- Editor, CHANG SHU JIH PAO, Chang-shu,
   Kiangsu (1943) (IDC-H 2562)

  Shan-ming -- Chief, General Affairs, Ministry of
   Education, Nanking (1943)

  Shao-jen -- See Chou Tsao-jen

  Shih-chueh -- Member, Committee for Application of
   Constitution (1943)

  Shih-yu -- Inspector, China Office, East Asia
   League (1943)

-15-

CHINESE

Chao Shu-jung (Chao Shu-yung) -- Former follower of
Gen. Huang Fu; General Manager, CHUNG HUA
JIH PAO, The Central China Daily News,
Shanghai; Minister, Agriculture and Mining,
Wang Ching-wei's government; Wang's contact
man in dealings with Wang Ke-min (3/22/40;
OSS-Ms.); member, Invited Committee, Cen-
tral Political Council (12/38; IDC); Execu-
tive Director, Sino-Japanese Cultural Asso-
ciation, Shanghai Branch (IDC 1943);
Honorary member, China Journalists Asso-
ciation; Secretary-General, Shanghai
Special Municipality; Inspector, China Of-
fice, East Asia League (1944) (49:164)

Shuang-feng -- Legislative member, Legislative
Yuan, Nanking (1943)

Tsun-yao -- Political Adviser, National Government,
Nanking (1943); Candidate Director, Sino-
Japanese Cultural Association; member,
National Economic Committee

Tsun-yueh -- Chief or General Secretary, Shanghai
Municipality; Chairman, West Shanghai
Food Preservation Committee; member, Com-
mittee for Preservation of Cultural Objects;
member, Committee for Custody of Real
Property of Absentee Owners; Adviser,
Citizens Savings Movement Committee,
Shanghai (49:164); member, Committee of
Political Councillors; member, Central
Political Council, Nanking; possibly suc-
ceeded Lin Po-sheng as Minister of Propa-
ganda; member, New Citizens' Movement
Promotion Committee

Wei-liang -- Director, China Educational Reconstruction Association, Anhwei Branch (1943)

Wen-yi -- Chairman, Women's Welfare Association,
Shanghai (1/43) (49:164)

Yang -- Magistrate, Ch'en Tsung-ai, under control
of Kwangtung Government (5/42) (51:232)

Yi-lin -- Deputy Head, Hua Chung Electrical Communications Company, Shanghai (8/5/43)
(49:164)

Yu-chang -- Chairman, Board of Directors, Shanghai
River Boat Corporation, Ltd. (8/5/43)
(49:164)

Yu-ch'in -- Head, Pei-fang Communications Company,
North China (52:231)

Yu-sung -- Member, Central Political Council, Nanking Kuomintang; Minister of Agriculture;
concurrently, Minister of Mining (3/31/41;
Oss-Ms.) Honorary Director, Sino-Japanese
Cultural Association; State Councillor,
Nanking; Executive Director, China Office,
East Asia League; Executive member, Committee on Application of Constitution
(49:132)

CHINESE

Chao Yung-pai -- Legislative member, Legislative Yuan,
        Nanking (1943)

Chau Lei-ko -- Consul General to Fengtien from Manchu-
        kuo (3/11/43 IDC)

    Wing-ting -- Works for Japanese Intelligence under
        Furukawa; operates in Amoy-Swatow Sector
        (9/41 OSS-Ms.)

Che Chih-ting -- Manager, Hsin Tai Bank, Shanghai
        (1943 IDC 7270)

Chei Chen, Reverend -- Priest, Li Shung Temple, Canton
        (51:232)

Ch'en -- Provincial Chairman, Japan-China Cultural
        Association, Canton Branch; Honorary Presi-
        dent (2/5/44) (51:232); Director-General,
        All-China Commercial Control Association,
        Kwangtung Branch; Executive member, Commodity
        Investigation Committee

Ch'en -- Director, Civil Administration Office, Hopeh
        Province (52:231)

Ch'en -- President, Shanghai Nan-shih Hospital (2/4/44)

    Ai-cheng -- Secretary, Kuomingtang Seventh Dis-
        trict Party Headquarters, Canton (12/43)
        (51:232)

    Chang-tzu (tsu), Lt. Gen. or Maj. Gen. -- Chief,
        Nanking Aviation Department, Wang Ching-wei's
        regime; arrived in Tokyo to inspect Japan's
        aviation (11/15/41 OSS-Ms.); Military Counsel
        or Aide de Camp, GEA Conference (0-57, 58);
        member, Central Executive Committee, Nanking;
        Chief, Army, Navy, and Air Force Armament
        Repair Department; member, New Citizens
        Movement Promotion Committee; Head, Chao-tung
        University (1943); member, National Economic
        Committee

    Chang-yen -- Chief, Statistics, Ministry of In-
        dustries (Interior), Nanking (1943)

    Chao-wei -- Chairman, Directors, Shanghai Realty
        Stock Company; Director, Greater Shanghai
        Gas Stock Company (1943) (7262 IDC)

    Ch'e -- Secretary, Ministry of Finance, Nanking
        (1943)

    Chen Chan-tsu -- Officer, Air Corps (10/10/43)

    Ch'eng -- Secretary, Control Yuan, Nanking (1943)

    Cheng-chang -- Director, Citizens Savings Move-
        ment Committee, Shanghai (1943) (49:164)

    Cheng-fan -- Director, Sino-Japanese Cultural
        Association, Shanghai Branch (1943) (49:164)

-17-

CHINESE

Ch'en Ch'eng-hun -- Chief, Bureau of Construction, Hupeh Province (1943); Chairman, Directors, Tobacco Leaves Association, Shanghai (IDC-V-1)

Chi-ch'eng -- Born, 1891, Tsinkiang, Kiangsu; Commander, 1st Army Corps; loyal to Chiang (9/35); Wuhan Garrison Commander (10/18/35); appointed Pacification Commander, Hon-Hup-Shen Borders (12/10/36); kidnapped with Chiang Kai-shek near Sianfu (12/12/36); released (12/25/36); replaced Chang Chih-chung as Dean, Central Military Academy, Nanking (4/8/37); Chairman, Board of Overseas Affairs Wang Ching-wei's regime (3/41); appointed Wang Ching-wei's Ambassador to Manchukuo; sent to Hsinking to replace Lien Yu (2/1/43) (OSS-Ms.); visited Wang Ching-wei and Foreign Minister Chu Min-yi (2/27/43); State Councillor, Nanking; Commissioner, National Government; Director, Sino-Japanese Cultural Association; Inspector, China Office, East Asia League; Honorary Chairman, Directors, China Educational Reconstruction Association (1943 IDC; O-42,59)

Chi-ju -- Manager, Central Reserve Bank, Wu Hsi Branch, Kiangsu (1943) (IDC 7270)

Chi-li -- Chinese actress, Hongkong (51:232)

Chi-p'o -- Secretary, Ministry of Information, Nanking (1943)

Chi-wu -- Professor, Fine Arts Department, Peking University (52:231)

Chia-ai -- Executive Director, Social Welfare Committee, East Asia League, Canton Branch (51:232)

Chia-mou -- With Japanese Huang Hsieh Chun, Yangloutung, commanding 1,000 men (6/39; OSS-Ms.)

Chia-poh -- Attache, Vichy Embassy (10/42 DIO)

Chieh -- China's Ambassador to Brazil (8/27/43); Ex-Ambassador to Germany (DIO 10/42)

Chien-kuo -- Head, Teachers Association and Education Bureau, Amoy (1/18/44) (49:164)

Chien-yuan -- Chief Secretary, Amoy Administration (1943) (49:164)

Chih-shih -- Member, Central Executive Committee, Nanking (1943); member, Executive Committee, All-China Economic Committee; Vice-Minister, Ministry of Finance; Candidate Director, Sino-Japanese Cultural Association; Vice-President, Central Reserve Bank, Nanking; member, China-Japan Returned Students Club; Inspector, China Office, East Asia League

CHINESE

Ch'en Chih-shuo -- Administrative Vice-Minister, Ministry of Finance, Wang Ching-wei's regime (3/41); appointed member and Chief Secretary, Commission for Control of Enemy Property (2/9/43) (OSS-Ms.)

Chin-hai -- Manager, Chung Tâ Commercial Bank, Shanghai (1943 IDC 7270)

Chin-ko -- Head, Hui Foo Branch Agency, Police Bureau, Canton (51:232)

Chin-chai -- Governor, Honan

Ch'ing-hsuan -- Chief, Bureau of Audits, Kwangtung (1943 IDC)

Ching-tsai -- Member, North China Political Council (1943)

Chiu-fang (feng) -- Director, Citizens Savings Movement Committee, Shanghai; Chief, Pao-chia Office, Second Department, First Police Office (1943) (49:164); Candidate Inspector, China Educational Reconstruction Association, Hankow Branch

Ch'iu-shih -- Inspector, East Asia League, Nanking Branch (1943)

Chu -- Director, Sino-Japanese Cultural Association, Nanking Branch (1943); President, Central University, Kiangsu (9/43) (49:154)

Chun -- Born, 1894, Kiangsu; B.A. Yale, M.A. Pennsylvania; expert in economics, Shanghai-Nanking Railway Administration; Minister of Interior, Nanking Reformed Government (3/28/38); made Minister, Wang Ching-wei's National Government (3/22/40); appointed Commissioner of Amoy Concessions when they were restored to Nanking (3/30/43); Standing Committee, Central Executive Committee, Nanking; Central Political Council member; State Councillor; member, National Military Council; Executive Director, New Citizens Movement Promotion Committee; President, Examination Yuan; Chairman, Compilation of History Committee, General Kuomingtang Headquarters; Executive Director, China-Japan Returned Students Club; Chairman, National History Editing Committee, Central Yuan, Nanking; Executive Director, East Asia League; Executive Director, Sin-Japanese Cultural Association (1943); Executive member, National Economic Committee; Executive member, Committee on Application of Constitution (OSS-Ms;IDC-1943)

Ch'un-f'u -- See Ch'en Chun-po

Chun-hoi -- See Ch'en Ch'un-hui

Chun-huei -- See Ch'en Ch'un-hui

-19-

CHINESE

Ch'en Ch'un-hui (Ch'en Chun-hoi; Chu Chien-huei; Ch'en
Chun-huei) -- Chinese National Government
Construction Minister; touring Japan; Com-
missioner, Tientsin Concession; Construction
member, National Government All-China
Economic Mission (7/18/43) (52:233); member,
Designated Committee, Central Political
Council (12/38); Minister of Interior; Min-
ister of Construction or Industry; member,
Executive Committee, National Government;
member, National Military Council; Commis-
sioner, Amoy (0-56); Governor, Kiangsu
Province (9/11/42); Director, China Office,
East Asia League; Executive Director, Sino-
Japanese Cultural Association; Vice-President,
Central Reserve Bank, Nanking (IDC 1943);
decorated by Japanese Emperor (3/23/44)
(R&A 2565 etc.)

Ch'un-kwei -- Minister, Commerce and Industry,
Department of Interior (1938); made statement re basic counter-measures for stabilization of commodity prices (1/13/44)

Ch'un-p'u -- (See also Chin Kun-kei; Chin Shun-po)
Brother-in-law of Wang Ching-wei; Born,
Singapore, family fron Sunwei, Kwangtung;
with Canton Government (1926); Manager,
Nanking Central News (1928); with Railway
Ministry (1928); with Finance Ministry
(1929); joined Wang Ching-wei's party,
Shanghai (1938); Deputy Chief-Secretary,
Orthodox Kuomingtang; Commissioner, Chinese
Overseas Affairs, National Government,
Nanking (3/22/40); Secretary-General, Execu-
tive Yuan (3/41); member, Commission for
Control of Enemy Property (2/9/43)(OSS-Ms.)
Chairman, Organization Committee, Central
Kuomingtang Headquarters; Director, Central
Reserve Bank; member, Executive Committee,
All-China Economic Committee; member, Cen-
tral Executive Committee; member, Central
Political Council; Executive Director, New
Citizens Movement Promotion Committee; Vice-
Secretary General, Supreme National Defense
Council; Chairman, Managers, Commodity In-
vestigation; Director, China Office, East
Asia League (1943); Minister of Construction,
Nanking (51:232)

Chung -- Ex-Director, Manufactured Goods Inspection Bureau, Shanghai; Adviser, Ministry of
Industries; Chief, General Affairs Department, Ministry of Construction, Nanking
(R&A 2565)

Chung-ch'ung -- Member, Central Political Council,
Nanking Kuomingtang (3/31/41); Minister
without Portfolio; member, Political Commission (8/41) (OSS-Ms.)

CHINESE

Ch'en Chung-fu -- Born, Soochow, Kiangsu, 1882; educated in Japan; member, T'ung Men Hui; one time Finance Commissioner, Anhwei; one time administrative member, Southwest Political Council; member, Hopeh-Chahar Political Council; Chairman, Foreign Affairs Committee (1935); resigned, Chairman of Foreign Affairs, Peiping; went to Canton when revolt broke out there (6/2/36); went to Japan; returned to Peiping (OSS-Ms.); member, National Government, Nanking (1943); State Councillor, Nanking

Chung-hsing -- Candidate Inspector, China Educational Reconstruction Association (1943)

Ch'ung-kuang -- Editor-in-Chief -- HSIN MIN PAO, Peiping (1943); Director, Committee for Airplane Donations (1944) (52:231)

Dao-chia -- Attache, Swiss Embassy (10/42 DIO)

En-chin -- Chief Prosecutor, Supreme Court, Nanking (1943)

En-pu -- Procurator General; appointed Chief Judge, Special Court, Nanking Government (3/44); appointed Minister of Justice (7/44); appointed Seimu Sansan (1/13/45)

Eugene -- See Ch'en Yu-jen

Fan-chang -- High Official, Hsin Min Hui; to supervise joint local meetings of Hsin Min Hui (6/17/44)

Fu-k'ang -- Director, Citizens Savings Movement Committee, Shanghai (1943) (49:165); Chairman, Directors, Auctions Association (IDC 7264)

Fu-ming -- Acting Chief, Supreme Court, Nanking (1/43 IDC)

Fu-mu -- Honorary Director, Sino-Japanese Cultural Association; Adviser, Citzens Savings Movement Promotion Committee, Shanghai (1943); resigned, Secretary General TUNG YA LIEN MENG, Shanghai Branch (9/43 IDC) (49:165); member, Central Executive Committee; Director, China Office East Asia League

Hai-ch'ao -- Special Delegate to Chekiang, Ministry of Foreign Affairs (1943); Inspector, China-Japan Returned Students Club

Hai-ch'iu -- Managing Director, Wharf Labor Union, Shanghai (1943) (49:165)

Han-pin -- Appointed, Chairman, Reconstruction and Rehabilitation Committee and Commander, Civilian Defense Army, Tsing Yun Hsien (11/6/44)

Hao-ming -- Chief, Executive Department, Police Bureau, Anking, Anhwei (R&A 2565)

-21-

CHINESE

Ch'en Hiang-yung -- Member, Committee of Academia Sinica, Nanking Government (6/18/43) (IDC)

Ho-chung -- Chief, Postal Affairs, Ministry of Construction, Nanking (1943)

Ho-tzu -- Member, Social Committee, China Writers Club (1943)

Hsian-fen -- Chief of Police, Hankow (12/2/43) (IDC 2213)

Hsiang -- Chief, Public Welfare Section, Ministry of Social Welfare, Nanking (1943)

Hsiang-ling -- Editor, HSIEN CHENG YEN CHIU, a monthly, Nanking (1943) (IDC-H 2562); Executive member, China Journalists Association

Hsiao-fen -- Inspector, East Asia League, Hupeh Branch (1943)

Hsien-liang -- Head, Police Tax Unit, Canton Bureau of Police (First Section) (1/6/44) (51:232)

Hsien-mo -- Secretary, Kuomingtang Sixth District Party Headquarters, Canton; Director, Social Welfare Committee, East Asia League, Canton Branch (1943) (51:232)

Hsien-yun -- Editor, PING PAO. Shanghai (1943) (IDC 7266)

Hsu-kwan -- Director, Peiping Chamber of Commerce (5/18/43) (52:231)

Hsueh-tan -- Vice-President, Mutual Relief Association, Kwangchowan (8/15/43) (IDC-R)

Hsun -- Minister, Department of Commerce, Nanking (10/28/44) (IDC)

Hu -- Secretary, Executive Yuan, Nanking (1943)

Hua -- Chairman, Trustees, Brass Foil Manufacturing Association, Shanghai (IDC 7264)

Hung-ch'ing -- Director, Citizens Savings Movement Committee, Shanghai, (1943) (49:165)

Hung-tz'u -- Judge and Chief, Kwangtung Province (1943) (51:233)

Jih-p'ing -- Adviser, Citizens Savings Movement Committee, Shanghai; member, Shanghai Newspaper Association; Inspector, Sino-Japanese Cultural Association (49:165); Economic Commissioner, Shanghai; Inspector, China-Japan Returned Students Club; Editor, HSIN WEN PAO

Ju-hao -- Editor, HSI MEN HSIN PAO, Hai-men, Kiangsu (1943) (IDC-H 2562)

CHINESE

Ch'en Jui-tsun -- Judge, Supreme Court, Nanking (1943)

K. P. -- Universal Trading Company, Shanghai
(7/15/44) (49:165)

Kao, Lt. Gen. -- Chief, Rites Office, Military
Adviser, National Government, Nanking (1943)

Ke -- Director, Newspapermen's Association,
Shanghai (1943); Editor, PING PAO, Shanghai

Ke-ying -- Director, Shanghai Education Committee; Director, Sino-Japanese Cultural Association; Inspector, China Educational Reconstruction Association (1943) (45:165)

Keng -- Mayor, Canton (8/29/44); Provincial Governor, Canton (51:233)

Ko -- Member, Shanghai Newspaper Association
(1943) (45:165)

Kuang -- Commander, 115th Division, Sino-Red
Army (3/15/44)

Kuang-chung -- Assistant Chairman, Investigation
Committee on Resources and Material Control,
Shanghai Office; member, Committee on Grain
Control; Chief, Bureau of Construction,
Kiangsu (49:165); Vice-Manager, Arbitration
Commission for Control of Commodities,
Shanghai; Chief, General Affairs Department,
Shanghai; Inspector, East Asia League, Nan-
king Branch (R&A 2565)

Kuei-ting -- With Japanese Huang Hsieh Chun,
Changhing, commanding about 1,000 men
(6/39;OSS-Ms.

Kung-po (Ch'en Tang-po; Cheng Pen-pow) -- Born,
1890, Kwangtung; B. A. New York; Editor,
Revolutionary Critic (1927-28); expelled from
Kuomingtang (7/29); reinstated (12/31);
Minister of Industries (1932-35); Chief,
Political Training Bureau (12/38); reported
arrested after Wang Ching-wei's flight from
Chungking; reported safe in Hanoi (7/2/39);
in Shanghai with Wang Ching-wei in charge of
pro-Japanese organization, The Reorganization
Fellowship of the Kuomingtang of China
(5/27/39); President, Legislative Yuan, Nan-
king (3/22/40); falsely reported assassi-
nated (12/4/40); member, Military Affairs
Commission, Nanking (3/41); still President,
Legislative Yuan and concurrently Mayor,
Shanghai (10/10/41); organizing official,
Shanghai International Settlement and French
Settlement (7/23/43); Head, Police Bureau,
Shanghai (7/27/43); Chairman, Committee to
Collect Funds for War Planes (12/3/43); Chief,
First and Eighth Districts (1943); Chairman,
Committee to Investigate Resources and Materi-
als (1943); Honorary Chairman, Directors,
Shanghai Education Committee (1943); Adviser,
Citizens Savings Movement, Shanghai (1943);
Executive Director, East Asia League (1943)

CHINESE

Ch'en Kung-po (con't) -- Chairman, Directors, Sino-
Japanese Cultural Association (1943); Chief,
First and Third Police Offices (1943); Chief,
Office of Village Pacification (1943); Chair-
man, Board of Directors, People's Foreign Re-
lations Stimulation Committee (1/43); Head,
Youth Corps and Model Youths' Corps; attended
All-China Commercial Control General Association (6/8/44); Acting Chairman, Supreme National Defense Council; President, Constitution Realization Movement; Chairman, National
Military Council; Chairman, New Citizens Movement Promotion Committee; Honorary Chairman,
Directors, China Educational Reconstruction
Association; Acting President, National Government of China upon death of Wang Ching-wei as
well as Chairman, National Military Council
(11/12/44) (45:165)

Kuo-cheng -- Member, Nanking Government, Kwangtung
Province (51:233)

Kuo-ch'i -- Secretary, Executive Yuan, Nanking
(1943)

Kuo-feng -- Director, General Affairs Department,
Ministery of Foreign Affairs, Nanking (R&A
2565)

Kuo-shih -- Director, China Educational Reconstruction Association, Hankow Branch (1943)

Li-min -- Chief, Police Bureau, Swatow (R&A 2565)

Liang-chao -- Manager, Arbitration Commission for
Control of Commodities and Capital, Shanghai
Office (1943) (R&A 2565)

Liang-lieh -- Training Head, Kuomingtang Fourth
District Party Headquarters, Canton (12/43)
(51:233)

Liao-shih -- Executive Inspector, China Writers
Club (1943)

Lien-pei -- Chairman, Preparation Committee, Main
Relief Association, Hongkong (51:233)

Mapa, Miss -- Musician, Hongkong (51:233)

Mo -- Inspector, Wharf Labor Union, Shanghai
(49:166)

Ou-sie -- Consul General to Guatemala (DIO 10/42)

Pai-heng -- Chief, Examinations, Examination Yuan,
Nanking (1943)

Pai-li -- Member, Chinese Language Society, Hongkong (5/15/44) (51:233)

Pan-chun -- Chairman, Directors, Patriotic Transportation Association, Shanghai (IDC 7264 1943)

Pao-yi -- Director, Sino-Japanese Cultural Association, Shanghai Branch (49:166)

CHINESE

Ch'en P'ei-shun -- Secretary, Kuomingtang Ninth District
        Party Headquarters, Canton (12/43) (51:233)

    Pi-chun (Mrs. Wang Ching-wei) -- Wife, Wang Ching-
        wei; ardent revolutionary worker; member,
        Central Political Council, Nanking Kuoming-
        tang; sister, Chan Yao-tsu, Governor, Canton;
        member, Standing Committee, Central Supervis-
        ory Committee (1943); Executive Director,
        East Asia League (1943) (OSS-Ms.; R&A 2565)

    Pin-ho -- See Ch'en Ping-huo

    Pin-so -- Lecturer, auspices of Press Federation
        and Chamber of Commerce, Shanghai (10/30/44)

    Ping-huo (Ch'en Pin-ho; Ch'en Ping-sho) -- Member,
        Committee on Peace and Order, Municipal Coun-
        cil, Shanghai (5/44); President and Editor,
        SHEN PAO, Shanghai; Vice-President, China
        Newspaper Association; Honorary Director,
        Sino-Japanese Cultural Association, Shanghai
        Branch; Inspector, Citizens Savings Movement
        Committee; Managing Director, Labor and Busi-
        ness Social Union; Assistant General-Secretary,
        Citizens Welfare Association; President,
        HIAN PAO; appointed, President, Translation
        Office, "Cultural Data Translation Office",
        established by Shanghai Publishing Institu-
        tion (49:166); Director, Shanghai Press Asso-
        ciation

    Po-fan -- Head, Match Enterprise Trade Association,
        National Trade Control General Association,
        Shanghai (49:166); member, Central Executive
        Committee, Nanking; President, Match Enterprise
        Trade Association; Director, China-Japan Re-
        turned Students Club; Director, Central China
        Railroad Stock Company; Inspector, China Office,
        East Asia League

    Po-hua -- Secretary, Pao-chia Office, First Police
        Office, Shanghai (49:166); Candidate Inspec-
        tor, China Educational Reconstruction Associa-
        tion (1943); Chairman, Directors, Central
        Reserve Bank, Canton Branch

    Pu -- Committee of Political Councillors, Nanking;
        Editor-in-Chief, CHUNG SHAN JIH PAO (R&A 2565)

    Saho-kuan, Admiral -- Minister of Navy (DIO 1941)

    Sen-tu -- See Ch'en Ch'un-p'u

    Shan-kan -- Puppet Brigade Commander, East Shantung;
        killed (51:233)

    Shang-tao -- Chief, Protective Police, Canton
        Bureau of Police (1/6/44) (51:233)

    Shao -- President, Shanghai Railway (49:166)

    Shao-chun -- Judge, Administrative Court, Nanking
        (1943)

-25-

CHINESE

Ch'en Shao-hsiang -- Member, Central Electrical Communications Corporation, Hongkong Branch (1943) (IDC-H 2562)

Shao-wei -- Director, Labor and Business Social Union, Shanghai; Director, Citizens Welfare Association; Inspector, Sino-Japanese Cultural Association, Shanghai Branch; Chairman, Board of Directors, Shanghai Property Corporation; Director, Greater Shanghai Gas Corporation (49:166)

Sheng-neng -- Head, Water Patrol Corps, Canton (51:233)

Sheng-wei -- Manager, Tung Yuan Commercial and Savings Bank, Shanghai (IDC 7270 1943)

Shih-ch'iu -- Director and Chairman, Literary Movement Committee, China Educational Reconstruction Association (1943)

Shih-te -- Member, Oil and Grain Special Committee, National Trade Control General Association, Shanghai (49:166)

Shiu-ching -- Director, National Commercial Control Association (1943)

Shu-chen -- Manager, Chao Hsing Commercial Bank, Chekiang (IDC 7270 1943)

Shu-chou -- Secretary, China Educational Reconstruction Association (1943)

Shui-li -- Director, National Trade Control General Association, Shanghai (49:166); Manager, Hua Chiao Bank (IDC 7270 1943)

Sing-fong -- Cooperating with Nanking Government; Ex-Commander, Patriotic National Salvation Army (9/5/42)

Sse-p'u -- Chief, Criminal Affairs, Ministry of Justice, Nanking (1943)

Sueh-tao -- Manager, Shanghai Commercial and Savings Bank (IDC 7270 1943)

Sun-yi -- Professor, formerly at Nanking University (4/30/44)

Ta-chun -- Commissioner, Directorate-General of Pacification, North China Political Commission (7/40 OSS-Ms.)

Ta-hsun -- Legislative member, Legislative Yuan, Nanking (1943)

Ta-pei -- Executive Director, China Writers Club (1943)

Ta-sheng -- Head, Mass Education Association, Shanghai (IDC 7265 1943)

74

-26-

CHINESE

Ch'en Ta-tsai -- Executive Director, China Writers Club (1943)

Tang-po -- See Ch'en Kung-po

Te-chao -- Accounting Office, Forestation Office, Ministry of Industry, Nanking (1943)

Te-chiung -- Director, China Educational Reconstruction Association, Hankow Branch (1943)

Te-yung -- Manager and Director, Shanghai Wharf Labor Union (49:166)

Te(h)-Kuang -- Member, Central Political Council, Shangtung; State Councillor (51:233)

Teng-shih -- See Ch'en Tso-shih

Ti-pu -- Councillor, National Government (1/19/45)

Ti-ting -- Councillor, Chinghsiang Administration, Hangchou Sector (6/8/43 IDC)

T'iao-ch'in -- Control Officer, Ta Pu Ward, Hsin Chieh, Hongkong (51:233)

Tieh-yi -- Publisher, CH'UN CH'IU, a monthly, Shanghai (49:166)

T'ing -- Javelin thrower; holds record, Nanking

T'ing-fang -- Member, Sugar Enterprise Special Committee, National Trade Control General Association, Shanghai (49:166)

T'ing-pao -- Chairman, Central Relief Association, Hongkong (1944) (51:233)

Tsai-p'ing -- Member, Committee on Culture, China Office, East Asia League (1943); Chief, Publicity Bureau of Hsin Min Hui (1/20/43 OSS-Ms.) Propaganda Chief, General Headquarters, New People's Society (7/6/44)

Tse-ching -- Head, Central Electrical Communications Corporation, Yang-chou Branch (1943) (IDC-H 2562)

Tse-min -- Governor, Kiangsu (1940); Inspector, Control Yuan, Nanking (1943)

Tseng-an -- Candidate Director, Education Committee, Shanghai (49:166)

Tseng-shih -- Member, Committee for Stopping Breakage at Chung-mon of Huang-ho (1943)

Tsi-cheng -- Ambassador, Nanking; asked to appoint general commander for important harbor of Kwangtung (10/3/44)

Tso-shih (Teng-shih) -- Chief Secretariat, Hopeh Province; appointed Provincial Governor, Hopeh (3/2/44); Head, Agricultural Department, North China Political Council (3/1/45) (52:231)

-27-

CHINESE

Ch'en Tsu-hsiang -- Executive Director, China Educational Reconstruction Association, Shanghai Branch (49:166)

Tsu-shang -- Legislative member, Legislative Yuan, Nanking (1943)

Tzu-yi -- Chairman, Oil and Grain Special Committee (R&A 2565)

Tsui-yun -- Director, China Writers Club (1943)

Tsung-yu -- Secretary and Chief, Printing Office, National Government, Nanking (1943)

Tuan-chih -- Editor, CHIAO YU CHIEN SHI, a monthly, Nanking (1943); member, Social Welfare Committee, China Office, East Asia League and Director, Nanking Branch; Executive Director and Chief, Publication Section, China Educational Reconstruction Association

Tung-ling -- Publisher, JIH YU HSUEH HSI, a monthly, Shanghai (49:167)

Tung-pai -- Director, Special Municipality Journalists Association, Shanghai; Adviser, Citizens Savings Movement Committee; Head, Shanghai News Company (49:167); Executive member, China Journalists Association

Tzu-shou -- Manager, Shanghai Chih Chung Commercial and Savings Bank (IDC 7270 1943)

Tzu-tang -- Manager, Shanghai Industrial Bank (IDC 7270 1943)

Tzu-yi -- Chairman, Oil and Grain Special Committee, National Trade Control General Association, Shanghai; member, Committee on Grain Control, Shanghai; Director, Citizens Savings Movement Committee (49:167)

Wang-li -- Head, Tihwa Bureau, China News (0-58)

Wang-wah -- Kwangtung industrialist; founded Kwangtung Prosper Asia Scholarship Association in sixteenth year of Showa (3/1/44)

Wei-cheng -- Chief, Bureau of Political Affairs and Financial Commissioner, Hupeh Province (1943); Executive Inspector, East Asia League, Hupeh Branch

Wei-jen -- Candidate Director, China Educational Reconstruction Association, Anhwei Branch (1943)

Wei-yi -- Member, Social Welfare Committee, China Office, East Asia League (1943)

Wei-yuan -- Member, National Military Council (R&A 2565)

Wen-chao -- Member, National Military Council (R&A 2565)

CHINESE

Ch'en Wen-sin -- Commander, 2nd and 4th Artillery Brigades, Pantung Volunteer Corps (9/20/44)

Wen-yun -- Member, National Military Council (R&A 2565)

Weng-yu (Weng-ku) -- President, Shanghai Security Exchange (7/25/43) (49:167)

Won-lu -- Member, Committee of Territories and Borders, Municipal Council, Shanghai (49:167)

Ya-fu -- Director, Sino-Japanese Cultural Association, Shanghai Branch (49:167)

Yao-tsu -- Wang Ching-wei's brother-in-law; Acting Governor for Ch'en Kung-po, Kwangtung Province (5/10/40); Governor, Kwangtung Province (11/25/40); Provincial Chairman, Canton Pacification Office (9/24/41); appointed member, Military Affairs Council, Nanking, with rank of Lt. Gen. (1/14/42); member, Central Political Council; Director, China Office, East Asia League; assassinated (4/44) (51:234)

Yeh-ming -- Head, First Unit, Chinghsiang Administration, Hangchou Sector (6/8/43 IDC)

Yen-ju -- Candidate Director, China Educational Reconstruction Association, Chekiang Branch (49:167)

Yen-shan -- Accounting Office, Forestation Office, Ministry of Industries, Nanking (1943)

Yen-sheng, Lt. Gen. -- Vice-Commander, 3rd Division, 1st War District Army (O-57)

Yen-t'ung -- Secretary, National Government, Nanking (1943)

Yen-yun -- Inspector, Citizens Savings Movement Committee, Shanghai; Director, Shanghai Special Municipality Journalists Association; member, Shanghai Newspaper Association

Yi -- Assistant Secretary, Pao-chia Office, 1st Police Office, Shanghai; Assistant Chairman, China Educational Reconstruction Association (49:167)

Yi-chiung -- Legislative member, Legislative Yuan, Nanking (1943)

Yi-wen -- Director, China Educational Reconstruction Association, Shanghai Branch (49:167)

Yien-tan -- Director, Agriculture and Forestry Board, Ministry of Industry, Nanking (R&A 2565)

Ying-chung -- Head, Nan An Branch Agency, Canton Police Bureau (1/16/44 IDC) (51:234)

Ying-jung -- Head, Sha Mien Branch Agency, Canton Police Bureau (51:234)

-29-

CHINESE

Ch'en Ying-tung -- Deputy Chief, Economic Police, Canton Bureau of Police (51:234)

Yu-chih -- With Japanese Huang Hsieh Chun, Chungyang and its vicinity, commanding 3,000 men (6/39; OSS-Ms.); Commander, 21st Division, Nanking Army (3/30/42 IDC)

Yu-jen (Eugene Chen) -- Cantonese; born, 1878, Trinidad; studied law, England; practised, West Indies; Adviser, Minister of Communications; Editor, Peking Gazette (1914-16); arrested for anti-Japanese utterances; pardoned and released (1917); Editor, Shanghai Gazette (1918-19); Southern Delegate, Paris Peace Conference (1919); Acting Minister, Foreign Affairs (1926); Minister, Foreign Affairs, Wuhan (1927); relieved of duty after split between Nanking and Wuhan factions; went to France (1930); member, abortive "People's Government", Foochow (11/33); expelled from Kuomingtang (1934); left China; arrived, Kwangsi to join anti-Japanese and anti-Chiang movement (8/3/36); in favor with Chungking since commencement of Sino-Japanese war (8/3/39); in Hongkong, controlling China Times; captured by Japanese (12/25); removed to Shanghai; refused to join Nanking Government (3/27/43); arrived in Shanghai (5/20/44) (49:164)

Yu-nung -- Head, Clerical Unit, Canton Bureau of Police, First Section (51:234)

Yu-san -- Chairman, Board of Directors, National Trade Control Association, Kwangtung Branch (51:234)

Yuan -- Advised Magistrate, Nanao hsien, that relief had been authroized (11/6/44)

Yueh-lou -- Director, Sino-Japanese Cultural Association, Shanghai Branch (49:167)

Yueh-tsu -- Governor, Shangtung Province; assassinated (52:232)

Yuen-ti -- Member, Education Committee, Shanghai Municipal Council (5/13/44) (49:167)

Yun-wen -- Member, Committee of Political Councillors; President, Central Police Officers School; Inspector, China Office, East Asia League

Yun-wu -- Inspector, East Asia League, Hupeh Branch (1943)

Yung-pak -- Representative of Chinese People, Hongkong (51:234); member, Council "to increase number of free schools" (10/16/44)

Yung-san -- Chief, Auditing, Ministry of Auditing, Chekiang Branch (1943)

CHINESE

Ch'en Yung-wen -- Member, Committee for Investigation of Resources and Materials, Shanghai (49:167); Political Adviser, National Government, Nanking (1943)

Cheng, C. L. -- Former employee, National City Bank of New York; Japanese speaking Chinese national; Chief Internment Superintendent for Hongkong aliens after Japanese invasion (OSS-Ms.)

Chan-chi -- Manager, Anhwei Local Bank (IDC 7270 1943)

Ch'ao-fan -- Secretary, Examination Yuan, Nanking (1943)

Ch'eng-yi -- Secretary, Legislative Yuan, Nanking (1943)

Ch'i-liu -- Political Adviser, National Government, Nanking (1943)

Ch'i-tung -- Inspecting member, China Journalists Association (1943)

Chi-ying -- Head, Electrical Communications Corporation, Hangchow Branch (49:167) Publisher, CHEKIANG JIH PAO, Hang-chou, Chekiang (49:167)

Chia-ting -- Director, Social Welfare Committee, East Asia League, Canton Branch (51:234)

Chia-yu -- Counsellor, National Government, Nanking (1943)

Chieh -- Inspector, China Writers Club (1943)

Chieh-shan -- Head, Te Sun Branch Agency, Canton Police Bureau (51:234)

Chien-p'o -- Director, Citizens Savings Movement Committee, Shanghai (49:167)

Chih -- Chief Judge, High Court, Huaihai Province (R&A 2565);Chief, Su-huai Special District, North China Political Council (1943)

Chih-liang -- Director and Chief, Planning Office, Citizens Savings Movement Committee, Shanghai; Secretary, Paochia Office, 3rd Police Office (49:167)

Chih-min -- Publishers Committee, China Writers Club (1943)

Chih-nung (pung) -- President, TUNG YA CH'EN PAO, Tientsin (1943) (52:232)

Chu-lu -- Director, Shangtung Coal Production and Marketing Company (8/5/43) (52:232)

Chui-hsiu -- Director, Central China City Bus Stock Company, Shanghai (1943)

-31-

CHINESE

Cheng Chun-li -- Chief, Land Affairs, Ministry of
Interior, Nanking (1943)

Chung -- Director, Newspapermen's Association,
Shanghai (1943)

Chung-ch'uan -- Director, Special Municipality
Journalists Association, Shanghai; Director,
Shanghai Newspaper Association; Inspector,
Citizens Savings Movement Committee (49:167);
Editor, HSIN WEN PAO

Han -- Councillor, Chinghsiang Administration,
Hangchou Sector (6/8/43 IDC)

Han-ch'ing -- Director, East Asia League, Hupeh
Branch (1943)

Heng -- Secretary-General, Directorate-Governor
of Posts, North China Political Commission
(7/40;OSS-Ms.)

Hsi-chang -- Director, Munitions Bureau, Ministry of the Navy (R&A 2565)

Hsia-cheng -- Editor, CHU CHIANG MIN KUO JIH PAO,
Yun-chou, South China (51:234)

Hu -- See Hu Cheng

Hung-nien -- Born, 1874, P'an-yu, Kwangtung;
Vice-Minister of Finance, Nanking Government (1924-28); Political Vice-Minister of
Industry (1929-31); Vice-Minister of Communications (Tuan Chi-jui's Government); appointed President, Central China Railway
(1943); Mayor, Shanghai (1/15/44) (49:168)

Hung-yen -- Inspector, Citizens Savings Movement
Committee, Shanghai; member, Shanghai News-
paper Association (49:168); Editor, HSIN WEN
PAO (IDC 7266 1943)

I-ping -- Candidate Director, Newspapermen's
Association, Shanghai (1943)

Keng-hsin(g) -- Secretary General, North China
Political Council (1943); Secretary General,
Huaihai Province

Kuan-hsun -- Reported Assistant Commander-in-
Chief, Peace Preservation Corps, Canton,
under Puppet Government (12/13/41); Commander, 30th Division, Nanking Army (3/30/42);
Executive Director, Social Welfare Committee, East Asia League, Canton Branch (1943)
(51:234)

Kun-hui -- Industry and Construction Minister,
National Government; attended reorganization
meeting, All-China Commercial Control General Association (6/8/44)

Kuo-chun -- Chairman, Directors, Cork Association, Shanghai (IDC 7264 1943)

CHINESE

Cheng Liang-pin -- Director, Citizens Savings Movement Committee, Shanghai (49:168); Chief, Shanghai Branch, Ministry of Construction (R&A 2565); Chairman, Directors, Machine Factories (IDC 7264)

Lien-shih (Cheng, S. G.) -- Special Commissioner of Foreign Affairs, Peiping (1935-36); joined Peiping Provincial Government (1939); appointed Superintendent of Customs; assassinated, British Concession, Tientsin (4/7/39)

Liu -- Publisher, YUNG AN YUEH K'AN, a monthly, Shanghai (49:168)

Min -- Director, China Educational Reconstruction Association, Shanghai Branch (49:168)

Ming-ch'ao -- Inspector, Sino-Japanese Cultural Association, Wu-ch'ang and Hankow Branch (1943); Honorary Director, China Educational Reconstruction Association, Hankow Branch

Nien-p'eng -- Head, Wool Weaving Enterprise Trade Association, National Trade Control General Association, Shanghai (49:168); Chairman, Directors, Woolen Textile Factories; Manager, Chung Hua Commercial and Savings Bank

Pai-yuan -- Training Head, First District Party Headquarters, Kuomingtang Headquarters, Canton (12/43) (51:234)

Pao-yuan -- Manager, Education Department, Kwangtun Province (51:234)

Pen-pow -- See Chen Kung-po

, S.G. -- See Cheng Lien-shih

, S. J. -- Appointed by Japanese as one of superintendents, Japanese Internment Camp for British, Stanley Prison, Hongkong (OSS-Ms.)

Sai-hoi -- Reported doing Japanese intelligence work, Hongkong, under Furukawa, Chief of Japanese Naval Intelligence, Macao (9/41; OSS-Ms.)

Sheng-t'ien -- Chief, Nanking Branch Office, Ministry of Construction (R&A 2565)

Shih-chang -- Chief, General Affairs, Ministry of the Navy, Nanking (1943)

Shih-chun -- Commissioner, Directorate-General of Reconstruction, North China Political Commission (7/40;OSS-Ms.)

Sui-sheng -- Manager, Chung Nan Bank, Peking Branch (1943) (IDC 7270 1943)

-32-

CHINESE

Cheng Tai-chang, Lt. Gen. -- Assistant Director, Military Training (12/38); Chief, Military Counselors' Board, Nanking; member, Central Executive Committee (O-57;R&A 2565)

Tak-hang, Lt. Gen. -- Military (Counsel Advisory) Board; appointed to rank of full General (10/10/44)

T'ao -- President, Supreme Court, National Government, Nanking (3/31/41;OSS-Ms.)

Tao-chou -- Inspector, China Educational Reconstruction Association, Chekiang Branch (49:168)

Te-hiang -- Candidate Inspector, China Educational Reconstruction Association, Shanghai Branch (49:168)

Tso-ch'ing -- Manager-Inspector, Post Office Labor Union; Manager-Director, Readjustment Committee, National Post Office Labor Union, Shanghai (49:168)

Tsung-yen -- Inspector, China Educational Reconstruction Association, Chekiang Branch (49:168)

Tung-pai -- Manager-Director, Special Municipality Journalists Association, Shanghai (49:168)

Tzu-hziu -- Inspector, China Educational Reconstruction Association, Hankow Branch (1943)

Wan-chun -- With Japanese Huang Hsieh Chun in region near Taihu, commanding about 7,000 men (6/39;OSS-Ms.)

Ya-yu -- Editor, TUNG YA CH'EN PAO, Tientsin (1943) (52:232)

Yi-kuei -- Staff member, Secretary's Office, Hankow Municipal Government (R&A 2565)

Yi-p'ing -- Candidate Director, Special Municipality Journalists Association, Shanghai (49:168)

Yu-shu -- Manager, Ho Cheng Bank, Shanghai Branch (IDC 7270 1943)

Yuan-hsing -- Chairman, Directors, Cold Storage and Ice Plants, Shanghai (IDC 7264 1943)

Yung-chi -- Police student sent to Formosa for training; now assigned to Police Branch Bureau, Sha-ho (Canton) as liaison officer (1/6/44) (51:234)

Yung-kung -- Publisher, CHUNG KUO CHING CHI, a bi-monthly, Shanghai (49:2562)

Cheung Koo-shan -- Officer, East Asia Cultural Association, Asiatic Affairs Bureau, Hongkong (51/234)

CHINESE

Cheung Suk-shun -- Member, Executive Committee, Bankers'
Association, Hongkong (51:234)

Chi Ching -- Legislative member, Legislative Yuan,
Nanking (1943); Honorary Director, China-
Japan Returned Students Club

Ch'uan -- Member, Committee for Stopping Breakage
at Chung-mon of Huang-ho

Chung-chiao -- Manager, Hui Chung Bank, Shanghai
(IDC 7270 1943)

Hsie-yuan -- See Chi Hsieh-yuan

Hsieh-yuan (Chi Hsueh-wan; Chih Che-yuan; Chi
Hsie-yuan) -- Born, 1879, Ningpo, Chihli;
graduate, Peiyang Military Academy (1906);
officer before Republic; Commander, 6th Division and Defense Commander, Nanking (1917-
20); Deputy High Inspecting Commander,
Kiangsu, Anhwei, and Kiangsi with brevet
rank of full general (1920); High Inspector,
Kiangsu, Anhwei, Kiangsi with rank of Mar-
shall (1923-25); fled to Japan after defeat
by Chang Chung-ch'ang (Fengtien Army) (1924);
joined Northern Coalition against Nanking
(1930); selected by Japanese to succeed
Hsiao as Mayor, Tientsin, but turned down
by Sung Che-yuan (6/13/36); appointed member,
HCPC (8/4/36);member, Standing Committee,
Head of Peace Maintenance, North China and
Commander, North China Pacification Corps
(12/38); member, North China Political Commission since establishment (3/30/40);
concurrently Director-General, Pacification,
North China, under Japanese (7/40);member,
Military Affairs Commission, Wang Ching-wei's
regime (3/41); Chief, Public Order, new
Provisional Government of China, Peking
(12/14/41); Commander, pro-Japanese "First
Peace Movement Army", North China; reported
making trouble for Japanese near Nanyuan,
Wang trying to mediate (1/1/43); Commander,
97,700 troops, Hopeh-Shantung-Shansu area
(OSS-Ms.); Supervisor, Department of Pacifi-
cation, Peking; Chairman, Anti-Communist
League; present at inaugural meeting, new
Communist Eradication Committee (5/2/43);
Director, Public Peace; Chairman, inaugura-
tion of Anti-Communist League, Peking (7/1/43);
resigned, Director-General, Public Safety
Headquarters and Commander-in-Chief, Pacifi-
cation Force (1/16/44); Managing Commissioner,
Chief of Education; decorated by Japanese
Emperor (3/23/44); Vice-Minister, Justice
(52:232)

Hsueh-wan -- See Chi Hsieh-yuan

Hua -- Legislative member, Legislative Yuan, Nanking (1943); Chief, Economic Committee

Hung-fu -- Training Head, Kuomingtang Sixth District
Party Headquarters, Canton (12/43) (51:234)

-34-

CHINESE

Chi Ju-ku -- Member, Social Committee, China Writers Club (1943)

K'ai-mo -- Publisher, SHIH TAI, a weekly, Shanghai (49:168)

Kuo-chang -- Born, Hupeh; formerly had amusement arcade; after Japanese occupation of Hankow, made Head, Wuhan Peace Maintenance Society (11/25/38;OSS-Ms.)

Kuo-fang -- Commander, pro-Japanese troops; with Japanese Huang Hsieh-chun in Taifu, commanding about 500 men (6/39;OSS-Ms.)

Shu-ying -- Candidate Director, China Educational Reconstruction Association, Hankow Branch (1943)

Tai-feng -- Director, East Asia League, Nanking Branch (1943)

Tsuguo -- Director, General Affairs Bureau, Shinta Special Municipality; appointed Minister and concurrently Counselor, attached to Chinese Embassy, Tokyo (5/5/43)

Wen-liang -- Chairman, Directors, Funeral Clothes and Coffins Association, Shanghai (IDC 7264)

Wen-ping -- Commander, pro-Japanese troops; with Japanese Huang Hsieh Chun in Lintsin, Tungho, Ishih, commanding 4,000 men (6/39; Oss-Ms.)

Yen-ju -- Commissioner, Directorate-General of Industry, North China Political Commission (7/40;OSS-Ms.)

Yun-pang -- Manager, Lu-ta Mining Industrial Company (over half capital of this company owned by Shantung Mining Industrial Company (8/5/43) (52:232)

Yung-kuei -- Assistant Chief, Police, Chia-Hsing District Office, First Police Office, Shanghai (49:168)

Hua -- Member, Committee on Grain Control, Shanghai (49:167)

Chia-la-li-ting -- Inspector, China Office, East Asia League (1943)

Chia Li-fu -- Editor, HSIANG TAO JIH PAO, Hongkong (1943) (51:234)

No-fu -- Editor-in-Chief, KUNG CHEN PAO, Canton (51:234)

P'u -- Publisher, HAN SHAN HSIN PAO, Han-shan Anhwei (1943) (IDC-H 2562)

Shih-yi -- Finance Commissioner, Nanking (1944; OSS)

CHINESE

Chia Te-yueh, Gen. -- Born, about 1887, Hofei, Anhwei; graduate, War College, Tokyo, specializing in infantry; ex-Chihli party member; Premier under Tuan Chi-jui (1924); member, Hopeh-Chahar Autonomous Council and Head, Foreign Affairs Commission (OSS-Ms.)

Yi-sheng -- Editor, HSIN HSI JIH PAO, Wu-hsi, Kiangsu (1943) (IDC-H 2562)

Chiang Ch'ao-chung -- See Chiang Chao-tsung, Gen.

Chao-tsung, Gen. (Chiang Ch'ao-chung; Kiang Chao-tsung) -- Born, 1863, Anhwei; Commander, Gendarmerie and Deputy Lt. Gen., Bordered Red Chinese Banner of Imperial Army at time of Revolution (1912); Acting Premier under President Li Yuan-hung (1917) (OSS-Ms.); rose to rank of General (1917); lived in retirement, Peiping (since 1917); emerged from retirement when Japanese occupied Peiping (7/37); Mayor, Peiping (Who's Who in China 1940); member, North China Political Commission (12/38); Delegate, North China Political Council (3/40) (52:232)

Chen-san -- Inspecting member, Control Yuan, Nanking (1943)

Ch'i-chun -- Candidate Inspecting member, China Journalists Association (1943)

Ch'i-shih -- Legislative member, Legislative Yuan, Nanking (1943)

Chia-chou -- Chief, Bureau of Highways, Ministry of Communications, Nanking (OSS-Ms.)

Chien-li -- Executive Director, China Educational Reconstruction Association, Anhwei Branch (1943)

Chih-fan -- Director, China Educational Reconstruction Association, Chekiang Branch (49:168)

Chih-kang -- Director, Shanghai Chamber of Commerce (49:168)

Chih-zwun -- Chief, International Section, Shanghai (49:168)

Ching-hsin -- Assistant Head, Tai-lan Branch, (#3) Shanghai Police (IDC 2973 1943)

Feng-mei (Chang Feng-ping) -- Chief, Tangshan Administrative Office Headquarters, North China Peace Preservation Corps (1944); Head, Second Administrative District, Hopeh Province (1944) (52:232)

Han-ch'ing -- Inspector, Shanghai Municipality Wharf Labor Union (49:169)

Hang-hu -- See Chiang Kang-hu

-36-

CHINESE

Chiang Hao-jen -- Secretary, Judicial Yuan, Nanking (1943)

Hsiao-kuang -- Inspector, Shanghai Special Municipality Journalists Association (49:169)

Hsin-chao -- Auditor, Ministry of Auditing, Nanking (1943)

Hu -- Vice-President, Control Yuan, under Wang Yi-tang in Wang Ching-wei's National Government (3/22/40;OSS-Ms.)

Hua-chin -- Chief, Public Health, Nanking (12/2/43); Candidate Director, Sino-Japanese Cultural Association, Wu-ch'ang and Hankow Branch (1943) (IDC 2273)

Hung -- Director, Magazines Association, Shanghai; Publisher, TAI P'ING YANG CHOU PAO (49:169)

Hung-geh (Chiang Hung-chih; Kiang Hung-geh) -- Born, 1876, Anhwei; graduate, Meiji University, Tokyo; entered diplomatic service, Vice-Consul, Yokohama (1907); Chinese Legation, Tokyo (1915-38); joined Nanking Reformed Government (1939); Minister of Communications, Nanking (Who's Who in China 1940)

Hung-pin -- Executive member, Flour Special Committee, National Trade Control General Association, Shanghai (49:169)

Hung-t'ang -- Reported by Japanese to be "second cousin of Chiang Kai-shek and to have deserted to Japanese side" (1/43;OSS-Ms.)

K'ai-sheng -- Secretary, Ministry of Justice, Nanking (1943)

K'ang-hu (Kiang K'ang-hu) -- Born, 1883, Kiangsi; Confucian scholar; studied in China, Japan, Belgium, and America; Hon. D. Litt., University of California; founder and leader, Social-Democratic Party of China (1912-13); proscribed; took refuge in America (1915); Professor, Chinese subjects, California University (1914-20); returned to China and organized Southern University, Shanghai, was president (1922); Professor, Chinese studies, McGill University, Montreal (1930-33); consultant on Chinese, Library of Congress, Washington, D. C.; Promoter, Association of Chinese and Foreign Cultural Relations, Shanghai (1935); Standing Committee member, Central Political Council; Vice-President, Examining Board, Nanking (1938); announced participation in Wang Ching-wei's peace movement (10/10/39); acting President, Examination Yuan, also Vice-President, Examination Yuan and concurrently, Minister of Personnel (3/31/41); member, Central Political Council (1943); Director, Sino-Japanese Cultural Association (1943); member, Committee on Application of Constitution; Postal Commissioner, Nanking Special Municipality; Inspec-

CHINESE

Chiang K'ang-hu (Con't) -- tor, China-Japan Returned
Students Club; Executive Inspector, China
Branch, East Asia League; decorated by
Japanese Emperor (3/23/44) (0-56;OSS-Ms.;
Who's Who in China 1940)

Kang-yuan -- Member, Peace and Order Committee,
Shanghai Municiapl Council (5/13/44) (49:169)

K'e-sheng -- Chief, Marine Products Administration, Ministry of Industries, Nanking (1943)

Ku-huai -- Inspecting member, Control Yuan,
Nanking (1943)

Kuang-ch'i -- Member, National Economic Committee (1943)

Kuo-chen -- Manager, Chien Hua Commercial Bank,
Nanking (IDC 7270 1943)

Lu-ch'ien -- Political Vice-Minister under Minister of the Interior, Wang Ching-wei's regime
(3/31/41;OSS-Ms.)

Mao-ch'ing -- Editor, AN CHING HSIN PAO, Anching
Anhwei (1943)

Nan-ch'un -- Member, All-China Economic Committee (OSS-Ms.)

P'ang-chung -- Member, National Economic Committee (1943)

Pang-tao -- Executive Director, China Educational
Reconstruction Association (1943)

Po-hsiang -- Head, Chung Kuo Communications Company, North China (1943) (52:232)

Shang-ta -- Managing Director, Chamber of Commerce,
Shanghai; Director, Labor and Business Social
Union; Director, Citizens Welfare Association;
Director, National Trade Control Association
(49:169); member, All-China Economic Commit-
tee (1943)

Shao-chieh (Kiang Shao-chieh) -- Director, Directorate General of the Interior, North China
Political Commission (7/40;OSS-Ms.)

Shih-chih -- Executive member, Oil and Grain
Special Committee, National Trade Control
General Association, Shanghai (1943) (49:169)

Shou-t'ung -- Director, Citizens Savings Movement
Committee, Shanghai (49:169)

Shui-yi -- Director, Public Health, Huaihai
Province (OSS-Ms.)

Su -- See Chang Su-min

Tao-yuan -- Special Commissioner, Municipal Government, Hankow (12/2/43 IDC)

-38-

CHINESE

Chiang Tho-hsuan (Chiang Tso-suan) -- Vice-Minister of
Construction; appointed Vice-Minister of Industry and Commerce (10/5/43); Chief, Bureau of War Transportation (0-57)

T'ien-ching -- Publisher, HSIN SHENG PAO, Hsin-hsiang (1943) (IDC-H 2562)

T'ing-hua -- Judge, Supreme Court, Nanking (1943)

Ts'an-po -- Former Magistrate, Mengtsze; left
Yunnan Provincial Government, joined Wang Ching-wei's party (1940;OSS-Ms.)

Tse-hsuan -- Vice-Minister of Construction, Nanking (1943)

Tsi-chwang -- Governor, Chekiang and Chief,
Chekiang Financial Board (1/3/45)

Tso-hsu -- Vice-Minister, Industry, Nanking
(10/29/44)

Tso-hsuan -- Member, Committee for Investigation
of Resources and Materials, Shanghai (49:169);
Vice-Minister, Ministry of Industry, Chunking
(1943); Chief, Second Office, National Economic Committee

Tso-suan -- See Chiang Tho-hsuan

Tsu-kang -- Inspector, Citizens Savings Movement
Committee, Shanghai (49:169(

Tsu-yu (Tang Hsu-yu) -- Police Commissioner, Nanking; appointed Governor, newly established
government, Chukuang, Shansi Province (5/7/43);
also reported as Governor, Kiangsi

Tsun-wei -- Counsellor, Directorate-General of the
Interior, North China Political Commission
(7/40;OSS-Ms.)

Tsung-tao -- Executive member, China Journalists
Association (1943)

Wei-hang -- Manager, Pu Tung Bank, Shanghai (IDC
7270 1943)

Wei-tsung -- See Ch'ien Wei-tsung

Wen-pao -- Chief, Office of Social Welfare, Nanking (1943); Director, East Asia League,
Chunking Branch (IDC)

Ya-ch'en -- Member, Sugar Enterprise Special Committee, National Trade Control General Association, Shanghai (49:169)

Yin-chiao -- Director, North China Salt Corporation, Tientsin Branch (1943) (52:232)

Yu-shan -- Manager, Hui Yuan Bank, Shanghai (IDC
7270 1943)

CHINESE

Chiang Yu-shi -- Head, Cultural Chinese Theatrical Cooperative Association (6/21/44)

Yun-chang -- Candidate Director, Special Municipality Journalists Association, Shanghai (49:169)

Yung-k'un -- Police Chief, Amoy (OSS-Ms.)

Chiao Chi -- Delegate, North China Political Council (52:232)

Jung -- Member, Central Executive Committee, Nanking; member, Central Political Council (OSS-Ms.)

Wan-hsuan -- Member, Committee of Political Councillors (1943); Director, Administrative Bureau for Abolition of Extraterritorial Rights; appointed Associate Judge, Special Court, National Government; Chairman, Supreme Court to serve concurrently with appointment as Director, Special Court (7/44)

Yi-yuan -- Represented former Governor at inauguration of Yang Yu-cheun (52:232)

Ying -- Member, Designated Committee, Central Political Council (12/38); member, Central Council, Nanking Kuomingtang (3/31/41)(OSS-Ms.); Director, China Office, East Asia League (1943)

Yung -- Inspector, Control Yuan, Nanking (1943);

Chien Ai-tsu -- Commander, pro-Japanese troops; with Japanese Huang Hsieh Chun in Tungling, Tatung, Kweichih, commanding about 800 men (6/39;OSS-Ms.)

Ch'ien -- Judge and Chief, High Court, Kiangsu Province (49:169); Inspector, China-Japan Returned Students Club

Chien-wu -- Member, Anti-Anglo-American Association (6/3/43); Inspector, China Office, East Asia League (1943)

Chih-shih -- Member, Committee for Investigation of Resources and Materials, Shanghai (49:169)

Ching-ts'an -- Inspector, China Educational Reconstruction Association, Anhwei Branch (1943)

Chiu-wei -- Legislative member, Legislative Yuan, Nanking (1943)

Feng-kao -- Manager, Shanghai Industrial and Commercial Bank (IDC 7270 1943)

Fu-hen -- Member, Finance Committee, Municipal Council, Shanghai (5/13/44) (49:169)

Hsiang-i -- Director, Standing Committee, Newspapermen's Association (1943)

-40-

CHINESE

Chien Hsiang-yi -- Manager and Director, Special Municipality Journalists Association, Shanghai (49:169)

Hsien-lai -- Assistant Manager, Central Reserve Bank, Nanking (IDC 7270 1943)

Kung-chu -- Chairman, Trustees, Buttons Association, Shanghai (IDC 7264)

Kung-hsia -- Director, Magazines Association, Shanghai; Director, Sino-Japanese Cultural Association; Publisher, TA CHUNG, a monthly (49:169)

Kuo-ch'eng -- Secretary, Pao-chia Office, 1st Police Office, Shanghai (49:169)

Lou -- Inspecting member, Control Yuan, Nanking (1943)

Lu-tsung -- Assistant Chairman, China Educational Reconstruction Association (1943)

Po-yuan -- Collector of Revenue, Hankow (12/243) (IDC 2213)

P'u-l'ai -- Inspector, China Educational Reconstruction Association, Hankow Branch (1943)

Sen -- Appointed Associate Judge, Special Court, National Government (3/11/44)

Sheng-chiao -- Judge and Chief, Supreme Court, Nanking (1943)

Shu-ni -- Assistant, General Affairs Section, China Educational Reconstruction Association (1943)

Ta -- Director, East Asia League, Shanghai Branch (49:169)

Ta-huai -- Member, Committee of Political Councillors, Nanking (1943); member, All-China Economic Committee; Vice-Governor, Central Reserve Bank of China (1/7/44)

Ta-k'uei -- Vice-President, Central Reserve Bank, Nanking (1943); Political Adviser, National Government, Nanking (1943); member, National Economic Committee, Nanking (1943)

Ta-tun -- Vice-President, Central Reserve Bank, Nanking (IDC-7270 1943)

Tao-tsun -- Director, East Asia Cultural Association; President, Peking University (8/27/44); member, Committee of Academia Sinica, Nanking Government (6/18/43) (52:232)

Te-kuang -- Secretary-General, National Economic Committee (1/43); member, National Government, Nanking (1943); Candidate Director, Sino-Japanese Cultural Association; Director, China Office, East Asia League; Inspector, China-Japan Returned Students Club

-41-

CHINESE

Chien Tsung-fan -- Chairman, Directors, Undertakers
      Association, Shanghai (IDC 7264 1943)

    Wei-hsiu -- Publisher, TUNG YA WAN PAO, Hongkong
        (IDC 1943)

    Wei-tsung -- Member, National Economic Committee
        (1943); Commissioner, Bureau of Education,
        Anhwei (1943); member, New Citizens Movement
        Promotion Committee; Head, Chekiang Univer-
        sity; Chairman, Directors, China Educational
        Reconstruction Association, Anhwei Branch

    Wen -- Control Officer, Shan Wang Tai Ward, Hong-
        kong (51:235)

    Yeh-cheng -- Head, Tung Ti Branch Agency, Canton
        Police Bureau (1/6/44) (51:235)

    Yi-fei -- Publisher, SHIH SHIH JIH PAO, Fu-shan,
        South China (IDC 1943) (51:235)

    Yuan-chung -- Counsellor, National Government,
        Nanking (1943)

    Yung-ming -- Vice-President, Central Reserve Bank,
        Nanking (10/29/44)

Chih -- Chairman, Chamber of Commerce, Canton (3/24/44)
      (51:235)

    Che-yuan -- See Chi Hsieh-yuan

    Han-fen -- Manager, Shanghai Iron Industry Bank
        (IDC 7270 1943)

    Tzu-ch'ing -- Inspector, Social Welfare Committee,
        East Asia League, Canton Branch (51:235)

Chin Chang -- Director-General, Directorate-General of
      Posts, North China Political Commission
      (7/40;OSS-Ms.)

    Chia-feng -- Member, Central Executive Committee,
        Nanking (1943); Director, China Office, East
        Asia League

    Chien-poi -- Central Reserve Bank, Hangchow, Chekiang
        (IDC 7270 1943)

    Chih-hao -- Member, Publishers Committee, China
        Writers Club (1943)

    Chih-hsun -- Director, International Affairs Bu-
        reau, Ministry of Foreign Affairs, Nanking
        (OSS-Ms.)

    Chin-tseng -- Assistant Chief, Kuo-sze Branch (#1),
        Shanghai Police (IDC 2973 1943)

    Ching-hsiu -- Candidate Director, China Education-
        al Reconstruction Association, Anhwei Branch
        (1943)

    Fu-sheng -- Chief, Office of Finance, Amoy (49:170)

-42-

CHINESE

Chin Fun-ka -- Vice-President, newly formed China Newspaper Association; publisher, Shanghai ...
newspaper (9/21/44) (49:170)

Han-chang -- Director, China Educational Reconstruction Association, Chekiang Branch (49:170)

Han-ching -- Divisional Commander, 2nd Nanking
Gendarmerie Corps (2/29/44; IDC 2463)

Hsuing-pai (-pao, -po) -- Manager Director, News-
paper Association, Shanghai Branch; Director,
East Asia League, Shanghai Branch; member,
Committee on Application of Constitution;
Executive Director, Sino-Japanese Cultural
Association; Publisher, P'ING PAO (49:170);
Executive Director and Chief, Investigation
Section, China Educational Reconstruction
Association

Hua -- Commissioner, Directorate-General of Pacification, North China Political Commission
(7/40;OSS-Ms.)

Ji-chang -- Director, Kako Commercial Block,
Shanghai (49:170)

Jun-ch'ing -- Managing Director, Chamber of Commerce, Shanghai (49:170); Manager, Development Bank of China (IDC 7270 1943)

Jung-kuei -- Governor, Fengtien Province (0-41)

Kang-hou -- Manager, Kuan I Commercial and Savings
Bank, Shanghai (IDC 7270 1943)

Kuan-hsien -- Manager, Chekiang Chien Yeh Bank,
Shanghai (IDC 7270 1943)

Kun-kei (Japanized reading) -- (See also Chen
Ch'un-p'u; Chin Shun-po) Chief, Business
Bureau, Nanking Government; Head, Industry
Department; Chief, Provisions Department;
involoved in graft scandal; Governor, Kwangtung
Province (4/44); appointed, Head Construc-
tion Department, National Government (4/44)
(51:235)

Liang-kung -- Inspecting member, Control Yuan,
Nanking (1943)

Lung-te -- Commander, pro-Japanese troops; with
Huang Hsieh Chun, in Kingshan, Tienmen and
Yuehkou, commanding 3,000 men (6/39:OSS-Ms.)

Mien-kou -- Inspecting member, Control Yuan, Nanking (1943)

Mien-tseng -- Assistant Chief, Police, Hui-sze
District Office, First Police Office, Shanghai
(49:170)

Mo-sen -- President, MIN KUO JIH PAO, Nanking;
Executive Director, Central Electrical Commu-
nications Corporation (1943); Director, China-
Japan Returned Students Club; member, Propa-

CHINESE

Chin Mo-sen (Con't.) -- ganda Committee, China Office, East Asia League

Pu-ying -- Inspector, Shanghai Municipality Wharf Labor Union (49:170)

Shao-fu -- Officer, 5th District, (P'u-tung-pei), Shanghai (OSS-Ms.)

Shao-wei -- Commissioner, Directorate-General of Industry, North China Political Commission (7/40;OSS-Ms.)

Sheng -- Publisher, SHANG LAI YING T'AN, a monthly, Shanghai (49:170)

Shou-liang -- Member, National Military Council (OSS-Ms.)

Shou-o -- Publisher, CH'UAN MIEN, a weekly, Shanghai (49:170)

Shun-po -- Head, Construction Department, Nanking; reported appointed Provincial Governor, Canton (4/44); See also Chin Kun-kei and Chen Chun-p'u (51:235)

Szuaan -- Member, Publishing Committee, China Writers Club (1943)

, ... Su -- Director, Shanghai Office, Enemy Property Disposal Committee (1/22/44) (49:170)

Ta-chih -- Head, Hsin-min Communications Company, North China (1943) (52:232)

T'ien-sheng -- Director, Shanghai Municipality Wharf Labor Union (49:170)

Tsung-ch'eng -- Manager Director, Citizens Savings Movement Committee, Shanghai (49:170)

Ya-hsiu (Yan-hsiu) -- Chief, Cotton Control Office, Nanking District, Ministry of Industry (1943); Inspector, East Asia League, Nanking Branch; Director, China Writers Club

Ching Chan-shen -- See also Kian Chang-chuan; President, North China Christian Association (8/12/44)

Hsiung-pai -- Director, Citizens Savings Movement Committee, Shanghai (49:170)

Hsuan-lu -- Chinese student in Japan (DIO 7/44)

Ke-sun -- Member, Council, Overseas China Association (O-58)

Pi-ch'eng -- Chief, Paochia Office, 4th Department, Shanghai (49:170)

Shao-fu -- Chief, 5th District, P'u-tung-pei, Shanghai (49:170)

Te-kuang -- Member, Invited Committee, Central Political Council (12/38)

CHINESE

Ching Tsung-ch'eng -- Director, Chamber of Commerce, Shanghai (49:170)

  Wei-chi -- Governor, Honan Province; made statement re attitude of Japanese in Hongkong toward war (4/21/44;51:235)

  Yuan -- Director, Sino-Japanese Cultural Association, Shanghai Branch (49:170)

Ch'iu An-t'ai -- Chairman, Inspectors, Shanghai Municipality Wharf Labor Union (49:170)

  Cho-hui -- Inspector, Social Welfare Committee, East Asia League, Canton Branch (51:235)

  Fu-to -- Director, Sino-Japanese Cultural Association, Shanghai Branch (49:170)

  Hsiung-po -- Editor, PING PAO, Shanghai (IDC 7266 1943)

  Kwai-cheung -- See Chao Kwei-chang

  Shen-yuan -- Editor, YU NAN JIH PAO, Huang-ch'uan (1943) (IDC-H 2562)

  Shih -- Editor, HAN SHAN HSIN PAO, Han-shan, Snhwei (1943) (IDC-H 2562)

  Shih-mu -- Inspector, Shanghai Special Municipality Journalists Association (49:170)

  Tang-mo -- Chief, Income Tax Office, Ministry of Finance, Nanking (1943)

  Ting-kuo -- Member, Directing Committee, China Office, East Asia League (1943)

  Yun-to -- Staff member, HSIN CHUNG KUO PAO, Shanghai (OSS-Ms.)

Cho Fu-hai -- See Chou Fu-hai

  I-lin -- Vice-President, Central China Telephone Company, Shanghai (O-67)

  Ju-san -- Chungking; deserted to Nanking? (DIO 6/43)

  Mau-in -- Professor, Japanese Literature, Peking University

  Po-hai -- Nanking Minister of Finance; visited Japan (3/15/42 DIO)

  Sui-chang -- Mayor, Nanking (Special Mayor, 1942); made survey of Youth Movement; Head, Felicitation Group to Manchukuo 10th Anniversary (9/2/42)

  Tien-an -- Chairman, Directors, Hemp Products Association, Shanghai (IDC 7264 1943)

Chong Pao-yuan -- Editor, EN PING JIH PAO, En-ping, South China (1943) (51:235)

-45-

CHINESE

Chou -- Commissioner, Administrative Affairs, Kwangtung; Commissioner, Political Works Corps for Village Pacification (3/13/44) (51:235); Vice-Minister, Foreign Affairs (4/25/43)

Chou, Gen. -- Deputy Chief, General Staff, National Government Military Council (2/17/43)

Chen -- Chairman, Political Affairs Bureau, North China (52:233)

Cheng-chi -- Legislative member, Legislative Yuan, Nanking (1943); Inspector, China Educational Reconstruction Association

Chi-tao -- Member, Propaganda Committee, China Office, East Asia League (1943)

Ch'ien -- Inspecting member, Control Yuan, Nanking (1943)

Ch'ien-k'ang -- Director, Citizens Savings Movement Committee, Shanghai (49:171)

Ch'in-hao -- Editor, CHAO SHENG YUEH KAN, a monthly, Swatow (49:171)

Chin-ting -- Chairman, Directors, North China Import and Export Trade Association, Shanghai (IDC 7264 1943)

Ching -- Head, Fang Tsun Branch Agency, Canton Police Bureau (51:235)

Ching-an -- Chairman, Directors, Fertilizers Association, Shanghai (IDC 7264 1943)

Ching-fang -- Vice-Secretary General, Executive Yuan (1/26/43); Minister of Finance, Nanking; Secretary General, Supreme National Defense Council; Secretary General, All-China Economic Committee

Ch'ing-man -- Director, North China Communications Corporation; Chief, Railroad Bureau, Tientsin Office (1944)

Ch'uan-sun -- Member, All-China Economic Council (OSS-Ms.)

Chueh -- Minister residing in Ministry of Foreign Affairs, Nanking (1943)

Chueh-seng -- Publisher, HSIN TAI HSING JIH PAO, T'ai-hsing, Kiangsu (1943) (IDC-H 2562)

Chung-ch:ing -- Head, Metal Enterprise Trade Association, National Trade Control General Association, Shanghai (1943) (49:171); Chariman, Directors, Smelting and Casting Factories, Shanghai (IDC 7264)

Chung-kuang -- Member, Association of Teachers, Amoy (49:171)

-46-

CHINESE

Chou Fo-hai -- See Chou Fu-hai

Fo-han -- Member, Judicial Department; made statement to press: judicial authorities will not pardon illegal acts, even by high ranking officials (3/13/44)

Fu-hai (Cho Fu-hai; Chu Fu-hai; Chow Fu-hai) -- Born, 1897, Hunan; B. A., Tokyo Imperial University; Director, Political Department, Central Military Officers' College; member, Central Executive Committee, Kuomingtang; Commissioner of Education, Kiangsu Province (since 1932); Vice-Director and Acting Director, Central Publicity Council Kuomingtang (1937-38); member, Designated Committee, Central Political Council, Department of Police Affairs (12/38); fled from Chungking with Wang Ching-wei (12/19/38); member, Chairman, Standing Committee, Central Executive Committee, Orthodox Kuomintang (8/39); Minister of Finance in Wang Ching-wei's Nanking Government; concurrently, Chief of Police; important liaison officer with the Japanese Army (3/22/40); member, Military Affairs Commission under Wang Ching-wei's regime (3/41); Finance Minister and Governor, Reserve Bank (8/3/42-9/7/44); Honorary Director, Sino-Japanese Cultural Association (1943); Special Envoy to Manchuria (4/9/43); member, Supreme Council, National Defense (1943); Vice-President, Executive Yuan (1943); Head, Special Committee, Control of Enemy Property (6/2/44); Chairman, Committee for Deliberation of Commodity Prices; visited Japan as Acting Chinese President (8/25/44); Vice-President, Executive Yuan (12/27/44); Chief, Shanghai Police; assumed post, Mayor, Shanghai (1/17/45); President, Central Reserve Bank (49:171; OSS-Ms.; Who's Who in China 1940); Vice-Secretary General, Supreme National Defense Council; Vice-Chairman, National Military Council; Vice-Chairman, All-China Economic Council; Chairman, Party Finance Committee, Central Kuomintang; Executive Director, New Citizens Movement Promotion Committee; Chief, Village Pacification Committee; Secretary General and Executive Director, China Office, East Asia League; Inspector, China- Japan Returned Students Club; Honorary Chairman, Directors, China Educational Reconstruction Association; Vice-Chairman, National Economic League

Hsiang-ching -- Manger, Yung Feng Commercial Bank, Shanghai (IDC 7270 1943)

Hsiao-ping -- Publisher, YING CHU, semi-monthly, Shanghai (49:171)

Hsing-tang -- Manager, Hankow Commercial Bank, Hupeh (IDC 7270 1943)

CHINESE

Chou Hsueh-ch'ang (Chow Hsieh-chang) -- Mayor, Nanking; arrived, Fukuoka for meeting (12/9/43); Chief, Office of Resources and Material Control; Chief, Office of Social Affairs (1943); Assistant Secretary-General, China Office, East Asia League, Nanking Branch; Chairman, China Movie Association, Nanking Office

Hua-jen -- Adviser, Citizens Savings Movement Committee, Shanghai; Executive Director, Sino-Japanese Cultural Association (49:171); member, Central Executive Committee, Nanking; member, All-China Economic Committee; Executive Director, New Citizens Movement Promotion Committee; Vice-Minister, Education; Director, China Office, East Asia League; Director, Central Electrical Communications Corporation; member, Chinese Journalists Association

Huan-chang -- Vice-President, Chung Chiang Industrial Bank, Hankow, Hupeh (IDC 7270 1943)

Hun-jen -- Administrative Vice-Minister, under Minister of Railways, Wang Ching-wei's regime (3/41;OSS-Ms.)

Hung-hsi -- Director, Central China Electrical Communications Stock Company, Shanghai (1943)

Kuan-hsiang -- Vice-President, North China Christians Association (8/11/44) (52:233)

Kuan-hung -- Chief, Bureau of Construction, Kiangsi (IDC 1943)

K'uang -- Legislative member, Legislative Yuan, Nanking (1943); member, Propaganda Committee, China Office, East Asia League

Kung-sheng -- Secretary, Executive Yuan, Nanking (1943)

Lang-siang -- See Chou Lung-hsiang

Li-an -- Manager Director, Magazines Association, Shanghai; Executive Director, Sino-Japanese Cultural Association; Publisher, KU CHIN, a semi-monthly (49:171)

Li-k'e -- Secretary General, China-Japan Returned Students Club (1943)

Lo-shan -- Executive Inspector, China Educational Reconstruction Association (1943)

Lung-hsiang (Chou Lung-kuang; Chou Lung-yang; Chou Lung-yuang; Chou Lang-siang; Chou Lung-shen) -- Born, 1885, Tingyuan, Anhwei; LLB., Tokyo Imperial University; Councillor, Ministry of Justice (1925-28); Director, Asiatic Affairs (1928); Hopeh-Chahar Council (1930); working with Japanese (since 1931); Counsellor, Tsingtao City Government (1931-33); Director, Intelligence and Publicity, Japanese controlled Peking Provisional Government (1939);

-48-

CHINESE

Chou Lung-hsiang (con't) -- reported in trouble for alleged embezzlement of official funds (1/15/40); Administrative Vice-Minister under Minister of Foreign Affairs, Wang Ching-wei's regime (3/31/41) (OSS-Ms.); Vice-Minister, Foreign Affairs; State Councillor, Nanking; Minister, Foreign Affairs (1/19/43); member, National Economic Committee; Secretary General, Executive Yuan, Nanking (9/10/43); member, Committee for Taking over French Concessions, Shanghai; member, Commission for Control of Enemy Property; Director, Central Electric Communications Corporation (1943); decorated by Japanese Emperor (3/23/44); member, New Citizens Movement Promotion Committee; Assistant Secretary General, China Office, East Asia League; China-Japan Returned Students Club; Director, China Office, East Asia League

Lung-kuang -- See Chou Lung-hsiang

Lung-shen -- See Chou Lung-hsiang

Lung-yang -- See Chou Lung-hsiang

Lung-yuang -- See Chou Lung-hsiang

Min-yi -- See Chu Min-i

Ming -- Publisher, CHIANG YIN JIH PAO, Chiang-ying, Kiangsu (1943) (IDC-H 2562)

Nai-wen -- Vice-Minister, Cotton Control Office, Ministry of Industry (1943); Vice-Minister, Ministry of Grains; Vice-Chief, Foodstuffs Department, National Government; dismissed on suspicion of illegal dealing (3/13/44)

Pang-chun -- Chairman, Directors, Soap and Candles Factories, Shanghai (IDC 7264)

Pang-tsun -- Honorary Director, Sino-Japanese Cultural Association, Shanghai Branch (49:171)

Pao-yi -- Director, China Educational Reconstruction Association (1943)

P'ei-ping -- Vice-President, North China Communications Corporation (1944)

Ping-san -- Special Delegate to Kwangtung, Ministry of Foreign Affairs (1943)

Po-kan -- Member, Social Welfare Committee, China Branch, East Asia League (1943)

Shao -- Head, Civilian Defense, West District, Canton, and Maritime District, Canton (IDC 10/6/44)

Shao-jen -- Director General, Education, North China Political Council (1942) (52:233)

Shen -- See Chu Shen

CHINESE

Chou Shou-chen -- Director, East Asia Bank; Director, Chung Hus Department Store; Chairman, Chinese Discursive Association, Hongkong (51:235)

Sung-sheng -- Commissioner, Directorate General of the Interior, North China Political Commission (7/40;OSS-Ms.)

Ta-wen -- Inspector, North China Electrical Industry Company, Peiping (8/5/43) (52:233)

Tao-jan -- See Chou Tsao-jen

Tao-min -- Manager, Chin Cheng Bank, Shanghai (IDC 7270 1943)

Tao-tseng -- Counsellor, Directorate General of Finance, North China Political Commission (7/40;OSS-Ms.)

Ti-nien -- Architect, Hongkong; member, China Discursive Association (51:235)

Ti-yu -- Chief, Construction, North China Political Council (1943)

Ting-ming, Maj. -- Chinese officer, captured by Japanese; now deceased (DIO 5/29/44)

T'ing-na -- Member, Committee on Application of Constitution, Nanking (1943)

Tsao-jen (Chou Tso-jen; Chou Tao-jen; Chou Tsuo-jen; Chao Shao-jen) -- State Councillor, Nanking; Head, Education, North China Political Council (1942); Vice-Chairman, Hsin Min Association (11/14/42); member, Committee to Restore National Research Department; Chairman, East Asia Cultural Council and President, Executive Committee (11/26/43); Executive Director, New Citizens Movement Promotion Committee (1943); President, East Asia Cultural Association, Peking (8/27/44) (52:233)

Tsing-lai -- Head, Department of Communications (12/38)

Tso-fen -- State Councillor, Nanking (1943)

Tso-jen -- (See Also Chou Tsao-jen) Honorary Chairman, Directors, China Educational Reconstruction Association (1943); Executive member, National Economic Committee; member, North China Political Council

Tso-min -- Born, 1882, Huai-an, Kiangsu; studied in Japan; Managing Director, Kincheng Banking Corporation (since 1918); member, Hopeh-Chahar Political Affairs Commission (12/11/35); reported gone over to Wang Ching-wei's party (7/31/39) (OSS-Ms.); Inspector, National Trade Control General Association, Shanghai (1943); Managing Director, Kincheng Banking Corporation, Shanghai (49:171); appointed member, All-China Economic Committee, Shanghai (2/5/43; OSS-Ms.); member, Municipal Advisory Committee

-50-

CHINESE

Chou Tsuo-jen -- See Chou Tsao-jan

Tu-hai -- Member, National Economic Committee, Nanking (1943)

Wang-hsien -- See Changh Chieng-ch'u

Wei -- Legislative member, Legislative Yuan, Nanking (1943); Chief, Military Affairs Committee

Wen-lung -- Abandoned command as battalion chief, Communist 8th Route Army, surrendered himself to Japanese fostered Peiping Government through intermediary of Ch chow magistrate (5/27/40;OSS-Ms.)

Wen-mei -- Chairman, Directors, Glass Factories, Shanghai (IDC 7264)

Wen-sui -- Manager, Chung Bank, Shanghai (IDC 7270 1943)

Yao-nien -- Member, Council of Chinese Representatives Association, Hongkong (1942-) (52:235)

Yi-tseng -- Editor, WAN PAO, An-ch'ing, Anhwei (1943) (IDC-H 2562)

Ying-hsiang -- Political Affairs Commissioner, Kwangtung Province; Director, Political Work Corps for Village Pacification; Head, Kwangtung Village Pacification Training Schools (51:236)

Yu-chang -- Director, Shanghai Inland Steamship Stock Company (IDC 7262 1943)

Yu-jen -- Candidate Inspecting member, China Journalists Association (1943); Director, China Writers Club

Yu-wen -- Secretary, Ministry of Justice, Nanking (1943)

Yu-ying -- Chief, Social Welfare Office, Shanghai; Adviser, Citizens Savings Movement Committee (49:171)

Yueh-jan -- Director, Sino-Japanese Cultural Association, Shanghai Branch (49:171); member, National Education Committee; member, New Citizens Movement Promotion Committee; member, National History Editing Committee; Editor, HAI FENG; President, Commercial Press

Yuen-tiou -- Left Chungking camp, joined National Government (2/8/43)

Yun-ch'ing -- Editor, TANG T'U JIH PAO, Tai-ping (49:171)

Yung -- Training Head, 4th District Party Headquarters, Kuomintang, Swatow (12/43)

Chow Chung-yueh (Chow Chung-you) -- Minster of Interior, Nanking (1/1/42; 9/23/43)

100 -51-

CHINESE

Chow Fu-hai -- See Chou Fu-hai

Hsieh-chang -- See Chou Hsueh-ch'ang

Lum -- Head, Bicycle and Tricycle Syndicate, New Territory, Hongkong and Kowloon (51:236)

Sir Shouson -- Chairman, Chinese Cooperative Council (1942-); Chairman, Council of Chinese Representatives Association, Hongkong (51:236)

Tao-jen -- Member, Committee for Restoration of National Research Department, Nanking (6/8/43)

Chu Chan-ming -- Chairman, Directors, South China Import and Export Trade Association, Shanghai (IDC 7264)

Chang-yi -- Secretary, Ministry of Finance, Nanking (1943)

Chao-lin -- Chairman, Directors, Thread Making Association, Shanghai (7264 1943)

Chen-chih -- Manager, Chekiang Hsing Yeh Bank, Tientsin Branch (52;233)

Ch'eng -- Secretary, China Educational Reconstruction Association, Chekiang Branch (49:171)

Ch'eng -- President, Judicial Yuan (1/1/42)

Ch'eng-yuan -- Director, East Asia League, Hupeh Branch (1943)

Ch'i-chen -- Director, Citizens Savings Movement Committee, Shanghai (49:171)

Ch'iao-yao -- Legislative member, Legislative Yuan, Nanking (1943)

Chien-huei -- (52:233); See also Ch'en Ch'un-hui

Chin-pu -- Manager, Cheng Ming Commercial and Savings Bank, Shanghai (IDC 7270 1943)

Ch'ing-lai -- Japanese educated; former professor of economics, Shanghai; member, Chinese National Socialist Party; member, Invited Committee, Central Political Council (from 12/38); Minister of Communications, Wang Ching-wei's National Government, Nanking (3/22/40); Minister of Police, Nanking Government (1941); removed from post as Head, Police (8/20/41) (OSS-Ms.); Honorary Director, Sino-Japanese Cultural Association (1943); member, Central Political Council; Vice-President, Legislative Yuan; Executive Director, China-Japan Returned Students Club; Executive Director, China Office, East Asia League; Honorary Chairman, Directors, China Educational Reconstruction Association; member, Committee on Application of Constitution

Ching-mai -- Inspecting member, Control Yuan, Nanking (1943)

-52-

CHINESE

Chu Ch'uan-ho -- Member, Committee for Stopping Breakage at Chung-mon of Huang-ho (1943)

Ch'un-po -- Member, Sugar Enterprise Special Committee, National Trade Control General Association, Shanghai (IDC 1943;49:171)

Ch'ung-ch'ing -- Minister, Ministry of Foreign Affairs (1943)

Chung-hua -- Manager, Chao Hsing Hsien Farmers' Bank, Chekiang (IDC 7270 1943)

Chung-lu -- Executive member, China Journalists Association (1943); Director, China Writers Club

Chung-lun -- Inspector, Citizens Savings Movement Committee, Shanghai (49:172)

Fan -- Member, North China Political Council, Education Department (2/8/43) (52:233)

Fu-hai -- See Chou Fu-hai

Hai-chu -- Manager, Shanghai Industrial Bank (IDC 7270 1943)

Hao-yuan -- Member, Committee for Stopping Breakage at Chung-mon of Huang-ho (1943)

Ho-hai -- Vice-President, Legislative Yuan, National Government; attended reorganization meeting of All-China Commercial Control General Association (6/8/44)

Hong-hi -- Director, Central China Telephone Company, Shanghai (49:172)

Hsin-ch'en -- Commander, pro-Japanese troops; with Japanese Huang Hsieh Chun in Honan (6/39; OSS-Ms.)

Hsing-yuan -- Born, 1880, Tahsin, Peking; graduate, Peking Imperial University; studied in Japan two years, Chung Yin Academy; on return from Japan, appointed Counsellor, Ministry of Foreign Affairs; first class secretary, Chinese Legation, Washington (1913); full secretary, Ministry of Foreign Affairs, concurrently Counsellor to same Ministry (1918); Secretary, Ministry of Communications (1919); Commissioner, Foreign Affairs for Chihli (1920; 1925-26); Director, Political Bureau, North China Political Commission; Chief, Board of Foreign Affairs, North China Political Commission (7/40) (OSS-Ms.); Head, Political Affairs Department, Political Council, North China (1942;52:233); member, North China Political Council (1943)

Hsu -- Secretary, Ministry of Foreign Affairs, Nanking (1943)

CHINESE

Chu Hsueh-fan -- Former Head, Shanghai General Labor
        Union; President, Chinese Association of
        Labor (49:172)

Hui-sheng -- Manager, Yung Heng Bank, Shanghai
        (IDC 7270 1943)

Hung -- Editor, CHE TUAG WAN HUA, a monthly, Ningpo,
        Chekiang (42:172)

I-chieh (Chu Yi-k'ai) -- Secretary General, Japanese
        fostered North China Political Commission
        (7/40;OSS-Ms.)

I-chiu -- Appointed to reorganize Hsin-hui Merchants
        Association, Canton (51:236)

Ju-tang -- Manager, Shanghai Commercial and Savings
        Bank (IDC 7270 1943)

Jun-sheng -- Director, China Educational Reconstruc-
        tion Association, Shanghai Branch (49:172)

Kang -- Publisher, YANG CHOU HSIN PAO, Yang-chou,
        Kiangsu (1943) (IDC 2562)

Keng-hsing -- Member, Sugar Enterprise Special Com-
        mittee, National Trade Control General Asso-
        ciation, Shanghai (49:172)

Li-ho -- See also Chu Lu-ho; Standing Committee
        member, Central Political Council (12/38);
        Vice-Minister, Judicial Yuan (12/38); Vice-
        President, Judicial Yuan (under Wen Tsung-yao
        (3/22/40;OSS-Ms.); Honorary Director, Sino-
        Japanese Cultural Association (1943); Execu-
        tive Director, China Office, East Asia League;
        Chief, Committee for Punishment of Central
        Officials

Li-yuan -- Chief, Secretariat, North China Politi-
        cal Council (1943)

Lu-ho -- See also Chu Li-ho; Born, 1884, Kashing,
        Chekiang; received advanced education, Eng-
        land; joined Nanking Reformed Government as
        Vice-Minister of Justice (1938); Minister of
        Justice (1940) (Who's Who in China 1940)

Min-yi -- Brother-in-law, Wang Ching-wei; born, 1884,
        Nanzing, Chekiang; went to Japan, 1903,
        studied political science and economics;
        travelled in Europe with Chang Chin-kiang
        (1908); joined with Tung Ming-hui at Singa-
        pore; lived in France; returned to China
        after outbreak of World War; returned to
        Paris where he studied medicine, histology;
        received M.D. and B.A. in pharmacy, Stras-
        bourg University; assisted in establishment,
        Universite de Lyons, served as first presi-
        dent (1921); returned to China (1924); Vice-
        President, University of Kwantung (1925);
        elected reserve member, Central Executive
        Committee, Kuomintang (1925); member, Central
        Executive Committee, Kuomintang (1927); sent
        to Europe to "study health conditions"(1928);

-54-

CHINESE

Chu Min-yi (Con't.) -- In Belgium (1930); Chief Secretary, Executive Yuan (1932-35); member, Standing Committee, Central China Political Council (12/38); Vice-President, Executive Yuan (12/38); joined Wang Ching-wei's peace movement (1939); elected Secretary General, Orthodox Kuomintang (8/39; Founder and President, China-Japan Cultural Association (10/4/42; 7/17/44); member, Standing Committee, National Economic Council (2/9/43); Foreign Minister, National Government of China (1943, 1944); signed agreement with Italian Ambassador (Taliani) providing restitution of administrative rights over Italian Legation quarters in Peking to Nanking Government (3/13/43; OSS-Ms.); Chairman, Preparatory Committee for National Research Department (1943); State Councillor; Special Envoy, Japan and Manchukuo (1943); decorated by Emperor of Japan (4/23/43); Adviser, Sino-Japanese Cultural Association, Shanghai Branch (1943; 49:172); Chairman, National Central Research Insititue (3/12/44); Chairman, Southeast Asia Medical Conference (4/12/44); Director and first Chairman, Sino-Japanese Buddhist Research Society (8/3/44); appointed President, Tungjen Medical College (9/11/44); member, Committee on Return of Concessions; member, Supreme National Defense Council; member, National Economic Council; Chairman, Directors, China-Japan Returned Students Club; President, All-China Athletic Association; Chairman, Committee Academia Sinica, Nanking Government; Executive Inspector, China Branch, East Asia League; Honorary Chairman, Directors, China Educational Reconstruction Association; member, Committee for Application of Constitution

Pao-heng -- Manager Director, Special Municipality Journalists Association, Shanghai; member Shanghai Newspaper Association; Editor, CHUNG HUA JIH PAO, Shanghai (49:172); member, Committee on Culture, China Office, East Asia League; Executive member, China Journalists Association

Ping-ch'ing -- Candidate Director and Assistant, China Educational Reconstruction Association (1943)

Po-ch'uan -- Member, Education Committee, Citizens Welfare Association, Shanghai; Executive Director, Sino-Japanese Cultural Association; member, Financial Consultation Committee, West Shanghai; Publisher, CHIA T'ING, a monthly (49:172); Manager, China Industrial Bank (IDC 1943); Chairman, Directors, Real Property Association (IDC 7264 1943)

Po-hsiung -- Manager Director, Post Office Labor Union; Manager Director, Readjustment Committee, National Post Office Labor Union, Shanghai (49:172)

104   -55-

CHINESE

Chu P'u -- Publisher, KU CHIN, a semi-monthly, Shanghai (49:172); member, All-China Economic Committee (1943); Inspector, China Office, East Asia League; honorary member, China Journalists Association

Sen -- Hongkong representative, Chinese Language Society (5/15/44) (51:236)

Shao-tseng -- Director, Shanghai Education Committee (49:172)

Shen -- Born, 1879, Yungtsin, Hopeh; graduate, Law Department, Tokyo Imperial University; appointed Procurator -General, Supreme Court, Peking (1915); Minister of Justice (1918-19); concurrently Interior Minister (1919); Premier (1919-20); in exile, Dairen and Japan for some years after (1920); Commissioner, Metropolitan Police, Peking (1925); joined Peiping Provisional Government (12/37); Chief, Judicial Affairs, Peking Provisional Government (12/37); Head, North China Political Affairs Bureau (12/38); member, North China Political Commission (1940); President, North China Electrical Company (1940-43;OSS-Ms.); decorated by Emperor of Japan (5/14/43); appointed by Wang Ching-wei, Chairman, North China Affairs Committee (2/8/43); died (7/2/43) (52:233; OSS-Ms.; Who's Who in China 1940)

Shih-to -- Manager, Fu Hsing Industrial Bank, Shanghai (IDC 7270 1943)

Shin -- See Shu Chen

Shu-k'un -- Editor, SAN LIU CHIU HUA PAO, a weekly, Peiping (1943); Publisher, HSI CHU PAO (52:233)

Shu-shen -- Head, Chin-hua Communications Company, North China (1943) (52:233)

Shu-yuan -- Director, North China Electrical Industry Company, Peiping (8/5/43); Assistant Director-General, General Affairs Bureau, North China (52:233)

Szu-huang -- Head, Bank Association, Shanghai (IDC 7265 1943)

T... -- President, North China Electrical Industry Company, Peiping (8/5/43) (52:234)

Ta-chang -- Legislative member, Legislative Yuan, Nanking (1943); member, Directing Committee, China Office, East Asia League

Tao-yen -- Member, Committee on Application of Constitution, Nanking (1943)

Tien-chi -- Member, Association of Teachers, Amoy (49:172)

-56-

CHINESE

Chu Tso-chun -- Director, China Writers Club (1943)

Tsung-chou -- Judge, Supreme Court, Nanking (1943)

T'ung-chueh -- Commissioner, Office of Public Health, Nanking (1943)

Tung-lu -- Chairman, Directors, Ginssen and Birds Nest Association, Shanghai (IDC 7264)

Tzu -- President, North China Electric Corporation, Peiping (52:234)

Tzu-ming -- Of Chungking; surrendered (4/26/43; IDC)

Wei -- Inspector, Social Welfare Committee, East Asia League, Canton Branch (51:236)

Wei-p'u -- Inspector, China Educational Reconstruction Association, Anhwei Branch (1943)

Wen-hsiang -- Candidate Director, China Educational Reconstruction Association, Shanghai Branch (49:172)

Wen-keng -- Secretary, Executive Yuan, Nanking (1943)

Yao-ju -- Director, Shantung Coal Production and Marketing Company (52:234)

Yeh-ping -- Director, Committee for Airplane Donations, Peiping (8/2/44) (52:234)

Yi -- Chief, Political Affairs, North China Political Council (1943); Commissioner, Civil Affairs, Huaihia Province

Yi-ju -- Secretary, Control Yuan, Nanking (1943)

Yi-k'ai -- See Chu I-chieh

Yi-men -- Inspector, Citizens Savings Movement Committee, Shanghai (49:172)

Yin-po -- Secretary, Ministry of the Navy, Nanking (1943)

Yu -- Chief, Higher Education, Ministry of Education, Nanking (1943); member, Culture Committee, China Office, East Asia League

Yu-cheh -- Chief, 6th District, P'u-tung-nan, Shanghai (49:172)

Yueh -- Executive Director, China Educational Reconstruction Association, Chekiang Branch (49:173)

Yung-k'ang -- Manager Director, Special Municipality Journalists Association, Shanghai; Inspector, Citizens Savings Movement Committee, Shanghai; Director, Sino-Japanese Cultural Association, Shanghai Branch (49:173)

CHINESE

Ch'uan -- Chief, Organization of Special Affairs, Ningpo;
  attended ceremony opening Kang-ling Bridge
  (3/20/43 IDC)

  Shin-shuo -- Governor, Chekiang Province; ap-
    pointed Construction Minister (9/15/44)

Chuang Shih-ju -- President, Tsinan Electric Corporation, Tsinan (IDC 6699 1943)

  Sze-ch'uan (Ssu-ch'uan) -- Editor, WU HAN PAO,
    Hankow, Hupeh (1943); Director, Sino-Japanese
    Cultural Association, Wu-ch'ang and Hankow
    Branch

  Wei-p'ing -- Member, Committee for Stopping
    Breakage at Chung-mon of Huang-po (1943)

  Yueh-hu -- Chief, Construction Office, Hopeh
    Province; appointed Chief, Secretariat
    (3/2/44) (52:234)

Chuck En-ching -- Manager, An Hua Commercial Bank,
  Shanghai (IDC 7270 1943)

Ch'ui K'an -- Inspecting member, Control Yuan, Nanking
  (1943)

Chun Yeng-tang -- Director, North China Chinese Raw
  Drug Association, Tsingtao (1943) (52:234)

Chung -- Director, European-American Bureau, Foreign
  Department, Nanking

  Chang-yao -- Chairman, Directors, Medical Instru-
    ments Stores, Shanghai (IDC 7264)

  Che-sho (Che-shu) -- Finance Minister, Standing
    Committee, National Economic Council (2/14/43)

  Chia-hsiang -- Chief, Currencies, Ministry of
    Finance, Nanking (1943)

  Chien-hun -- Military Advisor, National Govern-
    ment, Nanking (1943)

  Fu -- Training Head, Tenth District Party Kuoming-
    tang Headquarters, Canton (51:236)

  Fun-Chen-an -- General Secretary, North China
    Political Council; witness to revised by-
    laws of National Government by North China
    Political Council (10/8/43) (52:234)

  Hung-sheng -- Named Director, Supreme Investiga-
    tions Bureau, Ministry of Justice (7/44)

  Jen-shou (Jen-shuo) -- Vice-President, New China
    Youth Corps (1943); Chief, Secretary, General
    Affairs Council, Executive Yuan, Nanking;
    member, Propaganda Committee, China Office,
    East Asia League

  Kin-fo, Dr. -- Vice-Chairman, Model Peace Zone,
    Fukien Province (9/14/42) (49:173)

-58-

CHINESE

Chung Lin-teh -- Member, Chinese Representative Council, Hongkong (51:236)

Po-chuan -- Member, Educational Committee, Municipal Council, Shanghai (5/13/44) (49:173); member, Municipal Advisory Committee

Po Chuan-shih -- Member, Finance Committee, Municipal Council, Shanghai (5/13/44) (49:173)

Sao -- Head, People's Consumers Council, Hongkong (51:236)

Shan -- Magistrate, Pao Wen Hsien; under control of Government of Kwangtung (51:236)

Tang -- Head, Tai Ping Branch Agency, Canton Police Bureau (51:236)

Tsun -- Director, China Educational Reconstruction Association, Chekiang Branch (49:173)

Tzu-ming -- Candidate Director, China Educational Reconstruction Association (1943)

Yu-ts'ai -- Inspector, China Educational Reconstruction Association (1943)

Chuo Tepa-chap -- Member, Invited Committee, Central Political Council (12/38)

Cou Ming -- Executive Inspector, China Educational Reconstruction Association, Chekiang Branch (49:173)

Ei Ri-kan, Lt. Gen. -- Military Attache, Chinese Embassy, Japan (7/19/44 DIO)

En Bu-shen -- Ex-Vice Minister of Food; Director, Internal Affairs, Judicial Yuan, Nanking (0-56)

K'e Pa-t'u -- State Councillor, representing North China Political Council (52:234)

Fan Ch'ao -- Candidate Director, China Educational Reconstruction Association, Chekiang Branch (49:173)

Chen-ya -- Candidate Director, China Educational Reconstruction Association, Chekiang Branch (49:173)

Ch'un-yang -- Publisher, WAN PAO, An-ching, Anhwei (IDC 2562)

Chung-yun -- President, National Central University under Minister of Education, Wang Ching-wei's regime (3/41;OSS-Ms.); member, Sino-Japanese Cultural Association; member, Central Executive Committee, Nanking (1943); member, Committee of Political Councillors; member, New Citizens Movement Promotion Committee; Director, China Office, East Asia League; Honorary Chairman, Directors, China Educational Reconstruction Association; Honorary member, China Journalists Association

-59-

CHINESE

Fan Fo-kung (Fu-kung) -- Secretary, Former French Concession, Shanghai (49:173)

Hui-chun -- Manager, Chia Ting Commercial Bank, Shanghai (IDC 7270 1943)

Hui-kuo -- Honorary Director, Sino-Japanese Cultural Association, Shanghai Branch (49:173)

Hung-t'ai -- Honorary Director, China Educational Reconstruction Association, Hankow Branch

Ko-kung -- Director, European-American Bureau, Ministry of Foreign Affairs, Nanking (OSS-Ms)

Ngo -- Inspector, China Writers Club (1943)

O -- Chief, General Affairs, Ministry of Information, Nanking (1943)

Po-shang -- Member, Legislative Yuan, Nanking (1943)

Tsai-tsung -- Formerly in union labor activity in Shanghai, now in Chungking (49:173)

Tsung-tse -- Managing Director, New Cultural Bodies in China (1944); proposed Sino-Japanese conference in Peking to further cultural exchange between two countries (2/2/44) (52:234)

Yu-kuei -- Member, North China Political Commission (12/38) (52:234)

Yun-chih -- Inspector, China Educational Reconstruction Association, Chekiang Branch (49:173)

Yung-tseng -- Commissioner, Bureau of Land Administration; Advisor, Citizens Savings Movement Committee, Shanghai (49:173)

Fang Er-liang -- Manager, Central Reserve Bank, Pang Pu Branch, Anhwei (IDC 7270 1943)

Huan-ju -- Head, Propaganda Office, Chinghsiang Administration, Hankow Sector (1943); Head, Department of Political Affairs, Huaihai Province; Publisher, CHIANG HAN JIH PAO, Hankow, Hupeh; Director, East Asia League, Hupeh Branch; Executive Director, Sino-Japanese Cultural Association, Wu-ch'ang and Hankow Branches; Honorary Director, China Educational Reconstruction Association, Hankow Branch

Jih-liang -- Head, Si Tan Branch Agency, Canton Police Bureau (51:236)

Jo -- Member, North China Political Council (1943)

Li-hsiang -- Director, Central Electrical Communications Corporation (1943); Inspecting member, China Journalists Association

-60-

CHINESE

Fang Shang-ming -- Publisher, HSIN WAN JIH PAO, Ho-fei, Anhwei (IDC 2562)

Tsing-ao -- Director, Directorate-General of Education, North China Political Commission (7/40;OSS-Ms.)

Fat(?) Po-hang -- Head, Cereal Control Board, Naking; reported cooperation between Bureau, farmers and people (9/25/43)

Fei Cheng-yung -- Manager, Pu Tung Commercial and Savings Bank, Shanghai (IDC 7270 1943)

Fu-heng -- Honorary Director, Sino-Japanese Cultural Association, Shanghai Branch (49:173); member, National Economic Committee

Hsieh-ching -- Chairman, Directors, Machine-made Rope Factories, Shanghai (IDC 7264 1943)

Kung-hsie -- Chief, Taxation, Ministry of Treasury, National Government, Nanking (1943)

Yu-k'ai -- Member, Committee for Stopping Breakage at Chung-mon of Huang-ho (1943)

Yun-ch'ing -- Inspector, National Trade Control General Association, Shanghai; Manager Director, Chamber of Commerce, Shanghai; Manager Director, Citizens Savings Movement Committee (49:173)

Fen Su-chih -- Appointed Governor, Shansi Province by North China Political Council (1/29/43; OSS-Ms.)

Feng Cheng -- Committee member and Head, Organization Section, Kuomintang's Headquarters, Kwangtung Province; former Medical Officer, Canton-Shanshui Railroad; Head, Medical Affairs Section, Bureau of Public Health, Canton City Government; graduate, Chung Medical School (51:236)

Chi -- Adviser, Publicity Minister, National Government, Nanking

Chi-yu -- Chief, Military Personnel, Ministry of the Navy, Nanking (1943)

Chieh -- Adviser, Citizens Savings Movement Committee, Shanghai; Honorary Director, Sino-Japanese Cultural Association (49:173); member, New Citizens Movement Promotion Committee; Chief, Bureau of Information, Shanghai Branch; Director, China Office, East Asia League; Director, China Educational Reconstruction Association; Director, China Movie Association

Ch'ih -- Former Construction Commissioner, Chekiang Province (OSS-Ms.)

Ching-an -- Chairman, Trustees, Silver Articles Association, Shanghai (IDC 7264)

110   -61-

CHINESE

Feng Ch'u-pai -- Chief, Shanghai Office, Ministry of
Industry (OSS-Ms.)

Hao -- Control Officer, Yuamati Ward, Kowloon
(51:236)

Ho-yi -- Publisher, T'IEN TI, a monthly, Shanghai
(49:173)

Hsia -- Training Head, Kuomintang Eighth District
Party Headquarters, Canton (51:236)

Hsin-ting -- Chairman, Directors, Rug Dealers,
Shanghai (IDC 7264 1943)

Jui-sheng -- Assistant Chief of Police, Yu-Ling
District Office, First Police Office,
Shanghai (49:173)

Kuo-hsun -- Honorary Director, China-Japan Returned
Students Club (1943)

Ming-yu -- Publisher, HSIN CHIN TAN JIH PAO,
Chin Tan, and JU KAO JIH PAO, Ju-kao,
Kiangsu (IDC 2562)

Pei-sheng -- Head, Chien Chien Branch Agency,
Canton Police Bureau (51:236)

Pi-chiao -- Chief of Economic Police, Canton
Bureau of Police; Chief Detective, Canton
Bureau of Police; Head, Canton Bureau of
Police (51:236)

Pi-hsiao -- Head, Bureau of Police, Kwantung Provincial Government; called meeting of
financiers and asked their cooperation with
government for stabilization of financial
conditions; Propaganda Head, Kuomintang
Third District, Party Headquarters, Canton
(51:237)

Ping-nan -- Financial Consultation Committee member, West Shanghai (49:174); member, Municipal Advisory Committee (1943)

Tzu-kuang -- Head, Electrical Communications
Corporation; Publisher, CHIANG SU JIH PAO,
Soochow (49:174)

Tzu-yin -- Member, Council of Chinese Representatives Association, Hongkong (51:237)

Wen-kuang -- Chairman, Directors, Silk Textile
Factories, Shanghai (IDC 7264)

Yi -- Chief, Bureau of Construction, Chekiang
(49:174)

Yu-hsiang -- Interested in liberating Formosa;
wrote for Formosan Revolutionary Alliance
(IDC)

Yueh-chun -- Secretary, China Educational Reconstruction Association (1943)

-62-

CHINESE

Fong, K. P. -- Friend of Dr. Walter Chang; participated in Japanese propaganda broadcasts to U. S.; member, Public Health Department, Shanghai Municipality; allegedly graduate, Columbia University (49:174)

Foo, P. S. -- Spokesman (DIO 10/42)

Fow Wen-yunn, Gen. -- War Minister, China (2/15/43)

Fu Chien -- Executive Director, Sino-Japanese Cultural Association, Shanghai Branch (49:174)

Chih-hao -- Member, ... Committee, Shanghai Municipal Council (5/13/44) (49:174)

Chin-t'ang -- Director, Citizens Savings Movement Committee, Shanghai (49:174)

Chong-ying -- Vice-Chief, Political Training Bureau, (12/38); Vice-Chairman, Military Advisory Board (0-57)

Chun-shih -- Chief, Bureau of Finance, Anhwei (1943)

Fang-yung -- Director, Su Min Bank, Wu Hsi Agency, Kiangsu (IDC 7270 1943)

Hsiao-en -- Ex-Mayor, Shanghai (49:174)

Nan-hsun -- Manager, Ta Fu Commercial and Savings Bank, Hankow, Hupeh (IDC 7270 1943)

Pi -- Inspecting member, Control Yuan, Nanking (1943)

Ping-ch'ang -- Ambassador, Russia (1/43)

Sheng- Kwei -- Manager, Chung Yung Commercial Bank, Shanghai (IDC 7270 1943)

Shih-shuo -- Minister of Railroads, Wang Ching-wei's government (3/22/40); Governor, Chekiang; Director, Sino*Japanese Cultural Associa-
tion; Execut**tion**Director, China-Japan Returned Students Club (49:174); member, Central Executive Committee, Nanking (1943); member, Central Political Council; Minister of Construction; Director, China Branch, East Asia League; Honorary Chairman, Directors, China Educational Reconstruction Association

Shuan-gin (Shuang-ying),-Lt. Gen. -- Military Counsel; promoted to rank of full General (10/10/44); Chief of Staff, Army Training and Organization Headquarters; Chief of Staff, North Kiangsu Camp; Vice-Chairman, Military Advisory Board (1943)

Shuang-ying -- See Fu Shuan-gin

Tung -- Member, State Council, National Government, Nanking (12/38)

Yen-ch'ang -- Executive Director, China Writers Club (1943)

CHINESE

Fu Yu-keng -- Assistant Chairman, Oil and Grain Special
Committee, National Trade Control General
Association, Shanghai (49:174)

Fung Ch'i -- Head, Fifth Unit, Chinghsiang Administration, Hangchou Sector (IDC 6/8/43)

Ping-nan -- Member, ... Committee, Municipal Council, Shanghai (49:174)

Tsung-lung -- Doctor, died as result of Chungking
(1/2/43)

Gen Bun-hei, Lt. Gen. -- Attached to Pacification Bureau:
Provincial Governor, Honan Province (52:234)

Go Ten-shin -- Native of Canton; Chief, Economic Bureau,
Shanghai Special Municipality; formerly
Commander, 11th Corps, New Canton Army;
Chief, General Affairs, National Government
(49:174)

Goshin Shun -- Chief Accountant, Central Bank of China
(3/6/44)

Ha Er-k'ang -- Secretary, Examination Yuan, Nanking
(1943); Executive Inspector, China Writers
Club

Hae P'eng-chu -- See Hao P'eng-chu

Hai Chu-fu -- Reported President, Central Reserve Bank
of China and Minister of Finance (7/29/42;
DIO)

Han Chang-yuan -- Head, Evidence Examination Unit,
Third Section, Canton Bureau of Police
(51:237)

Chen-po, Gen. -- Commander, Chungking's 26th Peace
Preservation Corps; surrendered with 350
of his men (3/31/43)

Ch'ing-chien -- Member, Central Executive Committee,
Nanking (1943); Inspector, China Office,
East Asia League

Ch'ing-t'ing -- Member, Legislative Yuan, Nanking
(1943)

Kuo-ju -- Member, Ministry of Education (O-56)

Su-chung -- Honorary Director, Sino-Japanese Cultural Association (1943)

Wen-ping, Gen. -- Commander, Air Force (OSS-Ms.)

Hang Ku -- Chairman, Chinese Representative Council,
Hongkong (51:237)

Lu-kuang -- Advisory member, Ministery of Personnel,
Nanking (1943)

Hao Chi-kuang -- Judge, Supreme Court, North China
Branch (7/17/43) (52:234)

-64-

CHINESE

Hao P'eng-chu (Hae P'eng-chu),-Lt. Gen. -- Chief,
Administrator, Northern Kiangsu Special
Administrative Area (1943); appointed Com-
mander, Peace Preservation Corps, Suchow,
Kiangsu Province (11/25/43); Governor,
Huaihai Province; Governor, North Kiangsu
(1/44); attended joint conference between
Japanese military and civil authorities and
administration officials (6/29/44); Admin-
istrative Chief, Su Huai Special District,
(9/43); member, Committee of Political
Councillors; member, National Military
Council; member, New Citizens Movement Pro-
motion Committee; Chief, East Asia League,
Su Huai Branch; Administrator, Su-huai
Special District (1943)

Hau Cheng-hsun -- Chairman, Directors, Coarse and Fine
Dyes and Miscellaneous Goods Stores,
Shanghai (IDC 7264)

Han-ching -- Manager, Ta Lu Bank, Shanghai (IDC
7270 1943)

Li-ch'iu -- Member, Shanghai Magazines Association
(49:174)

Shih-hua -- Editor, HUO MIN HSIN WEN, Shanghai
(IDC 7266 1943)

Hei Hei-kin -- Councillor, Satsuroya District; pledged
allegiance to Nanking (2/27/44)

Heng Shan-chang -- Assistant to Japanese Advisor,
Special Municipal Government, Amoy (OSS)

Hi Shang-ming -- Advisory member, Ministry of Foreign
Affairs, Nanking (1943)

Hil Li-ling -- Overseas Chinese Bank; elected Manager,
Hongkong Chinese Bankers Association (51:237)

Hisao Yi-ch'eng -- Inspector, East Asia League, Nanking
Branch (1943)

Ho -- Head, Bureau of Food, Kwangtung Province, Canton;
Executive member, Commodity Investigation
Committee (51:237); Head, Tapo Stocks Ex-
change (7/17/44)

Bun-rei -- See So Bun-rei

Bun-ye (Japanized reading) -- Chief, Army Department
(1943); member, Supreme National Defense
Council (1943)

Ch'en-jo -- Secretary, Executive Yuan (1943)

Chia-mei -- Editor, HAI NING HSIN PAO, Chia-shih,
Chekiang (IDC 2562)

Chieh-tung -- Head, Ha Min Branch Agency, Canton
Police Bureau (51:237)

Chien -- Minister of Interior, Nanking (1941)

114 -65-

CHINESE

Ho Chih-hang -- Director, Central China Railroad Stock
       Company, Shanghai (1943)

   Chih-kang -- Manager, Chwan Kang People's Commercial
       Bank, Shanghai Branch (IDC 7270 1943)

   Chih-p'ing -- Inspector, China Educational Recon-
       struction Association, Chekiang Branch
       (49:174)

   Chih-ts'ai -- Member, Legislative Yuan, Nanking (1943)

   Ch'ing-hsiang -- Chief Secretary, City of Shanghai;
       Chief, Financial Department (1/3/45)
       (49:174)

   Chiuan-sheng -- Member, Committee on Grain Control,
       Shanghai (49:174)

   Cho-hsien -- Attended National Economic Conference
       (1/43); member, National Economic Committee

   Ch'u-hsin -- Secretary, 5th District Party Headquar-
       ters, Kuomintang, Swatow (IDC)

   Chung, Maj. Gen. -- Attended meeting, Central Public
       Health Association, Nanking (2/4/44)

   Chung-ying -- Inspector, China Educational Recon-
       struction Association (1943)

  Ch'uo-hsin -- Member, All-China Economic Committee
       OSS)

   Ei-shin (Japanized reading) -- Vice-President,
       Central News Service; visiting Japan

   Feng-lin, Gen. -- Born, 1873, Pingyin, Shantung;
       educated, Peiyang Military Academy, Tientsin;
       Minister of War, Peking Government (1927);
       with Chang Hsiao-liang (1930); Chief, Body-
       guard Training Department, North China
       Political Commission (7/40) (OSS-Ms.)

   Hai-ming -- Member, Committee for Application of
       Constitution, Nanking (1943); member,
       Publishers Committee, China Writers Club

   Han-lan, Vice-Admiral -- Commander, Naval Headquar-
       ters, Canton (51:237)

   Hsia-ch'ang -- Executive Inspector, East Asia League,
       Hupeh Branch (1943); Director, Sino-Japanese
       Cultural Association, Wu-ch'ang and Hankow
       Branch

   Hsing -- Publishers Committee member, China Writers
       Club (1943)

   Hsing-ch'ang -- Food Commissioner, Kwangtung Province
       (51:237)

   Hu -- Inspector, China Educational Reconstruction
       Association, Anhwei Branch (1943)

-66-

CHINESE

Ho I-hai -- Commander, Harbor of Kwangtung (10/3/44)
(51:237)

Jih-ju -- Control Officer, Wan Tzu Ward, Hongkong
(51:237)

Kin-shu -- See Ho Rin-shu

Kom-tong -- Chairman, Stewards, Hongkong Race Course
(51:237)

Kuo-wang (Kuo Kwang-ho), Gen. -- Commander, Air
Defense (8/42)

Mo-ch'i -- Special member, Ministry of Social Welfare (1943)

P'ei-yung -- Honorary Chairman, Directors, Sino-
Japanese Cultural Association, Wu-ch'ang
and Hankow Branches (1943)

Ping-hsien -- Member, Central Executive Committee
(1943); Chief, Quartermaster General Department, National Military Council; Inspector,
China Office, East Asia League; Director,
Central Reserve Bank, Nanking

Ping-sung -- Head, China Literary Society, Shanghai
(IDC 7265 1943)

Ping-yao -- Manager, Central Reserve Bank, Nanking
(IDC 7270 1943)

Rin-shu (Kin-shu) (Japanized reading) -- Ex-Director, Internal Affairs, Judicial Yuan, Nanking; appointed to Office of Foreign Affairs, Kiangsu Province (10/2/43) (0-58)

Shih-chang -- Director, Central China Sea Products
Stock Company, Shanghai (1943)

Shih-chen -- Member, Standing Committee, Central
Executive Committee, Nanking (OSS)

Shu-chun -- Editor, CH'ING NIEN JIH PAO, Shanghai
(49:174)

Su -- Inspector, China Writers Club (1943)

Ta-yung -- Correspondent in Japan of HSIN SHEN PAO,
Shanghai (OSS)

Tao-ch'i -- Chief, Aviation, Ministry of Construction, Nanking (1943)

Tao-yun -- Chief, Postal and Electric Communications
Department, Ministry of Construction (1943);
Director, China-Japan Returned Students
Club

Te-huei -- Chief of Police, Chung-Yang District
Office, Third Police Office, Shanghai
(49:174)

Te(h)-kuang -- Control Officer, East Ching Ward,
Hongkong (51:237)

CHINESE

Ho T'eng-lin -- Member, National Economic Committee (1943)

T'ing-chen -- Directing Committee member, China Office, East Asia League (1943)

T'ing-liu -- Member, Committee for Application of Constitution, Nanking (1943); Assistant Chairman, Culture Committee, China Office, East Asia League (1943); Director, China-Japan Returned Students Club

Tseng-p'ei -- Director, China Educational Reconstruction Association, Anhwei Branch (1943)

Tung, Sir Robert -- Financier, Hongkong (51:237)

Wen-chieh -- Secretary, National Economic Committee, Nanking (1943)

Wen-hai -- Counsellor, National Government, Nanking (1943)

Wu-liang -- Director, Citizens Savings Movement Committee, Shanghai (49:174)

Yi-chih -- Inspector, Shanghai Education Committee (49:175)

Ying-ch'in, Gen. -- Military Affairs, Nanking (1/1/42)

Ying-chun -- Police student sent to Formosa for training; assigned now to various bureaus in Tai-p'ing-ching and Hai T'ien-shou for additional training (51:237)

Yo-ko (Japanized reading) -- Chief, General Affairs Bureau, Propaganda Ministry; appointed to War Ministry

Yu-hsin -- Editor, HSIN CHEN PAO, Chen-chiang, Kiangsu (IDC 2562)

Yuan-p'o -- Candidate Inspector, China Educational Reconstruction Association, Hankow Branch (1943)

Yuen-chin -- President, Hongkong Tunghwa Hospital; to manage business affairs of hospital (2/26/44) (51:237)

Yun-kuei -- Commander, pro-Japanese troops; with Japanese Huang Hsieh Chun, Hangchow, commanding about 2,000 men (6/39;OSS-Ms.)

Yung-yuan -- Head, Central Electrical Communications Corporation, Chia-hsing Branch (IDC 2562)

Hou -- Chief, Public Safety Bureau, National Government, Nanking (2/4/44); Governor, Kiangsu (?) (1/11/45)

Chien-heng -- Inspector, China Educational Reconstruction Association, Anhwei Branch (1943)

Fu-sang -- Chief, North China Anti-Epidemic Office; North China delegate to GEA Medical Conference (4/20/44) (52:234)

CHINESE

Hou Hsiang-chuan -- Member, German Medical Experimental Laboratory, Shanghai (OSS)

Ta-chuang -- Chief, Office of Grain Control, Kiangsu (49:175)

Wen-an -- Civil Magistrate, Tung-huan hsien; named Deputy Commissioner, Political Works Corps for Village Pacification, Kwangtung Province (51:237)

Hseng Yang-fu -- Minister of Communications (1/1/42)

Hsi Ching-chou -- Head, Coal Trade Association, National Trade Control General Association, Shanghai (49:175)

Jun-keng -- Chairman, Directors, Western Dyes Stores, Shanghai (IDC 7264)

P'ei-wen -- Adviser, Citizens Savings Movement Committee, Shanghai (49:175); Inspector, East Asia League, Nanking Branch (1943)

Shih-hsien -- Head, Central Electrical Communications Corporation, Nantung Branch (IDC 2562)

Tse-wen -- Vice-Minister and Chief, People's Political Direction, Ministry of Social Welfare, Nanking (1943); Executive Inspector, China Educational Reconstruction Association

Wei-t'ing -- Head, Tobacco Enterprise Trade Association, National Trade Control General Association, Shanghai (49:175)

Hsia Chi-fang -- See Hsia Chi-feng

Chi-feng (Hsiao Chi-pung) -- Born, 1889, Yangchow, Kiangsu; graduate, Nanhui Middle School, Shanghai (1911); went to France as interpreter-foreman with Chinese Labor Corps of British Army (1916); returned to China after armistice; wrote about conditions in Europe; labor and diplomatic editor, Eastern Times, Shanghai (1919); helped organize Returned Chinese Laborers Association; became president; Europe, special correspondent, Eastern Times (1921); member, Information Section, League of Nations, Geneva (1923-28); member, Treaty Commission, Ministry of Foreign Affairs (1929-37); Vice-Minister of the Interior, Nanking Reformed Government (3/38); Minister, Foreign Affairs succeeding the late Chen Lu (8/39); Minister of Audit, Wang Chin-wei's regime (3/31/41;OSS-Ms.); member, Central Executive Committee, Nanking (1943); Minister of Commerce; Minister of Audits, Central Yuan; Minister, Nanking Foreign Office, in charge of taking over Shanghai French Concessions; Candidate Director, Sino-Japanese Cultural Association; Director, China Office, East Asia League (O-56;OSS-Ms.)

Chian -- Chief, Economic Department, Shanghai (1/3/45) (49:175)

CHINESE

Hsia Chung-ming -- Member, National Economic Committee (1943)

Hsia-ling -- Manager, Chung Ho Commercial and Savings Bank, Shanghai (IDC 7270 1943)

Huan-wen -- Enspector, China Educational Reconstruction Association, Chekiang Branch (49:175)

Jen-lin -- Executive member, China Journalists Association (1943)

Kung-li -- President, Tatung Coal Mine Corporation, Chang-chia-kow (IDC 6699 1943)

Pao-lo -- Member, Directing Committee, China Office, East Asia League (1943); Director, China Educational Reconstruction Association

Peng -- See Bang How

Tsung-te -- Director, Central Reserve Bank, Nanking (IDC 7270 1943)

Wei-ho -- Vice-President, South China Office, National Buddha Association; compiled book, "The Buddha Temples in Canton" soon to be circulated (2/23/44) (51:237)

Wen-chao -- Chairman, Directors, Waste Fiber Association, Shanghai (IDC 7264 1943)

Yo-wen -- Executive Director, China Educational Reconstruction Association, Anhwei Branch (1943)

Yu -- In Shanghai, private secretary to Wang Ching-wei after his flight from Chungking and Hanoi (5/27/39; OSS-Ms.)

Hsiang Chien -- Inspecting member, Control Yuan, Nanking (1943)

Ch'ien-an -- Secretary, Ministry of Grains, Nanking (1943)

Chih-chuang, Gen. -- Vice-Minister, Foreign Affairs; member, Supreme National Defense Council; Former Chief, Central Affairs Department, National Military Council; Finance Commissioner, Chekiang Province; Governor, Chekiang; Head, Pacification Headquarters, Hangchow (1944)

Chin-chuan, Gen. -- Chief, Office for Public Safety, Kiangsu Province (1/43); Chief, Ministry of Public Security, Kiangsu Province; seceeded and joined Nanking (2/1/43; OSS-Ms.)

Hsun -- Director, Trade Mark Bureau, Executive Yuan, Nanking (1943); Advisor, Ministry of Industries

-70-

CHINESE

Hsiang K'ang-yuan -- Director, Shanghai Labor and Business Social Union; member, Citizens Savings Movement Committee (49:175); Chairman, Directors, Can Factories Association; member, All-China Economic Committee

Shu-siang -- Manager, Chekiang Hsing Yeh Bank, Shanghai (IDC 7270 1943)

Hsiao Ch'i-pin, Lt. Gen. -- Military Advisor, National Government, Nanking; Director, China-Japan Returned Students Club (1943)

Chi-pung -- (49:175); see also Hsia Chi-feng

Chi-p'ing -- Chief of Education, Nanking (1943); Executive Inspector, China Educational Reconstruction Association, Hankow Branch

En-ch'eng -- Member, Legislative Yuan, Nanking (1943)

Fu-hsiang -- Member, Committee for Punishment of Central Officials, Nanking (1943)

Kang -- Secretary, Paochia Office, 3rd Police Office, Shanghai (49:175)

Kuang-chou -- Director, Wharf Labor Union, Shanghai (49:175)

Mien-tsai -- Chairman, Directors, Rawhide Store, Shanghai (IDC 7264)

Shih-yu -- Director and Secretary, China Educational Reconstruction Association, Hankow Branch (1943)

Shu-hsuan, Gen. -- Member, Central Political Council, Nanking (1943); Chairman, Military Advisory Council, Nanking; decorated by Japanese Emperor (3/23/44); Director, China Office, East Asia League

Shu-i -- Member, Designated Committee, Central Political Council (12/38)

Hsieh Chih-hsiang -- Assistant Chief, Hsin-cha Branch (#1), Shanghai Police (IDC 2973)

Chih-ying -- Editor, KUO MIN HSIN WEN, Shanghai (IDC 7266 1943)

Chung-fu -- Advisory member, Ministry of Foreign Affairs, Nanking (1943)

Chung-lo -- Chairman, Directors, Waste Cotton Association, Shanghai (IDC 7264)

En-kao -- Director, Sino-Japanese Cultural Association, Shanghai Branch (49:175)

Feng-yuan -- Deputy Secretary General, Executive Yuan, Nanking (DIO 11/5/43)

CHINESE

Hsieh Hsi-p'ing -- Editor, CHANG CHIANG HUA PAO, a
monthly, Hankow (1943); Director, Sino-
Japanese Cultural Association, Wu-ch'ang and
Hankow Branch

Hsiao-chu -- Chairman, Directors, Chemical Raw
Material Stores, Shanghai (IDC 7264)

Hsiao-hsueh -- Candidate Director, Newspapermen's
Association (1943)

Hsueh-fan -- Director, Shanghai Special Municipality Journalists Association (49:175)

Hu-cheng -- Manager, Chekiang Hsing Yeh Bank,
Hangchow (IDC 7270 1943)

Hui-tzu -- Director, China Writers Club (1943)

Hung -- Member, Shanghai Newspaper Association
(49:175)

Ke -- Chief, Bureau of Political Affairs,
Kiangsu (49:175)

Ke-yao -- Inspector, China Educational Reconstruction Association, Chekiang Branch
(49:175)

K'o -- Commissioner, Political Affairs, Kiangsu
Province (OSS)

Kuan-sheng -- See Hsieh Kwan-sheng

Kwan-sheng (Kuan-sheng) -- Minister of Judicial
Administration (1/1/42); Minister of Justice (9/23/43) (DIO)

Li-ch'ien -- Judge, Supreme Court, North China
Branch (1/17/43) (52:234)

Li-sheng -- Inspector, East Asia League, Hupeh
Branch (1943)

Mei-sheng -- Director, Shanghai Chamber of Commerce (49:175)

Nan-kuang -- Interested in liberating Formosa;
wrote for Formosan Revolutionary Alliance
(IDC)

Pao-sheng -- Director, Citizens Savings Movement
Committee, Shanghai; Assistant Chief, Office
of Police Affairs, Kiangsu (49:175)

Po-chin -- Director, East Asia League, Hupeh
Branch (1943)

Tien-hui -- Publisher, TIEN SHENG PAO, Tientsin
(52:234)

Ting-pu -- Manager, Ta Lai Commercial and Savings
Bank, Shanghai (IDC 7270 1943)

Tse-fu -- Head, reorganizing, Nan-hai Merchants
Association, Canton (51:238)

CHINESE

Hsieh Tse-min, Maj. Gen. -- Military Advisor, National
Government, Nanking (1943)

Tse-t'ung -- Chief, Office of Village Pacification, Anhwei

Tsu-yuan -- Minister and Counsellor, Chinese
Embassy, Japan; Ministry of Foreign Affairs
(1943)

Tsu-yuen -- Charge d'Affairs, Chinese Embassy,
Japan (DIO 11/12/43)

Ts'ung-tao -- Member, Legislative Yuan, Nanking
(1943)

Tzu-yi -- Head, Tien-men Communications Company,
North China (1943) (52:234)

Wen-ta -- Commander, 10th Division, Nanking
Army (IDC 3/30/42)

Yu-chi -- Chairman, Directors, Rubber-wheel
Hand Truck Association, Shanghai (IDC 1943)

Yung-fu -- Inspector, Shanghai Wharf Labor Union
(49:175)

Hsien Ping-hsi -- Director, District Affairs Bureau,
Hongkong; Officer, Wards Control (51:238)

Hsin-hui -- Magistrate, Yu Hsi Hsien; under control of
Government of Kwangtung (51:238)

Hsing Chi-liang -- Manager, Shanghai Hui Yuan Bank,
Wu Hsi Branch, Kiangsu (IDC 7270 1943)

Hsun -- Chief, Trade Mark, Ministry of Industries,
Nanking (1943)

Shou-heng -- Secretary, Civil Office, National
Government, Nanking (1943)

Yu-chieh -- Publisher, HSIN HONAN PAO, K'ai-feng,
Honan (IDC 1943)

Hsiu Feng-kuo -- Vice-Minister, Publicity, National
Government of China; concurrently President,
Central Press Service of China (5/10/44)

Hsiung Chao-chou -- Prosecutor, Supreme Court, North
China Branch (52:234)

Chien-tung -- Member, Military Council (1942-43)

Chuang-tung -- Official, Peace Preservation
Corps, Shanghai (OSS)

Han-ying -- Candidate Director, China Educational
Reconstruction Association, Hankow Branch
(1943)

Hengo-po -- Director, China Educational Reconstruction Association, Hankow

CHINESE

Hsiung Sung-ch'uan -- Director, Sino-Japanese Cultural Association, Shanghai Branch (49:175)

Yang-hsi -- Publisher, CHING CHIANG HSIN PAO, Ching-chiang, Kwantsu (IDC 2562)

Hsu -- Section Head, Education Bureau, Amoy (49:175)

Hsu -- Magistrate, Nanao Hsien, Government of Swatow

Chang-keng -- Chairman, Directors, Gift Stores, Shanghai

Chen -- Candidate Inspector, China Educational Reconstruction Association (1943)

Chen-p'u -- Chairman, Preservation Committee (name changed to Changchow Autonomous Council) (51:238)

Cheng-ch'uan -- Assistant Chief of Police, Li-Yang Road District Office, First Police Office, Shanghai (49:175)

Chi-chiao -- Head, Fourth Unit, Chinghsiang Administration, Hangchou Sector (IDC 6/8/43)

Chi-hsiang -- Administrative Vice-Minister under Minister of Navy, Wang Ching-wei's regime (3/31/41;OSS-Ms.)

Chi-jun -- Chairman, Directors, Central Reserve Bank, Soochow Branch (IDC 1943)

Chi-mao -- Chief, Municipal Department, Shanghai (1/3/45) (49:176)

Chi-tun -- Chairman, Directors, China Educational Reconstruction Association, Chekiang Branch; Chief, Bureau of Education, Chekiang; Special Village Pacification Supervisor, 2nd District (49:176); member, New Citizens Movement Promotion Committee; Assistant Chairman, China Educational Reconstruction Association; Chairman, China Movie Association, Chekiang Branch

Chiang -- Director, Silk Revenue Department, Ministry of Finance, Nanking (1943); Economic Commissioner, Shanghai

Chien-p'ing (Hsu, Jabin) -- Born, 1889, Shanghai; Interpreter.(1908); Editor, YU SHANG PAO, (1909); went to Michigan University (1911); returned to China (1915); with British law firm; with China Press; confidential secretary to H. H. Kung (1928); joined Wang Ching-wei (1939); Director, Inquiry Department, Central Reserve Bank (3/41) (OSS-Ms.)

Chien-t'ing -- Member, National Military Council; Vice-Chief, Naval Operations, Ministry of the Navy; Nanking Harbor Commander under Minister of Navy, Wang Ching-wei's regime (3/31/41) (OSS-Ms.)

-74-

CHINESE

Hsu Chien-yeh -- Manager Inspector, Shanghai Wharf
  Labor Union (49:176)

Chin-yuan -- Chief of Staff, Peace Preservation
  Corps, Shanghai (OSS)

Ch'ing-ch'i -- Member, Culture Committee, China
  Office, East Asia League (1943)

Ching-chuan -- Assistant Head, Li-Yang Boad Branch,
  (#1), Shanghai Police (IDC 2973 1943)

Ching-sheng -- Member, Propaganda Committee, China
  Office, East Asia League (1943)

Chiu-ch'eng -- Chief Prosecutor, North China
  Supreme Court (1/17/43) (52:234)

Ch'iung-yu -- Executive Inspector, Social Welfare
  Committee, East Asia League, Canton Branch
  (51:238)

Chu-chung -- Peking University; to study in Japan;
  see also Hsu Chou-chung (52:234)

Ch'uan-ying -- Assistant Chief, Village Pacification Affairs Bureau, Nanking (1943)

Ch'uan-yung -- Editor, HSIN LUN YUEH KAN, a monthly
  Peiping (1943) (52:234)

Ch'ui -- Member, Committee for Application of the
  Constitution, Nanking (1943)

Chui-ch'eng -- Chief Prosecutor, North China Branch,
  Supreme Court (1943)

Ch'un-sheng -- Director, Shanghai Wharf Labor Union
  (49:176)

Chung-chih -- Born, Kwangtung; once Commander,
  Civil Affairs, Kwangtung Provincial Govern-
  ment; State Councillor (since 1/32); Vice-
  President, Control Yuan (since 12/35); in
  Hankow (7/38); member, National Government
  State Council, Chungking; concurrently Vice-
  President, Control Yuan (7/40); captured
  by Japanese, Hongkong, day of occupation
  (12/25/41) (OSS-Ms.)

Chung-jen -- Anhwei Provincial Government; member,
  Pao-chia Promotion Committee; Chief, Office
  of Police Affairs, Anhwei (1943)

Feng-tsao -- Commander, pro-Japanese troops; with
  Japanese Huang Hsieh Chun, Changshu, commanding about 1,500 men (OSS-Ms.)

Han-wen -- Inspector, China Educational Reconstruction Association, Chekiang Branch (49:176)

Ho-ming -- Chairman, Directors, Cotton Processing
  Association, Shanghai (IDC 7264)

Hsi(?) -- Inspecting member, Control Yuan, Nanking
  (1943)

CHINESE

Hsu Hsi-chao -- Chairman, Directors, Textile Factories, Shanghai (IDC 7264)

Hsi-ch'ing -- Director, Citizens Savings Movement Committee, Shanghai; (49:176); Secretary, Education Department, New China Youth Corps; Executive member, China Journalists Association; Executive Director, East Asia League, Nanking Branch (1943)

Hsi-ch'uan -- Member, Propaganda Committee, China Office, East Asia League (1943)

Hsi-chung -- Secretary, Department of Education, China Central Youth Institute (0-56)

Hsian-ch'u -- Director, Shanghai Labor and Business Social Union; Director, Shanghai Chamber of Commerce (49:176)

Hsiang-sheng -- Secretary, Paochia Office, 3rd Police Office, Shanghai; Inspector, Citizens Savings Movement Committee, Shanghai (49:176)

Hsiao-ch'u -- Manager Director, Shanghai Citizens Welfare Association; Director, Labor and Business Social Union (49:176); Director, New Medicine Company, Shanghai (IDC 7264)

Hsiao-jung -- Executive Director, Social Welfare Committee, East Asia League, Canton Branch (IDC 1943)

Hsin-shih -- Mayor, Peking (3/1/45) (52:235)

Hsin-yu -- Publisher, YING CHU HSIN WEN, a semi-monthly, Shanghai (49:176)

I-chin -- Candidate Director, Newspapermen's Association, Shanghai (1943)

I-tsung -- Director, Asia Bureau, Foreign Ministry, Nanking (0-56)

, Jabin -- See Hsu Chien-p'ing

Kuan-ch'un -- Manager Director, Labor and Business Social Union, Shanghai; Manager, Director, Citizens Welfare Association; Manager Director, Citizens Savings Committee; Director, National Trade Control General Association (49:176)

Kung-mei -- Member, Committee on Culture, China Office, East Asia League (1943); Executive Director, China Educational Reconstruction Association; Inspector, China Writers Club

Kuo-lu -- Directing Committee member, China Office, East Asia League (1943)

Kuo-yuan -- Member, Legislative Yuan, Nanking (1943)

-76-

CHINESE

Hsu Li-ch'iu -- Manager Director, Shanghai Newspaper Association; Director, Shanghai Magazines Association; Executive Director, East Asia League, Shanghai; Honorary Director, Sino-Japanese Cultural Association; President, CHUNG HUA JIH PAO; Publisher, various papers; proposed general organ of newspaper of GEA (49:176)

Liang, Dr. (Yang Lieng?) -- Minister, Foreign Affairs, Wang Ching-wei's regime (3/41); switched posts with Ch'u Min-yi who returned to Nanking as Foreign Minister while Hsu went to Tokyo as Ambassador to Japan (11/1/41) (OSS-Ms.); Chinese Ambassador to Japan, State Councillor (1943); member, North China Political Council; stated China should work in cooperation with Japan (3/8/43); relieved of post as Ambassador to Japan (3/31/43); Candidate Director, Sino-Japanese Cultural Association (1943); Executive Director, East Asia Cultural League, China Office (52:235); Inspector, China-Japan Returned Students Club (0-58-59)

Liang-ch'iu -- Candidate Director, China Educational Reconstruction Association (1943)

Liu-sheng -- Commander, Sixth Regiment, Nanking Army (IDC 3/30/42)

Mien-ch'u -- Head, Third Unit, Chinghsiang Administration, Hangchou Sector (IDC 6/8/43)

Mien-t'ang -- Commissioner, Directorate General of Reconstruction, North China Political Commission (7/40;OSS-Ms.)

Min-i -- See Chu Min-yi

Mou-tang -- Manager, Chung Hui Bank, Shanghai (IDC 7270 1943)

Nai -- Leader, Green Circle Society, Ch'ing Pang, Shanghai (OSS)

Nien-ch'u -- Chief, Office of Peace Preservation, Chekiang (49:176)

Nien-li -- Chief, Peace Preservation Bureau, Chekiang (OSS-Ms.)

Pai-cheng -- Trustee, Lu-ta Mining Industrial Company (52:235)

Pai-lin -- Chinese student of Japanese culture in Tokyo (10/5/43)

Pany-hao -- Assistant Secretary, Paochia Office, 1st Police Office, Shanghai (49:176)

Pen-ch'ien -- Member, Committee for Punishment of Central Officials, Nanking (1943); member, Propaganda Committee, China Office, East Asia League; Inspector, China-Japan Returned Students Club

CHINESE

Hsu Peng -- Publisher, KUNG YEH CH'ANG SHIH, a weekly, Shanghai (49:176)

Po-ming -- Silk Goods Industry Bank, Shanghai (IDC 7270 1943)

Pu-cheng -- Commander, pro-Japanese troops; with Japanese Huang Hsieh Chun, Kashing, commanding about 5,000 men in First District, Third War Zone (6/39;OSS-Ms.)

Shang-wu -- Member, Association of Teachers, Amoy (49:176)

Shao-ch'ang -- Chief Secretary, China Movie Association (1943)

Shao-jung -- Mayor, Swatow (R&A 2565)

Shao-nien -- Manager, Shanghai Special City Fu Hsing Bank (IDC 7270 1943)

Shen-wu -- Director, East Asia League, Hupeh Branch (1943); Inspector, Sino-Japanese Cultural Association, Wu-ch'eng and Hankow Branch

Shih-hua -- Member, Shanghai Newspaper Association (49:177)

Shou-cheng -- Chairman, Directors, Raw Hemp Association, Shanghai (IDC 7264 1943)

Shou-chung -- See also Hsu Chu-chung; Chinese authoress; leaving for Japan to study things Japanese under leading Japanese scholars (1/24/44)

Shu-ch'en -- Assistant Chief of Police, P'u-t'o Road District Office, First Police Office, Shanghai (49:177)

Shun-ch'ing -- Assistant Chief of Police, Hui-Shan District Office, First Police Office, Shanghai (49:177)

Shun-hsiang -- Assistant Head, Kuo-chan Branch (#1), Shanghai Police (IDC 2973 1943)

Su-chung -- Member, Central Executive Committee, Nanking (1943); Director, Secretariat, Civil Officials Board; Vice-President, Control Yuan; Chief Councillor, Political Advisory Board; Honorary Director, Sino-Japanese Cultural Association; Executive Inspector, China Branch, East Asia League

Sui-chang -- Manager, Shih Ming Commercial and Savings Bank, Shanghai (IDC 7270 1943)

Sun-king -- Ex-Assistant Manager, China Commercial Bank; President, Japanese Raw Silk Association, Shanghai (49:177)

Sung-shih -- Inspector, Shanghai Education Committee (49:177)

CHINESE

Hsu Ta-chien -- Commander, pro-Japanese troops; with pro-Japanese forces in Honan, near Luyi, commanding about 2,000 men (6/39;OSS-Ms.)

Ta-yu -- Prize winner, North China Labor Association (5/31/43) (52:235)

T'ien-ch'en (-shen) -- Director, East Asia League, Shanghai Branch; Chief, Bureau of Economics, Municipality of Shanghai; adviser, Citizens Savings Movement Committee, Shanghai (49:177); member, Central Executive Committee, Nanking

Ting-cho -- Head, Hsiao Fei Branch Agency, Canton Police Bureau (51:238)

Tsao-shih -- Commissioner, Directorate-General of Finance, North China Political Commission (7/40;OSS-Ms.)

Tsun-kung -- President, Central China Raw Silk Company, Shanghai (OSS)

Wen-chao -- Inspector, Citizens Savings Movement Committee, Shanghai (49:177)

Wen-chi -- Secretary, Executive Yuan (1943)

Wen-chien -- Chairman, Directors, Jewlery Association, Shanghai (IDC 7264)

Wen-chuan -- Inspector, China Educational Reconstruction Association, Chekiang Branch (49:177)

Wen-huan -- Commander, pro-Japanese troops; with Japanese Huang Hsieh Chun, Shantung Border, commanding about 3,000 men (6/39;OSS-Ms.)

Wen-piao -- Chairman, Directors, Silk Textile Factories, Shanghai (IDC 7264)

Yang, Dr. -- Chinese Ambassador, Tokyo (9/2/42)

Yang-chih -- Former Chief, Social Affairs Bureau, Hankow; Head, Public Utilities Bureau (2/8/41) (OSS-Ms.); Inspector, Sino-Japanese Cultural Association, Wu-ch'ang and Hankow Branch; Honorary Director, Chinese Educational Reconstruction Association, Hankow Branch

Yeh -- Commissioner, Directorate-General of Finance, North China Political Commission (OSS-Ms.)

Yen-sheng -- Inspector, Shanghai Special Municipality Journalists Association (49:177)

Yi-chin -- Candidate Director, Shanghai Special Municipality Journalists Association (49:177)

Yi-tsung -- Director, Asia Bureau, Ministry of Foreign Affairs, Nanking (OSS-Ms.)

Yu-chih -- Candidate Director, Shanghai Special Municipality Journalists Association (49:177)

CHINESE

Hsu Yu-ti -- Candidate Director, Newspapermen's Association, Shanghai (1943)

Yu-tien -- Manager, China Fishery Industrial Bank, Shanghai Branch (IDC 7270 1943)

Yuan-ch'ing -- Executive member, China Journalists Association (1943); Director, China Writers Club

Yun-ch'uan -- Advisory member, Ministry of Interior, Nanking (1943)

Hsuan Lung-sse -- Editor, HSIN WU HAN, a magazine, Hankow

Hsueh Chih-ch'ing -- Assistant Chief of Police, Hsin-cha District Office, First Police Office, Shanghai, at Yang-shu-p'u, Hu-tung-kung-she

Chih-ying -- Director, Newspaper Association, Shanghai (49:177)

Ching-ch'un -- Secretary, Paochia Office, 3rd Police Office, Shanghai (49:177)

Feng -- Chief of Propaganda, Office of Nanking Special Municipality (1943); Director, China Movie Association

Feng-yu -- Minister residing in Ministry of Foreign Affairs, Nanking (1943)

Feng-yuan -- Head, Asia Bureau, Shanghai; representative, Executive Bureau (49:177)

Hsiao-hsueh -- Candidate Director, Shanghai Special Municipality Journalists Association (49:177)

Ke-li -- Publisher, LIU HO HSIN PAO, Liu-ho, Kwangsu (IDC 2562)

Keng-hsing -- Chief of Police, Mai-Lan District, Third Police Office, Shanghai (49:177)

Kuang-yung -- Chief, Accounting, Ministry of Finance, Nanking (1943)

Lu -- Editor, HSIN KUANG TSA CHIH, a monthly, Peiping (1943) (52:235)

Hsuing Chao-chou -- Prosecutor, North China Branch Supreme Court (1943)

Hsun Su-chung -- Executive Director, China-Japan Returned Students Club (1943)

Hu An-ku -- Member, Publishers Committee, China Writers Club (1943)

Cheng (Cheng Hu) -- Director, Marine Products Bureau, National Government; relieved of post for illegal dealings (3/44); adjudged guilty of graft and executed by firing squad (3/16/44)

-80-

CHINESE

Hu Chih-ming -- Publisher, HSIN TAN YANG PAO, Tan-yang, Kiangsu (IDC 2562)

Chih-ning -- Chief, Public Welfare Office, Ministry of Public Welfare, Nanking (1943)

Chuang-ta -- Commissioner of Finance, Huaihai Province (1943)

Chun -- Member, Committee on Culture, China Office, East Asia League (1943)

Chun-yi -- Inspector, Education Committee, Shanghai (49:177)

Fang-chun -- Director, Shanghai Magazines Association (49:177); Editor, NU SHENG (Woman's Voice)

Hai-hai -- Head, Shih-wen Communications Company, North China (1943) (52:235)

Hai-kan -- Head, Si Pei Branch Agency, Canton Police Bureau (51:238)

Han-ching -- Manager, Yu Tsin Bank, Tientsin (1943) (52:235)

Hsiung-fan -- Secretary, Social Welfare Office, Shanghai (49:177)

Hwa-wen -- See Wu Wha-wen

I-yung -- Manager, China Yung Shang Bank, Shanghai (IDC 7270 1943)

Keng-pei -- Chairman, Directors, Eyeglasses Association, Shanghai (IDC 7264 1943)

Kuan-sheng -- President, Joint Relief Association and all Philanthropic Organizations, Peking (1/20/44) (52:235)

Kuei-keng -- Director, Chamber of Commerce, Shanghai (49:177)

Kung-p'u -- Candidate Director, China Educational Reconstruction Association, Hankow Branch (1943)

Kuo-hua -- One of the heads, Propaganda Corps, Kwangtung Province (51:238)

Lan-ch'eng -- Political Vice-Minister under Minister of Publicity, Wang Ching-wei's regime (3/41; OSS-Ms.); member, Central Executive Committee, Nanking (1943); member, All-China Economic Committee; Inspector, China Office, East Asia League; Honorary member, China Journalists Association

Ming -- Inspector, China Educational Reconstruction Association, Shanghai Branch (49:177)

CHINESE

Hu Ping-sheng -- Manager, The Agricultural and Industrial City Bank, Tientsin (1943) (52:235)

Shan -- Publisher, HSIANG TAO JIH PAO, Hongkong; Publisher, KUNG CHEN PAO, Canton (51:238)

Shan-ch'en -- Judge and Chief, Administrative Court, Nanking (1943)

Shan-ch'eng -- Chief Arbitrator, Executive Yuan, Nanking (OSS)

Shou-ch'i -- Chairman, Secretary, Shanghai Municipality Social Welfare Bureau, Shanghai (49:178); special member, Ministry of Social Welfare (1943)

Ta-kang -- Assistant Chairman, China Educational Reconstruction Association, Anhwei Branch (1943)

Tao-wei -- Member, Committee for Application of Constitution, Nanking (1943)

T'ing-hsi -- Publisher, WU HU HSIN PAO, Wu-hu, Anhwei (IDC 2562)

Tse-chih -- Editor, WU HU HSIN PAO, Wu-hu, Anhwei (IDC 2562)

Tse-chun -- Attended National Economic Conference (1/43)

Tse-wu -- Head, Nanking Ministry of Justice, General Affairs Office, Shanghai (1943); member, All-China Economic Committee; Director, China Office, East Asia League; member, Committee for Application of Constitution

Tsung-chun -- Former division Commander under Marshal Wu Pei-fu; Head, "All Hupeh Self-Protection Corps", established Hankow area after Japanese occupation (8/26/38) (OSS-Ms.)

Tun-fu -- Director, Shanghai Education Committee, (1943); Honorary Director, Sino-Japanese Cultural Association, Shanghai Branch; member, New Citizens Movement Promotion Committee

Wen-hu -- See Aw Boon Haw

Wen-yao -- Director, Sino-Japanese Cultural Association, Shanghai Branch (49:178)

Yang-wu -- Manager, Ta Hsin Bank, Shanghai (IDC 7270 1943)

Yi-ai -- Candidate Inspector, China Educational Reconstruction Association, Hankow Branch (1943)

Yi-kung -- Manager Director, Post Office Labor Union, Shanghai (49:178)

Ying-chou -- Chief, Office of Grains, Hupeh Province (1934); Vice-President, Central News Agency; Advisory member, Ministry of Information

CHINESE

Hu Yu-chan (-chun) -- Special representative, National Government Military Council, North China; office established at Peking (3/17/44) (52:235)

Yu-k'un, Lt. Gen. -- Formerly of the Mukden party (16th Army); member, Hopeh-Chahar Autonomous Coucnil (12/11/35); reported to have pro-Japanese army of 200,000 men in Honan (7/18/39; Oss-Ms.); Head, North China Branch, National Military Council, Peiping; representative, Military Council, Peiping; Commander, Honan Border Region (11/18/43); Head, Supreme National Defense Council, North China (52:235)

Yun-fei -- Chairman, Directors, Chinese and Foreign Goods Department Stores, Shanghai (IDC 7264)

Hua Chen -- Member, Committee for Punishment of Central Officials, Nanking (1943)

Han-kuang -- Executive Director, China Writers Club (1943)

Hsien -- Magistrate, Sun Ch'eng-chih Hsien; under control of Government of Kwangtung (51:238)

Hung-hsi -- Editor, HSIN LIU, a monthly, Nanking (IDC 2562)

Nan-kuang -- Propaganda Committee member, China Office, East Asia League (1943)

Huang -- Head, Public Health Experimental Section, National Government, Nanking (2/4/44)

Chao -- Secretary, General Committee for promotion of farm production (5/25/44)

Ch'eng-piao -- Director, Social Welfare Committee, East Asia League, Canton Branch (51:238)

Ch'i-chung -- Member, Legislative Yuan, Nanking (1943)

Ch'i-hsing -- Member, National Military Council; member, China-Japan Returned Students Club (OSS)

Chia-mo -- Inspector, Shanghai Special Municipality Journalists Association (49:178)

Chiang-ch'uan -- Head, Alcohol Enterprise Trade Association, National Trade Control General Association, Shanghai; Inspector, National Trade Control General Association, Shanghai; Chairman, Sugar Enterprise Special Committee, National Trade Control General Association, Shanghai; Manager Director, Shanghai Labor Business Social Union; Manager Director, Shanghai Chamber of Commerce (49:178)

Chin-kuei -- Chairman, Directors, Shoe Leather Nailing and Moulding Association, Shanghai (IDC 7264 1943)

132   -83-

CHINESE

Huang Chin-tsai -- Director, Central Electrical Communications Corporation (IDC 2562)

Ch'ing-chung -- Member, Legislative Yuan and
Chief of Laws and Regulations Committee,
Nanking (1943)

Ching-ning (?) -- Executive Inspector, China Educational Reconsturction Association (1943)

Ching-tsai -- Manager Director, Shanghai News-
paper Association; Director, East Asia League,
Shanghai Branch; President, KUO MIN ER;
Editor, KUO MIN HSIH WEN, Shanghai (49:178)

Ching-wan -- Director, Citizens Savings Movement
Committee, Shanghai (49:178)

Chu-an -- Chairman, Directors, Bamboo, Rattan,
and Straw Business, Shanghai (IDC 7264)

Chu-cheh -- Chief, Special Information Section,
Propaganda Department, Chekiang (1/3/45)

Chun-ti -- Publisher, HSIN HSI JIH PAO, Wu-hsi,
Kiangsu (IDC 2562)

Chung -- Member, Political Division, General
Affairs Bureau, Kowloon District (51:238)

Chung-hu -- Propaganda Head, Kuomingtang Sixth
District Party Headquarters, Canton (51:238)

Chung-su -- Director, Sino-Japanese Cultural
Association, Shanghai Branch (49:178)

Chung-t'ang -- Director, China Educational Reconstruction Association, Hankow Branch (1943)

En-mu -- Head, Huang Sha Branch Agency, Canton
Police Bureau (51:238)

Fu-ming -- Secretary, Judicial Yuan, Nanking (1943)

Hsi -- Chief, Military Affairs, Ministry of the
Army, Nanking (1943)

Hsiang-ku -- Political Vice-Minister under Minister of Personnel, Wang Ching-wei's regime
(3/31/41;OSS-Ms.); Inspector, China Office,
East Asia League (1943)

Hsiao-p'ing -- Counsellor, Directorate-General of
Industry, North China Political Commission;
Commissioner, Directorate-General of Indus-
try (7/40) (OSS-Ms.); Trustee, North China
Aluminite Mining Industrial Company, LTD
(52:235)

Hsin-po -- Manager, China United Reserve Bank,
Tsinan Branch, Shantung (52:235)

Hsun -- Chief, Central Seamen's Training Office,
Ministry of the Navy, Nanking (1943)

-84-

CHINESE

Huang Huan-hsin -- Advisor of Party Affairs, Kuomintang
    Headquarters, Kwangtung Province; graduate,
    Chungshan University; once propaganda member,
    Canton Party Headquarters (51:238)

Hui-yuan -- Member, Association of Teachers,
    Amoy (49:178)

Ju-liang -- Chairman, Directors, Glass Stores,
    Shanghai (IDC 7264)

Ke-min (Ko-min) -- Chief of Staff, Peace Preser-
    vation Corps, Kwangtung Province (1943);
    Chairman, North China Political Affairs
    Council, Tientsin (12/4/43); first Head,
    Bureau of Rural Pacification Affairs (12/1/43);
    appointed Acting Chairman, Headquarters of
    Purification (4/6/44) (51:238)

Koh-min -- See Huang Koh-min; also (51;239)

Kuei-hsun -- Propaganda Head, 4th District Party
    Headquarters, Kuomintang, Swatow (IDC)

Lo-i -- Manager, Chung Nan Bank, Shanghai (IDC
    7270 1943)

Mao-ch'ien -- Secretary, Control Yuan, Nanking
    (1943)

Min-chung -- Chief, Bureau of Finance, Kiangsu
    (49:178)

Nan-p'eng, Maj. Gen. -- Commander, 2nd Army Corps,
    Paoting, Hopeh, of the Peace Preservation
    Army, North China Political Commission
    (7/41;OSS-Ms.); Chief Commander, Pacifica-
    tion Corps; appointed Commander, Gendarmerie
    and the Superior School of Gendarmery, North
    China (6/19/44) (52:235)

Pao-shu -- Formerly connected with a Hongkong
    newspaper, published with support of Formosan
    Government; appointed by Formosa to repre-
    sent her in General Affairs Office, Hongkong
    (51:239)

Pen-jen -- Commander, pro-Japanese troops; with
    Japanese Huang Hsieh Chun, Honan, commanding
    about 1,000 men (OSS-Ms. 6/39)

Ping-chen -- Director, Trade Mark Bureau, Minis-
    try of Industry, Executive Yuan, Nanking (OSS)

Ping-hsing -- Member, Chinese Ministry of Edu-
    cation (residing in Chinese Embassy, Tokyo)
    (1943)

Ping-kun -- Head, Chen Tang Branch Agency, Canton
    Police Bureau (51:239)

Po-ch'in -- Control Officer, Shen Shui Ward,
    Kowloon (51:239)

Pu -- Director, China Ship Corporation, Shanghai
    (49:178); Director, Central China Steamship
    Stock Company (IDC 7264 1943)

CHINESE

Huang P'u-huan -- Member, Legislative Yuan (1943);
Chief of Editors, Legislative Yuan, Nanking;
Executive Director, Chinese Educational Re-
construction Association

P'u-sheng -- Counsellor, Shanghai Municipality
(1943) (49:178); Chief, Propaganda Directing, Ministry of Information, Nanking (1943);
Superintendent, Ch'ao-Hai-Kuan

Shan-ku -- Member, National Economic Committee
(1943)

Shao-hung (Japanized reading) -- Vice-Mayor,
Shanghai (1944) (49:178)

Shao-ku -- Interested in liberating Formosa;
wrote for Formosan Revolutionary Alliance
(IDC)

Shih-kuang -- Inspector, East Asia League, Hupeh
Branch (1943); Executive Director, Sino-
Japanese Cultural Association, Wu-ch'ang,
Hankow Branches; Executive Director, Chinese
Educational Reconstruction Association

Shu-hai -- Executive Director, Chinese Educational
Reconstruction Association (1943)

Ta-chung -- Chief, Bureau of Education, Hupeh
Province (1943); member, New Citizens Move-
ment Promotion Committee; Director, China
Office, East Asia League; Chairman, China
Movie Association, Wu-Han Office

Ta-wei, Gen. -- Native, Kwangtung; studied military science, Belgium; military counsellor,
Provisional President of the Republic (Dr.
Sun Yat-sen), Nanking (1912); Commander, 1st
Route Army, Kwangtung Provincial Army (1921);
appointed Commander, First Army by Dr. Sun
Yat-sen (1923); concurrently Field Commander,
Border Defense, Kwangtung and Fukien; resigned when Kuomintang reorganized and ad-
mitted Communists (1924); lived in Shanghai
and Kuling, Kiangsi; joined Wang Ching-wei's
peace movement (11/39); organized "Peace and
National Salvation Army" in Kwangtung in
support of Wang; proclaimed himself Commander-
in-Chief of the Army (11/15/39) with headquarters in Swatow (Who's Who in China 1940)

Tah-huan -- President, Tsining Business Firms
Association; presented donation to Japanese
Military Liaison Office (6/4/44) (52:235)

Tai-chun(g) -- Director, Foodstuffs Bureau,
Kiangsu Province; relieved for illegal dealings (3/44); also relieved of Directorship
Kiangsu Province Headquarters, Kuomintang,
(3/44); adjudged guilty of graft and executed
by firing squad (3/16/44) (41:278)

Tao-ming -- Editor, HSIN CHIN YUEH KAN, a monthly,
Peiping (1943) (52:235)

-86-

CHINESE

Huang T'i-lien -- Member, Legislative Yuan, and Chief, Finance Committee, Nanking (1943)

Tien-cho -- Head, First Section, Canton Bureau of Police (51:239)

T'ien-tso -- Director, Sino-Japanese Cultural Association, Shanghai Branch (49:178)

Ting-sung -- Special Envoy, Chinese Ministry of Education to National Government

Tsai -- Head, Chang Shou Branch Agency, Canton Police Bureau (51:239)

Tse-cheng -- Member, Association of Teachers, Amoy (49:178)

Tu-pen, Dr. -- President, Peiping Technical School; school designated to carry out inspection of survey of work done under Education Department for increase of food production (6/17/44) (52:235)

Tung-yuan -- Manager, Hua Hsing Commercial Bank, Pang Pu Branch, Anhwei (IDC 7270 1943)

Tzu-ch'iang -- Inspector General, Organization and Training, Nanking; Director, Political Affairs Department, National Military Council; member, New Citizens Movement Promotion Committee (O-57;OSS-Ms.)

Yen-ching -- Principal, Hongkong Kuang Hua Middle School; Assistant to Chairman, Hongkong Lower Middle School Board; Manager, Bureau for Preservation of Morals; member, China Discursive Association (51:239)

Yen-t'ang -- Director, Citizens Savings Movement Committee, Shanghai (49:178)

Yi-chen -- Chief, Publicity Bureau, North China Political Affairs Commission (52:236)

Yin-tai -- Officer, North China Political Affairs Council, Tientsin (12/4/43) (52:236)

Yu-kwan -- Manager, China Industrial Bank, Shanghai (IDC 7270 1943)

Hui Pin -- Influential leader, Chinese Residents, Hongkong; known as richest man in Hongkong; residing in Macao since shortly before outbreak of war; pledged cooperation with Japanese (51:239)

Shu-sheng -- Assistant Chief, Pu-to Road Branch, (#1), Shanghai Police (IDC 2973 1943)

Yang -- Magistrate, Sun Sheng-su Hsien; under control of Government of Kwangtung (51:239)

Hun Kai-keh -- President, Council of Protestant Ministers, Amoy; attended celebration commemorating formation of Council (11/21/43) (49:179)

CHINESE

Hung Chen-liang -- Manager, China Tobacco Industrial
Bank, Shanghai (IDC 7270 1943)

Chou (chu) -- Secretary General, Examination Yuan,
Nanking (1943)

Chung-hao -- Presented 5,000 yen to Hongkong Government General (12/14/42) (51:239)

Han-pao -- See Hung Han-pin

Han-pin (-pao) -- Assistant Chief of Police, Lao-
cha District Office, First Police Office,
Shanghai (49:179)

Hsueh-chow -- Manager, Central Reserve Bank,
Changchow Branch, Kiangsu (IDC 7270 1943)

Hsun -- Inspector, East Asia League, Nanking
Branch (1943)

Kwang Hsin-chang -- Witness to by-laws revised by
North China Political Council (10/8/43)
(52:236)

Tien-ching -- Member, Association of Teachers,
Amoy (49:179)

Wang -- Editor, SHEN PAO, Shanghai (IDC 7266 1943)

Yuan -- Member, Association of Teachers, Amoy
(49:179)

Yum-sum -- Director, Experimental Station, Kwangtung University (51:239)

Huo Hsia-min -- Editor, NAN YUEH JIH PAO, Fu-shan,
South China (IDC 2562)

I Chin -- President, Ming Chiang Electric Corporation,
Chang-chia-kow (IDC 66 1943)

Fu-chu -- Head, Tai Tung Branch Agency, Canton Police
Bureau (51:239)

Hsien-kuan -- See Kuan I-cien

Lang-chao -- Manager, Wei Yeh Commercial and Savings
Bank, Shanghai (IDC 7270 1943)

Pao-san -- Commander, pro-Japanese troops; with
Japanese Huang Hsieh Chun, commanding 900
men, Tohsien, Chingkou area (6/39;OSS-ms.)

Po-szu -- Head, Asiatic Cultural Association, Shanghai
(IDC 7265 1943)

Tieh-sun -- Editor-in-Chief, CHUNG PAO, Nanking (IDC
7267 1943)

Tzu-kan -- Director, Central Reserve Bank, Nanking
(IDC 7270 1943)

Yang -- Chief, Organization Department, Hsin Min Society; made inspection trip (8/18/43)

CHINESE

In Dung -- Head, North China Labor Association; once
            Managing Director, Peiping Army (Chungking
            8/31/42) (52:236)

Ing Tung -- Vice-President, Hsin Min Society, Peking
            (52:236)

Iu Feng -- Editor, HSIN CHUNG KUO PAO, Shanghai (IDC
            7266 1943)

Jan San-sheng -- Manager, Lun I Commercial and Savings
            Bank, Shanghai (IDC 7270 1943)

    Yen-tao, Admiral -- See Jen Yuan-tao

Jen Chia-chu -- Member, Committee for Punishment of
            Central Officials, Nanking (1943)

    Chung-tai -- Member, Inter-State Catholic Goodwill
            Federation (6/27/44)

    Feng-pao -- Manager, Yen Yeh Bank, Shanghai (IDC
            7270 1943)

    Hsi-p'ing -- Member, Central Political Council,
            Nanking (1943); member, All-China Economic
            Committee

    Li -- See Chang Jen-mu

    Yuan-tao, Admiral (Yen Ling-tao; Jan yen-tao) --
            Graduate, first class, Paoting Military
            College; served successively, commander,
            40th Infantry Regiment, 55th Brigade, and
            Garrison Commander, Tientsin-Pukow and
            Peiping-Hankow Railways; member Foreign
            Relations Committee, Hopeh-Chahar Political
            Council, Peiping; Pacification Minister,
            Nanking Reformed Government (since 1938);
            for a time, concurrently held post, Director,
            Nanking Municipal Administration (Who's Who
            in China (1940); made Minister, Public
            Safety, Nanking Reformed Government; Acting
            Chief, Pacification Department (3/28/38;
            OSS-Ms.); Acting Chief, Military Advisory
            Council (12/38); member, Designated Commit-
            tee, Central Political Council (12/38); Min-
            ister of Navy; Head, Navy Department (1938-
            43); member, Military Affairs Commission
            under Wang Ching-wei's regime; Commander-in-
            Chief, 1st Military District Army (2/15/43);
            Commander, 652,000 puppet troops, Kiangsu-
            Chekiang-Anhwei area (5/20/43); member,
            National Military Council; Governor, Kiangsu
            Province; Director, China Office, East Asia
            League; decorated by Japanese Emperor
            (3/23/44)

    Yun-p'eng -- Chief Manager, Newspaper Association,
            Shanghai; Director, Special Municipality
            Journalists Association; Chief, Managing
            Office, Citizens Savings Movement Committee
            (49:179)

Jo Haku-oi (Japanized reading) -- Ex-Director, Federal
            Reserve Bank of China (3/27/43)

CHINESE

Jo Min-tai -- Director, Peace Preservation Office, Chekiang (49:179)

Ryo -- Chinese Ambassador, Tokyo

Ju Hsing -- Head, Ta-t'ung News Company, Shanghai (49:179); Editor-in-Chief, NING PO KUNG PAO (IDC 7267 1943)

Wan -- Chief, Section for Abolition of Extra-territoriality Affairs, Ministry of Foreign Affairs, Nanking (IDC 3/11/43)

Jui Hsin-yung -- Director, Shanghai Special Municipality Journalists Association; Editor, NING P'E KUNG PAO, Shanghai (49:179)

Jung Chen -- Member, National Military Council, Nanking

Ching, Lt. Gen. -- Permanent Chairman, Anti-Communist Commission, North China (8/5/43); member, National Government Military Affairs Commission (1943) (52:236)

Tse-hong -- See Jung Tsu-heng

Tsu-heng (Jung Tse-hong; Jung Tu-heng) -- Commander-in-Chief, South Shantung and North Kiangsu Army; "gone over to peace camp", pledged allegiance (7/10/43) (52:236)

Tsu-pao, Gen. -- Chairman, Supreme War Command, North China (6/11/43) (52:236)

Tu-heng -- See Jung Tsu-heng

Kai Gi-so (Japanized reading) -- Ex-Director, Federal Reserve Bank (3/27/43)

Kaku Shuu-kei -- Vice-President, newly formed China Newspaper Association; President, Central ... Newspaper (9/20/44)

Kan -- Chief, Information Board, Central Council; attended conference, Peiping (52:236)

Chuan-chu -- Commander, 7th War District; killed in action (2/16/44)

Chin-chai -- Artist, Canton (51:239)

Kuki -- Head, Hopeh Interpretation Office, Education Administration, North China (52:236)

Po-cheng -- Chairman, Economic Committee, North China Political Council; witness to revised by-laws of National Government by North China Political Council (10/8/43) (52:236)

Tou-nan -- Chairman, Directors, Thermos Bottle Factories, Shanghai (IDC 7264 1943)

Yok-ken -- Vice-President, China Newspaper Association; President, North China Propaganda Association; Publisher, North China Daily News (9/20/44) (52:236)

-90-

CHINESE

Kang Che -- Interested in liberating Formosa; wrote for Formosan Revolutionary Alliance (IDC)

Hsi-tung -- Director, China Educational Reconstruction Association, Shanghai Branch (49:179)

T'ao-shou -- Member, Legislative Yuan, Nanking (1943)

Yu-t'ing -- Executive Inspector, East Asia League, Nanking Branch (1943)

Kao Cheng -- Commander, Police Corps, Anking Municipal Government (OSS)

Ch'i-hsien -- A secretary, Ministry of Foreign Affairs, Nanking (1943)

Ch'i-wu -- Editor-in-Chief, PING PAO, Tientsin (52:236)

Han -- Director of Propaganda, Huaihai Province (OSS)

Hua -- Editor-in-Chief, YEH CHIANG JIH PAO, Canton (51:239)

Kuan-wu -- Born, 1892, Tsungming Island, Kiangsu; graduate, Paoting Military College; Senior Counsellor, Headquarters of Generalissimo (Dr. Sun Yat-sen); Chief-of-Staff, Headquarters, Military Governor, Kweichow; Vice-Commander, 10th Nationalist Army; Garrison Commander, Shanghai Woosung Area; Chief Counsellor, Headquarters, Director-General of Bandit Suppression in Shensi and Szechwan; joined Japanese (1935); became Senior Adviser, "East Hopeh Anti-Communist Administration" under Yin Ju-ken; Vice-Minister of Pacification, Nanking Reformed Government (3/38); Mayor, Nanking (1940) (Who's Who in China 1940); member, Central Executive Committee, Nanking (1943); member, National Military Council; Governor, Anhwei; Chairman, Village Pacification Committee, Anhwei; Honorary Director, Sino-Japanese Cultural Association; Director, China Office, East Asia League; Governor, Kiangsi Province (1944); decorated by Japanese Emperor (1944)

Liang-mei (Kao Ling-mei) -- Chief of Public Works, Hankow (1943); Honorary Director, China Educational Reconstruction Association, Hankow Branch

Ling-han -- Training Head, 2nd District Party Headquarters, Kuomintang, Swatow (IDC)

Ling-mei -- See Kao Liang-mei

Ling-wei -- Born, 1868, Tientsin, Commissioner, Education, Hupeh (1906); Vice-President, Bank of Agriculture and Commerce (1921); Minister of Finance, Interior and Communications; Premier and then Director-General, Customs Revenue Administration (1923-24); member, Hopeh-Chahar Political Council (1935);

CHINESE

Kao Ling-wei (Con't) -- organized and headed, Tientsin Peace Maintenance Commission (1937); Mayor, Tientsin; Governor, Hopeh; member, Legislative Council, Peiping Provisional Government; died, Peiping (3/7/40) (Who's Who in China (1940)

    Ming-hua -- Candidate Director, China Educational Reconstruction Association, Shanghai Branch (49:179)

    Po-hsun -- Director, Sino-Japanese Cultural Association, Wu-ch'ang and Hankow Branch (1943); Executive Director, China Educational Reconstruction Association; Honorary Director, China Educational Reconstruction Association, Hankow Branch

    Po-mien -- Executive Director, Sino-Japanese Cultural Association, Wu-ch'ang and Hankow Branches (1943)

    Shih-mao -- Chairman, Directors, Handmade Nets and Bags, Shanghai (IDC 7264 1943)

    Shu-ying -- Assistant Manager, Nanking General Office, Central Reserve Bank of China; Head, new Branch Office, Hsuchow (2/17/44)

    T'ien-ch'i -- Executive Director, China Writers Club (1943)

    Tsun-wu -- Executive Director, China Educational Reconstruction Association, Anhwei Branch (1943)

    Tsung-hsin -- Director, Shanghai Education Committee; Director, Sino-Japanese Cultural Association, Shanghai Branch; Chief, Office of General Affairs, Sino-Japanese Cultural Association, Shanghai Branch (49:179)

    Wei-hua -- Prosecutor, Supreme Court, Nanking (1943)

    Wen-min -- Chief, Affairs Promotion Section, Ministry of Social Welfare, Nanking (1943)

    Yen -- Newly appointed Chief of ... organization; attended opening of Kang-ling Bridge (IDC)

    Yu-t'ung -- Counsellor, Directorate-General of Pacification, North China Political Commission (7/41;OSS-Ms.)

Ke Chih-min -- Executive member, China Journalists Association (1943)

    Hsin-no (Hsing-o) -- Financial Consultation Committee member, West Shanghai (12/42) (49:179); Inspector, China Office, East Asia League

    Hsing-o -- See Ke Hsin-no

    Lan-p'ei -- Publisher, CHUNG KUO FU CHIA CHI K'AN, a quarterly, Shanghai (49:179)

-92-

CHINESE

Ke Lang -- Chairman, Directors, Bittersauce Manufacturers, Shanghai (IDC 7264 1943)

   Liang-ch'ou -- Director, East Asia League, Nanking Branch (1943)

   Ti-fu -- Director, Shanghai Special Municipality Journalists Association; member, Shanghai Magazines Association (49:179)

Keh Tei-ken (Japanized reading) -- Mayor, Municipality of Hankow (10/19/43)

Kei Sho -- Lives in Toshu, China; reputedly donated 1 plane to Japanese Air Force (9/18/43)

(Ken Ito) -- Formerly Superintendent of Education Provincial Government; appointed first President, Anhwei Province Branch, China-Japan Cultural Society (10/4/42)

Ken To-sen (Japanized reading) -- Professor, Peiping University; attended 6th Deliberative Committee meeting, East Asia Cultural Conference, Peiping University (8/31/42) (52:236)

   Yao-fu -- Provincial Governor, Canton (51:239)

   Yng-fu -- Governor, Kwantung Province; attended 78th anniversary of birth of Sun Yat-sen (11/13/43)

Keng Chia-chi -- Director, East Asia League, Shanghai Branch (49:179)

   Fu-lu -- Director, China Educational Reconstruction Association, Hankow Branch (1943)

   Hsueh-kun -- Chairman, Directors, Warehouse and Storage Association, Shanghai (IDC 7264 1943)

Ki Sho-rei (Japanized reading) -- Secretary, Federal Reserve Bank of China (3/27/43)

Kian Chang-chuan -- (52:236); See Ching Chan-shen

Kiang Chao-tsung -- See Chiang Chao-tsung

   Hung-geh -- See Chiang Hung-geh

   Kang-hu -- See Chiang Kang-hu

   Shao-chieh -- See Chiang Shao-chieh

Kiat, G. H. -- President, Shonan Sports Association (OSS)

Kin -- Vice-Director, Finance Section, National Government of China (3/11/44)

Kiu Kiang -- Governor, Anhwei Province, Nanking

   Kuk -- Director, Trading Union, Hongkong (51:239)

Ko Ch'ao-p'ing -- Director, Shanghai Chamber of Commerce (49:179)

CHINESE

Ko Chieh-chen -- Chairman, Directors, Woolen Material
       Stores, Shanghai (IDC 7264)

Chuang-fa -- One of 7 students to study movie photog-
       raphy in Japan; arrived Moji enroute to
       Tokyo (7/1/43;OSS-Ms.)

Hoo-koo -- Chief, Bureau, Provisions Department,
       Kiangsu Provincial Administration; to be
       tried on charges of food conspiracy (3/12/44)

Liang-tao -- Manager, Nanking Hsing Yeh Bank (IDC
       7270 1943)

Pao-hua -- Inspector, Citizens Savings Movement
       Committee, Shanghai (49:179)

Soku-kin, Lt. Gen. (Japanized reading) -- Chief,
       Pacification Bureau, Provincial Governor,
       Hopeh Province (52:236)

Soku-shi (Japanized reading) -- Member, Board of
       Standing Directors, North China Political
       Council (11/11/43) (52:237)

Son-bun -- Tried to start Chinese Revolution; heart
       taken to Nanking (3/25/42) (52:237)

Ti-fu -- Editor, KUO MIN HSIN WEN, Shanghai (1943);
       Director, Newspapermen's Association

Ting-yuan -- Member, National Military Council,
       Nanking (OSS)

Wen-tsu -- Leader, South Seas Chinese Merchants
       (51:239)

Yung-chi -- Manager, Chang Cheng Commercial and
       Savings Bank, Shanghai (IDC 7270 1943)

Kong From -- Lihon Bank; Vice-Chairman, Hongkong Chinese
       Bankers Association (51:239)

    Kai-chung -- President, (Hwshwa) Jih Pao, Hongkong
          (51:239)

    Kai-tung -- Press Official, Hongkong (51:239)

    Po-tin -- Officer, East Asia Cultural Association,
          Asiatic Affairs Bureau, Hongkong (OSS)

Koo Chuu-setsu (Japanized reading) -- Vice-Chief, ...
       Bureau, North China Political Council;
       Chief, Finance Bureau, North China Politi-
       cal Council; Vice-Chief, General Affairs
       Bureau, North China Political Council
       (11/11/43) (52:237)

    Kuan-wu -- Mayor, Nanking (0-58)

    Roo-rin -- Chief, Business Affairs Bureau, Central
          (Headquarters), Hsin Min Society (8/12/44)

    Shi-ki -- President, Branch Office, China Reserve
          Bank, National Government; Standing Direc-
          tor, Nanking General Office (F-9)

CHINESE

Kotewall, Sir Robert -- See Lo Kuk-wo

Ku -- Chairman, Executive Yuan, Nanking (1/43)

Cheng-kan (Cheng-kang) -- Minister, Social Affairs,
Nanking (1/1/42; 9/23/43)

Chi-wu -- Political Vice-Minister under Minister of
Social Affairs, Wang Ching-wei's regime
(3/41; OSS-Ms.); Chief, Poachia Office
(First Police Office), Shanghai (49:179);
member, Central Executive Committee, Nanking;
member, Committee of Political Councillors;
Inspector, China Office, East Asia League;
Honorary member, China Journalist Association

Chih-lien -- Chairman, Directors, Porcelains Association, Shanghai (IDC 7264)

Chung-chen -- Vice-President, Examination Yuan
(under Liang Hung-chih), Wang Ching-wei's
regime (3/22/40; OSS-Ms.)

Chung-lao -- President, CHUNG PAO, Nanking (7267
1943)

Chung-pao -- Member, Inter-State Catholic Goodwill
Federation (6/27/44)

Chung-shen -- President, Control Yuan (1943); member, Central Supervisory Committee; Executive Inspector, China Branch, East Asia
League

Chung-tan -- Member, Standing Committee, Central
Political Council (12/38)

Chung-tao -- Publisher, CHUNG PAO, Nanking (IDC 2562)

Chung-yi -- Director, Sino-Japanese Cultural Association, Shanghai Branch (49:179)

Fei-jan -- Publisher, HUA YING YEN CHIU, weekly,
Shanghai (49:180)

Hai-chiu -- Commander, 12th Independent Brigand (OSS)

Hsi-hsi -- Editor, T'AI TSANG HSIN PAO, Tai Tsang,
Kiangsu (IDC 2562)

Huai-ch'ing -- Editor, HSIN HSING JIH PAO, Hsing Hua,
Kwangsu (IDC 2562)

Huan-chang -- Head, Leather Enterprise Trade Association, National Trade Control General Association, Shanghai (49:180)

Huang-chuan -- Battalion Commander, Tinghsien Peace
Preservation Corps; killed in action (2/12/44)

K'an -- Publisher, WU YU, a monthly, Peiping (1943)
(52:237)

144   -95-

CHINESE

Ku Keng-yang -- Manager, Chia Shan Hsien Local Farmers
        Bank, Chekiang (IDC 7270 1943)

Ki-kan (?) -- Head, Interpretation Office, Hopeh
        (1944) (52:237)

Leng-kuan (Ling-kuan) -- Director, Shanghai Maga-
        zines Association; Publisher, HSIAO SHUO
        YUEH PAO, a monthly, Shanghai (49:180)

Li-fu -- Editor-in-Chief, HSIANG TAO JIH PAO,
        Shanghai (IDC 7267)

Ling-kuan -- See Ku Leng-kuan

Min-cheng -- Minister (11/27/42)

Nan-ch'un -- Chairman, Public Welfare Committee,
        Citizens Welfare Association, Shanghai;
        Director, Citizens Savings Movement Commit-
        tee, Shanghai (49:180)

Pao-heng -- Administrative Vice-Minister, Ministry
        of Industry and Commerce, Wang Ching-wei's
        regime (3/41; OSS-Ms.); Minister of Food-
        stuffs, Nanking (1943); Vice-President,
        Central Reserve Bank; member, Executive
        Committee, All-China Economic Committee;
        Director, Central Bank of China, Nanking;
        dismissed for graft (5/11/44); Inspector,
        China Office, East Asia League; member,
        National Economic Committee

Po-chu -- Manager, Kiang Su Bank, Shanghai Branch
        (IDC 7270 1943)

Shen -- Member, Committee on Culture, China Office,
        East Asia League (1943)

Shien -- Hongkong newspaper representative (51:240)

Shih -- Advisory member, Ministry of Justice (1943)

Ta-i -- Manager, Hai Ning Hsien Farmers Bank, Yung
        Kang, Chekiang (IDC 7270 1943)

T'ien- tsan -- Candidate Director, China Educational
        Reconstruction Association (1943)

Tse-po (Tsu-po) -- Member, Shanghai Newspaper Asso-
        ciation (49:180); Editor, HSIN WEN PAO

Tsung-shen -- Honorary Director, Sino-Japanese Cul-
        tural Association

Wen-sheng -- Director, Shanghai Chamber of Commerce
        (49:180)

Y. S. -- Vice-Minister of Education, Nanking (9/23/43)

Yung-chin -- Director, East Asia League, Shanghai
        Branch (49:180); Secretary, Ministry of In-
        formation; Director, China Educational Re-
        construction Association (1943); Inspector,
        China Writers Club

-96-

CHINESE

Kuan Cheng-pin -- Director of Economics, Huaihai
    Province (OSS)

Ch'i-yu -- Editor, MIN KUO JIH PAO, Nanking (1943);
    member, Propaganda Committee, China Office,
    East Asia League; Director, China Writers
    Club

Chia-mei -- Chairman, China Movie Association,
    Su-Hai Office

Chia-tung -- Publisher, JU KAO JIH PAO, Ju-kao,
    Kiangsu (IDC 2562)

Ch'ing-hua -- Director, Sino-Japanese Cultural
    Association, Shanghai Branch (49:180)

Chu-tsun -- Journalist; Editor, Central Electrical
    Communications Corporation (IDC 2562)

Ch'un-yi -- Manager Director, Shanghai Magazines
    Association; Publisher, SHEN PAO YUEH K'AN,
    a monthly (49:180)

Chung-hsi -- Counsellor, National Government,
    Nanking (1943)

Hsin-yen -- Control Officer, Kowloon Tang Special
    Ward, Kowloon (51:240)

I-chien (Kuan I-hsien; I Hsien-kuan) -- Director,
    Board of Information, North China Political
    Affairs Commission (3/27/44); Publisher,
    SHIH PAO, Peiping (1943) (52:237) (see also
    Kuan Yi-hsien)

Lu -- Director, Citizens Savings Movement Commit-
    tee, Shanghai; Director, Sino-Japanese Cul-
    tural Association, Shanghai Branch (49:180)

Se-chow -- See Shau Quei-chang

Wu -- Discussed new reconstruction of North China
    and its food supply (10/1/43) (52:237)

Yi-hsien -- Publisher, SHIH PAO, Peiping (1943);
    President, North China News Agency; Vice-
    President, new China Newspaper Association
    (9/26/44) (see also Kuan I-cien)

Yi-ming -- Editor, HUAI NAN PAO, Tsao-hsien,
    Anhwei (IDC 2562)

Yu-lin -- Secretary, Kuomintang Fifth District
    Party Headquarters, Canton (51:240)

Yuan-ch'un -- Secretary, Village Pacification
    Affairs Bureau, Nanking (1943)

K'uang Ch'i-kuang -- Member, Legislative Yuan, Nanking
    (1943)

Ch'-tung -- Publisher, NAN HUA JIH PAO; Director,
    South China Daily News; Commissioner, Propa-
    ganda Department, National Government; mem-
    ber, China Discursive Association; member,
    Council, Chinese Representatives Association

CHINESE

Kuang Chia-ting -- Secretary, Kuomintang Fourth District
Party Headquarters, Canton (51:240)

Hung-tsao -- Director, East Asia League, Shanghai
Branch (49:180)

Yun-wen -- Member, Legislative Yuan, Nanking (1943);
Director, East Asia League, Nanking Branch

Kuei Ming-chih -- Candidate Inspector, China Educational
Reconstruction Association, Anhwei Branch
(1943)

Kui Shing, Col., C.I. -- Assistant Military Attache,
Manchukuo Embassy, Nanking (0-60)

K'un Yao-kuang -- Candidate Executive member, China
Journalists Association (1943)

Kung -- Chief, Finance Bureau, Hankow; represented
China at Sino-Japanese conference re concessions at Hankow (4/6/43)

Chao-yao -- Judge, Supreme Court, Nanking (1943)

Ch'ih-p'ing -- Chief, Special Propaganda, Ministry
of Information, Nanking (1943)

Ching-ning -- Manager, Hua Mao Bank, Shanghai (IDC
7270 1943)

H. H. -- Asked for report on Criterion Trading
Company, Shanghai (49:180)

Han-tiao -- Member, Publishers Committee, Chinese
Writers Club (1943)

Hsiang -- Acting Secretary-General, Legislative
Yuan, Wang Ching-wei's regime (3/31/41;
OSS-Ms.); member, Legislative Yuan, Nanking
(1943)

Hsien-chien (K'ung Hsien-k'eng) -- Born, 1898,
Nanhai, Kwantung; LL.M. Paris University;
Ph. D. Economics, Brussels University;
Principal, Law School, Kwantung National
University; Professor, Chungshan University,
Canton; Director, Bureau of Statistics, Na-
tional Government; Senior Secretary, Examina-
tion Yuan, Nanking; newspaper work, Shanghai,
Nanking and Canton; practiced law Shanghai;
joined Nanking Reformed Government as Coun-
sellor, Education Ministry; Director, Pub-
licity Bureau, Nanking (1940) (Who's Who in
China 1940); Administrative Vice-Minister,
Ministry of Publicity, Wang Ching-wei's
regime (3/41;OSS-Ms.); Director, China Branch,
East Asia League (1943); member, National
Economic Council, Nanking; member, Central
Executive Committee, Nanking (1943); Vice-
Minister, Ministry of Justice; member, All-
China Economic Committee; Official, Judicial
Administration, Wartime Special Court; mem-
ber, Central Electrical Communications Cor-
poration; member, Social Welfare Committee,
China Office, East Asia League; member, Com-
mittee for Application of Constitution

CHINESE

Kung Hu -- Candidate Director, Shanghai Special Municipality Journalists Association (49:180)

Liang-lu (Lu Kung-liang) -- Commander of 29th Division; deceased (5/4/44)

Ping-ch'uan -- Chief, Office of Police Affairs, Hupeh Province (1943)

Sheng -- Chief, Fire Department, Canton Police Bureau (51:240)

Sin-yen -- Cooperating with Nanking Government; former leader, Young Men's Service Corps (9/5/42)

Wei-yu -- Head, Second Section, Canton Bureau of Police (1/6/44); Chairman, Peace Preservation unit (51:240)

Wen-shiu -- Assistant Chief of Police, Yang-shu-p'u District Office, First Police Office, Shanghai (49:180)

Yung-ting -- Manager, Ta Kung Commercial and Savings Bank, Shanghai (IDC 7270 1943)

Kuo -- President, Army Hospital, Chunking (2/4/44)

Ch'en-yuan -- Chief of Agriculture, Ministry of Industries, Nanking (1943)

Ch'i -- Candidate Director, China Educational Reconstruction Association, Chekiang Branch (49:180)

Chi-yun -- Candidate Director, China Educational Reconstruction Association, Hankow Branch (1943)

Ch'ien-yaun -- Director, Agriculture and Forestry Board, Executive Yuan, Nanking (1943)

Chuan -- Director, Yung An Bank, Hongkong; Manager, Yung An Company; Chairman, Pu I Importing Association; member, China Discursive Association

Chun-hua -- Chairman, Directors, Second-hand Goods Association, Shanghai (IDC 7264)

Chun-t'ao -- Interested in liberating Formosa; wrote for Formosan Revolutionary Alliance

Hsien-hung -- Control Officer, Tung Lo Wan Ward, Hongkong (51:240)

Hsiu-feng -- Chief, Central Telegraph Bureau, Executive Yuan (1943); Executive Director, Central Electric Communications Corporation; member, New Citizens Movement Promotion Committee; member, China-Japan Returned Students Club; member, Propaganda Committee, China Office, East Asia League; Inspecting member, China Journalists Association; Assistant Chairman, China Movie Association; President,

CHINESE

Kuo Hsiu-feng (Con't) -- Central China News Agency;
Vice-President, new China Newspaper Association (1944); resigned, Vice-Minister, Propaganda and Publicity (6/44)

Hua -- Editor, YUEH CHIANG JIH PAO, Canton (51:240)

Hung -- Deputy Chief, Narcotic Prohibition Headquarters, Shanghai (49:180); Chief, National
Weight and Neasures, Ministry of Industries

Kwang-ho -- See Ho Kuo-kwang

Lien-ch'eng -- Chief, Army Hospital, Ministry of
the Army, Nanking (1943)

Pao-huan -- Chief, Kwantung Propaganda Office,
Ministry of Information (1943)

Shu-liang -- Chief, Social Sample Insurance, Ministry of Social Welfare, Nanking (1943)

Shun -- Inspector, National Trade Control General
Association, Shanghai; member, Peace and
Order Committee, Municipal Council, Shanghai
(5/13/44); Manager Director, Shanghai Chamber
of Commerce; Director, Labor and Business
Social Union (49:180); Chairman, Directors,
Department Stores

Siu-feng -- President, Central Press Service, Nanking (9/26/44)

Te-chun -- Commander, pro-Japanese troops; with
Japanese Huang Hsieh Chun, commanding about
1,000 men, Honan (6/41; OSS-Ms.)

Te-lin -- Commander, pro-Japanese troops; with
Japanese Huang Hsieh Chun Commanding troops
in Hsingtai (6/39; OSS-Ms.)

Tsan -- Vice-President, Hongkong China Merchants
Association; Chinese Director, Bank of
France; member, China Discursive Association; member, Council, Chinese Representatives Association

Tsan-li -- Hwaliang Association, Haichow (F-15)

Wei-min -- Former Chief, Police Affairs Office,
Shangtung Province (51:240)

Wen-ch'i -- Publisher, WU CHIN JIH PAO, Chang Chou,
Kiangsu (IDC 2562)

Yen-t'ing -- Director, Citizens Savings Movement
Committee, Shanghai (49:180)

Kwan Hoy -- Head, Dai-au Autonomous Council, Hongkong
(10/5/44) (51:240)

Kwang Chang-po -- Former Chairman, Board of Directors,
... Hospital and Orphan 9home), Hongkong;
re-elected director of the institution
(51:240)

-100-

CHINESE

Kwang Lin-po -- Director, Finance Department, Kiangsu
    Provincial Government (7/22/44)

    Ming-fu -- Magistrate, Tsininghsien, Shantung;
        presented donation to Japanese Liaison
        Office (6/14/44) (52:237)

Kwei Ming-chung -- Accounting Unit, Canton Bureau of
    Police, First Section (51:240)

Kwok Chuen -- Representative for Foreign Goods, Chamber
    of Commerce, Hongkong (51:240)

Kwong Kuh-chung -- Representative of Chinese in Hongkong
    in discussion of food problem (51:240)

Kyo Caku-mei -- Chairman, Supreme War Council (6/11/43)

    Kei-koo (Japanized reading) -- Member, Bureau of
        Industry and Business, National Government;
        dismissed for illegal activities (5/44)

Kyoo Sa-sen (?) -- Vice-Chief, Industrial Department,
    Kiangsu Administration; named Vice-Head,
    Provisions Department (3/12/44)

Kyu Kaku-ju (Japanized reading) -- Supreintendent,
    Education, North China; attended 6th Deliber-
    ative Committee meeting, East Asia Cultural
    Conference, Peiping University (8/31/42)
    (52:237)

Lai Ch'un-kuei -- Director, General Affairs, Hupeh
    Province (OSS)

    Kong-sun -- Representative, Firewood Merchants,
        Hongkong (51:240)

    Yuk-tam -- Addressed winning teams, Hongkong
        Athletic Federation (11/9/44)

Lam Fei -- Nanking's agent in Hongkong, (successor to
    Wang Ki, Police Commissioner, Canton) under
    Takeda, Head, Special Service Section and
    officially attached to Japanese Consulate
    General, Hongkong (9/41; OSS-Ms.); with
    45 Senior Agents under him, is mainly inter-
    ested in the collection of military infor-
    mation in Hongkong for Wang Ching-wei
    (51:241)

Lan Li-ting -- Member, Association of Teachers, Amoy
    (49:180)

Lang Ching-shan -- Director, Sino-Japanese Cultural
    Association, Shanghai Branch (49:181)

    Kang -- Secretary, 4th District Party Headquarters,
        Kuomintang, Swatow (1943)

    Tank-lan -- Leader, group from Hsin Min Society of
        Peking on tour of Manchukuo (5/17/44)
        (52:237)

    Yi-shan -- Secretary, Committee for Application
        of Constitution, Nanking (1943)

CHINESE

Lao Feng -- Treasurer, Central Relief Association, Hongkong (51:241)

    Sui-yuan -- Secretary, Ministry of Social Welfare, Nanking (1943)

    Yet-sen -- Vice-Chairman, Hongkong Christian Association (51:241)

Lau -- Mayor, Canton (51:241)

    Hip-tsing, Rev. -- Speaker at 5-day Christian revival sponsored by Hongkong Chinese Christian Association (8/15/44) (51:241)

    Tit-sing -- Member, Chinese Representatives Council; Manager, Bank of Communications; Chief, Executive Department, Chinese Relief Association, Hongkong; Chairman, Bankers Association (51:241)

    Tsi-shing -- Appointed Head, Business Affairs Department, Hongkong Chinese General Relief Association and Chinese Benevolent Association (51:241)

Le Yung-hu -- Member, Kwangtung Social Affairs Committee; concurrently Head, Kwangtung Bureau of Social Welfare (51:241)

Lee -- Chairman, Cooperative Area, North China (9/26/43) (52:237)

    Fung -- Nanking Minister to Roumania; appointed concurrently Minister to Hungary (2/24/42)

    Jee-chor -- Member, Council, Chinese Representatives Association, Hongkong (51:241)

    Kiang-yuan -- See Ya Hsiel-lien

    Shan-wu -- Nanking Ambassador, Berlin and Denmark (2/24/42)

    Sheng-pu -- Head, East District, Civilian Defense, Canton (51:241)

    Ta-kung, Miss -- Former woman Communist of Hopeh Province who decided to work for new China (52:237)

    Ting-kuo -- Head, Civilian Defense, North District, Canton (51:241)

    Wang-ching (Lin Wang-king; Ling Wang-ching) -- President, Medical College; former Head, University of Amoy; cooperating with Japanese organized Shonan Chinese Merchants Association; Chairman, Chinese Association of Shonan City

    Yao -- Head, Civilian Defense, Central District, and Maritime District, Canton (51:241)

    Ying-lun, Dr. -- President, Lingnan University, escaped (2/12/42)

CHINESE

Lei Chen-yuan -- Member, Shanghai Newspaper Association (49:181); Editor, CHUNG HUA JIH PAO

Fair Mu-fu -- Chairman, Treasury Committee, North China Political Council; witness to revised by-laws of National Government by North China Political Council (10/8/43) (52:237)

Hsien-chih -- Director, Citizens Savings Movement Committee, Shanghai (49:181)

Hui-ming -- Head, Ming Tung Memorial School; graduate, Chungshan University; Committee member, Kuomintang Headquarters, Kwangtung Province; former Head, First Middle School, Canton City (51:241)

Hung-sse -- Member, Legislative Yuan, Nanking (1943)

Lo-er -- Head, Shanghai Pa Szu Te Research Institute (IDC 7265 1943)

Pao-shu -- Secretary, First District Party Headquarters, Kuomintang Headquarters, Canton (51:241)

Shou-yung -- Member, Foreign Affairs Committee, Hopeh-Chahar Autonomous Council; formerly connected with Luantung Retrocession Commission under Huang Fu; returned student from Japan (OSS-Ms.)

Sun-yen -- Head, Shanghai Police Inspection Party, touring Manchukuo (5/12/44) (49:181)

Yi-min -- Director, East Asia League, Nanking Branch (1943)

Yu-chun -- Head, Opium Suppression Bureau, Kwangtung Province (51:241)

Leng Chia-chi -- Member, Hopeh-Chahar Autonomous Council (12/11/35); former Head, Peiping Chamber of Commerce (OSS-Ms.); Manager, China Agricultural and Industrial Bank, Peking Branch (1943) (52:237); member, North China Political Council

Yu-tsai -- Head, Central Electrical Communications Corporation, Yang-chou Branch (IDC 2562)

Leung Sui-ping -- See Liang Sui-ping

Li -- Publicity Minister (11/19/43); Propaganda Minister (1/10/44); see also Ling Po-sheng

Bon-um -- Shanghai Commercial Bank; member, Committee of Bank of Communications, Hongkong (51:241)

Chai -- Director, National Commercial Control Association (1943)

Ch'ang-chiang -- Commander-in-Chief, First Group Army; Deputy Director-General, Military Advisory Board, Nanking; Vice-Chairman, Military Counsellors Board

-103-

CHINESE

Li Ch'ang-liu -- Secretary, First District Party Headquarters, Kuomintang, Swatow

Ch'ao -- Publishers Committee, China Writers Club
(1943)

Chao-chih -- Director, East Asia League, Shanghai
Branch; Director, Sino-Japanese Cultural
Association, Shanghai Branch (49:181)

Chen-chung -- Head, Police Affairs Unit, Second Section, Canton Bureau of Police (51:241)

Chen-pang -- Chairman, Directors, Travelling Agencies,
Shanghai (IDC 7264 1943)

Chen-yuen -- Made study of economic conditions,
Kwangtung (1/20/44) (51:242)

Chi-chih -- Inspector, China Educational Reconstruction Association, Hankow Branch (1943)

Ch'i-fen -- Head, Public Health Division, Kwangtung;
made observation tour, Tung-huan District
(51:242)

Chi-fong -- Elected Chairman, General Affairs Committee at second meeting, General Relief
Association (6/2/44)

Ch'i-hsin -- Control Officer, Hsi Ying Pan Ward,
Hongkong (51:242)

Chia-feng -- Inspector, China Educational Reconstruction Association, Hankow Branch (1943)

Chia-hsin -- Chief, Education Administrative Office,
Su-hai (1943)

Chia-kan -- Commissioner of Education, Huaihai
Province (OSS)

Chian-shi -- Head, Research Institute, Shanghai
(49:181)

Chiang-chuan, Dr. -- Professor, Peking University;
in attendence at Japanese Medical Conference
in China (1944) (52:237)

Chien -- Director, Shanghai Wharf Labor Union
(49:181)

Chien-chi -- Head, Meng Shen Branch Agency, Canton
Police Bureau (51:242)

Chien-nan -- Born, 1890, Port Arthur; attended
Anglo-Chinese College, Tientsin; Phillips
Academy, Andover, Mass., and Columbia Uni-
versity, New York; Section Chief and Secre-
tary, Office of the Commissioner of Foreign
Affairs, Tientsin; Secretary, Civil Governor,
Chihli Province (1914-19); Secretary, Minis-
try of Communications, Peking; Research Mem-
ber, Versailles Treaty, Ministry of Foreign
Affairs, Peking (1920-21)(Who's Who in China)
Commissioner of Customs, Shanghai; Head, Salt
Affairs, Ministry of Finance (1943)

-104-

CHINESE

Li Chih-ch'ien -- Director, China Educational Reconstruction Association, Chekiang Branch (49:181)

Chih-hsin -- Editor-in-Chief, TIEN SHENG PAO, Tientsin (1943) (52:237)

Chih-hung -- Director, East Asia League, Hupeh Branch (1943)

Chih-wen -- Editor, MIN SHENG JIH PAO and other papers, Canton (51:242)

Chin-wo -- Publisher, HUA CH'IAO SHANG PAO, Foochow (49:181)

Ching-han -- Director, Shanghai Education Committee; Executive Director, China Educational Reconstruction Association, Shanghai Branch (49:181)

Ching-kang -- Member, Legislative Yuan, Nanking (1943)

Ching-shao -- Chief, Paochia Office, 5th Department, Shanghai (49:181)

Ching-to -- Publisher, CHENG CHOU HUA PEI JIH PAO, Cheng-chou, Honan (IDC 1943)

Ching-wu -- Member, All-China Economic Committee (National Economic Council) (1943)

Chiu -- Member, Council, Chinese Representatives Association, Hongkong (51:242)

Choh-sen -- Head, 5th Section, Ministry of Military Affairs (1/4/45)

Chu-fong -- Chinese Councillor; commented on importation of rice and firewood into Hongkong (8/28/44) (51:242)

Ch'uan-shih -- Chairman, Economic Committee, Citizens Welfare Association, Shanghai (49:181); member, All-China Economic Committee

Ch'un-ch'ao -- Obtained license to operate mines in Nanhai, Kwangtung (51:242)

Chun-to, Maj- Gen. -- Chief, General Affairs Office, Nanking (1943)

Chung-chao -- Head, Branch Office of Police, Shameen, Canton (51:242)

Chung-fu -- Chairman, Tung Hua San Yuan, Hongkong; Director, Asia Company; member, Council, China Representatives (Discursive) Association (51:242)

Chung-hao -- Representative, Information Committee, Shanghai (49:181)

Chung-sheng -- Commander, Third Brigade, Independent Nanking Army (IDC 3/30/42)

154 -105-

CHINESE

Li Chung-yu -- Inspecting member, China Journalists Association (1943)

Fan-ch'ang -- Executive Director and Inspector, East Asia League, Hupeh Branch (1943)

Fang (Li Fang-ch'ang; Lien Fang) -- Minister to Rumania (also Minister Extraordinary and Plenipotentiary to Hungary) (1943); Candidate Inspector, Sino-Japanese Cultural Association, Wu-ch'ang and Hankow Branch

Fei-- President, Central China Salt Industry Company, Shanghai (OSS)

Fu-sun -- Manager, Chekiang Industrial Bank, Shanghai (IDC 7270 1943)

Han -- Principal, Tekning School; Chairman, Relief Committee for Education, Hongkong (51:242)

Han-hun -- "Formerly an able military man"; Governor, Kwangtung (?) (51:242)

Hao-chu -- Postmaster, Shanghai (1943); member, National Economic Committee

Hao-jan -- Editor-in-Chief, HSIN WEN PAO, Shanghai (49:181)

Haui-chi -- Vice-Minister, Navy Department, Nanking (1/3/45)

Hen-ying -- Commander, pro-Japanese troops; with Japanese Huang Hsieh Chun, North Shantung, commanding about 3,000 men (6/39; OSS-Ms.)

Ho-yi -- Commander, pro-Japanese troops; with Japanese Huang Hsieh Chun, Canton, commanding 4,000 men (6/39; OSS-Ms.)

Hong-ching -- Manager, Fu Chin Commercial Bank, Changchow, Kiangsu (IDC 7270 1943)

Hsi-peng -- (Commander), pro-Japanese troops; with Japanese Huang Hsieh Chun, Huangpo and Hsiaokan area, commanding 5,000 men (6/39; OSS-Ms.)

Hsia-fu -- Publisher, NAN YUEH JIH PAO, Fu-shan (IDC 2562)

Hsiang-ching -- Director, China Educational Reconstruction Association, Hankow Branch (1943)

Hsiao-chen -- Commander, pro-Japanese troops; with Japanese Huang Hsieh Chun, commanding 800 men, Ningchin, Hopeh (6/39; OSS-Ms.)

Hsieh-t'ang -- Editor, NAN HUA JIH PAO, Hongkong (51:242)

Hsien-ying -- Publisher, HSIN TU CHOU K'AN, a monthly, Shanghai (49:181)

CHINESE

Li Hsing-chieh -- Director, Shantung Coal Production and Marketing Company (52:238)

Hsing-poi -- Editor, CHUNG KUO SHANG PAO, Shanghai (49:181)

Hsu-an, Lt. Gen. -- Vice-Minister of War, Nanking (0-57)

Hsuan-t'i (-ao) -- Member, Committee of Political Councillors, Nanking (1943); Vice-Minister, Executive Yuan; member, National History Editing Committee; Inspector, China-Japan Returned Students Club; Vice-Minister of War

Hsuan-wei -- Director, North China Electrical Industry Company, Peiping (52:238)

Hsueh-tseng -- Judge, Supreme Court, North China Branch (1/17/43) (52:238)

Hua -- Head, Miscellaneous Goods Enterprise Trade Association, National Trade Control General Association, Shanghai (49:181)

Hui -- Commander, Nanking Defense Corps; appointed Police Commissioner, Nanking; to hold both positions concurrently (5/7/43)

Hui-chi -- Chief, Military Supplies, Ministry of the Navy, Nanking (1943)

Hung-fei -- Chairman, Directors, Huai Nan Salt Industry Stock Company, Shanghai (IDC 7262 1943)

Ju-ching -- Head, Shanghai Police Inspection Party to Japan (OSS)

K.C. -- Reorganized Wah Chang Company, Shanghai (49:181)

K'ai-ch'en -- Executive Director, East Asia League, Shanghai Branch (49:181)

Kan-huang -- Chief, Peace Preservation Office, Anhwei Province (OSS)

Keng-hsi -- Nanking District Commander under Minister of Navy, Wang Ching-wei's regime (3/31/41; OSS-Ms.)

King-hong -- Education Representative, Chinese Cooperative Council, Hongkong (1942-?) (51:242)

Kuan-chun -- Vice-Chairman, Chinese Cooperative Council, Hongkong; Chairman, China Merchants Association, Hongkong; Chairman, Hongkong Exchange Shops Association; Director, Tao Heng Bank, Hongkong; Vice-Chairman, China Representatives Discursive Association

Kuan-hua -- Chief of Police, Lo-Yang Road District Office, Third Police Office, Shanghai (49:181)

CHINESE

Li Kuang-chih -- Member, Social Welfare Committee,
China Office, East Asia League (1943)

Kuang-wo -- Publisher, CHUN SHAN JIH PAO, Canton
(51:242)

Kuang-yuan -- Candidate Director, Sino-Japanese Cultural Association, Wu-ch'ang and Hankow
Branch (1943)

Kuei-lui -- Publisher, TIEN YING PAO, Peiping (1943)
(52:238)

Kung-ti -- Manager, Szechwan Mei Feng Bank, Shanghai
Branch (IDC 7270 1943)

Kuo-ch'ang -- Member, Committee on Culture, China
Office, East Asia League (1943)

Kuo-fei -- Head, Hua-chung Salt Corporation, Shanghai
(49:181)

Kuo-liang -- Graduate, National Chungshan Univer-
sity; Committee member, Kuomintang Head-
quarters, Kwangtung Province; Former Chief,
Kwangtung Boy Scouts Leaders Training
School; Supervisor, Department of Education,
Kwangtung Government; Head, Provincial
Second Middle School; Director, Social Wel-
fare Committee, East Asia League, Canton
Branch (51:242)

Kuo-yi -- Commander, 20th Division, Nanking Army
(IDC 3/30/42)

Kusi-liu -- Editor, TIEN YING PAO, Peiping (52:238)

Li-wen -- Member, All-China Economic Committee (1943)

Liu-hsiao -- Publisher, CHING PAO, Nanking (IDC 2562)

Liu-yao -- President, CHING PAO, Nanking (IDC 7267)

Mien -- Judge and Chief, Supreme Court, Nanking
(1943)

Min -- Councillor, Chinghsiang Administration,
Hangchou Sector (IDC 6/8/43)

Ming-chang -- Director, Shanghai Wharf Labor Union
(49:181)

Ming-shen -- Chunking's prefectural governor,
Chuhsien, Shansi; saw "true intentions of
Japan" (1/27/43; OSS-Ms.)

Mo-pei -- Director, Shanghai Special Municipality
Journalists Association (49:181); Editor-in-
Chief, CHUNG KUO SHANG PAO, (IDC 7267)

Ou-yi -- Chief, Nanking Police Force; member, National Military Council

Pai-sheng -- See Ling Po-sheng

Pao-lien -- Commander, 11th Division, Nanking Army (IDC)

-108-

CHINESE

Li P'ei-ch'iu -- Member, National History Editing Committee (1943)

Ping-chian -- China (?Hung) Men Association (IDC 6/3/43)

Po-chin -- Director, Central China Silk Stock Company, Shanghai (1943)

Seng-wu -- National Government of China; Honorary Chairman, Directors, China Educational Reconstruction Association (1943)

Shao-han -- Chief of Finance, Hankow; Director, East Asia League, Hupeh Branch

Shao-hou -- Special Delegate, Ministry of Foreign Affairs, to Hupeh (1943)

Shao-keng -- Foreign Minister (3/29/44)

Shao-p'ing -- Head, Hua-pei News Company, North China (1943) (52:238)

Shen-lin -- Special Delegate, National Supreme Defense Council (7/8/43)

Sheng-chun -- Manager, Hua Hsing Commercial Bank, Hangchow Branch and in Kiangsu (IDC 1943)

Sheng-hung -- Manager, Ya Chou Bank, Shanghai (IDC 1943)

Sheng-nan -- Deputy Chief of Fire Department, Canton Police Bureau (51:242)

Sheng-po -- Director, Shanghai Labor and Business Social Union (49:182); member, All-China Economic Committee

Sheng-wu -- Member, Department of Justice and Administration (12/38); Minister of Justice, Wang Ching-wei's regime (3/40; OSS-Ms.); Minister of Judicial Administration and Concurrently member, Central Political Council, Nanking Kuomintang (3/41; OSS-Ms.); member, Central Political Council (1943); member, Central Executive Committee; Minister of Education, Nanking; member, Committee for Return of Concessions; Executive Director, New Citizens Movement Promotion Committee; Adviser, Sino-Japanese Cultural Association, Shanghai Branch; Director, China Office, East Asia League; Inspector, China-Japan Returned Students Club; Nanking Ambassador, Germany and Denmark

Shi-ch'un -- Member, Designated Committee, Central Political Council (12/38); Director, China Office, East Asia League; Died (9/11/43)

Shih -- Inspector, Shanghai Special Municipality Journalists Association (49:182); Correspondent, HSIN SHEN PAO; Inspector, China Office, East Asia League

158

-109-

CHINESE

Li Shih-chen (Lin Shih-chen ?) -- Commissioner, Directorate General of Reconstruction, North China Political Commission (7/40; OSS-Ms.)

Shih-ch'un -- Former Governor, Kiangsu Province; member, Central Political Council and Minister, Police Administration (3/31/41; OSS-Ms.); appointed Head, Investigation and Statistics Bureau, Military Council (8/41; OSS-Ms.); decorated by Japanese Emperor (3/23/44)

Shih-fe -- Part owner, Hu-yi Company; granted permission to operate coal mines, Nanhai and Kang-t'ou; granted permission to operate coal mines at Tan-ts'un, 6th District, P'anyu-hsien (IDC 5/29/42)

Shih-fen -- Obtained license to operate mines in Nanhai, Kwangtung (see Li Shih-fe) (51:243)

Shih-fu -- Special Officer, Department of Information, Kwangtung Province (51:243)

Shih-heng -- Inspector, China Educational Reconstruction Association (1943)

Shih-hsien -- Chairman, Peace Maintenance Committee, Amoy (49:182)

Shih-mou -- Graduate, Tokyo Military Cadets School; Directorate-General, Military Training, Nanking (1934); "considered Pro-Japanese and follows same police as adopted by Generalissimo Chiang Kai-shek" (OSS-Ms.)

Shih-pu -- Commander, 12th Brigade, Independent Nanking Army (IDC 3/30/42)

Shih-shun -- Ex-Governor, Kiangsu Province; decorated by Japanese Emperor (3/23/44)

Shih-yuan -- Trustee, North China Aluminite Mining Industrial Company, Ltd. (52:235)

Shing-po -- Shanghai textile industry magnate (12/26/44)

Sho-me -- Vice-Minister, Civil Service (1/43)

Shou-hei -- Inspector, China Office, East Asia League (1943)

Shou-mo -- Member, Committee for Application of Constitution, Nanking (1943)

Shou-shan -- Control Officer, Hung Kan Ward, Kowloon (51:243)

Shu-pen -- Director, China Educational Reconstruction Association, Shanghai Branch (49:182)

Shu-shih, Maj. Gen. -- Counselor, Military Affairs Department, Nanking (O-57)

-110-

CHINESE

Li Sing-hui -- Farming Bank; committee member, Hongkong Chinese Bankers Association (51:243)

Ssu-hao -- Former Director of Finance, old Peking Government; President, Central News Agency (1943); Chairman, Board of Directors, Ssu Ming Commercial Bank; President, new China Newspaper Association (1944)

Ssu-hsien -- Mayor, Amoy Special Municipality

Su-yu -- Deputy Commissioner; Director, Judicial Section, Shanghai Police Force (4/18/44) (49:182)

Sung-chieh -- Vice-Chief of Police, Kwangtung Province (51:243)

Sung-ch'ing -- Control Officer, Chih Chu Ward, Hongkong (51:243)

Sung-hsia -- Deputy Chief, Police Administration, Kwangtung; sent to make survey in San-shui hsien (51:243)

Szu-hao -- Director, Citizens Welfare Association, Shanghai (49:182)

Szu-hsien -- Mayor, Amoy (49:182)(same as Ssu-hsien?)

Ta-chang -- Executive Director, China-Japan Returned Students Club (1943)

Tai -- Commander, pro-Japanese troops; with pro-Japanese Huang Hsieh Chun, Honan, commanding about 1,000 men (6/39; OSS-Ms.)

T'ai-fang -- Member, National History Editing Committee (1943)

Tai-fen -- Professor, Teachers University, Peiping (8/13/44) (52:238)

T'ai-yao -- Member, Committee for Editing the National History, Nanking (1943)

Tao-shuan -- Commander, pro-Japanese troops; with Japanese Huang Hsieh Chun, commanding 1,000 men, Hsikiang, Paisha (6/39; OSS-Ms.)

Te-hsin -- Former Chief of Staff to General Wang Ching-tsai; surrendered to Japanese with 4,000 men (3/5/43; OSS-Ms.)

Te-ming -- Judge, Supreme Court, North China Branch (1/17/43) (52:238)

Tei-chi -- Chairman, Honan Province (O-58)

T'en-ju -- Inspecting member, Control Yuan, Nanking (1943)

Teng-hui -- Head, World Students Association, Shanghai (IDC 7265 1943)

CHINESE

Li Ti-chu -- Chairman, Directors, Bicycles Association, Shanghai (IDC 7264 1943)

Tien-chang -- Commissioner, Directorate-General of Industry, North China Political Commission (7/41; OSS-Ms.)

Ting-shih -- Inspecting member, Control Yuan, Nanking (1943)

Tsai-chung -- Commissioner, Directorate-General of Pacification, North China Political Commission (7/40; OSS-Ms.)

Tse -- Director, National Trade Control General Association, Shanghai (49:182)

Tsu-fan -- Head, Soap and Candle Enterprise Trade Association, National Trade Control General Association, Shanghai; Director, National Trade General Association, Shanghai (49:182); Chairman, Directors, Chemical Goods Association (1943)

Tsu-yu -- Graduate, Waseda University; sometime Judge, Supreme Court; Commissioner, Civil Affairs, Fukien Provincial Government (since 4/34); Author, two volumes on general principles of obligations in civil laws, etc; Administrative Vice-Minister under Minister of Communications, Wang Ching-wei's regime (3/41; OSS-Ms.); member, Committee of Political Councillors, Nanking (1943); member, China-Japan Returned Students Club; Candidate Director, Sino-Japanese Cultural Association (1943) (52:238); Director, China Office, East Asia League

Tsun-yuan -- Chief, Military Education, Ministry of the Army, Nanking (1943)

Tsung-t'ang -- Inspecting member, Control Yuan, Nanking (1943)

Tung-hsia -- Deputy Chief, Police, Canton (51:243)

Tze-feng -- Treasurer, Committee on Relief and Culture Exhibition, Hongkong (51:243)

Tzu-fang -- Office holder and member of Council, Chinese Representatives Association (1942-?) Hongkong; Vice-Chairman, Hongkong Bankers Association; Chairman, General Affairs Committee, General Relief Association (51:243)

Tzu-tung -- Chief, 2nd District Office, Central District, Shanghai (49:182)

Wang -- Vice-Chief, Political Training Bureau (12/38)

Wei -- Member, Association of Teachers, Amoy (49:182)

Wei-ning -- Director, Sino-Japanese Cultural Association, Shanghai Branch (49:182)

-112-

CHINESE

Li Wen-chi -- Propaganda Head, Kuomintang Eighth District Party Headquarters, Canton (51:243)

Wen-fei -- Financial Consultation Committee member, West Shanghai (12/42) (49:182)

Wen-li, Gen. -- According to Japanese report, surrendered to Nanking with 25,000 men (4/43; OSS-Ms.); joined "Peace Camp" (3/15/44; 52:238)

Wen-pin -- Administrative Vice-Minister, Minister of Interior, Wang Ching-wei's regime (3/31/41; OSS-Ms.); member, Committee of Political Councillors, Nanking

Ya-fans -- Commander, Fifth Brigade, Independent Nanking Army (IDC 3/30/42)

Yang-chou -- Chief, Protective Office, Ministry of Justice, Nanking (1943)

Yang-lou -- Councillor, Chinghsiang Administration, Hangchou Sector (IDC 6/8/43)

Yin-kuang -- Training Head, Kuomintang Second District Party Headquarters, Canton (51:243)

Yin-nan -- Graduate, Government and Law School, Meiji University and Kyshu Imperial University; Committee member, Kuomintang Headquarters, Kwangtung Province; former Secretary, National Central Bank; consultuant to Executive Yuan; Financial Specialist, Central Political Committee; President, Kwangtung Bank; Executive Director, Social Welfare Committee, East Asia League, Canton Branch

Yin-ping, Maj. Gen. -- Reportedly went over to Nanking with his command (3/19/43; OSS-Ms.)

Ying -- Commander, pro-Japanese troops; with 1st Division, pro-Japanese Huang Hsieh Chun on Honan Border, commanding about 3,000 men (6/39; OSS-Ms.)

Ying-mao -- Assistant Chairman, Flour Special Committee, National Trade Control General Association, Shanghai (49:182)

Ying-pen -- In command, puppet troops, Shansi (1942); near Lishih, revolted with troops, killed puppet commander at Wanglingshan, joined Chungking forces (9/42; OSS-Ms.)

Young-p(o)ing, Gen. -- Pinhai Shantung Province; joined "Peace Camp" (3/15/44) (52:238)

Yu-lin -- Chief, Pacification Commission, Hsuchang (OSS)

Yu-sheng -- Auditor, Ministry of Auditing, Nanking (1943)

CHINESE

Li Yu-wen -- Propaganda Head, Kuomintang Fifth District
　　　　Party Headquarters, Canton (51:243)

Li Yuan-chi, Dr. -- Director-General, National Health
　　　　Administration, Executive Yuan; appointed
　　　　Vice-Chairman, Southeast Asia Medical Con-
　　　　ference (4/12/44) (49:143)

　　Yuan-fu -- Editor, HUA CH'IAO SHANG PO, Foochow
　　　　(49:182)

　　Yun-cheng -- Leader of resistance against bandits,
　　　　Hopeh Province (52:238)

　　Yun-chieh -- Manager, Chwan Yen Bank, Shanghai
　　　　Branch (IDC 7270 1943)

　　Yung-chen -- Member, Publishers Committee, China
　　　　Writers Club (1943)

　　Yung-ting, Gen. -- Forsook Chungking regime (52:238)

Lia Kia-fan -- Controller of Fuel, Hongkong (51:243)

Lian Kuan-tsun -- Manager, Kwangtung Bank, Shanghai
　　　　Branch (IDC 1943)

Liang Chan-hsun -- Publisher, YUEH CHIANG JIH PAO,
　　　　Canton (IDC 1943)

　　Chao-hui -- Graduate, National Chungshan Univer-
　　　　sity; committee member, Secretary General,
　　　　and Head, General Affairs Section, Kuomin-
　　　　tang's Headquarters, Kwangtung Province;
　　　　Former Secretary, Kwangtung Provincial
　　　　Government; Chairman, Social Movement Com-
　　　　mittee, Kwangtung; Head, Bureau of Social
　　　　Affairs, Canton City Government (51:243)

　　Chi -- Control Officer, Chien Sha Chu Ward,
　　　　Kowloon (51:244)

　　Chiang-chin -- Police student sent to Formosa for
　　　　training; assigned now to various bureaus in
　　　　Tai-p'ing-ching and Hai T'ien-shou for addi-
　　　　tional training (51:244)

　　Chou-tung -- Propaganda Head, Kuomintang Second
　　　　District Party Headquarters, Canton (51:244)

　　Heng-chang -- Deputy Chief, Protective Police,
　　　　Canton Bureau of Police (51:244)

　　Hsia-hsin -- Publisher, YEH CHIANG JIH PAO, Canton
　　　　(51:244)

　　Hsiu-yu -- Manager Director, Committee for Estab-
　　　　lishment of China's Broadcasting Business,
　　　　Shanghai; Chief, Bureau, Office of Propa-
　　　　ganda; Executive Director, Sino-Japanese Cul-
　　　　tural Association, Shanghai Branch; Advisor,
　　　　Citizens Savings Movement Committee, Shanghai:
　　　　(49:182); Executive Committee member, China
　　　　Broadcasting Enterprise and Reconstruction
　　　　Association (1943); member, Directing Com-
　　　　mittee, China Office, East Asia League;
　　　　Director, China Movie Association

-114-

CHINESE

Liang Hung-chih -- President, Executive Yuan (1938); President, Examination Yuan (3/22/40) (OSS-Ms.); member, Executive Committee, Central Political Council; President, Control Yuan, Nanking; granted Order of Rising Sun by Japanese Emperor (4/22/43); decorated by Japanese Emperor (5/14/43); Executive Inspector, China Office, East Asia League (49:182); Honorary Director, Sino-Japanese Cultural Association; member, Committee for Application of Constitution

   Pi-ch'un -- Counsellor, National Government, Nanking (1943)

   Shang-ling -- Publisher, KAI PING JIH PAO, Kai Ping, South China (51:244)

   Shih -- Inspector, Shanghai Special Municipality Journalists Association; (49:182); Deputy Editor-in-Chief, CHUNG HUA JIH PAO

   Sui-ping (Leung Sui-ping) -- Chairman, Hongkong Athletic Federation (51:244)

   Ting-ch'uan -- Graduate, Kwangtung Legal School; formerly worked for Salt Administration of Kwangtung; Head, Section of Organization, Kuomintang Headquarters, Kwangtung Province (51:244)

   Ya-p'ing -- Counsellor, Directorate-General of Education, North China Political Government (7/40; OSS-Ms.)

   Yen-ts'ai -- Publisher, EN PING JIH PAO, En-ping, South China (51:244)

Liao Chia-nan -- Vice-Minister, Construction, Nanking (1943); member, Committee of Political Councillors; Inspector, China Office, East Asia League

   En-tao -- State Councillor, Nanking (OSS)

   Lien-neng -- Member, Legislative Yuan, Nanking (1943)

   Ping-chi -- Born, Swatow; spent some time in Japan and Germany (7/8/40; OSS-Ms.)

   Po-hsien -- Director, China Educational Reconstruction Association, Hankow Branch (1943)

Lien Fang -- See Li Fang

   Yu -- Appointed Ambassador to Manchukuo for Wang Ching-wei (1941); recalled to Nanking (2/1/43) (OSS-Ms.); Director, Office of Ambassadors, Ministry of Foreign Affairs, Nanking; Executive Director, China-Japan Returned Students Club (1943); Executive Inspector, China Branch, East Asia League (OSS); Plenipotentiary Ambassador residing in Ministry of Foreign Affairs, Nanking

CHINESE

Lieu Chien-cheng -- Manager, Hongkong Communications
        Bank (51:244)

    Tsung-fan -- Vice-President, Peiping Technical
        School (6/17/44) (52:238)

    Tung-chuen -- Indo-Chinese doctor, posthumously
        named a Chevalier of Legion of Honor; with
        Dalat Hospital(DIO)

Lim Chong-pang -- Council member, Overseas Chinese Asso-
        ciation; leading local Chinese and member,
        Singapore Consultative Board (6/29/44)

Lin -- Head Educational Department; President, Canton
        Branch, Japan-China Cultural Association
        (51:244)

Lin -- Section Head, Propaganda, Amoy (49:182)

    Ch'ao-hui -- Executive Director, Social Welfare
        Committee, East Asia League, Canton Branch
        (51:244)

    Ch'eng-liang -- Training Head, 1st District Party
        Headquarters, Kuomintang, Swatow (IDC)

    Chi -- Chief Secretary, Shanghai Municipality
        (49:183); Chief, General Affairs Department
        (1943)

    Chia-min (mim) -- Head, Bureau of Information,
        Kwangtung; Publisher, MIN SHENG JIH PAO and
        MIN SHENG WAN PAO, Canton (1943) (51:244)

    Chien -- Commander, pro-Japanese troops; with
        Japanese Huang Hsieh Chun, commanding 1,000
        men, Samsui (6/39; OSS-Ms.)

    Chien-chih -- Chief, Police Bureau, Chia-hsing,
        Chekiang (OSS)

    Chien-yin -- Member, Committee of Labor Procure-
        ment, Hongkong and Kowloon; member, Chinese
        Discursive Association, Hongkong; member,
        Council, Chinese Representatives Associa-
        tion; President, Laborers Association (51:244)

    Chih-chun -- Formosan; formerly head, Chinese
        Workers Welfare Association, Shanghai (49:183)

    Chih-kiang, Col. -- Director, Poison Gas Research
        Institute, Chiang Kai-shek regime; appears
        to have deserted the Chungking Government for
        Wang Ching-wei (1941; OSS-Ms.)

    Ch'ih-min -- Inspector, Control Yuan, Nanking (1943)

    Chih-yen -- member, Central Executive Committee,
        Nanking (OSS)

    Chiung-an -- Executive Director, Sino-Japanese Cul-
        tural Association, Shanghai Branch; Chairman
        Director, China Educational Reconstruction
        Association, Shanghai Branch (49:183) Com-
        missioner, Education, Shanghai; Executive Di-
        rector, China Educational Reconstruction Asso-
        ciation

CHINESE

Lin Chong-pang -- Chinese leader, Singapore (0-59)

Chu-hsuing -- Manager, Chien Hua Bank, Shanghai (IDC 7270 1943)

Chu-tang -- Manager, Chung Yuan Commercial and Savings Bank, Shanghai (IDC 1943)

Han-chih -- Publishers Committee member, China Writers Club (1943)

Hsiang-fu -- Chairman, Directors, Flags and Mats Association, Shanghai (IDC 1943)

Hsiao-k'un -- Interested in liberating Formosa; wrote for Formosan Revolutionary Alliance (IDC)

Huang-chu -- Attended meeting, Shanghai Municipal Council; represented heads of committees (6/7/44) (49:183)

Jo-shih -- Former Naval Officer; former Major General and Adviser to Government; follower of Sun Yat-sen; being pushed by Canton people for post of General Commander, Kwangtung harbor (10/3/44) (51:244)

Ju-hang (Lin Ju-heng) -- Chief Executive Director and Secretary General, Social Welfare Committee, East Asia League, Canton Branch; President, National Chekiang Ministry of Education (51:244); Political Adviser, National Government, Nanking (1943); member, Committee of Political Councillors, Nanking; Education Commissioner; member, Committee of Academia Sinica, Nanking Government (6/18/43); member, New Citizens Movement Promotion Committee; Publisher, CHUNG SHAN JIH PAO, Canton (1943); Inspecting member, China Journalists Association; Executive Inspector, China Educational Reconstruction Association

Ju-heng -- See Ling Ju-hang

Ju-hsuing -- Head, Bureau of Education, Kwangtung Provisional regime; spoke, Canton University, on ideas of participating in present war (1/30/43) (51:244)

Kai-sheng -- See Ling Po-sheng

K'ang-hou -- Member, Municipal Advisory Committee, Shanghai (1943); member, National Trade Association; Secretary General, Banking Association; Director, National Commercial Control Association; Chief Commissioner of Control, National Trade Control Association (6/18/44)

Kuang-chi -- Counsellor, Business Office, Sino-Japanese Cultural Association, Shanghai Office (49:183)

Kuo-hsun -- Executive Director, China Educational Reconstruction Association, Shanghai (49:183)

CHINESE

Lin Kuo-ts'ai -- Member, Legislative Yuan, Nanking (1943)

Ling-hsi -- Inspector, China Educational Reconstruction Association, Shanghai Branch (49:183)

Nai-shih -- Executive Director, China Educational Reconstruction Association, Shanghai Branch (49:183)

Pai-sheng (Lin Pao-sheng; Lam Pak-sang) -- Minister of Publicity, Nanking; addressed East Asia Journalists Convention with Wang Ching-wei (8/2/41; OSS-Ms.); Chairman, Board of Directors, China Broadcasting Enterprise and Reconstruction Association (1943); Minister of Publicity, Central Government; decorated by Japanese Emperor (3/23/44)

Piao -- President, High Administrative Committee, Executive Yuan (1943); Inspector, China Office, East Asia League

Po-sheng -- See Lin(g) Po-sheng

Po-shun -- See Lin(g) Po-sheng

Po-yen -- Commander, 16th Brigade, Guerrilla Forces, Chiang regime, Wuting Area Shantung (1/27/45) (52:238)

Sen -- President (1/1/42); died (5/43) (DIO)

Shang-chih -- Inspector, East Asia League, Hupeh Branch (1943)

Shih-chen -- See Li Shih-chen

Shou-kang -- Editor, HUA MAN HSIN JIH PAO, South China News Daily (51:245)

Shu-kuang -- Director, Hongkong Kuo Min Bank, Shanghai Branch (IDC 7270 1943)

Ta-chung -- Ex-Chief, Economic Affairs, Nanking (1943); Chief, Chekiang Construction Department (1/3/45)

Ta-wen -- Judge and Chief, Supreme Court, Nanking (1943)

T'ing-shen -- Prosecuter, Supreme Court, Nanking (1943)

Tsung-yang -- Professor, Peiping University; delegate from North China to GEA Medical Conference (4/20/44) (52:238)

Wang-king -- See Lee Wang-ching

Wei-in -- Member, Publication Committee, China Writers Club (1943)

-118-

CHINESE

Lin Wen-hai -- Member, Culture Committee, China Office, East Asia League (1943); Secretary, Executive Yuan (1943); Auditor and Chief, Anhwei Office, Ministry of Auditing

Wen-lung -- Chief, Publicity Board, North China Political Commission (7/40; OSS-Ms.)

Wu -- Propaganda Head, 2nd District Party Headquarters, Kuomintang, Swatow (IDC)

Yen-do (Japanized reading) -- Chief, Navy Department (1943); member, Supreme National Defense Council (1943)

Yin -- Magistrate, Haitan Island (OSS)

Yu-ken -- Commissioner of Customs, Canton (1943) (51:245); Kwantung Customs, Salt Affairs

Ling Chen-ling -- Publisher, TZU LO LAN, a monthly, Shanghai (49:183)

Chen-tsun -- Director, Shanghai Magazines Association (49:183)

Chia-min -- Publisher, MIN SHENG JIH PAO, Canton (51:245)

Chiung-an -- Advisor, Citizens Savings Movement, Shanghai; Chief, Shanghai Bureau of Education (49:183)

Chun-hoa -- Member, ... Committee, Municipal Council, Shanghai (5/13/44) (49:183)

Fu-yuan -- Publisher, HSIN PEI CHING PAO, Peiping (1943) (52:238)

Ho-tsai -- Editor, HUA NAN HSIN JIH PAO, Amoy (49:183)

Hong-fat -- Chief Executive, General Labor Association, Hongkong and Kowloon (51:245)

Hsiao -- Political Vice-Minister, Ministery of Navy, Wang Ching-wei's regime (3/31/41); first Nanking Attache to Japan; arrived Japan (6/21/41; OSS-Ms.); member, National Military Council (1943); acting Minister, Navy, Executive Yuan; Executive Director, China-Japan Returned Students Club; Inspector, China Office, East Asia League

Hsien-wen -- Advisor, Citizens Savings Movement Committee, Shanghai; Executive Director, East Asia League, Shanghai Branch; Honorary Director, Sino-Japanese Cultural Association, Shanghai Branch (49:183); member, Central Executive Committee, Nanking; Commissioner, Social Affairs, Shanghai (1943); Executive Director, China Educational Reconstruction Association; member, National Economic Committee

CHINESE

Ling Ju-heng -- Chief, Bureau of Education, Kwangtung;
Publisher, CHUNG SHAN JIH PAO, Canton
(51:245)

K'ang-fa -- Chairman, Hongkong-Kowloon Labor
Union; Chairman, Restaurant Industries Association; member, China Discursive Association; member, Council, Chinese Representatives Association (51:245)

K'ang-hou -- Member, Education Committee and Com-
mittee on Peace and Order, Shanghai Munici-
pal Council; Managing Supervisor, Shanghai
Chamber of Commerce; Assistant Chairman,
Shanghai Citizens Welfare Association;
member, Committee on Grain Control; Vice-
Chairman and Managing Director, Citizens
Savings Movement Committee, Shanghai; Man-
ager Director, Labor and Business Social
Union

Kong -- Editor, HUA NAN HSIN PAO, Amoy (49:183)

Ku -- Publisher, HUA NIN HSIN JIH PAO, and other
papers, Amoy (49:183)

Kuang-chi -- Executive Director, Sino-Japanese
Cultural Association, Shanghai Branch (49:184)

Lin(g) Po-sheng(Li; Li Pai-sheng; Lin Kai-sheng; Lin
po-shen; Lin Po-shun) -- Adviser, Sino-
Japanese Cultural Association, Shanghai
Branch; President, CHUNG HUA JIH PAO;
(49:184); member, Designated Committee,
Central Political Council, (12/38); represented Wang Ching-wei, Kwangtung "Movement
for Reconstruction"; Chairman, Publicity
Department, Kwangtung (1942); Publicity Minister, Nanking (1943, 1944); Head, Information Bureau, National Government, Nanking
(2/10/43); Propaganda Minister, National
Government, Nanking (7/28/42; 7/29/43);
Mayor, Shanghai (1944); decorated by Japanese
Emperor (3/23/44); attended inaugural ceremony for new China Newspaper Association
(9/26/44); replaced as Minister of Propaganda (1/17/45) (51:245); sent to Japan to
study organization of Japanese Youth Corps
(9/42); Chairman, Directors, Central Elec-
trical Communications Corporation; Secretary-
General, New Citizens Movement Promotion
Committee; Governor, Anhwei Province; member,
Supreme National Defense Council; President,
New China Youth Corps; Executive Director,
China Office, East Asia League; Executive
Director, Sino-Japanese Cultural Associa-
tion; Honroary Chairman, Directors, China
Educational Reconstruction Association;
Chairman, China Movie Association

Ling Shang-kang -- Director, Shanghai Magazines Association (49:184)

Ta-chung -- Chief, Office of Economics, Nanking

-120-

CHINESE

Ling Ta-t'ing -- Director, Sino-Japanese Cultural Association, Shanghai Branch (49:184)

Wang-ching -- See Lee Wang-ching

Wen-li -- Manager, Tung Ya Bank, Shanghai (IDC 7270 1943)

Yang-wu -- Executive member, Oil and Grain Special Committee, National Trade Control General Association, Shanghai (49:184)

Yi-shin -- Mayor, Peking (1943); member, North China Political Council (2/8/43) (52:238)

Liong Kang-hou -- Member, Education Committee, Shanghai Municipal Council (49:184)

Liu -- Head of a Unit -- Department of Public Health, National Government, Nanking (2/4/44)

Ch'ang-ming -- Assistant Chief of Police, Chung-Yang District Office, First Police Office, Shanghai (49:184)

Chang-yi -- Commander, pro-Japanese troops; with pro-Japanese Huang Hsieh Chun, North Honan, commanding 1st Route Army (6/39); just before Japanese offensive against Chengchow, revolted with troops, killed Japanese officers inspecting, rejoined Chiang Kai-shek's armies (9/41) (OSS-Ms.)

Ch'ao -- Inspector, China Office, East Asia League (1943)

Chao-lin -- Director, Hospital, Peiping University; delegate from North China to GEA Medical Conference (4/20/44) (52:239)

Chen-sheng -- Head, Chung-wen Communications Company, North China (52:239)

Chen-ya -- Chief, Bureau of Political Affairs, Kiangsi

Chi -- Secretary, Legislative Yuan, Nanking (1943)

Chi-hung -- Commander, 3rd Army (1942) (52:239)

Chi-lan -- Publisher, TIEN CHING SHIH PAO, and other papers, Tientsin (52:239)

Ch'ien -- Secretary General, Directorate-General of pacification, North China Political Commission (7/40; OSS-Ms.)

Chih -- Interested in liberating Formosa; wrote for Formosan Revolutionary Alliance (IDC)

Ching-chen -- Chief, Ration Board, Shanghai (1/3/45) (49:184)

Chu-chen -- Governor, Kwantung Province; Chief Secretary, (Specification) Committee, National Government, Canton, South China; reviewed 4,000 member, Youth Corps (51:245)

CHINESE

Liu Chu-san -- Manager, Min Fu Commercial and Savings Bank, Shanghai (IDC 7270 1943)

Ch'un-po -- Director, East Asia League, Hupeh Branch (1943)

Chun-yang -- Head, Police Department, Huaihai Province (OSS)

Chung-chu -- Head, Executive Department, Peiping (52;239)

Ch'uo-pak -- Chief, Hongkong Opium Commission (51:245)

Erh-ku -- Chairman, Directors, Chao-shan Sacrificial Money Association, Shanghai (IDC 7264)

Feng-chang -- Judge, Supreme Court, North China Branch (1/17/43) (52:239)

Feng-ch'ih, Maj. Gen. -- Commander, First Army Corps, Peiyuan, Peking, of the Peace Preservation Army, North China Political Commission (7/40; OSS-Ms.)

Hah-ju -- Secretary, Paochia Office, 1st Police Office, Shanghai (49:184)

Hai-shu -- Honorary Director, Sino-Japanese Cultural Association, Shanghai Branch (49:184)

Hsi-chih -- Chief of Police, Hsiao-Tung-Men District Office, Third Police Office, Shanghai (49:184)

Hsi-hao -- Member, Publication Committee, China Writers Club (1943)

Hsi-p'ing -- Director, Shanghai Special Municipality Journalists Association (1943) (49:184)

Hsiang-kuo -- Commander, 22nd Division, Nanking Army (IDC)

Hsiao-lan -- Publisher, TIENTSIN SHIH PAO and PING PAO, Tientsin (1943) (52:239)

Hsieh-t'ang -- Editor-in-Chief, NAN HUA JIH PAO, Hongkong (51:245)

Hsing-ch'en -- Councillor, Chinghsiang Administration, Hangchow Sector; President, Chekiang Provincial Bank, Hangchow Branch (49:184); Executive Inspector, China Educational Reconstruction Association

Hsu-kuang -- Director, East Asia League, Nanking Branch (1943)

, John -- Intelligence agent, Hongkong, for Furukawa who is Chief, Japanese Intelligence, Macao; claims to be member, Shanghai Tai Fing Insurance Company; headquarters, 19-20 Connaught Road, West, 3rd floor, Hongkong; another John Lui, boatswain, SS Antinous, reported sailing out of Baltimore to Far East (9/41; OSS-Ms.)

-122-

CHINESE

Liu Ju-hsiang -- Director, Central Reserve Bank, Nanking
(1943); Inspector, China-Japan Returned
Students Club; Chief of Public Debts, Finance
Ministry

Keng-ying -- Assistant Chief of Police, Cheng-Tu
Road District Office, First Police Office,
Shanghai (49:184)

Kun-ming -- Editor-in-Chief, HSIN PEI CHING PAO,
Peiping (52:239)

Kung-lung -- Commander, pro-Japanese troops; with
Japanese Huang Hsieh Chun, North Shantung
(6/39; OSS-Ms.)

Li-fan -- Director, East Asia League, Hupeh Branch
(1943)

Lien-sheng -- Candidate Inspector, China Educational Reconstruction Association, Anhwei
Branch (1943)

Ling-fan -- Head, Detention Unit, Third Section,
Canton Bureau of Police (51:245)

Liong -- Director, Citizens Savings Movement Committee, Shanghai (49:184)

Lo -- Trustee, North China Aulminite Mining Industrial Company (1943) (52:239)

Lung-kuang -- Editor, HUA PAI TSO CHIA YUEH PAO,
a monthly, Peiping (1943) (52:239)

Mo-ch'ing -- Director, East Asia League, Shanghai
Branch (49:184)

Pai-hsu -- Commander, Second Army, Nanking Army
(IDC 3/30/42)

P'ei-hsu -- Vice-Chief, General Staff (1938);
member, National Military Council (1943)

Pen-ho -- Commander, pro-Japanese troops; with
Japanese Huang Hsieh Chun, Chuyeh, command-
ing 400 men, in Chuyeh, Tsining, 900 in
Yuncheng, 1,000 in Kuantao (6/39; OSS-Ms.)

P'ing -- Member, Publications Committee, China
Writers Club (1943)

Ping-san -- Manager, Chung Hua Chuan Kung Bank,
Shanghai (IDC 7270 1943)

Po -- Chief, Office of Grain Control, Nanking

Po-mai (Hei) -- Publisher, HSIN TIEN CHING PO,
Tientsin (52:239)

Shao-so -- Commander, 2nd Army (1942) (52:239)

Shih-chen -- Inspector, China Educational Reconstruction Association, Hankow Branch (1943)

172   -123-

CHINESE

Liu Shih-k'e -- Director, Sino-Japanese Cultural Association, Shanghai Branch (49:184); Inspector, China Writers Club (1943)

Shih-yuan -- Commissioner, Directorate-General of Education, North China Political Commission (7/40; OSS-Ms.); Trustee, North China Aluminite Mining Industrial Company (1943; 52:239)

Song -- Member, Huang Tao Hui; arrested September 1938 in connection with murders of Dr. Herman G. E. Liu and Tsai Tiao Tu (OSS-Ms.)

Shou-hua -- Propaganda Head, 5th District Party Headquarters, Kuomintang, Swatow (IDC)

Shu -- Head, Transportation, Bureau of Highways, Ministry of Communication, Executive Yuan (OSS)

Tieh-ch'eng -- Office holder, Chinese Representatives Association, Hongkong (51:245)

T'ien-hsiung -- Director, East Asia League, Hupeh Branch (1943)

Tsu-sheng, Maj. Gen. -- Commander, Third Army Corps, K'aip'ing, Hopeh, of the Peace Preservation Army, North China Political Commission (7/40; OSS-Ms.)

Tsu-wang -- Chief, Bureau of Political Affairs, Anhwei Province

Ts'un-hou -- Candidate Inspector, China Educational Reconstruction Association (1943)

Ts'un-p'u -- Chief, Office of Social Welfare, Hupeh Province (1943); member, Social Welfare Committee, China Office, East Asia League

Tzu-ch'eh -- Councillor, National Government, Nanking (1943)

Wan-hsuan -- Member, Directing Committee, China Office, East Asia League (1943)

Wan-pang -- Inspector, China Educational Reconstruction Association (1943)

Wei-chun -- Chief, Insurance Supervision Bureau, Executive Yuan, Nanking (OSS)

Yang-shan -- Director, Shanghai Education Committee; Adviser, Citizens Savings Movement Committee, Shanghai; Chief Executive and Secretary-General, East Asia League, Shanghai Branch; Honorary Director, Sino-Japanese Cultural Association, Shanghai Branch; Chairman, Nationalist Party, Shanghai Branch (49:184); member, Central Executive Committee, Nanking (1943); member, Committee of Political Councillors; Vice-Commander, Model Youth Corps

CHINESE

Liu Wen-kuang -- Commander, pro-Japanese troops; with
Japanese Huang Hsieh Chun, Yingshan and
Haochiatien, commanding 1,000 men (6/39;
OSS-Ms.)

Yeh-p'ing -- Publisher, HUAI NAN PAO, Tsao-hsien,
Anhwei (IDC 2562)

Yi-han -- Inspector, China Writers Club (1943)

Yu-fen -- Native, Wanhsien, Chihli; graduate,
Paoting Military Academy; joined revolutionary party in Yunnan; staff officer to Feng
Yu-hsiang (1914); successful retreat, Kuomin-
chun army of 100,000 from Nankow, due in large
part to his efforts; Chairman,(Kansu) Province (1927-30); Commander, 7th Route Army
(OSS-Ms.); member, Designated Committee,
Central Political Council (12/38); joined
Wang Ching-wei's party, Shanghai (1939;
OSS-Ms.); Chief of Staff, National Salvation and Peace Preservation Army; relieved
of office of Chief of Staff (4/7/43); Inspector, China Office, East Asia League;
deceased ??

Yu-feng -- See Ming Yu-shen, Gen.

Yu-sheng -- Manager Director, Shanghai Magazines
Association; Publisher, FENG YU T'AN, a
monthly; Director and Chief, Office of Planning, Sino-Japanese Cultural Association,
Shanghai Branch (49:185)

Yu-ts'ui -- Counsellor, National Government, Nanking
(1943)

Yun -- Inspector, China Office, East Asia League
(1943)

Yun-fang -- Publisher, CHI YEH CHOU KAN, a weekly,
Shanghai (49:185)

Lo Chai-sing -- Assistant Director, Eastern District
Bureau, Hongkong Government (51:245)

Chao-liang -- Publisher, TA KUANG PAO, Hongkong
(51:245)

Cheng -- Inspector, Citizens Savings Movement Committee, Shanghai (49:185)

Ch'iang -- Executive Director, East Asia League,
Shanghai Branch (49:185)

Chien-tung -- Police student sent to Formosa for
training; assigned now to various bureaus in
Tai-p'ing-ching and Hai T'ien-shou for additional training (51:245)

Chih-ch'eng -- Secretary, Paochia Office, 3rd Police
Office, Shanghai (49:185)

Chih-hsueh -- Supervisor, National Commercial Control
Association, Shanghai (1943)

CHINESE

Lo Chin-cheng -- Director, Huai Nan Salt Industry
        Stock Company, Shanghai (IDC 7262 1943)

Ching-kwang -- Representative, Central News Agency,
        Hongkong Branch (51:246)

Cho-liang -- Publisher, TA KUANG PAO, Hongkong
        (51:246)

Chu-chin -- Manager, Bank of Communications; Chairman,
        Hongkong Chinese Bankers Association for
        third time (8/29/44) (51:246)

Chung-ch'iang (Lo Chun-ch'iang) -- Chairman, Com-
        mission on Mongolian and Tibetan Affairs
        (1938); member, Wang Ching-wei's new Kuomin-
        tang, Shanghai (1939; OSS-Ms.); Border Com-
        missioner or Frontier Affairs Commissioner
        (1940; OSS-Ms.); Minister of Justice (1943);
        Vice-Secretary General, Nanking; Governor,
        Anhwei Province; member, Central Political
        Council; member, National Military Council;
        Director, Central Reserve Bank, Nanking;
        Director, Sino-Japanese Cultural Associa-
        tion; member, New Citizens Movement Com-
        mittee; member, Committee on Abolition of
        Extraterritoriality; Director, China Office,
        East Asia League; Honorary Chairman, Direc-
        tors, Chinese Educational Reconstruction
        Association

Cu-quo -- See Kuk-wo

Hsu-ho -- Chairman, Chinese Representatives Asso-
        ciation, Hongkong (51:246)

Ku-po -- See Lo Kuk-wo

Kuang-lin -- Chief, Central Hospital, Ministry of
        Interior, Nanking (1943)

Kuk-wo (same as Sir Robert Kotewall, Kt., C.M.G.,
        LLD.; Lo Cu-quo; Lo Ku-po) -- Former unof-
        ficial member, British Executive Council
        (OSS-Ms.); Chairman, Hongkong Central Relief
        Association (51:246); member, Chinese Repre-
        sentatives Association; member, Chinese
        Benevolent Association

Lei-wei -- Propaganda Head, Kuomintang Third District
        Party Headquarters, Canton (51:246)

, M.K. -- Member, Chinese Cooperative Council (1942-),
        Hongkong (51:246)

Na-tsai -- Member, Committee on Grain Control,
        Shanghai (49:185)

San -- Living Buddha, Shansi Province

Shun-ch'iang -- Minister, Ministry of Justice,
        Nanking (1943)

Wen-chao -- Honorary Director, Sino-Japanese Cultural
        Association, Shanghai Branch (49:185)

-126-

CHINESE

Lo Wen-chin -- Lawyer; member, Council, Chinese Representatives (Discursive) Association, Hongkong (51:246)

Yen-li -- Chief of the Treasurery, Shanghai (49:185)

Yi-chih -- Candidate Director, Sino-Japanese Cultural Association, Wu-ch'ang and Hankow Branch (1943)

Yu-hsiang -- Director, China Educational Reconstruction Association, Hankow Branch (1943)

Yu-lan -- Director, Citizens Savings Movement Committee, Shanghai (49:185)

Yun-chi -- Chief, Department of Public Health, Nanking (2/4/44)

Yun-sheng (Luo Yun-sheng) -- Acting Chief, Business Department, North China Political Commission; concurrently Counsellor, Directorate-General of the Interior (7/40; OSS-Ms.)

Yung-ku -- Commissioner, Office of Social Welfare, Kwangtung (51:246)

Loh Fuk-woh -- Chairman, Chinese Representatives Council, Hongkong (51:246)

Lou Tzu-chiao -- Chairman, Directors, Umbrella Making Association, Shanghai (IDC 7264 1943)

Lu -- Executive Inspector, East Asia League, Nanking Branch (1943)

Lu -- Police Chief, Sanshui (51:246)

Ai-yun -- Member, Hongkong Branch, South China Physical Culture Association; Director, Chien Tung firm; member, China Representatives (Discursive) Association (51:246)

Ch'ang-ming -- Director, China Educational Reconstruction Association, Hankow Branch (1943)

Chao-yuan -- Commander, 23rd Division, Nanking Army (IDC 3/30/42)

Chen -- Candidate Director, Shanghai Special Municipality Journalists Association (49:185)

Chi -- Advisory member, Ministry of Industries (1943)

Chi-tseng -- Director, Sino-Japanese Cultural Association, Shanghai Branch (49:185)

Chia-yun -- Commander, pro-Japanese troops; with Japanese Huang Hsieh Chun, Huaiyuan, commanding 1,000 men (6/39; OSS-Ms.)

Chien-chih (Lu Jun-chih; Lu Jun-chin) -- Director, Health Bureau, National Government; represented China, 3rd East Asia Medical Conference (3/27/44); ordered to Japan to inspect health conditions; returned from Japan (8/10/44)

176

-127-

CHINESE

Lu Chih-hsueh -- Head, Chemical Enterprise Trade Association, National Trade Control General Association, Shanghai; Inspector, National Trade Control General Association (49:185)

Ching-ju -- President, Lung Yin Iron Mine Corporation, Chang-Chia-Kow (IDC 6699 1943)

Chung-en -- Publisher, JEN SHENG, a monthly, Shanghai (49:185)

Feng -- Director, Shanghai Newspaper Association; Manager, Shanghai Magazines Association; Director, Shanghai Special Municipality Journalists Association; Chairman, Publication Committee, Shanghai Special Municipality Journalists Association; Secretary-General and Director, Citizens Savings Movement Committee, Shanghai; Director, Sino-Japanese Cultural Association, Shanghai Branch; Editor, HSIN CHUNG KUO WAN PAO (49:185); Editor and Publisher, CHENG CHIH YUEH PAO (political monthly)

Hao-jan -- Chairman, Directors, Iron Bucket Dealers Association, Shanghai (IDC 7264)

Hsi-p'u -- Editor, YANG CHOU HSIN PAO, Yang-chou, Kiangsu (IDC 2562)

Hsiao -- Executive Director and Assistant, Employment Service Committee, China Educational Reconstruction Association (1943)

Ji -- Director, Administrative Department, Police Force, Shanghai (49:185)

Jun-chih -- (See also Lu Chien-chih); Chief, Bureau of Sanitation, Ministry of Personnel Affairs, National Government (1944)

Jung-ch'ien -- Police Commissioner, Kiangsi Province (OSS)

Jung-huan -- Manchukuo Ambassador to Nanking (4/1/44)

Kao-yi -- Director, Citizens Savings Movement Committee, Shanghai (49:185)

Kuang-chieh -- Manager Director, Shanghai Special Municipality Journalists Association; Director, Shanghai Newspaper Association; Inspector, Citizens Savings Movement Committee, Shanghai; Chairman, Propaganda Committee, Citizens Savings Movement Committee, Shanghai; Editor, PING PAO (49:185)

Kung-liang -- See Kung Liang-lu

Kuo-ching -- Member, Social Welfare Committee, China Office, East Asia League (1943)

Meng-ch'u (-shu) -- Editor, TUNG YA WAN PAO and HUA CHIAO JIH PAO, Hongkong (51:246)

CHINESE

Lu Mun-hsi -- News Editor, HUA CHIAO JIH PAO, Hongkong
(51:246)

Pai-hua -- Publisher, TA SHANG HAI, a weekly,
Shanghai (49:186)

Shan-chih -- Chief Secretary, Nanking Municipality
(1943)

Shao-kuang -- Director, China Educational Reconstruction Association (1943)

Tan-ju -- Chairman, Directors, Floss Silk Association, Shanghai (IDC 7264)

Wen-shao -- Director, Shanghai Chamber of Commerce,
Shanghai (49:186)

Yao -- Chairman, Directors, Haui Nan Coal Mine Stock
Company, Shanghai (IDC 7262 1943)

Yi-fan -- Advisory member, Ministry of Social Welfare (1943)

Yi-jan -- Director, Social Welfare, Huaihai Province
(OSS)

Ying -- Appointed Chief, Second Police Bureau,
Shanghai (7/27/44); Chairman, Paochia Committee, Shanghai; Chief, 2nd Police Office;
Chief, 7th District (Nan-shih); member,
Committee, Investigation of Resources and
Materials; Advisor, Citizens Savings Movement Committee, Shanghai; Director, East
Asia League, Shanghai Branch (49:186); member, Social Committee, China Writers Club
(1943); member, National Military Council
(1943); Inspector, China Writers Club

Yun-chih -- Chief, Bureau of Public Health, Nanking
(7/43)

Yun-khwan -- See Lu Yung-huan

Yun-sheng -- Manager, Chung Mao Bank, Shanghai (IDC
7270 1943)

Yung-ch'ien -- Chief, Office of Police Affairs,
Kiangsi

Yung-ch'uan -- Chief, Office of Economics, Amoy
(49:186)

Yung-huan (Lu Yun-khwan; Lu Jung-huan) -- Manchukuo
Ambassador, Nanking; on order of Emperor of
Manchukuo, presented Order of Blue Jade to
President Wang Ching-wei

Lue Po -- Advisory member, Ministry of Justice (1943)

Lui -- Mayor, Peking

Lui Che -- Prosecutor, Supreme Court, Nanking (1943)

Ch'ien-an -- Chief, Keangsu, Chekiang and Anhwei
Salt Affairs, Ministry of Finance (1943)

CHINESE

Lui Feng-chang -- Judge, Supreme Court, North China Branch (1943)

Po-shen -- General Secretary, New Peoples Movement, Nanking

Wei-tsun -- Chief, First Office, National Economic Committee, Nanking (1943)

Yu-wen -- Member, Committee for Punishment of Central Officials, Nanking (1943)

Luk Tan-lam -- Officer, East Asia Cultural Association, Asiatic Affairs Bureau, Hongkong (51:246)

Luke Oi-wan -- Chairman, South China Athletic Association (51:246)

Lun Ching-hun (-hon), Lt. Gen. -- Deserted Chungking Junta and joined National Government, Nanking; member, Military Committee (7/9/43)

Hsueh-p'u -- Inspector, Social Welfare Committee, East Asia League, Canton Branch (51:246)

Sho-lien -- Secretary, Protestant Council, Amoy (49:186)

Lung Hsiung -- Executive member, Flour Special Committee, National Trade Control General Association, Shanghai (49:186)

Min-hsun -- Member, New Citizens Movement Promotion Committee (1943)

Mu-hsun -- Member, Legislative Yuan, Nanking (1943)

Ping-hsun, Gen. -- Surrendered to Central Government; appointed Head, Pacification Headquarters, Kaifeng (9/15/44)

Shen -- Secretary General, Executive Bureau, GEA Conference (0-58)

Tai-hsung, Rear Admiral -- Commander-in-Chief, Hankow Naval Base (6/10/43) (49:186)

Tien-shi -- Representative of Chinese Merchants, Hongkong; collected money for Memorial Tower (51:246)

Luo Yun-sheng -- See Lo Yun-sheng

Ma -- Chairman, Chengchow Chamber of Commerce (8/3/44)

Chi-liang -- Chairman, Directors, Wood Dealers, Shanghai (IDC 7264 1943)

Chi-ts'ai -- Chief, Bureau of Construction, Anhwei Province (1943); Executive Director, China Educational Reconstruction Association, Anhwei Branch

Chih-hsiang -- Head, Ching-chi News Company, Communications Company, North China (52:239)

-130-

CHINESE

Ma Chin-jen -- Director, Sino-Japanese Cultural Association, Shanghai Branch; Inspector, China Educational Reconstruction Association, Shanghai Branch (49:186)

Ching-ch'ih -- Counsellor, National Government, Nanking (1943)

Fu-liang -- Outstanding Moslem leader in China; member, Chinese Moslem Mission to India, headed by Ai Sha (1938; OSS-Ms.)

Hsiao-t'ien -- Director, Political Police Bureau under Minister of Police Administration, Wang Ching-wei's regime (3/41; OSS-Ms.); member, National Military Council (1943); Vice-Commander, Gendarmerie, Nanking; Director, China Office, East Asia League, Nanking Branch

Hung-chi -- Assistant Chairman, China Educational Reconstruction Association, Anhwei Branch (1943)

I-teh -- Chief Procurator, North China Branch, Supreme Court, North China Political Commission (7/40; OSS-Ms.)

Kiam -- Vice-Chairman, East Asia Cultural Association, Asiatic Affairs Bureau, Hongkong (51:247)

Kung-yu -- Director, Sino-Japanese Cultural Association, Shanghai Branch (49:186)

Liang -- Native, Hopeh; Mohammedan; formerly, Officer, Peiyang Army (Who's Who in China, 1940); member, North China Political Commission; delegate, North China Political Council (52:239)

Lu-sun -- Manager, Su Min Bank, Soochow (IDC 7270 1943)

Mi-chih -- Publisher, T'AI P'ING YUEH K'AN SHA, a monthly, Shanghai (49:186)

Ping-nan -- Executive Inspector, China Educational Reconstruction Association, Shanghai Branch (49:186)

Tien-ju -- Member, Executive Committee, Nanking (OSS)

Wu -- Member, Publication Committee, China Writers Club (1943)

Ya-ting -- Inspector, China Educational Reconstruction Association, Hankow Branch (1943)

Yin-liang -- Director, Shanghai Newspaper Association (49:186); Editor, SHEN PAO

Ying -- Representative, Rice Importers Association, Hongkong (51:247)

Yu-po -- Head, Census Unit, Second Section, Canton Bureau of Police (51:247)

CHINESE

Ma Yun-t'eng -- Mayor, Anking (OSS)

Mai Cheng-ming -- Director, Manufactured Goods Inspection Office, Shanghai (OSS)

    Hsun -- Head, Personnel Unit, Canton Bureau of Police (First Section) (51:247)

    T'ao-ch'u -- Chief, Business Office, Shanghai Cotton Industry Management Bureau (OSS)

    Tzo-p'ing -- See Mei Ssu-p'ing

Mao Ching-fan -- Magistrate, Shang-yu Hsien, Chekiang (OSS)

    Hung-pin -- Commissioner, Directorate-General of Finance, North China Political Commission (7/40; OSS-Ms.)

    Sung-liang -- Counsellor, Directorate-General of Education, North China Political Council (7/40; OSS-Ms.)

    Tzu-ming -- Chief, Office of Social Welfare, Kiangsu Province (49:186)

Mei Ase-p'ing -- Minister of Interior, National Government, Nanking (1943); member, National Economic Committee; member, Committee on Astronomy and Meteorology; Chairman, Committee on Preservation of Cultural Objects

    Che-chih -- Director, Central Reserve Bank and Agricultural and Commercial Bank, Nanking (1943); Inspector, China Office, East Asia League

    Ch'ing-fen -- Executive Inspector, Social Welfare Committee, East Asia League, Canton Branch (51:247)

    En-ping -- Minister of Interior, Central Government; decorated by Japanese Emperor (3/23/44)

    Ho-chang -- Member, Committee for Punishment of Central Officials, Nanking (1943)

    Lan-feng (-fang) -- Honorary Director, Sino-Japanese Cultural Association, Shanghai Branch (49:186); famous actor and female impersonator

    Shou-fen -- Chief, Military Doctors, Ministry of the Army, Nanking (1943)

    Ssu-p'ing (Mei Tso-p'ing; Mai Tzo-p'ing; Mei Sze-p'ing; Mei Szu-p'ing) -- Minister, Commerce and Industry, Nanking (12/38-7/13/43); member, Designated Committee, Central Political Council, Nanking (12/38); in Shanghai with Wang Ching-wei; in charge of pro-Japanese organization, "Anti-Communist National Salvation League"; worked with Chen Kung-po and Chu Min-yi for establishment of new central government under Wang Ching-wei (5/27/39; OSS-Ms.); Minister, Industry and Commerce, National Government, Nanking (3/22/40); ap-

-132-

CHINESE

Mei Ssu-p'ing (Con't) -- pointed concurrently member, Commission for Control of Enemy Property (2/9/43; OSS-Ms.); elected Chairman, Local Cooperative Association (10/19/43); decorated by Japanese Emperor (3/23/44); Minister, Interior; Chairman, National Price Policy Committee; member, Central Political Committee; Honorary Director, Sino-Japanese Cultural Association; member, Executive Committee, All-China Economic Committee; Chairman, Directing Committee, China Office, East Asia League; Executive Director, New Citizens Movement Promotion Committee; Executive Director, China Office, East Asia League

Sze-p'ing -- See Mei Ssu-p'ing

Szu-p'ing -- See Mei Ssu-p'ing

Tso-p'ing -- See Mei Ssu-p'ing

Men Chih-chung -- Member, National Military Council (OSS)

Meng Ch'i -- Director, China Writers Club (1943)

Chih-wo -- Publisher, CHANG SHU JIH PAO, Ch'ang-shu, Kiangsu (IDC 2562)

Hsiu-chuang, Rear Admiral -- Chief, Naval Office, Hankow (1943)

Hsuan -- Chief of Abolishing Extraterritoriality, Nanking; in Consular Office, Shenyang (3/10/43)

Ti-chi -- Director, East Asia League, Hupeh Branch (1943)

Miao Chia-nan -- Political Advisor, National Government, Nanking (1943); Chief, Central Agricultural Experimental Station, Ministry of Grains

Pin (Ping) -- Born, 1899, Wusih,Kiangsu; graduate, Nanyang University, Shanghai; radio instructor, Whampoa Military Academy (1924); joined Peiping Provisional Government (1938); Director, Hsin Min Hui (1939) (Who' Who in China, 1940); reported to have been granted $1,000,000 by North China Japanese Special Service Section to promote anti-Wang Ching-wei movement (4/40; OSS-Ms.); member, Central Executive Committee (1943); member, Central Political Council; Vice-President, Legislative Yuan, Nanking; Ex-Vice-President, Examination Yuan; member, National Military Council; Honorary Director, Sino-Japanese Cultural Association; Chairman, Culture Committee, China Office, East Asia League; member, Committee for Application of Constitution

P'u-sun -- Director, Sino-Japanese Cultural Association, Shanghai Branch (49:186)

Min Chung-hui -- Manager, Hui Tung, Nan Tung, Kiangsu (IDC 7270 1943)

-133-

CHINESE

Min Hsing-yung -- Director, China-Japan Returned Students Club (1943)

Kan -- Executive Director, China Writers Club (1943)

To-bi -- Selected to matriculate in Japanese University; from Hongkong (51:247)

Ming Hsin -- Chief, Kiangsu Propaganda Office, Ministry of Information (1943)

Kan -- Member, Propaganda Committee, China Branch, East Asia League (1943); member, Social Committee, China Writers Club; Chairman, China Movie Association, Kiangsu Office

Nan-ch'un -- Chairman, Planning Committee, Citizens Savings Movement Committee, Shanghai (49:186)

Yu-shen (Liu Yu-feng), Gen. -- Chief, General Staff, Nanking Government (2/19/43)

Miu Ch'iu-sheng -- Director, Citizens Savings Movement Committee, Shanghai (49:186)

Pin -- Member, Invited Committee, Central Political Council (12/38)

Mo Kuo-k'ang -- Director, East Asia League, Shanghai Branch (49:186); member, Legislative Yuan; Executive Director and Chairman, Mandarin Propagation Committee, China Educational Reconstruction Association (1943)

Kuo-ying -- Assistant, Mandarin Propagation Committee, China Educational Reconstruction Association (1943)

Yi -- Director, Social Welfare Committee, East Asia League, Canton Branch (51:247)

Moy, Herbert Erasmus -- Chinese-American radio announcer, Shanghai (OSS)

Mu Chen-tung -- Head, Chong-chih News Company, North China (52:239)

Myo Ton-mei -- President, Malay-Shonan Chinese Merchants Association (8/42) (DIO)

Nai Chien -- Councillor, North China Political Council; witness of revised by-laws of National Government by North China Political Council (10/8/43) (52:239)

Nan Hai -- Magistrate, Li Tao-ch'un Hsien; under control of Government of Kwangtung (51:247)

Nao Li -- Japanese Ambassador to Bucharest; made China inspection tour

Ni -- Civil Magistrate, Sanshui (51:247)

Hung-weh -- Executive Director, China Educational Reconstruction Association, Anhwei Branch (1943)

-134-

CHINESE

Ni Po-tsai -- Chairman, Directors, Firewood and Charcoal Dealers Association, Shanghai (IDC)

Shou-fu -- Manager, Chang Chun I Fa Bank, Shanghai Agency (IDC)

Tao-hen -- Head, Huai Nan Coal Mine Corporation, Shanghai (49:186)

Tao-lang (Ni Tao-liang) -- Born, 1880, Fuyang, Anhwei; after 1925 lived in retirement in Tientsin where he became associated with the Special Service Section of the Japanese Army; joined Japanese (1938); Governor, Anhwei under jurisdiction of the Nanking Reformed Government (Who's Who in China, 1940); State Councillor, Nanking (1943); Inspector, China Office, East Asia League

Tao-liang -- See Ni Tao-lang

Tieh-sun -- Editor, CHUNG PAO, Nanking (IDC 2562)

Yuan -- Executive Director, East Asia League, Hupeh Branch (1943)

Nieh Lu-sheng -- Head, Cotton Products Trade Association, National Trade Control General Association, Shanghai (49:186); Chief, Cotton Goods Purchase Office, Cotton Control Association

Niki Teki-cho (Japanized reading) -- Chief Administrative Officer, Hsin Min Society (1943); Vice-President, Hsin Min Society (1943); taught National Central China University

Ning Li -- Member, Sugar Enterprise Special Committee, National Trade Control General Association, Shanghai (49:187)

Niu Chih-tzu -- Director, Shanghai Chamber of Commerce (49:187)

Hsun-ch'eng -- Member, Shanghai Newspaper Association (49:187)

Nu Chih-tzu -- Chairman, Directors, Silk and Satin Stores, Shanghai (IDC 7264)

O Ka-ho -- Executive Secretary, Federal Reserve Bank (3/27/43)

Koku-min -- Chairman, North China Political Council (7/4/43); formerly went to France; Former Chairman, Domestic Affairs; Former Chairman, Civil Administration Committee (52:239)

Mai-chih -- Central Electrical Communications Corporation, Canton Branch (51:247)

Mei-toku -- Official, Japan-China Christian Federation, Nanking; visited Japan at invitation of Yasuo Oki (7/14/43)

CHINESE

O Ta-ch'ing -- Head, Lei-tien Communication Company, North China (52:239)

Wang-ishi -- Living Buddha, Shansi Province

Ou Chi-fu -- Candidate Inspector, China Educational Reconstruction Association (1943)

Lin -- Head, General Affairs Unit, Canton Bureau of Police (First Section) (51:247)

Sun-hsi -- Head, Protective Unit, Second Section, Canton Bureau of Police (51:247)

Ta-ching -- In command, National Peoples Army, Canton (51:247)

Tao-kung -- Head, Department of Commerce, Kwangtung Province (51:247)

Yang -- Deputy Commissioner, Economic Council, Canton; Executive member, Commodity Investigation Committee (51:247)

Pa Na-to -- Head, Chen Tan Musieums, Shanghai (IDC 7265)

Pai Ching-chang -- President, Chinese Association in Burma (7/5/43)

Ch'ing-yun -- Candidate Executive member, China Journalists Association (1943)

Kung-chen -- Commanding Officer, Anti-Air Defense, Canton (51:247)

Kung-huan -- Commanding Officer, Air Defense, Canton (51:247)

Pen -- Member, Education Committee, Shanghai Municipal Council (49:187)

Pan -- President, Information Board, North China Political Affairs Commission (8/10/44) (52:239)

, Dr. C. -- Former Secretary General, Chinese Red Cross; figures in controversy between medical services in China (6/9/43; OSS-Ms.)

, C.C., Maj-Gen. -- Police Commissioner (OSS-Ms.)

Ch'ao-chun -- Manager Director, Post Office Labor Union, Shanghai; Manager Director, Readjustment Committee, National Post Office Union (49:187)

Ch'en-kung -- Director, China Educational Reconstruction Association, Shanghai Branch (49:187)

Ch'i-hsuan -- Secretary, Ministry of Personnel, Nanking (1943)

Chi-mei -- Manager, China Chih Yeh Bank, Shanghai (IDC 7270 1943)

-136-

CHINESE

Pan Chi-yen -- Manager, Ta Yuan Commercial and Savings
Bank, Shanghai (IDC 7270 1943)

Chih-wen -- Director, Citizens Savings Movement
Committee, Shanghai (49:187)

Feng-t'ang -- Candidate Inspector, China Educational Reconstruction Association, Anhwei
Branch (1943)

Fu-hsiang -- Graduate, School of Education, Chungshan
University; once teacher, various Middle
Schools, Canton; Head, Social Affairs Sec-
tion, Kuomintang Headquarters, Kwangtung
Province; Training Head, Kuomintang, Fifth
District, Party Headquarters, Canton; Deputy
Head, Social Affairs Committee, Kwangtung
Province

Hao-fen -- Member, Committee for Punishment of Central Officials, Nanking (1943)

Heng -- Secretary, Ministry of Industries, Nanking
(1943)

Hsu-sheng -- Director, Shanghai Chamber of Commerce
(49:187); Chairman, Directors, Moth Factories

Hsu-tsu -- Director, Sino-Japanese Cultural Association, Shanghai Branch (49:187)

Kan-cheng -- Commander, 28th Division, Nanking
Army (IDC 3/30/42)

Kuei-yi -- Director, Sino-Japanese Cultural Association, Shanghai Branch; Executive Director, China Educational Reconstruction Association, Shanghai Branch (49:187)

Kuo-chun -- Advisory member, Ministry of Social Welfare (1943)

Kuo-tsun -- Director, China Educational Reconstruction Association (1943)

O-nien -- Secretary, Ministry of Interior (1943);
Chief, Rites and Customs

Pei-wei -- Advisor, Party Affairs, Kuomintang Headquarters, Kwangtung Province; formerly worked
for Ministry of Railroads, Nanking, for Department of Civil Affairs, Kwangtung Government; graduate, Political Training School

Ping-hsun -- (52:239); See P'ang Ping-hsun, Gen.

, S. H. -- Member, Racing Committee, Hongkong
Jockey Club (51:248)

San-sheng -- Publicher, CHING CHI TAO PAO, a monthly,
Shanghai (49:187)

Shan-wen -- Manager, Chung Fu Bank, Peiping Branch
(52:240)

CHINESE

Pan Shen-cho -- Special Delegate, Ministry of Foreign
       Affairs, Kiangsu (1943)

Shou-heng -- Chief, Peoples Directive, Ministry of
       Social Welfare (1943); Assistant Chairman,
       China Educational Reconstruction Associa-
       tion, Anhwei Branch

Shou-peng -- Director, Hua Hsing Commercial Bank,
       Soochow and Wu Hsi Branches, Kiangsu (IDC)

Sung-hsien -- Member, Flour Special Committee,
       National Trade Control General Association,
       Shanghai (49:187)

Tzu-chi -- Manager, Wu Hsien Tien Yeh Bank, Soochow
       (IDC 1943)

Tzu-chun -- Director, Opium Suppression, Husihai
       Province (OSS)

Yang-yao -- Member, Education Committee, Citizens
       Welfare Association, Shanghai; Publisher,
       CHUNG KUO KUNG YEH, a monthly, Shanghai
       (49:187)

Yi-shan, Maj. Gen. -- Military Advisor, National
       Government, Nanking (1943)

Yu-hsien -- Magistrate, Ch'en Kung-yi Hsien; under
       control of Government of Kwangtung (51:248)

Yu-kuei (P'an Yu-kwei) -- Born, 1884, Yenshan,
       Hopeh; graduate, Waseda Law College, Tokyo;
       chu-jen (M.A.), Ching dynasty; appointed mem-
       ber, Hopeh-Chahar Political Council (1936);
       joined Japanese after fall of Peiping (8/37);
       Police Commissioner, Peiping (7/37); Mayor,
       Tientsin (1938-39); member, North China
       Political Commission since its establish-
       ment (3/40) (Who's Who in China 1940; OSS-
       Ms.)

Yu-kwei -- See Pan Yu-kuei

P'ang Hung-sheng -- Executive Director, China Education-
       al Reconstruction Association, Shanghai
       Branch (49:187)

Li-min -- Director, Hsin Min Youth Corps, North
       China (1944) (52:240)

Ping-chen -- Manager, Hsien Commercial Bank,
       Shanghai (IDC 1943)

Ping-hsun, Gen. (Pang Ping-sing; Pan Ping-hsun;
       Pang Ping-hsuin) -- Native, Honan; Commander,
       40th A. C.; loyal to Chiang; Honan (Controls
       39th Division and 5th Division); Chairman,
       Hopeh during Japanese occupation; concurrently
       Commander, 24th Group Army, Hopeh Chahar
       Special War Zone and controls N5A (N3-D,
       N4-D) and the 40A (106D)(12/19/41); Said to
       have been captured by Japanese (5/19/43);
       (OSS-Ms.); pledged allegiance to "Peace Camp"
       (7/10/43); member, National Military Council;
       Commander-in-Chief, 5th District Army (1944)

CHINESE

Pao An -- Magistrate, Liu Huan Hsien; under control of
Government of Kwangtung (51:248)

Chang -- Former Superintendent of Education; Honorary Vice-President, GEA Culture Deliberation Association, Peiping (11/27/43) (52:240)

Cheng-te -- Manager, Chiang Hai Bank, Shanghai (IDC
7270 1943)

Chi-chen -- Inspector, China Educational Reconstruction Association, Anhwei Branch (1943)

Chien-ching -- See Pao Teng-ching

Hai-ming -- Commander, pro-Japanese troops; with
Japanese Huang Hsieh Chun, Ching Shuiho,
commanding 900 men (6/39; OSS-Ms.)

Kuei-sheng -- Commander, pro-Japanese troops; with
Japanese Huang Hsieh Chun commanding 900 men
in area of Tashuwan (6/39; OSS-Ms.)

Pai-ping -- Chief Superintendent, Canton Bureau of
Police (51:248)

Teng-ching (Pao Chien-ching), Dr. -- Dean, Medical
College, Peiping University; Vice-Chairman,
Southeast Asia Medical Conference (4/12/44);
delegate from North China to GEA Medical
Conference (4/20/44) (52:240)

Tsun-hua -- Inspector, China Educational Reconstruction Association, Anhwei Branch (1943)

Wen-ting, Gen. -- Chief-of-Staff, Military Affairs
Council; decorated by Japanese Emperor
(3/23/44)

Wen-yueh, Gen. -- Born, Mukden; graduate, Tokyo
Military Officers College; infantry officer;
member, Peiping Branch, Military Council;
Lt. Gen.; formerly, Chief-of-Staff to Chang
Hsueh-liang (4/35); Acting War-Minister,
Wang Ching-wei's government (3/22/40);
Minister, Military Administration, Wang
Ching-wei's regime; also Political Vice-
Minister, Ministry of Military Administra-
tion (3/31/41)(OSS-Ms.); member, Central
Political Council, Nanking (1943); War Min-
ister, retired (4/43); Chief-of-Staff, Gen-
eral Military Affairs Committee, Central
China (started 4/43); Director, China Office,
East Asia League; decorated by Japanese
Emperor (3/23/44)

Yen-yu -- See Pao Wen-yueh

Yen-yuan -- See Pao Wen-yueh

Yi-wei -- Candidate Director, China Educational
Reconstruction Association, Shanghai Branch
(49:187)

Yung-shun -- Assistant Chief of Police, Hung-k'ou
District Office, First Police Office, Shanghai
(49:187)

CHINESE

Pau Yi, Admiral -- Commander, Nanking Navy, Wei Hai Wei

Pei -- Captain, 31st Company, North China Peace Preservation Corps, Weihsien (8/8/44) (52:240)

 Chih-chui -- Auditor and Chief, Keangsu Office, Ministry of Auditing (1943)

 Chung-hsi -- Vice Chief-of-Staff (DIO)

 Fu-heng -- Member, Central Executive Committee, Nanking; member, All-China Economic Committee; Principal, Commercial School, Shanghai (OSS)

P'eng Cheng-kuang -- Director, Shanghai Special Municipal Journalists Association (49:187)

 Chi-hua -- Commander, Second Brigade, Independent Nanking Army (IDC 3/30/42)

 Chih-te -- Civil Magistrate, Pao-an Hsien; named Deputy Commissioner of Political Works Corps for Village Pacification; Deputy Director, Training School for Pacification, Kwangtung Province (51:248)

 Hien -- Administrative Vice-Minister under Minister of Social Affairs, Wang Ching-wei's regime (3/41; OSS-Ms.)

 Hsi-min (-ming) -- Director, East Asia League, Shanghai Branch (49:187); Chief Secretary, Legislative Yuan

 Kuo-lien -- Training Head, Kuomintang Ninth District Party Headquarters, Canton (51:248)

 Nien -- Chairman, Social Affairs Committee, Central Kuomintang Headquarters, Nanking (1943); member, Committee of Political Councillors; Director, Social Welfare Committee, China Office, East Asia League; Honorary member, China Journalists Association

 Sheng-t'ien -- Chief, City Construction, Ministry of Construction, Nanking (1943)

 Szu-chien -- Director, Citizens Savings Movement Committee, Shanghai (49:187)

 Te-sheng -- Director, Shanghai Wharf Labor Union (49:187)

 Tung-yuan -- Inspector, Control Yuan, Nanking (1943)

 Yi-ming -- Secretary General, Legislative Yuan, Nanking (OSS)

 Yun-p'eng -- Secretary, Paochia Office, 1st Police Office, Shanghai (49:188)

P'i Ch'i-hao -- Director, East Asia League, Hupeh Branch (1943)

 Shu-chih -- Mayor, Hsuchow, Huaihai Province (OSS)

CHINESE

P'i Tse-yu -- Member, National Military Council (OSS)

Yang-chen -- Candidate Director, China Educational
Reconstruction Association, Anhwei Branch
(1943)

Pien Chin-piao -- Director, Shanghai Wharf Labor Union
(49:188)

Ho-chih -- Editor, WU CHIN JIH PAO, Ch'ang-chou,
Kiangsu (IDC 2562)

Hsiao-ching -- Member, Flour Special Committee,
National Trade Control General Association,
Shanghai (49:188)

Yu-fen -- Judge, Supreme Court, Nanking (1943)

Pih, C. C. -- Member, Racing Committee, Hongkong
Jockey Club (51:248)

P'ing Ching-ya (Chun-ya) -- Director, Shanghai Magazines
Association; Director, Sino-Japanese Cul-
tural Association, Shanghai Branch; Publisher,
WAN HSIANG, a monthly (49:188)

Po Hsiao-lah -- Chairman, Directors, Shanghai Wharf
Labor Union (49:188)

Lo -- Magistrate, Li Kuang-jung Hsien; under control
of Government of Kwangtung (51:248)

Poon Shunt-um -- Member, Executive Committee, Bankers
Association, Hongkong (51:248)

Pu Li-fu -- Chief, 4th District, Hu-hsi (West Shanghai)
(49:188)

Liang-chih -- Counsellor, Directorate-General of
Finance, North China Political Commission
(7/40; OSS-Ms.)

T'ing -- Member, Central Supervisory Committee,
Nanking (1943); State Councillor; Director,
Sino-Japanese Cultural Association; Inspec-
tor, China Branch, East Asia League

Wang -- Commander, 31st Regiment of 11th Division;
committed suicide (5/4/44)

Yu -- Chief, Office of Economics, Chekiang Province
(49:188); Member, Directing Committee, China
Office, East Asia League (1943); Head,
Supervisors, Chinghsiang Administration,
Hangchow Sector; China Educational Recon-
struction Association, Executive Director, and
Chairman, Employment Service Committee

Ren, S. D. -- Heavy loser in Wah Chang Company; now in
Universal Trading Company (7/15/44) (49:189)

Ri Choo-koo -- Commander, Headquarters, 1st Corps,
Military Council, Nanking Government; became
Vice-President, Military Council (12/22/43)

CHINESE

Ri Set-su (Setsu-fi) -- Governor, Chekiang-Kiangsi
Province; appointed Commissioner, Hangchow
(3/16/43)

Rin Do -- Vice-President, Hsin Min Society; Supervisor,
Central Supervisory Department, new Hsin
Min Youth Corps (12/4/42)

Rit Su-bun -- See also Ri Set-su; Governor, Kiangsu
Province; appointed Commissioner, Suchow
(3/16/43)

Roo Taiku-ai -- Learned man of North China whose works
will be published by North China Research
Institute (1944) (52:240)

Ryo Ko-shi -- Chairman, Board of Directors, Kako Commercial Bank, Shanghai (49:187)

Ryu Ippun (Japanized version) -- Chief, Military Council Staff (1943); member, Supreme National
Defense Council

Sa Fu-chou -- Believed to be son of Admiral Dah Chen-ping;
Commandant, Canton Naval Base under Japanese
(1941); appointed, Vice-Minister, Nanking
Navy Department, Wang Ching-wei's govern-
ment, replacing Chao Kwei-chang (9/28/42;
OSS-Ms.)

Hai-ro -- Manager, later Director, Central Bank of
China, Nanking (5/11/44)

Sai Hai -- Former Special Mayor, Nanking (8/31/42)

San Liang-cheng, Gen. -- Commander-in-Chief, 2nd Region;
member, Chinese Military Mission to Japan
(5/21/43)

Lu-chien -- Ex-Communist Guerrilla, operating in
Shantung Province; surrendered (8/3/43)

Shui-hsien -- Magistrate, Chu Yu-chun Hsien; under
control of Government of Kwangtung (51:248)

Sen Shi-sai, Col. -- Chief, Ordnance Department, new
5th Army; surrendered (4/26/43)

Tao-seng -- President, National Peiping University;
member, Art and Literature Council, Educational Ministry (11/12/42) (52:240)

To-ken -- Leader in establishment of organization
of literary men in China (3/31/44)

Setsu Ri -- See Ri Set-su

Shan Pu-shon, Madame -- Delegate, Central Executive
Committee, to open Lin Sing Middle School,
Canton University, Canton (51:248)

Rin -- Inspector, Shanghai Wharf Labor Union (49:189)

Swei-ming -- Ex-War Lord, Chungking General; now
with Nanking Government; younger brother of
Chang Hwei-yung; member, Military Committee,
Nanking (7/9/43)

CHINESE

Shao Ch'eng-p'o -- Chief, Personnel Cultivation, Ministry of Personnel, Nanking (1943)

Chih-feng -- Member, Shanghai Newspaper Association (49:189); Editor, PING PAO

Chih-kao -- Manager, Chungking Bank, Shanghai Branch (IDC 7270 1943)

Chou-wu -- Commander, 85th Army (5/4/44) (DIO)

En-k'ai -- (52:240); See Shao Wen-k'ai

Hsi-hien -- Chief, Office of Grains, Chekiang (49:189); Director, Charities and Affairs Promotion Office, Ministry of Social Welfare, Executive Yuan, Nanking (1943)

Meng-kang-- Manager, Tai Tsang Bank, Tai Tsang, Kiangsu (IDC)

Ming-chi -- Executive Director, and Assistant, Publication Section, China Educational Reconstruction Association (1943)

Shih-chun -- Publisher, CHUNG KUO SHANG PAO, Shanghai (49:189); Director, Central Reserve Bank, Nanking (IDC 7270 1943); Director of Taxation; Director, Customs Administration, Ministry of Finance, Executive Yuan (IDC 2562)

Tung-hu -- Director, North China Electrical Industry Company, Peiping (52:240)

Tzu-min -- Chairman, Directors, Flat Type Printing Association, Shanghai (IDC)

Wei-ming -- Control Officer, Shang Huan Ward, Hongkong (51:249)

Wen-k'ai, Lt. Gen. (Shao En-k'ai) -- Born, 1890, Liaoyang, Manchuria; graduate, Army Officers College (1919); Chief-of-Staff, Manchurian Army under Chang Hsueh-liang (1927); Commander, Peiping Gendarmes; held this post to end of (7/37); Chief, Gendarmerie, under new Japanese sponsored Peace Maintenance Association; Gendarmerie General under North China Political Commission (7/40) (OSS-Ms.); Commander, Gendarmerie and concurrently Commander, Gendarmes School of Honan Province (1944); Acting Governor, Honan, during T'ien Wen-ping's illness (5/29/44); Governor, Honan (6/44)

Yu-lin -- Interested in liberating Formosa; wrote for Formosan Revolutionary Alliance (IDC)

Quei-chang, Admiral (Kuan Se-chow) -- Nanking Naval Station (3/29/42)

Ch'ang-yin -- Member, Shanghai Newspaper Association (49:189); Editor, CHUNG HUA JIH PAO (IDC 7266 1943)

CHINESE

Shen Ch'ao -- Candidate Director, Shanghai Education Committee (49:189)

Ch'en-kang -- Member, National Military Council; Commander, Gendarmerie, Nanking; Director, China-Japan Returned Students Club (OSS)

Ch'i -- Director, China-Japan Returned Students Club (1943)

Ch'i-ch'ang -- Political Vice-Minister, Ministry of Audit, Wang Ching-wei's regime (3/31/41; OSS-Ms.); Inspecting member, Control Yuan, Nanking (1944)

Chieh-k'ang -- Inspector, East Asia League, Hupeh Branch (1943)

Chih-ch'en -- Commissioner, Directorate-General of Finance, North China Political Commission (7/40; OSS-Ms.)

Chin-chou -- Chairman, Directors, Briquettes Association, Shanghai (IDC 7264)

Chin-li -- Director, China Educational Reconstruction Association, Anhwei Branch (1943)

Ching-an -- Member, Social Welfare Committee, China Office, East Asia League (1943)

Chu-ch'en -- Director, East Asia League, Nanking Branch (1943)

Erh-ch'iao -- Minister, Ministry of Personnel, Executive Yuan (1943); Minister, Civil Service (8/43); Senior Administrative Official, East Chekiang Province; Director, China Office, East Asia League; Executive Inspector, China Educational Reconstruction Association (49:189)

Fan-szu -- Manager, Chekiang Hsing Yeh Bank, Peking Branch (52:240)

Fu-cheng -- Propaganda Head, Kuomintang Ninth District Party Headquarters, Canton (51:249)

Hsin-min -- Publisher, HSIN TANG SHAN PAO, Tongshan, North China (IDC 2562)

Hsin-wu -- Counsellor, National Government, Nanking (1943)

Hua-chen -- Chairman, Directors, Silk Factories, Shanghai (IDC 1943)

Huang-chuan -- Chairman, Directors, Inner-tube stores, Shanghai (IDC 1943)

Hung-lai, Admiral -- Minister, Agriculture and Forestry

Jen -- Candidate Executive member, China Journalists Association (1943); member, Social Committee, China Writers Club

-144-

CHINESE

Shen Ju-chang -- Editor, ANHWEI JIH PAO, Peng-pu, Anhwei (IDC 2562)

Lai-chou -- Chairman, Directors, Wool Yarn Stores, Shanghai (IDC 1943)

Lan-sheng -- Candidate Director, Shanghai Special Municipal Journalists Association (49:189)

Li -- Executive Inspector, China Educational Reconstruction Association (1943)

Liang-chao -- Chairman, Investigation Committee on Resources and Material Control, Shanghai Office (49:189)

Ling-ch'ing -- Member, Committee on Grain Control, Shanghai (49:189)

Liu-tsun -- Director, Shanghai Chamber of Commerce (49:189)

Nau-sheng -- Manager, Kuang Chung Commercial Bank, Shanghai (IDC 7270 1943)

Neng-yi -- See Sheng Neng-yi

Pa -- Chief, Ordinary Education, Ministry of Education, Nanking (1943); member, Committee on Culture, China Office, East Asia League; Secretary General, China Educational Reconstruction Association

Pa-o -- Member, Shanghai Newspaper Association (49:189)

Pan-mei -- Councillor, Chinghsiang Administration, Hangchou Sector; also (49:189)

Pi-ta -- Judge, Supreme Court, Nanking (1943)

Shi-liang -- Member, Education Committee, member, Peace and Order Committee, Municipal Council, Shanghai (49:189)

Sui-yang -- Vice-Chairman, Directors, Central China Mining Stock Company, Shanghai (1943)

Szu-liang (Sse-liang) -- Member, New Citizens Movement Promotion Committee (1943); also (49:189; 52:240)

Szu-pu -- Head, Shanghai Confucian Institute (IDC 7265 1943)

Te-chi -- Training Officer, Government Personnel, Ministry of Interior, Nanking (1943)

T'ing-shan -- Central Executive Committee member, Nanking (OSS)

Ts'ai-hsia -- Executive Director, China Educational Reconstruction Association, Anhwei Branch (1943)

T'ung -- Chief, Office of Economics, Kiangsu (49:189)

CHINESE

Shen Tzu-liang -- Executive Director, China Educational Reconstruction Association, Anhwei Branch (1943)

Wei-t'ing -- Managing Suprevisor, Shanghai Chamber of Commerce (49:189); Chairman, Directors, Cigarettes, Matches, Soaps and Candles Association, Tobacco Factories, Shanghai (IDC 7264)

Wei-ya -- Director, Shanghai Chamber of Commerce, (49:189)

Wen-hua -- Chief Manager, Committee for Application of Constitution (1943)

Ya-pin -- Inspector, Shanghai Education Committee (49:189)

Sheng An-sun -- Manager, Shanghai Coal Industry Bank (IDC 7270 1943)

Chang-tsao -- Executive Director, China Educational Reconstruction Association, Anhwei Branch (1943)

En-i -- Director, Central China Water and Electric Stock Company, Shanghai (1943)

Feng-tsai -- Editor, CHING PAO, Nanking (IDC 2562)

K'ai-wei -- Executive Inspector, East Asia League, Nanking Branch (1943)

Kuo-ch'eng -- Secretary, Ministry of Justice (1943); member, Committee on Culture, China Office, East Asia League

Lu-chai -- Editor-in-Chief, CHING PAO, Nanking (IDC 7267 1943)

Ming-t'ien -- Candidate Inspector, Shanghai Municipal Journalists Association (49:189)

Neng-yi (Shen Neng-yi) -- Native, Kasing, Chekiang; formerly engaged in newspaper work, Shanghai; Secretary to Gen. Chang Hsueh Liang; Director, Bureau of Engraving and Printing, Ministry of Finance, Peiping; Spokesman, Nanking Reformed Government (3/28/38); Vice-Minister of Industry (Who's Who in China 1940); Director, Hua Chung Fishing Corporation, Shanghai (49:189); Director, Central China Sea Product Stock Company, Shanghai (1943)

Yu-tu -- Director, Citizens Savings Movement Committee, Shanghai (49:189)

Shi Saku-lin -- Leader in organization of literary men of China (3/31/44)

Yu-ts'un -- Assistant Chairman, Sugar Enterprise Special Committee, National Trade Control General Association, Shanghai (49:190)

-146-

CHINESE

Shia Chang -- Head, Fujung Temple, Canton; "regarded as the greatest monk of South China (51:249)

Shih -- Mayor, Hankow (12/2/43); Chairman, Material Control Deliberative Council (4/1/43)

Chao-lung -- Commander, pro-Japanese troops; with Japanese Huang Hsieh Chun, Tungping, commanding 300 men (6/39; OSS-Ms.)

Ching -- Chief of Statistics, Ministry of Interior, Nanking (1943)

Chiu-lung -- Counsellor, National Government, Nanking (1943)

Fa-jen -- Director, Sino-Japanese Cultural Association, Shanghai Branch (49:189)

Fu-hou -- Executive member, Flour Special Committee, National Trade Control General Association, Shanghai (49:189)

Hao-jan -- Publisher, HSIN CHI TUNG PAO, Chi Tung, Kiangsu (IDC 2562)

Hsiao-ch'ing -- Appointed by Formosa to represent her as advisor, General Affairs Office, Hongkong (51:249)

Hsin-tan -- Director, China Writers Club (1943)

Hsing-ch'uan -- Mayor, Hankow; member, Central Executive Committee, Nanking; Executive Inspector, East Asia League, Hupeh Branch (1943); Honorary Director, Sino-Japanese Cultural Association, Wu-ch'ang and Hankow Branches; member, National Economic Committee

K'un-hou -- Inspector, China Educational Reconstruction Association, Hankow Branch (1943)

Lai-fu -- Chairman, Directors, Rickshaw Factories, Shanghai (IDC 7264 1943)

Shao-ch'ing -- Chief, General Affairs Department, Police Bureau, Anking Municipality (OSS)

Shih-che -- Chairman, Application of Simplified Primary School System, China Educational Reconstruction Association (1943)

Shun-yuan -- Member, Social Welfare Committee, China Office, East Asia League (1943)

Ting-yi -- Editor, HSIN TSUNG MING PAO, Tsung-ming, Kiangsu (IDC 2562)

T'o -- Editor, FU NU SHIH CHIEH, a monthly, Canton (51:249)

Yu-fu -- Inspector, Shanghai Education Committee (49:189)

Yu-ts'un -- Assistant Chairman, Sugar Enterprise Special Committee, Shanghai (1943)

196

CHINESE

Shin Ko-haku (Japanized version) -- Director, Shanghai
        Branch, China Cultural Federation (10/4/43);
        represented Wang Ching-wei at opening cere-
        mony of newly remodeled Central Military
        Police School of National Government of
        China (49:190)

    Po-chuan -- Director, Shanghai Citizens Welfare
        Association (49:190)

    Shin-ai -- Learned man of North China whose works
        will be published by North China Research
        Institute (1944) (52:240)

Sho Kei-cho, Vice-Admiral -- Vice-Chief, Naval Depart-
        ment, Nanking Government (10/14/43)

    Tani-wang -- President, Broadcasting Corporation of
        North China (6/6/43) (52:240)

Shou Lung-siao -- National Government of China

    Tso-jen -- Member, Committee of Academia Sinica,
        Nanking (6/18/43)

Shu Chen (Chu Shin) -- Chairman, North China Political
        Affairs Council (3/31/43) (52:240)

    Chih-san -- Counsellor and Secretary, Civil Office,
        National Government, Nanking (1943)

    Chuang-huai -- Member, Committee for Stopping
        Breakage at Chung-mon of Huang-ho (1943)

    Lang-hsien -- Chairman, Directors, Western Clothing
        Association, Shanghai (IDC 7264 1943)

    Maru-tei -- Appointed Special Mayor, Nanking;
        arrived Nagasaki (8/31/42)

    Shao-ja -- Chairman, Anti-Communism Committee,
        North China; member, Japan-China Economic
        Conference (12/17/42) (52:240)

    Sheng -- Chief, Peoples Direction, Ministry of
        Social Welfare (1943)

    Shih -- Director, China Educational Reconstruction
        Association, Chekiang Branch (49:190)

    Te-tsai -- Counsellor, National Government, Nanking
        (1943)

    Ying-kao -- Assistant Manager, Nanking Office,
        Central Reserve Bank of China

Shun-Te -- Magistrate, Su-te-shih Hsien; under control
        of Government of Kwangtung (51:249)

Si Kuo-yen -- Public State Minister; Head, Manchukuo
        Mission to North China (11/29/42) (52:240)

Siang, T. F. -- Director, Political Affairs (10/42)(DIO)

Sin -- President, Hsin Min Hui, Peiping (2/28/43)
        (52:240)

-148-

CHINESE

Sin, Mr. Peter -- Former Solicitor; member, one of
Japanese sponsored Chinese Cooperative Councils (9/2/42; OSS-Ms.)

, Peter H. -- See Hsien Ping-hsi

So Bun-rei (Ho Bun-re) -- Ex-Mayor, Hankow Special
Municipality; member, North China Political
Affairs Committee; Mayor, Tientsin Special
Municipality (10/20/43) (52:240)

Shaku-mo -- One of heads, Peace and Order Army
(1/4/44) (52:241)

Shi-bo, Gen. -- One of Heads, Peace and Order Army
(1/4/44) (52:241)

Son Toku-sei -- Connected with chemical company,
Shanghai (49:190)

Song Wu-cho, Dr. -- Head, Hongkong Buddhist Association;
in charge, Medical Center, (Al Badáni)
district (51:249)

Soo Hsi-wen -- Chief Secretary, Shanghai City Government; Acting Chairman, Provisional Government,
Canton (O-58)

Ti-jen -- See Su T'i-jen

Soong Kei-ying -- Chinese authoress; leaving for Japan
to study things Japanese under leading
Japanese scholars (1/24/44)

Soshi Bo, Gen. -- "Reformed"; leader against Communist
Army (1/4/44)

Sse Ma Tsung-chieh -- Member, Sugar Enterprise Special
Committee, National Trade Control General
Association, Shanghai (49:190)

Ssu Cheng-te -- See Su Ch'eng-te(h)

Su Ch'eng-te(h) (Su Ch'eng-toh; Ssu Cheng-te) -- Commissioner, Metropolitan Police, Wang Ching-
wei's regime, under Minister, Police Administration (3/31/41; OSS-Ms.); Assistant Chief,
First Police Office, Shanghai; Assistant
Chief, Third Police Office, Shanghai; Adviser,
Citizens Saving Movement Committee, Shanghai
(49:190); member, National Military Council
(1943); Deputy Commissioner, Police Bureau,
Shanghai; Inspector, China Branch, East Asia
League, Nanking Branch

Ch'eng-kuei -- Inspector, Citizens Savings Movement
Committee, Shanghai (49:190)

Chung-wu -- Secretary and Chief of General Affairs,
Ministry of Auditing, Nanking (1943)

Hsi-wen -- Chairman, Directors, Central China
Steamship Stock Company, Shanghai (IDC 7262
1943)

CHINESE

Su Ke-nien (Su Ko-nien) -- Chief, Police Affairs,
     Administrative Office, Su-huai (1943)

Ko-min -- Superintendent of Police, Huaihai Province
     (OSS)

Ko-nien -- See Su Ke-nien

(Lui) -- Mayor, Peiping; attended inauguration cere-
     monies for Anti-Communist League (7/1/43)
     (52;241)

Po-i -- Manager, Ta Sheng Bank; Manager, Ta Lu Bank,
     Tientsin (1943) (52:241)

Sheng-kuei -- Publisher, CH'ING NIEN JIH PAO,
     Shanghai (49:190)

Shin-rei -- Chief, Supervisors Bureau; Director,
     Federal Reserve Bank of China (3/27/43)

Soo-chung -- Director, Department of Civil Affairs

T'i-jen -- Born, 1889, Soohsien, Shansi; studied
     chemistry in Japan, then worked in factories
     there; returned to China (1916); Principal,
     Shansi Middle School; Dean, Shansi University;
     Secretary to Governor, Shansi; Commissioner,
     Foreign Affairs, Tientsin (1928-30); member,
     North China Political Commission (3/30/40)
     (OSS-Ms.); member, North China Political Com-
     mittee (12/38); member, Board of Standing
     Directors, North China Political Affairs
     Commission (1943); Industrial Administrator;
     Managing Commissioner and Chief of Construc-
     tion; member, Committee, Academia Sinica,
     Nanking Government (6/18/43); Director General,
     North China Political Council (11/18/43)
     (52:241)

Wen-hua -- Head, Ching Hai Branch Agency, Canton
     Police Bureau (51:249)

Sui Ch'in-li -- Chief of Estimation, Ministry of Per-
     sonnel, Nanking (1943)

Sun -- Inaugurated as new Vice-Minister, Ministry of
     Propaganda, Nanking (1/17/45)

Bin-shan -- Assistant Head, Chiang-ning Road Branch
     (#1), Shanghai Police (IDC 2973 1943)

Chai-chou -- Manager, Ta Sheng Bank, Shanghai (IDC
     7270 1943)

Cheng -- Editor, SHEN PAO, Shanghai (IDC 1943)

Chi-ch'ang -- Director, East Asia League, Hupeh
     Branch (1943)

Ch'i-min -- Assistant Chairman, China Educational
     Reconstruction Association, Shanghai Branch
     (49:190)

-150-

CHINESE

Sun Chi-wu -- Secretary, Civil Office, National Government, Nanking (1943); member, Legislative Yuan; member, Directing Committee, China Office, East Asia League

Chi-yao -- Executive Director, China Educational Reconstruction Association (1943)

Chien-ch'u -- See Chang Chieng-ch'u

Chih-chieh -- Director, General Affairs Department, Ministry of Interior, Nanking (1943)

Ching-hsuan -- Commander, pro-Japanese troops; with pro-Japanese forces in Honan, near Shangchiu, commanding about 1,000 men (6/39; OSS-Ms.)

Chu-tsai -- Member, Legislative Yuan, Nanking (1943)

Chu-tung -- Manager Director, Shanghai Post-Office Labor Union; Manager Director, Readjustment Committee, National Post-Office Labor Union (49:190)

Chun-shan -- Manager, Ta Chung Bank, Shanghai (IDC 7270 1943)

Chung-li -- Chairman, Flour Special Committee, National Trade Control General Association, Shanghai (49:190); member, All-China Economic Committee

Foo -- Interested in liberating Formosa; wrote for Formosan Revolutionary Alliance (IDC)

Hao -- Executive Inspector, China Educational Reconstruction Association, Shanghai Branch (49:190)

Hsiang-fu -- Member, National Military Council (OSS)

Hsing-chih -- Manager, Che Tung Commercial Bank, Ning Po, Chekiang (IDC 7270 1943)

Hsuan -- Counsellor, Directorate-General of Industry, North China Political Commission (7/40; OSS-Ms.)

Jui-huang -- Director, Shanghai Citizens Welfare Association (49:190)

Jui-kan -- See Sun K'uei-yuan

Jun-yu -- Born, 1879, Wuhsien, Kiangsu; old Ching dynasty scholar; graduate, Tokyo Law College; M.P.; Legation Secretary, Tokyo; Cabinet Secretary; member, Foreign Affairs Commission, HCPC (1937); Chairman, Tientsin Peace Maintenance Association (OSS-Ms.); Chief, Internal Affairs, North China Political Council (1943)

Kou -- Member, Major Staff, 7th War District Headquarters; war prisoner (2/16/44)

CHINESE

Sun Kuang-ch'uan -- Control Officer, Shih Tong Chu
Ward, Hongkong (51:249)

K'uei-yuan, Gen. (Sun Jui-kan) -- Member, National
Military Council (1943); Commander-in-Chief,
Northern Honan Communist Extermination Army;
to be Commander, 6th District Army (10/10/44)
(IDC)

Kwang-nien -- Chief, Chekiang Education Department
(1/3/45)

Kwong-yu -- Chairman, Relief Club, Hongkong (51:249)

Lang-chang -- See Sun Liang-cheng, Gen.

Li-fu -- Chief, Shanghai Office, Nanking Foreign
Ministry (4/7/43) (49:190)

Liang-cheng, Gen. (Sun Lang-chang; Tu Liang-cheng)--
Once noted Army leader under Chungking
regime (2/15/43); Commander-in-Chief, 2nd
Military District, China; Ex-Head, Keifeng
Pacification Corps; Head, National Government
Forces (1/21/44); active with North China
Peace Preservation Corps (3/29/44); appointed
Head, North Kiangsu Pacification Headquarters
(9/15/44) (52:241)

Liang-chun -- Left Chungking camp; joined National
Government (2/8/43)

Lin-kuo -- Consul General, Shenyang (1943)

Meng-hua -- Head, Central Electric Communications
Corporation, Wuhu Branch; Director, China
Writers Club (IDC 2562)

Ming -- Director, Shanghai Special Municipality
Journalists Association; Chairman, Welfare
Committee, Shanghai Special Municipality
Journalists Association (49:191)

Ming-ch'i -- Director, East Asia League, Shanghai
Branch; Chief, Bureau of Social Welfare,
Shanghai; Advisor, Citizens Savings Movement
Committee, Shanghai (49:191)

Pin-shan -- Assistant Chief of Police. Chiang-ning
Road District Office, First Police Office,
Shanghai (49:191)

Ping-chu -- Chairman, Trustees, Silverware Factories,
Shanghai (IDC 7264)

Shih -- Counsellor, Chinese Embassy, Japan (0-59)

Si-wen, Lt. Gen. -- Head Puppet, China Military
Party (o-57)

Sing-ying, Gen. -- Formerly commanded Chinese Unit;
now gone over to Puppet Government; joined
Peace Camp (4/43); defeated; went into retirement (7/9/43)

Sung -- Director, Sino-Japanese Cultural Association,
Shanghai Branch (49:191)

CHINESE

Sun Te-ching -- Commander, pro-Japanese troops; with pro-Japanese in Honan, near, Shangchiu, commanding about 1,000 men (6/39; OSS-Ms.)

Ti-san -- Member, Legislative Yuan, Nanking (1943)

Tien-ying, Gen. -- Formerly commanded 117th and 118th Division; invaded Ninghsia Province (winter 1933-34); appointed Commander-in-Chief, Peace Preservation, Northern Chahar (1/5/37); Commander, New 5th Army, under 24th Group Army, in Hopeh-Chahar Special War Zone (12/41); said to have deserted in Shansi to puppets with 30,000 soldiers under his command (5/28/43) (OSS-Ms.); Commander-in-Chief, 6th District Army (1944)

Tsu-chi -- Chief, Peoples Affairs and Chief, Insurance Supervision Bureau, Ministry of Interior, Nanking (1943); Commissioner, Finance, Huaihai Province

Tun-min -- Special delegate, Ministry of Foreign Affairs to Anhwei (1943)

Wei-yu -- Trustee, North China Aluminite Mining Industrial Company, LTD. (52:241)

Yu-fang -- Manager, Chung Fu Bank, Shanghai (IDC 7270 1943)

Yu-ts'ai -- Editor, CHIAO WU CHI KAN, a quarterly, Nanking (IDC 2562)

Yueh-chi -- Manager, Liang Che Commercial Bank, Hangchow, Chekiang (IDC 7270 1943)

Yueh-yuan -- Member, Association of Teachers, Amoy (49:191)

Yun-chang -- Chief, Bureau of Political Affairs, Chekiang (49:191)

Sung Ch'i-kuei -- Publisher, HAI NING HSIN PAO, Chiashih, Chekiang (IDC 2562)

Ching-tse -- Member, Shanghai Newspaper Association (49:191); Editor, KUO MIN HSIN WEN (IDC 7266 1943)

Ching-ying, Miss -- Peiping University; to study in Japan (52:241)

Hsin-teng -- Editor, HOPEH JIH PAO, Pao-ting, Hopeh (52:241)

Huai-yuan -- Executive Director, East Asia League, Hupeh Branch (1943)

, I.C. -- Treasurer, Universal Trading Company, Shanghai (49:191)

Mo-lin -- Chih Yeh Bank, Tientsin (1943) (52:241)

Pi-ju -- Inspector, Lu-ta Mining Industrial Company (over half capital owned by Shantung Mining Industrial Company) (52:241)

CHINESE

Sung Po-sen -- Candidate Director, China Educational
   Reconstruction Association, Shanghai Branch
   (49:191)

 Shang-wen -- Publisher, CHIA HSING HSIN PAO,
   Chia-hsing, Chekiang (IDC 2562)

 Shao-hsiung -- Chief, General Affairs Department,
   Water Police Office, Amoy Special Municipality
   (R&A 2565)

 Shao-yu -- Head, Pei Ching Cheng-wen Communication Company, North China (52:241)

 Ting-ying, Gen, (Sun Tien-ying) -- "Gone over to
   Peace Camp"; pledged alligance (7/10/43);
   Vice-Commander, 24th Army Corps (O-57)

 Yao-lin -- Inspector, China Educational Reconstruction Association, Hankow Branch (1943)

Szu Shih-pin -- Manager, Kiangsu Agricultural and
   Industrial Bank, Wu Chiang, Kiangsu (IDC
   7270 1943)

T'a Han-sheng -- Advisory member, Ministry of Foreign
   Affairs, Nanking (1943)

 Nai-liang -- Director, Newspapermen's Association,
   Shanghai (1943)

Ta'en Teh-kuang -- Chairman, Famine Relief Commission,
   Wang Ching-wei's regime (3/41; OSS-Ms.)

Tai, Gen. -- Chief Administrator, Hopeh Province; to
   tour Manchukuo (8/17/42)

 Ai-lu -- Member, ... Committee, Municipal Council,
   Shanghai; member, Committee on Grain Control
   (49:191); Vice-President, Central Reserve
   Bank, Nanking (IDC 7270 1943)

 Chi-t'ao -- President, Examination Yuan, Nanking
   (1/1/42)

 Chu -- Manager, Yung Chia Local Farmers Bank,
   Yung Chia, Chekiang (IDC 7270 1943)

 Han-sung -- Consul, Nagasaki, Japan; promoted to
   rank of Minister (4/1/43)

 Hsuan-ching -- Commander, pro-Japanese troops; with
   Japanese Huang Hsieh Chun, commanding 900
   men, Wu-chuan, Pailingmiao and Tamiao (6/39;
   OSS-Ms.)

 Jo-lan -- Control Officer, Kowloon, City Ward
   (51:249)

 Shou-hsien -- Manager, Wenchow Commercial Bank,
   Yung Chio, Chekiang (IDC 7270 1943)

 Si-lu -- Manager, Central Reserve Bank, Shanghai
   Branch (IDC 1943)

CHINESE

Tai Te -- Chief, Office of Accounting, Shanghai (49:191)

Ts'e -- Chief, Office of Overseas Chinese Affairs, Ministry of Foreign Affairs, Nanking (1943); Director, China Office, East Asia League, Nanking Branch

Wang-ing -- China's representative, GEA Economic Conference (11/27/42)

Ying-fu -- Political Vice-Minister under Minister of Education, Wang Ching-wei's regime (3/41; Oss-Ms.); Political Advisor, National Government, Nanking (1943); Assistant General Secretary, Committee of Promotion, New Citizens Movement; member, Central Executive Committee, Nanking (1943); member, Committee of Political Councillors; Candidate Director, Sino-Japanese Cultural Association; Editor, CHIAO YU CHIEN SHE, a monthly, Nanking; Assistant Secretary, New Citizens Movement Promotion Committee; Director, China Office, East Asia League; Chairman, Directors, China Educational Reconstruction Association; Honorary member, China Journalists Club

Tam Kwok-wa -- Works for Japanese Intelligence (9/41; OSS-Ms.)

Shu-kuei -- Mayor, Hangchow; assassinated (2/7/44) by assailants sent by Military Council of Chungking regime

, Mr. Thomas -- Prominent Hongkong Chinese; solicitor; member of one or another of Japanese sponsored and controlled Chinese councils (9/2/42; OSS-Ms.)

, William N. T. -- Member, Chinese Cooperative Council (1942-   ), Hongkong (51:249)

Tamilingsulung -- Commander, pro-Japanese troops; with Japanese Huang Hsieh Chun, commanding 900 men in Taolin, Hsingho, Shangtu (6/39; OSS-Ms.)

T'an Chih-min -- Manager, Hua Hsing Commercial Bank, Nanking and Wu Hu, Anhwei, Branches (IDC 7270 1943)

Chueh-chen -- Secretary, Civil Office, National Government, Nanking (1943); Head, Tokyo Branch, Central Electric Communication Corporation

Fu-hu (Tan Fu-yu) -- Leader, Hsin Min Association (1944); spoke at meeting of department chiefs (2/25/44)

Kung-pei -- Secretary, Kuomintang Eighth District Party Headquarters, Canton (51:249)

Mu-kung -- Publisher, HSIN LI SHUI PAO, Li-shiu, Kwangsu (IDC 2562)

Shu-ch'ien -- Director, East Asia League, Shanghai Branch (49:191)

CHINESE

T'an Shu-hui (-kuei) -- See T'an Shu-kuei

    Shu-kuei (-hui) -- Mayor, Hangchow, Chekiang; (49:191); Chief Secretary, Chinghsiang Administration, Hangchou Sector (1943)

    Tao-nan -- Honorary Director, Sino-Japanese Cultural Association, Wu-Ch'ang and Hankow Branches (1943)

    Tan-ch'en -- Executive member, China Journalists Association (1943)

    Tao-te -- Honorary Director, China Educational Reconstruction Association, Hankow Branch (1943)

    Tse-kai -- Honorary Director, Sino-Japanese Cultural Association, Shanghai Branch (49:191)

    Ya-shih -- Architect, Hongkong; member, China Representatives (Discursive) Association (51:249)

    Yu-chung -- Chief, Office of Finance, Nanking

T'ang Ch'en-lung -- Inspector, Committee for Establishment of China's Broadcasting Business, Shanghai (49:191); Supervisor, China Broadcasting Enterprise and Reconstruction Association (IDC 7268)

    Ch'en(g)-po -- Chairman, Board of Directors, Hua Chung Hydro-electric Corporation (49:191); Director, Central China Water and Electric Stock Company, Shanghai (1943); member, All-China Economic Committee; Inspector, China Office, East Asia League

    Ch'i-hsiang -- Editor, CHIANG SU JIH PAO, Soochow (49:191)

    Chi-yuan -- Inspector, China Office, East Asia League (1943)

    Chin-chiang -- Commander, 11th Division (5/4/44)

    Chien -- Inspector, North China Electrical Industry Company, Peiping (52:241)

    Chih-liang -- Chairman, Directors, Textile Stores, Shanghai (IDC 7264)

    Ching-jung -- Head, Hai Chuang Branch Agency, Canton Police Bureau (51:249)

    Chiu-wun -- Head, Divisional Bicycle Syndicate, Hongkong (51:249)

    Erh-ho -- Member, Standing Committee and Head, Education Bureau, North China (12/38); Chairman, Legislative Council, Legislative Yuan; Ex-Superintendent of Education, Nanking; Ex-Director General, Education Administration, South China Political Affairs Committee; decorated by Japanese Emperor (3/23/44)

-156-

CHINESE

T'ang Hsiang -- Director, East Asia League, Shanghai Branch (49:191)

Hsiung-feng -- Candidate Inspector, Shanghai Special Municiaplity Journalists Association (49:191)

Hsu-yu -- See Chiang Tsu-yu

Hui-min -- Member, Central Executive Committee, Nanking (1943); Inspector, China Office, East Asia League

Hui-sin -- Administrative Vice-Minister under Minister of Police Administration, Wang Ching-wei's regime (3/31/41; OSS-Ms.)

I-peng -- Judicial Administration, Tientsin; sent to inspect North China affairs (52:241)

Jen -- Connected with education (7/1/43)

K'ao-shan -- Director, Shanghai Wharf Labor Union (49:191)

Kuan-yuan -- Manager, Chekiang Local Bank, Shanghai (IDC 7270 1943)

Kung-teh -- Chinese student of Japanese culture in Tokyo (10/5/43)

Li-hsi -- Secretary, Ministry of Social Welfare, Nanking (1943)

Liang-li -- Born, 1901, native of Fukien; B. Sc., London; principal correspondent in Europe, Kuomintang Central Executive Committee (1929); Managing Editor, "The Peoples Tribune", Shanghai (since 1930); Director, International Publicity Bureau, Wang Ching-wei's regime (3/41) (OSS-Ms.); Honorary Director, Committee on Establishment of China Broadcasting Business, Shanghai; Honorary Director, Sino-Japanese Cultural Association, Shanghai Branch (49:191); honorary member, China Journalists Association; Honorary Director, China Broadcasting Enterprise and Reconstruction Association (1943); Minister, International Bureau, Ministry of Propaganda or Information; Director, Central Electrical Communications Corporation; Director, China Office, East Asia League; Plenipotentiary Ambassador, residing in Ministry of Foreign Affairs

Mang -- Director, Military Affairs Board, Nanking; member, National Military Council; Inspector, China-Japan Returned Students Club

Mao-hsi -- Secretary, Ministry of Construction, Nanking (1943)

P'ei-sheng -- Director, China Educational Reconstruction Association, Anhwei Branch (1943)

CHINESE

T'ang Po-chi -- Manager, Chen Yeh Commercial and Savings Bank, Shanghai (IDC 1943)

Sheng-- Director, East Asia League, Shanghai Branch (49:191)

Sheng-ming -- Member, National Military Council (OSS)

Shih-tsun -- Publisher, YU HANG HSIN PAO, Chekiang (IDC 2562)

Shou-min -- Born, 1891, Chinkiang, Kiangsu; sometime Assistant Manager, Shanghai Commercial Bank; Director, Central Mint; General Manager, Banking Department, Central Bank; General Manager, Bank of Communications (since 10/33); (OSS-Ms.); Former Chairman, Board of Directors, All-China Commercial Control General Association; appointed Auditor, Commercial Control General Association (6/44); member, Committee on Territories and Borders, Shanghai Municipal Council; Chairman, Directors, National Trade Control General Association; Director, Shanghai Labor and Business Social Union (49:192); member, Executive Committee, All-China Economic Committee (2/5/43); member, Advisory Committee, Shanghai Municipality

Ta-chang, Lt. Gen. -- Chief, Military Counsellors Board; promoted to full General (10/10/44)

Teng-p'o -- Political Vice-Minister under Minister of Industry and Commerce, Wang Ching-wei's regime (OSS-Ms.)

T'ien-te -- Editor, NAN HUI HSIN PAO, Nan-hui, Kwangsu (IDC 2562)

Tsu-yu -- Political Vice-Minister under Minister of Police Administration, Wang Ching-wei's regime (OSS-Ms.)

Wen-chieh -- Chief, Reserves Office, Ministry of Grains, Nanking (1943)

Wen-hsuan -- Chief, Paochia Office, 3rd Department, Shanghai (49:192)

Yang-tu -- Born, Shantung; Mohammedan; Mayor, Tsinan (1923); once Commissioner of Finance, Shantung Province; appointed Governor, Shantung (1/7/39); Governor, Hopeh (3/30/39) (OSS-Ms.); Director-General, Industry, North China Political Affairs Council (3/1/45) (52:241)

Yat-yan -- Representative, Overseas Chinese Bank, Hongkong (51:250)

Ying-huang -- Vice-Minister, Ministry of Justice, Executive Yuan (1943); member, Committee on Abolition of Extraterritoriality

-158-

CHINESE

T'ang Yu-lian -- Candidate Inspector, China Educational
Reconstruction Association (1943)

Tao Chuan-i -- Head, Editorial and Statistics Unit,
Canton Bureau of Police (First Section)
(51:250)

Hang-te -- Director, Sino-Japanese Cultural Association, Shanghai Branch (49:192)

Hsiao-chieh -- Special Village Pacification Supervisor, 1st District, Chekiang (49:192)

Kai -- Military Spokesman (8/26/43) (DIO)

K'ang -- Counsellor, Directorate-General of Finance,
North China Political Government (OSS-Ms.)

K'ang-te(h) -- Staff member, CHUNG HUA JIH PAO,
Shanghai; member, Editorial Staff, CHUNG HUA
YUEH PAO (OSS)

Kuo-hsien -- Member, Directing Committee, China
Office, East Asia League, Nanking Branch (1943);
Chief, Commerce and Mining, Ministry of In-
dustries

Shang-ming -- Director, North China Communications
Corporation (1944)

Shun-ch'u -- Secretary, Civil Office, and Counsellor, National Government, Nanking (1943)

Tun-li -- Executive Director, East Asia League,
Hupeh Branch (1943)

Yao-shan -- Chief Administrator, First Administrative District; led eleven officials of the
Police Association on inspection trip to three
new hsiens (1/17/45)

Yu-t'ian -- Counsellor, National Government, Nanking
(1943)

Yun -- Member, Publications Committee, China Writers
Club (1943)

Taui Ching-su -- Outstanding worker, receiving award
from Kaifeng Branch, North China Labor Association (10/5/44) (52:241)

Tcheng Loh -- See Chen Lu

Te Cheng-kung -- Director, North China Raw Drug Company,
Tsinan (1943) (52:241)

Teh Sin-kung -- Director, North China Raw Drug Company,
Tsingtao (1943) (52:242)

Tei Yuan -- Representative, Central Tsinan Financial
Association

Teng Chao-chien -- Director, Teng T'ion Fu Bank, Hongkong; Vice-President, Hongkong Automobile
Distribution Center; member, China Representatives (Discursive) Association (51:250)

CHINESE

Teng Chi-tung -- Investigator, Political Affairs Department, Kwangtung Province; Executive Head, Work Corps; Section Head, Education; Executive Director, Training School for Pacification (51:250)

Ch'iu-p'u -- Director, East Asia League, Nanking Branch (1943)

Hai -- Magistrate, Ch'en Fu-kuo Hsien; under control of Government of Kwangtung (51:250)

Heng, Maj. Gen. -- Military Attache, Manchukuo Embassy, Nanking (0-44)

Shih-chang -- Member, National Military Council (OSS)

Shou-ming -- Member, ... Committee, Municipal Council, Shanghai (49:192)

Shu-ku -- Director, China Educational Reconstruction Association; Director, China Writers Club

Tsan-ch'ing -- Chief, Office of Economics, Anhwei

Tsan-hsiang -- Commissioner, Economic Affairs, Anhwei Province (OSS)

Tsu-yu -- Governor, Kiangsi (0-59)

Ti Chia-chi -- Advisor, Citizens Savings Movement Committee, Shanghai (49:192)

Chiu-hua -- Assistant Secretary General, Advisor, and Inspector, Citizens Savings Movement Committee, Shanghai (49:192)

Wei-ch'eng -- Chief, Army Court Martial, Ministry of the Army, Nanking (1943)

Tiao Yu-ha -- Director, Trade Bureau, Nanking (0-57)

Tien -- Vice-President, Hsin Min Hui (2/28/43)

Pei-lin -- Head, Shanghai Moral Culture Institute (IDC 7265 1943)

Po -- President, Federal Reserve Bank of China; signed loan from Bank of Japan (9/13/44)

Shou-ch'eng -- Secretary, Civil Office, National Government, Nanking (1943)

Wen-ping -- Commissioner, Directorate-General of Pacification, North China Political Commission (7/40; OSS-Ms.); Governor, Honan Province (1944); relieved on account of illness (5/29/44); resigned (6/44)

Tieng Hsi, Maj. Gen. -- Chief, Nanking Air Force (0-57)

Tin Dee-shen -- Farmer, Contributed a plane, Shanghai (49:192)

-160-

CHINESE

Tin Kun-kei -- Chief, Industrial Department, Kiangsu
          Administration; named Head, Provisions Depart-
          ment (3/12/44)

Ting Ch'ao -- Chief, 3rd District Office, Cha-pei,
          Shanghai (49:192)

     Cheng-yen -- Member, Legislative Yuan, Nanking
               (1943)

     Chi-chang -- Commander, pro-Japanese troops; with
               Japanese Huang Hsieh Chun, commanding 900
               in Kweitou, Tenkou, Sahsien (OSS-Ms. 6/39)

     Ching-cohao -- Managing Director, Shantung Coal
               Production and Marketing Company (52:242)

     Cho -- Assistant Secretary, Paochia Office, 1st
               Police Office, Shanghai (49:192)

     Fang-yu -- Chairman, Directors, Cloth Stores,
               Shanghai (IDC 7264)

     Fang-yuan -- Director, Shanghai Chamber of Com-
               merce; Director, Citizens Savings Movement
               Committee, Shanghai (49:192)

     Hou-ch'ing -- Director, National Trade Control
               General Association, Shanghai (49:192);
               Manager, Kuang Hua Commercial and Savings
               Bank (IDC 7270 1943)

     Hsi-san -- Commander, 13th Division, Nanking Army
               (IDC 3/30/42)

     Hsiung-pai -- Member, Territories and Borders
               Committee, Municipal Council, Shanghai (49:192)

     Liang-chan -- Inspector, Shantung Coal Production
               and Marketing Company (IDC)

     Mei-chun -- See Ting Mo-tsun

     Mo-tsun (Mei-chun) -- Formerly member, "C.C."
               group, blue shirts, Nanking (OSS-Ms.);
               member, Designated Committee, Central Politi-
               cal Council (12/38); member, Central Execu-
               tive Committee, Nanking (1943); member,
               National Military Council; Minister, Social
               Welfare (7/29/43); Minister of Communications,
               Nanking; Director, Sino-Japanese Cultural
               Association, Nanking Branch; Executive Direc-
               tor, New Citizens Movement Promotion Committee;
               Executive Director and Chairman, Social Wel-
               fare Committee, China Office, East Asia
               League; Honorary Chairman, Directors, China
               Educational Reconstruction Association (O-56);
               Honorary member, China Journalists Associa-
               tion

     Shan-kwei -- Manager, Nanking Commercial and
               Savings Bank, Shanghai Branch (IDC 7270 1943)

     Ting -- Member, Committee on Culture, China Office,
               East Asia League (1943); Executive Director
               and Secretary, China Writers Club

210   -161-

CHINESE

Ting Tzu-ts'ai -- Inspector, China Educational Reconstruction Association, Anhwei Branch (1943)

Yen-tao -- Inspector, Citizens Savings Movement Committee, Shanghai (49:192)

Yu-yi -- Editor, CHIANG PEI HSIN PAO, Nan Tung, Kiangsu (IDC 2562)

Wei-fen -- Born, 1874, Jihchao, Shantung; graduate, Meiji University, Tokyo; member, KMT CEC (since 1924); Vice-President, Control Yuan (1932-35); member, Standing Committee, CEC KMT (12/31; OSS-Ms.)

To Boku-mei -- Director, Tientsin Bank; Director, Federal Reserve Bank of China (3/27/43)

Ju-min -- Managing Director, National Commerce Control Association (3/29/44)

Kai-jin -- Member, Board of Standing Directors, North China Political Council (52:242)

Sei-ei -- Sent by Hsin Min Society, Peiping, to Tokyo (52:242)

Tong Chi-tung -- Inspector, Department of Administrative Affairs, Kwangtung; concurrently Head, Educational Unit, Pacification of Villages; named Executive Director, Political Works Corps (IDC 3/13/44)

Ching-kan -- Chief, Kowloon Markets Bureau (51:250)

Ping-tat -- Representative, Nam Pak Hong Merchant Houses, Hongkong (51:250)

Shan-fu -- Head, Cultural Chinese Theatrical Cooperative Association (6/21/44)

Tou Kuang-pu -- Commander, 15th Division, Nanking Army (IDC 3/30/42)

Ts'ai Fu-t'ang -- Director, Shanghai Chamber of Commerce; Director, Shanghai Education Committee (49:192)

Hao-chang -- Chief, Military Affairs, Ministry of the Navy, Nanking (1943)

Hsiang-sheng -- Chairman, Directors, Coal Scrap Association, Shanghai (IDC 7264 1943)

Hsin-yuan -- Commander, 19th Regiment, Nanking Army (IDC 3/30/42)

Hung-t'ien -- Member, Central Executive Committee, Nanking; Director, China Office, East Asia League

Kan-shun -- Director, Pacification Bureau, Anhwei Provincial Government; appointed Chairman, First Pacification Supervisory Commission, Anhwei Province (3/7/44)

-162-

CHINESE

Tsai Kang -- Head, Hung Te Branch Agency, Canton
Police Bureau (51:250)

Ko-chien -- Managing Director, Central Reserve
Bank of China Shanghai Branch (OSS)

Kuo-chi -- Financial leader of China; Central
Reserve Bank, Shanghai (49:192)

P'ei (Ts'ia P'ei) -- Member, Political Affairs
Council, Central China; Chinese Ambassador
to Tokyo in place of Hsu Liang (1943-1944);
wrote article for "Sozo" (8/8/44); Director,
Sino-Japanese Cultural Association; Director, China-Japan Returned Students Club;
Director, China Office, East Asia League

Sheng-pai -- Director, National Trade Control
General Association (1943) (49:192); Head,
Silk Enterprise Trade Association

Shih-ming -- Inspector, Citizens Savings Movement
Committee, Shanghai (49:192)

Shu-ling -- Head, Arrest Unit, Fourth Section,
Canton Bureau of Police (51:250)

Shun -- Chief, Office of Prisons, Ministry of
Justice, Nanking (1943)

Sung-pu -- Manager, Tun Hsu Commercial and Savings
Bank (IDC 1943)

Ti-jen -- Manager, Tun Hsu Commercial and Savings
Bank, Shanghai (IDC 7270 1943)

Tzu-hsiang -- Chairman, Directors, Non-ferrous
Metals Association, Shanghai (IDC 7264)

Wen-shih (Tsai Yun-shih) -- Chief, Office of
Economics, Hupeh Province (1943)

Ya-t'ien -- Director, Shanghai Wharf Labor Union
(49:193)

Yu-san -- Manager, Liang Che Commercial, Hangchow,
Chekiang and Chekiang Industrial and Commercial Bank, Changchow (IDC 7270 1943)

Yun-shih -- See Tsai Wen-shih

Yung -- Secretary, Ministry of Finance, Nanking
(1943)

Tsang Cho -- Member, National Military Council (OSS)

Shan-hsiang -- Trustee, Lu-ta Mining Industrial
Company (over half capital of company owned
by Shantung Mining Industrial Company (IDC)

Tsao -- Administrator, First Administrative District,
Hopeh (12/16/44) (52:242)

Chen-kang -- Chairman, Directors, Photographic
Plates Industry, Shanghai (IDC 7264 1943)

212

CHINESE

Tsao Chi-ming -- Chairman, Directors, Cotton Association, Shanghai (IDC 1943)

Chien-wei -- President, NANKING WAN PAO (Evening Post) (1943); Executive member, China Journalists Association; Director, China Writers Club

Chu-shan -- Chief, Affairs Promotion Section, Ministry of Public Welfare, Nanking (1943)

Chung-chi -- Manager, Ya Hsi Industrial Bank, Shanghai Agency (IDC 1943)

Chung-ping -- Training Head, Kuomintang Seventh District Party Headquarters, Canton (51:250)

Han-mei -- Member, Publications Committee, China Writers Club (1943)

Hung-ch'uan -- Secretary, Ministry of Finance, Nanking (1943)

Hung-fei -- Chairman, Directors, Thread and Tapes Association, Shanghai (IDC 1943)

Ju-lin (Ts'ao Jun-tien) -- Born, 1875, Shanghai; graduate in law, Tokyo Imperial University; Chinshih, LLD, Imperial Exams; Junior Vice-President, Board of Foreign Affairs (1911); Senator (1913); Vice-Minister, Foreign Affairs (1913-16); Minister of Communications and concurrently Acting Minister of Finance (1917-19); Proscribed (1922); President, Bank of Communications and Industrial Bank of China; member, Provisional Government of Peking (12/14/37); High Adviser, North China Political Commission (7/40) (OSS-Ms.); President, Ching Ching Coal Mine Corporation, Peiping (52:242)

Mao-lin -- Commander, pro-Japanese troops; with pro-Japanese forces in Honan, near Tungshu and Chenliu, commanding about 2,000 men (6/39; OSS-Ms.)

Miao-sheng -- Assistant Manager, Provincial Bank, Hangchow, Chekiang (OSS)

Ming-lieh -- Chairman, Directors, Silk Stores, Shanghai (IDC 1943)

Nan-t'ien -- Chief, Military Council, Ministry of the Navy, Nanking (1943)

Pang, Lt. Gen. -- Vice-Chief, Military Affairs Office, Nanking (O-57)

Pang-yeh -- Director, Physical Education, Social Welfare Ministry, Nanking (O-56)

Pin -- Inspector, Citizens Savings Movement Committee, Shanghai (49:193)

Shih-yu -- Chairman, Directors, Medical Instrument Factories, Shanghai (IDC 1943)

-164-

CHINESE

Tsao Shu-jen -- Editor, CHENG PAO, Shih-men, North China (52:242)

Tsung-yin -- Counsellor, National Government, Nanking (1943)

Yu-kao -- Chairman, Directors, Embroidery Factories, Shanghai (IDC 7264)

Yun-fei -- Candidate Director, China Educational Reconstruction Association, Anhwei Branch (1943)

Tsen Hsi-yung -- Managing Editor, HUA CHIAO JIH PAO, Hongkong (51:250)

Wei-hsiu -- Publisher, HUA CHIAO JIH PAO, Hongkong (51:251)

Yeh-kuang -- Member, Central Political Council, Nanking Kuomintang (OSS-Ms.)

Tseng Ch'eng -- Magistrate, Huang En-li Hsien; under control of Government of Kwangtung (51:250)

Ching-lai -- Editor, CHIUNG HAI CHAO YIN, a monthly, Hai-kou, Chekiang (49:193)

Hsi-chun -- Secretary, National Economic Committee, Nanking (1943); Secretary, Ministry of Industries, Nanking (1943)

Hsiao-hing -- Judge, High Court, Hopeh (5/18/44) (52:242)

Hsing -- Member, Legislative Yuan, Nanking (1943); Director, China Office, East Asia League

Jung -- Control Officer, Wang Chueh Ward, Kowloon (51:250)

Kuang-ch'uan -- Executive Inspector, Social Welfare Committee, East Asia League, Canton Branch (51:250)

Kwang-ping -- Head, Tung Shan Branch Agency, Canton Police Bureau (51:250)

Kwong-kung -- Officer, East Asia Cultural Association, Asiatic Affairs Bureau, Hongkong (51:250)

Shou-ch'ao -- Control Officer, Shao Chi Wan Ward, Hongkong (51:251)

Ta-chun -- Commander, pro-Japanese troops; with Japanese Huang Hsieh Chun in area of Huangpo and Hsiaokan, commanding 5,000 men (6/39; OSS-Ms.)

Ta-chung -- Commander, pro-Japanese troops; with pro-Japanese Huang Hsieh Chun, near Changchiu, Honan, commanding about 700 men (6/39;OSS-MS.)

Ting-chung -- Head, Feng Yuan Branch Agency, Canton Police Bureau (51:251)

CHINESE

Tseng Ting-hsin -- Member, Association of Teachers, Amoy (49:193)

Ts'u-hsi -- Director, China Educational Reconstruction Association, Chekiang Branch (49:193)

Tz'u-ling -- Inspector, China Educational Reconstruction Association, Shanghai Branch (49:193)

Wan-pu -- Chairman, Directors, Raw Rubber Material Association, Shanghai (IDC 7264)

Wei-ch'i -- Publisher, HSIEN TAI T'I YU, a monthly, Shanghai (49:193)

Wen-ch'uan -- Executive Director, China Educational Reconstruction Association, Chekiang Branch (49:193)

Tsi Hsi-yuan -- Puppet General for Japan (12/42) (DIO)

Wai-yu -- Member, Finance, Committee, Municipal Council, Shanghai (49:193)

Tsiang, T. F. -- Government Spokesman (11/42) (DIO)

Tsmin Chang -- Deceased; was Vice-Commander, 81st Army (5/4/44) (DIO)

Tso Erh-liang -- Graduate, Kwangtung Legal Officers School; formerly Consultant, Ministry of Interior; Head, Third Bureau Section, Kuomintang Central Headquarters; Committee member and Head, Propaganda Section, Kuomintang Headquarters, Kwangtung Province (51:251)

Ju-liang -- One of Heads, Propaganda Corps, Kwangtung (51:251)

Tsun-chih -- Editor, NU SHENG, a monthly (49:193)

Tsou Cha-pao -- Chairman, Directors, Military Uniform Association, Shanghai (IDC 1943)

Ching-fang -- Member, Supreme National Defense Council; Chief Secretary, National Economic Commission (10/14/43); President, Peiping Trade Association (5/26/44) (52:242)

Ch'uan-sun -- Member, National Economic Committee, Nanking (1943)

Li-p'ing -- Secretary, Executive Yuan (1943)

Tso-jen -- Noted man of letters (IDC 1/15/44)

Tsu Chih-chu -- Member, China Inspection Party to Japan to study Youth Training Centers (10/25/43)

, M. -- Appointed by Japanese as one of Superintendents, British Internment Camp Stanley, Hongkong (OSS-Ms.)

-166-

CHINESE

Tsu Min-yi, Dr. -- See Ch'u Min-yi

Tsuei Tsai-fu -- Chairman, Directors, Truck Transportation, Shanghai (IDC 7264)

Ts'ui Cheng-sheng -- Secretary, Committee for Application of Constitution, Nanking (1945)

    Pei-chu -- Commander, pro-Japanese troops; with Japanese Huang Hsieh Chun, commanding 1,000 men, Hantan and Pengcheng (6/39; OSS-Ms.)

    Ping-hsi -- Manager, Tai Ho Hsing Bank, Shanghai (IDC 7270 1943)

    Pu-chi -- Vice-Chairman, North China Judicial Administration (5/18/44) (52:242)

    Pu-wu -- Executive Inspector, East Asia League, Nanking Branch (1943)

    Ssu-jui -- Candidate Director, China Educational Reconstruction Association, Anhwei Branch (1943)

    Yu-ming -- Inspector, China Educational Reconstruction Association, Chekiang Branch (49:193)

    Yuan-pei -- Founder (1927), Academia Sinica; closed (1937); reopened (7/1/43), Shanghai (49:193)

Tsung Chih-ch'iang -- Chief, Police Affairs, Kiangsu (49:193)

    Hua -- Magistrate, Li Pao-an Hsien; under control of Government of Kwangtung (51:251)

    Tong-zee -- Finish Consul General, Nanking (O-59)

    Wei-chih -- Publisher, CHEN PAO, (Morning Post), Peiping (52:242)

Tu Che-an -- Counsellor, National Government, Nanking (1943)

    Che-lien -- Special Police Agent, Nanking District; Secondary Head, Pao-chia Promotion Committee; Candidate Director, China Educational Reconstruction Association (1943)

    Chen-k'un -- Director and Secretary, China Educational Reconstruction Association, Hankow Branch (1943)

    Cheng-chien -- Assistant Chief, First Police Office, Shanghai (49:193)

    Chih-hua -- Head, Trial Unit, Third Section, Canton Bureau of Police (51:251)

    Ching-shan -- Candidate Director, China Educational Reconstruction Association, Chekiang Branch (49:193)

CHINESE

Tu Hao -- Head, 6th Section, Ministry of Military
        Affairs (1/4/45)

    Ho-yun -- Manager Director, Post Office Labor Union,
        Shanghai; Manager Director Readjustment Com-
        mittee, National Post Office Labor Union
        (49:193)

    Hsi-chun, Gen. -- Governor, Hupeh Province (12/2/43);
        Commander-in-Chief, North China Peace Preser-
        vation Corps; temporarily assumed position,
        Director-General, Public Safety Headquarters
        and Commander-in-Chief, Pacification Force
        on resignation of Chi Hsieh-yuan (1/16/44);
        member, North China Political Council
        (12/4/44) (52:242)

    Hsia-shih -- Chief, Pao-chia Office, 6th Department,
        Shanghai (49:193)

    Hsu-tiao (Tu Hsi Tiao) -- Supreme Commander, Pacifi-
        cation Corps, North China; Chief, Peace and
        Order Administration, Peiping (52:242)

    Hua-fang -- Chairman, Directors, Leather Tanning
        Association (IDC 1943)

    Liang-cheng -- See Sun Liang-cheng

    Ping-chun -- Candidate Director, China Educational
        Reconstruction Association, Anhwei Branch
        (1943)

    Tzu-chieh -- Candidate Inspecting member, China
        Journalists Association (1943)

    Yi-ch'ien -- Chief, Bureau of Peace Preservation
        and Village Pacification, Shanghai (49:193);
        member, National Military Council, Nanking
        (1943)

Tuan Ch'ing-p'ing -- Executive Inspector, China Edu-
        cational Reconstruction Association (1943)

Tung Chih-p'ing -- Member, Committee for Punishment of
        Central Officials, Nanking (1943)

    Chuan-ju -- Manager, Yu Yao Hsien Farmers Bank,
        Chekiang (IDC 7270 1943)

    Chung-li -- Inspector, China Educational Recon-
        struction Association, Hankow Branch (1943)

    Chung-wei -- Member, Council, Chinese Representa-
        tives Association, Hongkong (51:251)

    Hsien-ting -- Manager, Kuo Fu Commercial and
        Savings Bank, Shanghai (IDC 7270 1943)

    Hsin-po -- Director, Shanghai Chamber of Commerce
        (49:193)

    Jen-hsing -- Director, North China Raw Drug Com-
        pany, Kaifeng (52:242)

-168-

CHINESE

Tung Jon-fu -- Publisher, HSIN CHUNG HUA PAO, Tai Hsien, Kiangsu (IDC 2562)

K'ang -- Born, 1869, Wutsin, Kiangsu; Chinshih, Imperial Examinations; Chief Justice, Supreme Court (1914-18); President, Law Codification Commission (1918-20); again Chief Justice (1920); Minister of Justice (1921); Chief Justice, third time and concurrently Acting Minister of Finance and Director, Salt Administration (1922); in Europe and U.S.A (1923); Vice-Chairman on Extraterritoriality Commission (1923-26); Chairman, Chinese Committee to arrange for rendition of International Mixed Court, Shanghai (1925); in retirement, Shanghai (since 1926); member, new Peking Government (12/14/37); member, North China Political Commission (since 3/30/40) (OSS-Ms.); member, State Council, National Government; Delegate, North China Political Council (52:242)

Kuan -- Magistrate, Lu Pao-yung Hsien; under control of Government of Kwangtung (51:251)

Kuang -- Member, Committee for Punishment of Central Officials, Nanking (1943)

Lo-k'an -- Member, Publication Committee, China Writers Club (1943)

Lu-ch'ing -- Director, National Trade Control General Association, Shanghai (49:193)

Pang-kan -- Prosecutor, North China Supreme Court (52:242)

Sheng-to -- Manager, China Agricultural and Industrial Bank, Shanghai (IDC 7270 1943)

T'ai-hsing -- Director, North China Raw Drug Company, Tsingtao (1943) (52:243)

Tao-min -- Propaganda Head, Kuomintang Seventh District Party Headquarters, Canton (51:251)

Tao-ning -- Director and Manager, Shanghai Labor and Business Social Union (49:193)

Yu-min -- Chief, Cooperative, Ministry of Industries, Nanking (1943)

Tzo -- Minister of Commerce, National Government of China; addressed Material Control Deliberative Council, Shanghai (4/1/43) (49:193)

U Sho-kai -- Said by Japanese to head the GEA Moslem Society which has a membership of 560,000 Mohammedans (3/19/43; OSS-Ms.)

Wan Chuan-tang -- Director, North China Raw Drug Company, Tsientsin (1943) (52:243)

Hauoh-fang -- Director, Citizens Savings Movement Committee, Shanghai (49:194)

218

-169-

CHINESE

Wan Meng-wan -- Inspector, China Writers Club (1943)

Shao-chun -- Chief, Labor Bureau, North China Political Affairs Commission; visited Manchukuo on inspection tour (8/26/43) (52:243)

Ta-hua -- Justice, District Court, Hankow (OSS)

Yi-tai -- Director General, Industrial Administration, North China; represented North China, GEA Economic Conference (52:243)

Yu-chuan -- Vice-Minister, Commerce and Industry, Nanking (0-57)

Wang -- Chairman, North China Inter-city Athletic Meet (6/8/44) (52:243)

Wang -- Commissioner of Finance, Canton; Head, Kwangtung Social Affairs Committee; member, Kwangtung Government; Executive member, Commodity Investigation Committee (51:251)

Chai-liang -- Chief, Auditing Board, North China Political Commission (7/40; OSS-Ms.)

Chang-ju -- Central Reserve Bank, Ning Po Branch, Chekiang (1943) (IDC)

Chang-keng -- Chairman, Directors, Waste Paper Association, Shanghai (1943)

Chang-yuan -- Manager, Ta Ya Bank, Shanghai (1943)

Chao-chun -- Director, Central China Silk Stock Company (IDC 1943)

Chao-ming -- See Wang Ching-wei

Chei-min -- Chairman, North China Affairs Council (7/15/43) (52:243)

Chen-hua -- Commander, pro-Japanese troops; with Japanese Huang Hsieh Chun, commanding 900 men, Tsining, Liangcheng (6/39; OSS-Ms.)

Chen-kang -- Secretary, Committee for Application of Constitution, Nanking (1943)

Chen-shen -- Special Financial Delegate to Chekiang, Hupeh, and Kiangsi, Ministry of Finance (1943)

Ch'eng -- Director, China Educational Reconstruction Association, Hankow Branch (1943)

Ch'eng-ch'eh -- Secretary, Ministry of Finance, Nanking (1943)

Cheng-li -- Manager, Shen Chou Industrial Bank, Shanghai (1943)

-170-

CHINESE

Wang Ch'i -- Studied chemistry, Lyons University, France; Chairman, Headquarters Committee, Kuomintang of Kwangtung Province; former Secretary, Executive Yuan; Head, Department of Police and of Civil Affairs, Kwangtung Government; Mayor, Canton; Commissioner of Police, Kwangtung; to administer duties of Governor of Province until successor for Chen Yao-tze chosen (51:251); member, New Citizens Promotion Committee

Chi-min -- President, Chung Hua Medical Publications, Shanghai (OSS)

Chi-shuang -- Counsellor, Directorate-General of the Interior, North China Political Commission (7/40; OSS-Ms.)

Chia-chun -- Vice-Minister of Reconstruction, Executive Yuan, Nanking (1943-44); Chief, Office of Arbitration Commission for the Control of Commodities and Capital, Shanghai; Director, China-Japan Returned Students Club

Chia-kan -- Director, China Educational Reconstruction Association, Hankow Branch (1943)

Chia-li -- Chief, Bureau of Treaty Affairs, Nanking; appointed (3/10/43)

Chia-tsun -- Chief, Investigation Office, Committee on Resources and Material Control, Shanghai (49:194); Advisory member, Ministry of Industries

Chiao-i -- Editor-in-Chief, SHIH PAO, Peiping (1943) (52:243)

Ch'ien-kang -- Commissioner, Directorate-General of the Interior, North China Political Commission (7/40; OSS-Ms.)

Chien-min -- Director, Central China Railroad Stock Company, Shanghai (1943)

Chien-tien -- Former Head, Education Department, Peiping (3/1/45) (52:243)

Chih-ch'eng -- Executive Director, China Educational Reconstruction Association, Shanghai Branch (49:194)

Chih-hsia -- Head, Ya-pei Communications Company, North China; Chief, Social Welfare, Hankow (52:243)

Chih-hsin -- Manager, Hsin Hua Trust and Savings Bank, Shanghai (1943)

Chih-sheng -- Director, Sino-Japanese Cultural Association, Wu-ch'ang and Hankow Branch (1943); Director, China Educational Reconstruction Association

-171-

CHINESE

Wang Chin-hsia -- Executive Director, East Asia League, Hupeh Branch (1943); Chief, Social Welfare Bureau, Hankow; Candidate Director, Sino-Japanese Cultural Association, Wu-ch'ang and Hankow Branch

Ch'ing-fan -- Editor, CHU YUNG CHENG PAO, Chu-yung, Kiangsu (1943); member, Publications Committee, China Writers Club

Ching-hsia -- Honorary Director, China Educational Reconstruction Association, Hankow Branch (1943)

Ching-tsai, Gen. -- With temporary 43rd Division (1/43); captured by Japanese (3/5/43; OSS-Ms.)

Ching-tung -- Chairman, Directors, Rubber Goods Stores, Shanghai (1943)

Ching-wei (Wang Chao-ming) -- Born, 1885, Chekiang; graduate, Tokyo Law College, political science and sociology; High Adviser, Dr. Sun (1924); went to Europe, returning to China (1927); joined Northern Coalition (1930); expelled from party; went into hiding; returned to Nanking (about 1933) (OSS-Ms.); Chairman, National Military Council (12/38); Chairman, Model Peace Zone (1942); Premier or President, National Government, Nanking (1942, 1943, 1944); Chairman, Military Affairs Commission (1943); President, Economic Research Institute; President, National Economic Committee; Manager, Director, Bank of China; Chairman, North China Political Counci; President, Hsin Min Hui; Chief, Executive Yuan (1943); Chairman, Military Council (1943); Chairman, Supreme National Defense Council (1943); Chief, Office for Preservation of Peace, North Kiangsu (1943); received decoration, Order of Blue Jade, from Emperor of Manchukuo; Honorary Chairman, Sino-Japanese Cultural Association; Honorary Chairman, China-Japan Returned Students Club; Chairman, New Citizens Movement Promotion Committee; Chairman, Committee for Application of Constitution; died, Japan (11/12/44)

Ching-we, Mrs. -- See Ch'en Pi-chun

Ching-wu, Maj. Gen. -- Military Advisor, National Government, Nanking (1943)

Chu-ping -- Manager, Hang Li Bank, Shanghai (1943)

Ch'uan -- Candidate Director, China Educational Reconstruction Association, Shanghai Branch (49:194)

Ch'uan-ho -- Inspector, China Writers Club (1943)

Chueh-yi -- Editor, SHIH PO, Peiping (52:243)

Ch'un -- Director, Industry and Business Bureau, National Government dismissed for illegal activities (5/44)

-172-

CHINESE

Wang Chung-ch'i -- Inspector, China-Japan Returned
        Students Club (1943)

Chung-chun -- Chairman, Executive Board, Kwangtung
        Branch, National Advisory Committee for
        Materials Control (51:251)

Chung-hui -- Secretary General (11/42)

Chung-ta -- Minister of Education (2/26/44)

Er-fan -- Manager, Ta Chung Bank, Shanghai Branch
        (IDC 1943)

Feng-ch'ui -- Judge, Supreme Court, Nanking (1943)

Fu-chien -- Vice-Chairman and Financial Adviser,
        North China Political Council (2/8/43)
        (52:243)

Fu-ch'uan -- Member, Propaganda Committee, China
        Office, East Asia League (1943)

Fu-lin -- Commander, pro-Japanese troops; with
        pro-Japanese Huang Hsieh Chun, commanding
        about 800 men in Tzehsien, Hopeh (6/39; OSS-MS.)

Fu-sheng -- Chief, Production Increase Administra-
        tion, Nanking (1943)

Fu-wei -- Educated in Japan; member, Foreign
        Affairs Committee, Hopeh-Chahar Autonomous
        Council; formerly Vice-Minister of Communica-
        tions, Peiping (OSS-Ms.)

Fu-mu -- Trustee, Lu-ta Mining Industrial Company
        (over half capital owned by Shantung Mining
        Industrial Company (52:243)

Hak-kien -- Naturalized Citizen of Formosa; has
        spent some time in Germany and Japan (OSS-Ms.)

Han-chang -- Political Vice-Minister under Minis-
        ter of Judicial Administration, Wang Ching-wei's
        regime (3/41; OSS-Ms.)

Han-liang -- Chairman, Directors, Antiques Asso-
        ciation (1943)

Hao-jan -- Director, China Educational Reconstruc-
        tion Association, Anhwei Branch (1943)

Ho-fang -- Manager, Hopeh Provincial Bank,
        Tientsin (52:243)

Ho-tang -- Chairman, Directors, Air Lamps Associa-
        tion, Shanghai (1943)

Hou-ho -- Assistant Chairman, China Educational
        Reconstruction Association, Hankow Branch
        (1943)

Hsi-ho -- Executive member, Committee for Applica-
        tion of Constitution, Nanking (1943); In-
        spector, China Office, East Asia League

-173-

CHINESE

Wang Hsi-wen -- Councillor, Chinghsiang Administration, Hangchou Sector (IDC 6/8/43); see also (49:194)

Hsia-ts'ai -- Advisory member, Ministry of Industries (1943)

Hsiang (Wang Siang?) -- Appointed Governor, Shansi Province (6/19/44) (52:243)

Hsiang-chiu -- Inspector, China Educational Reconstruction Association, Anhwei Branch (1943)

Hsiang-ku -- Chairman, Military Commission, Peiping (52:243)

Hsiang-sheng -- Honorary Director, China Educational Reconstruction Association, Hankow Branch (1943)

Hsiao-feng -- Candidate Inspector, China Educational Reconstruction Association, Shanghai Branch (49:194)

Hsiao-p'o -- Executive Director, China Educational Reconstruction Association (1943)

Hsiao-shui -- Secretary General, Wheat and Flour Control Committee, National Trade Association, Shanghai (OSS)

Hsiao-ts'ang -- Advisor for Formosa in General Affairs Office, Hongkong (51:252)

Hsien -- Manchukuo Representative to Shanghai; member, Executive Committee, China Headquarters, Shao Wai-kai

Hsien-chieh -- Candidate Executive member, China Journalists Association (1943)

Hsing-huan -- Commander, pro-Japanese troops; with Japanese Huang Hsieh Chun, Honan (6/39; OSS-Ms.)

Hsiu -- Administrative Vice-Minister under Minister of Audit, Wang Ching-wei's regime (3/31/41; OSS-Ms.); Vice-Minister, Ministry of Auditing, Nanking (1943); Candidate Director, Sino-Japanese Cultural Association; Executive Director, China-Japan Returned Students Club

Hsiu-ho -- Director, Shanghai Education Committee (49:194)

Hsueh-nung -- Director, Central China Water and Electricity Stock Company, Shanghai (1943)

Hsun -- Director, China Educational Reconstruction Association, Hankow Branch (1943)

Hu-chen -- Publisher, KO HSUEH HUA PAO, a monthly, Shanghai (49:194)

CHINESE

Wang Hua-feng -- Chairman, Directors, Native Tobacco
Association, Shanghai (1943)

Huai-ling -- Chief, Protocol Section, Ministry of
Foreign Affairs and Director of Treaty
Bureau, Nanking (1943)

Huan-chang -- Chairman, Directors, Weights and
Measures Association, Shanghai (1943)

Huan-wen -- Director, North China Communication
Corporation (1944)

Hung-en -- Counsellor, National Government,
Nanking (1943)

I-chih -- Chairman, Directors, Feather and Fur
Association, Shanghai (1943)

I-t'ang, Gen. -- Born, 1877, Anhwei; attended
Tokyo Military Staff College; Vice-Roy of
Manchuria; studied military science in Ger-
many, France, and U.S.A.; made full General
(1912); Civil Governor, Kirin (1915-16);
chief promoter and organizer, Anfu Club;
ordered arrested; took refuge in Japan (1920-
24); member, Hopeh Chahar Political Pro-
visional Government of China, Peking (12/14/37)
(OSS-Ms.); member, North China Political
Commission (12/38); Head, Hopeh Political
Council (11/29/42;1943); Head, Interior
Department (1942); represented North China,
GEA Economic Conference (10/26/42); Chairman,
North China Political Affairs Commission
(1942; 1943); retired (2/43); Director,
General Affairs Bureau, North China Political
Commission (1943); Chief, Civil Affairs
Bureau, North China Political Affairs Com-
mission (1943); member, Supreme National De-
fense Council (1943); decorated by Japanese
Emperor (5/14/43); member, Board of Standing
Directors, North China Political Council
(11/11/43); Vice-Chairman, North China
Political Affairs Commission (11/43); Direc-
tor, General Affairs (Hsin Min Society?)
(12/8/43); President, Hsin Min Society,
Nanking; President, Examining Yuan, Nanking;
Chief, General Affairs Bureau, North China
Political Council

Ing-tai -- See Wang I-t'ang

Jen-chih -- Secretary, National Trade Control
Association, Kwangtung Branch (51:252)

Jen-ch'ing -- Director, Shanghai Chamber of Commerce (49:194)

Jun-chen -- Chinese father, Japanese mother;
formerly Department Chief, PH Railway; Adviser, Sung Che-yuan, S.M.R., and Yin Ju-keng;
went to Japan to discuss construction of
Tsangchow-Chentow Railway (5/4/36); Chief,
Board of Communications, North China Political Commission (7/40) (OSS-Ms.)

224   -175-

CHINESE

Wang Jun-min -- Commander, pro-Japanese troops; with pro-Japanese (6/39; OSS-Ms.)

Kai-shan -- Head, Education Section, Hongkong District Bureau; went on inspection tour of island's industries (51:252)

Ke-chin -- Chairman, Directors, Celluloid Dealers, Shanghai (1943)

K'e-min (Wang Kai-ming; Wang Keh-min) -- Born, Hangchow, Chekiang; attended Tokyo Military Staff College; Counsellor, Chinese Legation, Tokyo (1902-11); Minister of Finance (1917; 1923-24); Director, Finance Division, Peiping Political Council (since %/33); Mayor, Tientsin (6/35); member, Hopeh-Chahar Political Affairs Commission (12/11/35); Executive Chairman, Provisional Government of China, Peking (12/14/37); (OSS-Ms.); State Councillor; member, Executive Committee, Central Political Council (from 12/38); Head, Administrative Bureau, North China (12/38); decorated by Emperor of Japan (5/14/43); Chairman, North China Political Affairs Committee (7/28/43); Chairman, Board of Standing Directors, North China Political Council (11/11/43); Chairman, North China Political Affairs Commission, second time (7/20/43); Honorary President, GEA Cultural Deliberative Council (11/27/43); Manager, Pe Yang Pao Bank, Peiping (1943); active in program for constructing model districts and developing war resources (3/8/44); temporary Acting Director, Board of Education, North China Political Commission (7/44)

Ki -- Formerly Wang Ching-wei's representative, Hongkong; Police Commissioner, Canton (51:252)

Kuang-ch'i -- Assistant Chairman, China Educational Reconstruction Association, Anhwei Branch (1943)

Kuei-lin -- Inspector, North China Communications Corporation (1944)

Kwang-tin -- Graduate, Japanese University; returned from Germany; left Canton for Fort Bayard, Kwangchou wan (OSS-Ms.)

Lien -- Executive Director, China Educational Reconstruction Association, Chekiang Branch (49:194)

Lien-fang -- Director, Citizens Savings Movement Committee, Shanghai (49:194)

Lin -- Director, Education Affairs; representative at Hsin Min lecture meeting (12/8/43); Special Representative, Hsin Min Society, Peiping (52:244)

Lin-chung -- Assistant Chairman, China Educational Reconstruction Association (1943)

-176-

CHINESE

Wang Ling-kang -- Director, Chinese Broadcasting
Enterprise and Reconstruction Association
(1943)

Lu-hsun -- Chief, Education, North China Political
Council (1943)

Lung-yu -- Executive Director, China Educational
Reconstruction Association, Chekiang Branch
(49:194)

Man-jan -- Editor, HSIN CHI TUNG PAO, Chi Tung,
Kiangsu (IDC 2562)

Man-yun -- Political Vice-Minister under Minister
of Agriculture and Mining, Wang Ching-wei's
regime (3/41; OSS-Ms.); member, Central Executive Committee, Nanking (1943); member,
Committee of Political Councillors; Candidate
Director, Sino-Japanese Cultural Association; Chief, Village Pacification Affairs
Bureau; Director, China Office, East Asia

Meng-hsien -- Inspector, China Educational Reconstruction Association, Shanghai Branch
(49:194)

Min-chih -- Candidate Director, China Educational
Reconstruction Association, Shanghai Branch
(49:194)

Min-chung -- Administrative Vice-Minister under
Minister of Education, Wang Ching-wei's
regime (3/41; OSS-Ms.); member, Central Execu-
tive Committee, Nanking (1943); member, Com-
mittee of Political Councillors; Vice-
Minister of Interior; appointed Head, Pao-chia
Promotion Committee; Assistant Chairman,
Directing Committee, China Office, East
Asia League

Min-chung -- Chief of Finance, Kiangsu (39:194);
Political Advisor, National Government,
Nanking

Mu (Mo)-- Minister of Education, Education Ministry, North China (52:244)

On-ho, Lt. Gen. -- Director, Pacification Office,
Hupeh Province, Nanking Government (8/29/43)

Pao-chen -- Editor-in-Chief, TIEN TSIN SHIH PAO,
Tientsin (52:244)

Pe-jen -- See Wang Te-yen

P'ing -- Manager Director, Shanghai Special Munici-
pality Journalists Association; member,
Shanghai Newspaper Association; Director,
Sino-Japanese Cultural Association, Shanghai
Branch; Editor, HSIN CHUNG KUO PAO (49:194)

P'ing-yung -- Publisher, SHIH SHIH KUNG PAO,
Ningpo, Chekiang (IDC 2562)

CHINESE

Wang Po-yuan -- Manager Director, Shanghai Chamber of
Commerce; Director and Treasurer, Shanghai
Labor and Business Social Union; Director,
Shanghai Citizens Welfare Association;
Chairman, Savings Gift Bond Committee; mem-
ber, Citizens Savings Movement Committee
Shanghai (49:194)

Pu -- Commander, pro-Japanese troops; with
Japanese Huang Hsieh Chun, Yunghsiu and its
vicinity, commanding 1,000 men (6/39; OSS-Ms.)

Pu-lo -- Manager Inspector, Shanghai Wharf Labor
Union, Shanghai (49:194)

Shao-tiao -- Director, Hua Chung Silk Corporation,
Shanghai (49:194)

Shi -- Chief, Office of Police Affairs, Kwangtung
(51:252)

Shih-chen -- Candidate Director, Shanghai Education Committee (49:194)

Shih-chieh -- Minister of Publicity (1941) (DIO)

Shih-ching (Wang Shin-cheng; Wang Shis-kang) --
Head, Finance Bureau (12/38); member, Central
Political Council, Nanking (1943); member,
Executive Committee, All-China Economic
Committee; member, Standing Committee, North
China; manager, China United Reserve Bank,
Shanghai (3/11/43); decorated by Japanese
Emperor (3/23/44); Governor, Federal Reserve
Bank of China (9/13/44); Director, General
Economic Administration, Political Commission
of North China (9/13/44); Superintendent,
Department of Finance, Nanking; Financial
Administration, Peiping; signed loan from
Bank of Japan to Federal Reserve Bank of
China (9/13/44); Managing Commissioner and
Chief of Public Peace (4/24/44) (52:244)

Shih-ch'u -- Member, Shanghai Newspaper Association (49:194)

Shih-fen -- Commissioner of Education, North
China (7/21/44) (52:244)

Shih-huan -- Officer, North China Political
Affairs Council, Tientsin (12/4/43) (52:244)

Shih-tsung -- Director General of Finance, North
China Political Affairs Commission (52:244)

Shih-yi -- Counsellor, National Government,
Nanking (1943)

Shin-ching -- Governor, Federal Reserve Bank of
China (1944) (52:244)

Shou-p'eng -- Inspector, China Educational Reconstruction Association, Chekiang Branch
(49:195)

-178-

CHINESE

Wang Shou-shan -- Inspector, East Asia League, Hupeh Branch (1943)

Shu-ch'eng -- Candidate Inspector, Sino-Japanese Cultural Association, Wu-ch'ang and Hankow Branch (1943)

Shu-ch'un -- Formerly Director, Industry Department, Ministry of Industry, Executive Yuan; also Chief of Engineering, Ministry of Industry, Executive Yuan (1943)

Shu-go -- Ex-Chief, Economic Bureau, Shanghai; resigned (about 8/27/43) (49:195)

Shu-huai -- Chairman, Directors, China Educational Reconstruction Association, Hankow Branch (1943)

Shu-sheng -- Candidate Director, China Educational Reconstruction Association, Hankow Branch (1943)

Sung-hui -- Director, East Asia League, Hupeh Branch (1943)

Sung-nien -- Editor-in-Chief, CHEN PAO (Morning Post), Peiping (52:245)

Ta-te -- Honorary Director, China Educational Reconstruction Association, Hankow Branch (1943)

T'ai -- Control Officer, Yuan Hsiang Kang Ward, Hongkong (51:252)

Tao, Maj. Gen. -- Military Advisor, National Government (1943)

Tao-nan -- Inspector, East Asia League, Hupeh Branch (1943)

T'e-chang -- Candidate Inspector, China Educational Reconstruction Association and Director, Anhwei Branch (1943)

Te-kuang -- Chairman, Business Affairs Bureau, China People's Representative Assembly, Hongkong; member, Council, Chinese Representatives Association (51:252)

Teh-feng -- Secretary, Committee on Exhibition of Relief and Culture, Hongkong (51:252)

Te-yen (Wang Pe-jen) -- Son of Wang I-tang, Chairman, North China Political Affairs Council; Minister Extraordinary and Plenipotentiary to Spain; Secretary General, Committee for the Custody of Enemy Property, Shanghai Branch (49:195); member, Directing Committee, China Office, East Asia League, Nanking Branch; Executive Director, China Educational Reconstruction Association

Tieh-hsiang -- Commander, pro-Japanese troops; with Huang Hsieh Chun, commanding about 3,000 men, Hopeh Border (6/39; OSS-Ms.)

228

-179-

CHINESE

Wang T'ien-mu -- Deputy Chief, Office of Economics; Director, Sino-Japanese Cultural Association, Shanghai Branch (49:195)

Tien-shen -- Manager, Chung Hsing Bank, Shanghai (1943)

Tin-tai -- Director General, North China Financial Administration; attended session of Supreme National Defense Council (6/27/43) (52:245)

T'ing-chang -- Minister, residing in Ministry of Foreign Affairs, Nanking (1943)

Ting-kuei -- Chairman, Directors, Photographers Association, Shanghai (1943)

To-kuang -- Chairman, Business Affairs Bureau, Chinese People's Representative Assembly, Hongkong; member, China Discursive Association (51:252)

To-ping -- Manager, Chekiang Hsing Yeh Bank, Hankow Branch, Hupeh (1943)

Tsai-ping -- Commander, pro-Japanese troops; with Japanese Huang Hsieh Chun, Chengssu Islands, commanding Mobile Detachment (6/39: OSS-Ms.)

Tsu-tse -- Chief Prosecutor, North China Supreme Court (1/17/43) (52:245)

Tsung-chun -- Member, Committee of Political Councillors, Nanking (1943); Finance Commissioner; Food Commissioner; Chairman, Executive Board, Kwangtung Branch, National Trade Control Association, Kwangtung; Chief, Bureau of Finance; Chief, Office of Grain Control (51:252)

Tsung-shih -- Member, Directing Committee, China Office, East Asia League, Nanking Branch (1943)

Tu-feng -- Represented Wang Chien-tien, former Head of Education Department, on inauguration of Wen Yuan-mo, Peiping (3/1/45) (52:245)

Tu-hwei -- Vice-Minister of Education, North China (52:245)

Tung-hsin -- Assistant, Production Education and Research Committee, China Educational Reconstruction Association (1943)

T'ung-ming -- Superintendent, Hongkong-Kowloon Tung Ming Hospital; member, China Representatives (Discursive) Association, Hongkong (51:252)

Wei -- Inspector, China Educational Reconstruction Association, Anhwei Branch (1943)

Wei-fan -- Member, National Military Council (OSS)

-180-

CHINESE

Wang Wei-te -- Editor, HU CHIANG TUNG PAO, and other papers, Shanghai (49:195)

Wen-tsai -- Candidate Director, China Educational Reconstruction Association, Hankow Branch (1943)

Wu Chin-wei -- Managing Director, Bank of China, Shanghai (11/2/43) (49:195)

Ya-ch'en -- Director, Sino-Japanese Cultural Association, Shanghai Branch (49:195)

Yi-ch'ing -- Director, China Educational Reconstruction Association, Shanghai Branch (49:195)

Yi-fang (Chao Ju-heng; Chao Ju-hang) -- Head, Social Department, Ministry of Education, Nanking; Executive Director, China Educational Reconstruction Association (R&A 2565)

Yi-hsuan -- Editor, LU TUNG JIH PAO, Yen-tai, North China (52:245)

Yi-sheng -- Counsellor, National Government, Nanking (1943)

Yi-t'ang (See Also Wang I-tang) -- Member, Central Political Council, Nanking (1943); State Councillor; member, North China Political Council; temporary Chief, Reconstruction Department (1/43); Vice-Chairman, National Economic Conference (1/43); Honorary Director, Sino-Japanese Cultural Association (52:245); Executive member, Committee for Application of Constitution

Yin-k'ang -- Director, Committee for Establishment of China's Broadcasting Business, Shanghai (49:195)

Yin-t'ai -- Born, 1886, Shaohsing, Chekiang; studied in Japan (until 1906); took law course, Berlin University (1912); returned to China (1913); Counsellor, Bureau of Legislation; Diplomatic Service, Japan (1914-20); Advisor, Chang Tso-lin (1922-25); Minister, Foreign Affairs (1927); Minister of Justice (1928); practiced law, Shanghai (1930) (OSS-Ms.); member, Central Political Council, Nanking; member, Standing Committee and Head, Industry Bureau, North China (12/38-43); member, North China Political Council, Peiping; Supervisor of Industry, Commerce and Industry Ministry; Head, Industrial Bureau, Peiping; represented North China, GEA Economic Conference; decorated by Emperor of Japan (3/23/44); Director, Agricultural Affairs Bureau; first President, North China Food Corporation (5/21/44); member, Executive Committee, All-China Political Affairs Council; Honorary Director, China-Japan Returned Students Club (52:245); member, National Economic Conference

Ying -- Held office, North China Political Council (2/8/43) (52:245)

CHINESE

Wang Ying-ju -- Minister, residing in Ministry of Foreign Affairs, Nanking (1943)

Ying-kuo -- Magistrate, Pao-ying Hsien, Chekiang (OSS)

Yu -- Director, East Asia League, Hupeh Branch (1943)

Yu-chai -- Manager, Li Min Bank, Shanghai (IDC 7270 1943)

Yu-ch'en -- Director, China Educational Reconstruction Association, Chekiang (49:195)

Yu-chia, Lt. Gen. -- Chief, Rural Pacification Bureau, Hopeh Province; Chief, Office of Village Pacification (52:245)

Yu-chin -- Member, National Military Council (OSS)

Yu-ching -- Director, Central Reserve Bank, Tai Hsien Branch, Kiangsu (IDC 1943)

Yu-chung -- Executive member, China Journalists Association (1943)

Yu-lin -- Commissioner, Directorate-General of the Interior, North China Political Commission (7/40; OSS-Ms.); Supervisor, North China Salt Corporation, Tientsin Branch (1943) (52:245)

Yu-mei -- Head, General Affairs Bureau, Ministry of Interior; member, Pao-chia Promotion Committee (IDC 3/30/43)

Yu-sheng -- Member, Legislative Yuan, Nanking (1943)

Yuan-po -- Director, Sino-Japanese Cultural Association, Shanghai Branch (49:195)

Yuang -- "Well known educator"; member, North China Political Council (1943); resigned as Director General (7/31/44) (52:245); Candidate Director, China Educational Reconstruction Association

Yun-shih -- Director, Sino-Japanese Cultural Association, Shanghai Branch (49:195)

Yung -- See Wang Yuang

Yung-ch'uan -- Director, Directorate-General of Pacification, North China Political Commission (7/40; OSS-Ms.)

Yung-t'ien -- Counsellor, National Government, Nanking (1943)

Yung-nien -- Staff member, Construction Department, Hongkong (51:252)

We Ting-chang -- Detached Officer, Peace Preservation Corps, North China Political Commission (52:245)

CHINESE

Wei Ch'eng-tsai -- Member, Social Welfare Committee, China Office, East Asia League (1943)

Ching -- Deputy Chief Detective, Canton Bureau of Police (51:252)

Ching-hsing -- Secretary, Control Yuan, Nanking (1943)

Fan -- Publisher, HSIN SHEN PAO, Shanghai

Kuo-lun -- Representative, Central News Agency, Hongkong Branch (51:252)

Li-chou -- Candidate Director, China Educational Reconstruction Association (1943)

Li-huang -- Head, 14th Army; Head, 10th Division; in charge, bandit suppression, Hsiang-kung Area (Hunan, Hupeh, Kiangsi Provinces)(DIO)

Lun-sung -- Formerly connected with Hongkong newspaper published with support of Formosan Government; appointed by Formosa to be representative, General Affairs Office, Hongkong (51:253)

Nai-lun -- Member, Social Welfare Committee, China Branch, East Asia League (1943); also Executive Director, Nanking Branch, East Asia League; Director, China Movie Association

Nai-tun -- Manager Director, Committee for Establishment of China Broadcasting Business, Shanghai (49:195); member, Executive Committee, China Broadcasting Enterprise and Reconstruction Association; Director, China Writers Club

, Peter -- Member, Racing Committee, Hongkong Jockey Club (51:253)

Shan-fu -- Director, Shanghai Chamber of Commerce (49:195)

Tu-tung -- Police Commissioner, Anhwei Province (OSS)

Wen-chin -- Member, Legislative Yuan, Nanking (1943)

Wu-hsiang -- Executive Inspector, East Asia League, Hupeh Branch (1943)

Yun-wei -- Auditor and Chief of First Department, Ministry of Auditing, Nanking (1943)

Wen Ch'ing-ch'ai -- Secretary, Judicial Yuan, Nanking (1943)

Ch'ing-ch'eng -- Secretary, National Economic Committee (1943)

Ho-t'ing -- Chairman, Directors, Shanghai Labor and Business Social Union; Chairman, Directors, Shanghai Citizens Welfare Association (49:;95)

CHINESE

Wen Lan-t'ing -- Appointed Chairman, Board of Directors, All-China Commercial Control General Association (6/44); President, Chinese Society for Active Diplomacy; Chairman, Board of Supervisors, Chamber of Commerce, Shanghai; Chairman, Board of Directors, National Trade Control Association Headquarters; (49:195); Chairman, Directors, Textile Factories Association; member, Advisory Committee, Shanghai Municipality; Chairman, Cotton Control Association

Nan-lu -- Member, Committee on Peace and Order, Shanghai Municipal Council (49:195)

Shih-tseng -- Mayor, Tientsin (52:245)

Shih-chen -- Member, North China Political Council (1943)

Tsung-yao (Wen Tsung-chiao) -- Born, 1876, Kwangtung; graduate, Men's College, Hongkong; studied in America; returned to China (1903); appointed Delegate, Anglo-Chinese Convention for revision of commercial treaties; Secretary to Viceroy of Liang Kwang (1903-08); went to India concerning Tibet (1908); Chinese resident, Lhassa; joined new government in Canton (1918); quarreled with Sun Yat-sen; fled to Shanghai to seek refuge in concession (1920);President, Legislative Yuan, Nanking "Reformed Government" (3/28/38) (OSS-Ms.); member, Standing Committee, Executive Committee, Central Political Council (from 12/38); President, Judicial Yuan, Nanking (1943); decorated by Japanese Emperor (3/23/44); Honorary Director, Sino-Japanese Cultural Association; Executive member, Committee for Application of Constitution

Tzu-chen -- Member, Legislative Yuan, Nanking (1943)

Yuan-mo -- Formerly President, North China University; Head, Education Department, Peiping (3/1/45) (52:246)

Yung-ch'ang -- Secretary, Judicial Yuan, Nanking (1943)

Weng Chieh-fu -- Candidate Inspector, China Educational Reconstruction Association, Chekiang Branch (49:195)

(Chung-ta) -- Minister of Education (2/26/44) (DIO)

Ho -- Director, China Educational Reconstruction Association, Chekiang Branch (49:195)

Mo-shun -- Candidate Director, China Educational Reconstruction Association, Chekiang Branch (49:196)

Mon-fang -- National Commercial Savings Bank; elected committee member, Hongkong Chinese Bankers Association (51:253)

-184-

CHINESE

Weng Yung-ch'ing -- Member, Shanghai Newspaper Association; Inspector, Citizens Savings Movement, Shanghai (49:196); Editor, HSIN CHUNG KUO PAO (IDC 7266 1943)

Wo Ji-cho, Lt. Gen. (Japanized version) -- Chief, General Affairs Bureau, Military Affairs Committee; appointed Chief, General Affairs Bureau, Propaganda Ministry

Wong Hoi-tong -- Chairman, Hongkong Christian Association (51:253)

, Peter M. -- Journalist and Writer, Hongkong (51:253)

Tai-wah -- Head, Kowloon Division, Kowloon Bicycle and Tricycle Syndicate (51:253)

Tai-wei -- Former Commander-in-Chief, Kwangtung Peace National Establishment Army; deceased (51:253)

Wen-hao, Dr. -- Minister of National Economy (1/1/42)

Yat-chung -- Vice-Chairman, General Affairs Committee, General Relief Association, Hongkong (51:253)

Wu Chang-chia -- Left Chungking Camp; joined National Government (2/8/43)

Chang-tu -- Left Chungking Camp; joined National Government (2/8/43)

Chao-p'ing -- Candidate Inspector, China Educational Reconstruction Association, Shanghai Branch (49:196)

Chen-hsiu (hsin) -- Executive Committee member, All-China Economic Committee (1943); Manager Director, Central Reserve Bank of China, Shanghai Branch; Municipal Advisory Committee member, Shanghai; Director, National Commercial Control Association

Chen-nain -- China Bank

Chen-tse -- Secretary, Ministry of the Navy, Nanking (1943)

Ch'en-yu -- Member, Legislative Yuan and Chief, Diplomatic Committee, Nanking (1943); member, Committee for Application of Constitution

Ch'eng-chih -- Director, East Asia League, Shanghai Branch; Publisher, TSA CHIH (49:196)

Ch'eng-yu -- Inspector, China Office, East Asia League (1943)

Chiang-feng -- Director, Shanghai Magazines Association; Director, Sino-Japanese Cultural Association, Shanghai Branch (49:196)

CHINESE

Wu Chiang-tung -- Director, Shanghai Education Committee (49:196)

Ch'ien-k'uei -- Secretary, Legislative Yuan, Nanking (1943)

Chih-hao -- Member, Peace and Order Committee, Municipal Council, Shanghai (49:196)

Chih-p'u -- Director, China Educational Reconstruction Association, Hankow Branch (1943); high official, Hsin Min Hui

Ching-chi -- Chief, Hygienic Division, National Government of China (7/3/44)

Ching-shiu -- Member, Finance Committee, Municipal Council, Shanghai (5/13/44) (49:196)

Ch'ou -- Propaganda Head, 3rd District Party Headquarters, Kuomintang, Swatow (IDC)

Chuang -- Member, Committee for Application of Constitution, Nanking (1943)

Chung-pao -- Director, Propaganda Department, Chekiang (?) (1/3/45)

Han-pai -- Member, Publication Committee, China Writers Club (1943)

Hsi-chen -- Judge, Administrative Court, Nanking (1943)

Hsi-yung -- Chief, Financial Affairs, North China Political Council (1943)

Hsiang-chen -- Manager, Peiping Agricultural and Industrial Bank (52:246)

Hsiao-hou -- Director, Citizens Savings Movement Committee, Shanghai (49:196)

Hsiao-hsien -- Inspector, East Asia League, Nanking Branch (1943)

Hsi-yung -- Director, Directorate-General of Finance, North China Political Commission (7/40; OSS-Ms.)

Hsien, Gen. -- According to Japanese source, went over to Nanking from Shantung Province with troops (3/19/43; OSS-Ms.)

Hsien-ch'ing -- Executive Inspector, East Asia League, Nanking Branch (1943)

Hsien-hsiang -- Member, Legislative Yuan, Nanking (1943)

Hsien-tzu -- Inspecting member, Control Yuan, Nanking (1943)

Hu-fan -- Director, Sino-Japanese Cultural Association, Shanghai Branch (49:196)

CHINESE

Wu Hua -- Advisor, Bureau for Restoration of Commerce, Hongkong; Director and General Manager, Pita Firm; Director, Sheng Tai Construction Company; member, Chinese Representatives (Discursive) Association (51:253)

Hua-wen, Gen. -- Highest Commander, National Shantung Army, renamed the Third Army (7/29/43); interested in education (2/16/44); Head, Anti-Communist Army, Shantung Province (3/15/44)

Huan-ju -- Director, Citizens Savings Movement Committee, Shanghai (49:196)

Hui-po -- Manager, China Fishery Industrial Bank, Shanghai (IDC 1943)

Ju-k'ang -- Counsellor, National Government, Nanking (1943)

Jui-yuan -- Member, National Economic Committee (1943)

K'ai-hsien -- Member, Central Executive Committee, Nanking

K'ai-sheng -- Vice-Minister, Foreign Affairs, Nanking; Special Delegate to receive English Legation Quarters, Peiping, and French Concession, Hankow; Candidate Director, Sino-Japanese Cultural Association; Chairman, General Affairs Department, National Military Council (1943); Inspector, China Office, East Asia League; Nanking Minister to Italy and Crotia; member, Committee for Application of Constitution

K'ai-sho -- Nanking Ambassador to Rome; appointed concurrently Minister to Croatia (2/24/42)

K'e-jen -- In command, 117th Division, 67th Army Corps (under Wang I-che); stationed at Sian (9/35); moving into Kansu (10/35); with Japanese Huang Hsieh Chun, Peichiang and its vicinity commanding 4,000 men (6/39; OSS-MS.)

Ko-chuan -- Publisher, CHUNG SHAN MIN PAO, Chungshan, South China (51:253)

K'uai-sheng -- Honorary member, China Journalists Association (1943)

Kuan-li -- Executive member, China Journalists Association (1943)

Kwan-shen -- Director, Committee for Airplane Donations, Peiping (8/2/44) (52:246)

Lan-hsi (Wu Lan-mo) -- Vice-Secretary General, Executive Yuan (1/43)

Lien-te -- Director, East Asia League, Shanghai Branch (49:196)

CHINESE

Wu Liu-kung -- Member, Shanghai Newspaper Association; (49:196); Editor, HSIN CHUNG KUO PAO (IDC 7266 1943)

Lun-te -- Manager, Nan Yang Commercial Bank, Shanghai Branch (IDC 7270 1943)

Min -- Secretary, 3rd District Party Headquarters, Kuomintang, Swatow

Nien-chung -- Mayor, Hangchow; advisory member, Ministry of Information (1943)

Ou -- Secretary General, Directorate-General of the Interior, North China Political Commission (7/40; OSS-Ms.)

Pao-chung -- Candidate Inspector, Shanghai Special Municipality Journalists Association (49:196)

Pei -- Head, Third Section, Canton Bureau of Police (51:253)

Pei-chih -- Inspector, Shanghai Special Municipality Journalists Association (49:196)

Pei-chung -- Chairman, Directors, Brass Foil Ashes Association, Shanghai (IDC 7264 1943)

Pei-yuan -- Chief, Central News Agency, Hongkong Branch (51:253)

Peng-fei -- Captain, Shanghai Youth and Juvenile Corps, Model Youth Corps (OSS)

Pin -- Auditor and Chief, Second Department, Ministry of Auditing, Nanking (1943)

Po-chou -- Director, Huai Nan Coal Mine Stock Company, Shanghai (IDC 1943)

Po-shih -- Police student sent to Formosa for training; now assigned to Police Officers Academy, Canton (1/6/44) (51:253)

Shang-shih -- Chief, Water Police Patrol, Canton Police Bureau (51:253)

Shih-chin -- Secretary, Kuomintang Second District Party Headquarters, Canton; Manager, Ho Thai Commercial Bank, Shanghai (51:253)

Shu-ta -- Head, Bureau of Construction, Amoy (49:196)

Sia-cheng -- Chinese Ambassador to Italy; member, Committee taking over French Concessions, Shanghai (49:196)

Sung-kai -- Ex-Secretary General, Shanghai; Minister of Justice, National Government (1/13/45)

Sung-kao (-tao) -- Minister of Justice, Executive Yuan (1943); member, Committee on Return of Concessions; Special Delegate to receive Japanese Concessions; in Ministry of Foreign Affairs, Plenipotentiary Ambassador; member

CHINESE

Wu Sung-kao (-tao) (Con't) -- Central Executive Committee, Nanking; once Secretary General, Shanghai; Advisor, Citizens Savings Movement Committee, Shanghai (49:196)

Szu-ju -- Training Head, 3rd District Party Headquarters, Kuomintang, Swatow (IDC)

Tai-ch'iu -- Director, Sino-Japanese Cultural Association, Shanghai Branch (49:196)

Tao-cheng -- In Shanghai with Wang Ching-wei, working as assistant to Chen Kung-po who is in charge of "Reorganization Fellowship of the KMT of China" (5/27/39; OSS-Ms.)

Te-fang -- Chief, Land Surveying, Ministry of the Army, Nanking (1943)

Tien-feng -- Chairman, General Affairs Committee, North China Political Council; witness to revised by-laws of National Government by North China Political Council (52:246)

Tien-min -- Head, United Guard, Amoy (?) (49:197)

Ting-chang -- Special (detached officer), Peace Preservation Corps, North China Political Commission; concurrently Commander-in-Chief, North China Regular Army (11/19/43) (52:246)

T'ing-hsueh -- Inspecting member, Control Yuan, Nanking (1943); member, Committee for Editing the National History

To -- Athlete, Hongkong (51:253)

Toun-ting -- Editor, KAI PING JIH PAO, K'ai-ping, South China (51:253)

Tsan-chou -- Member, Political Affairs Commission, Peiping (52:246)

Tsun-t'ing -- Editor, K'AI P'ING JIH PAO, South China (1943) (same as Wu Toun-ting?)

Tsung-han -- Director, Sino-Japanese Cultural Association, Shanghai Branch (49:197)

T'u-nan -- Member, Legislative Yuan, Nanking (1943)

Tzu-keng -- Candidate Inspector, China Educational Reconstruction Association, Chekiang Branch (49:197)

Wei-ju -- Manager, Tung Lai Bank, Shanghai (IDC 7270 1943)

Wei-yun -- Director, Central Reserve Bank, Nanking (IDC 7270 1943)

Wen-chai -- Director, Standing Committee, Shanghai Press Association; Chairman, HSIN WEN PAO (IDC 1943)

238   -189-

CHINESE

Wu Wen-chung -- Advisory member, Ministry of Foreign
        Affairs, Nanking (1943)

Wen-hu -- See Aw Boon-haw

Wen-kuei -- Head, Bureau of Police, Amoy (49:197)

Wen-tai -- Member, Committee of Peace and Order,and
        Committee of Territories and Borders, Shanghai
        Municipal Council (49:197)

Wen-tse -- Control Officer, Race Course Ward,
        Hongkong (54:254)

Wen-sei -- Inspector, China Educational Reconstruc-
        tion Association (1943)

Yao-t'ing -- Director, Shanghai Wharf Labor Union
        (49:197)

Yen-pin -- Manager Director, Readjustment Committee,
        National Post Office Labor Union, Shanghai
        (49:197)

Yi-chih -- Candidate Director, Shanghai Educational
        Committee (49:197)

Yi-min -- Editor, HUA PAI TI YU, a publication,
        Peiping (1943) (52:246)

Yi-sheng -- Director, Shanghai Magazines Associa-
        tion; Publisher, JEN CHIEN, a monthly (IDC
        2562)(49:197)

Yun-wan -- Chief, Education Section, Peiping Munici-
        pal Bureau of Education (52:246)

Yun-fei -- Commander, pro-Japanese troops; with
        Japanese Huang Hsieh Chun commanding 900
        men in area of Kuyang, Shapatze, and
        Hsiaochetai (6/39; OSS-Ms.)

Yun-pu -- Secretary, Canton Bureau of Police (51:253)

Yun-tsai (-chai) -- Manager Director, Shanghai
        Labor and Business Social Union; Manager
        Director, Shanghai Newspaper Association;
        Manager Supervisor, Shanghai Chamber of Com-
        merce; Inspector, Sino-Japanese Cultural
        Association, Shanghai Branch; Publisher,
        HSIN WEN PAO (49:197)

Yung -- Acting Chief, Ministry of Foreign Affairs,
        Shanghai Office (1943)

Yung-hua -- Chairman, Directors, Automobile Parts
        Association, Shanghai (IDC 7264)

Wuan Hua-wen, Gen. -- Leader and member, Nanking
        Supreme War Council (7/29/43)

Wun Pa-chin -- Cooperating with Nanking Government;
        former Battalion Commander, Guerrilla Army,
        Patriotic National Salvation Army (9/5/42)

Wung -- Chief, Police Bureau, Hankow

-190-

CHINESE

Ya Hsiel-lien, Gen. (Lee Kiang-yuan) -- Inspector-
General, Military Divisions (2/15/43)

Sen-li -- Vice-Chairman, Nippon Press Association,
GEA Conference; Manchukuo Delegate; Editor-
in-Chief, Kangte Hsin Min

Yan Chen, Maj. Gen. -- Director, Information Bureau,
Nanking (1943)

Chung-hwa -- Divisional Commander, 2nd Mixed Division, Northwest China; attempted to revolt
(10/27/42)

Hai-keh -- Vice-President, Protestant Council,
Amoy (49:197)

Yang -- Governor, Wuhan (5/18/44)

Chao-- Head, Sha Ho Branch Agency, Canton Police
Bureau (51:254)

Chao-lei -- Mayor, Tahsien (9/24/44) (52:246)

Chen-lieh -- Special Delegate to National Supreme
Defense Council (7/8/43)

Cheng-yu -- Chief, Office of Education, Nanking
(1943); Executive Director, East Asia League,
Nanking Branch; Executive Director and
Chief, Research Section, China Educational
Reconstruction Association; Director,
China-Japan Returned Students Club

Chi-hsu -- Director, East Asia League, Hupeh
Branch (1943)

Chi-wu -- Chief of Staff, Hankow-Wuchang Branch,
National Military Council (2/15/43)

Chieh -- Chief, Board of Investigation and
Statistics, Political Affairs Office, Nan-
king (1943); Inspector, China Office, East
Asia League

Chih-ch'ing -- Judge and Commissioner of Civil
Affairs, Kiangsi (1943)

Ching-ch'en -- Member, Flour Special Committee,
National Trade Control General Association,
Shanghai (49:197)

Ching-hu -- Director, Shanghai Wharf Labor Union
(49:197)

Chiung-lang -- Manager Director, Shanghai Special
Municipality Journalists Association; Inspector, Citizens Savings Movement Committee,
Shanghai; Director, Sino-Japanese Cultural
Association, Shanghai Branch; Head, Electrical Communications Corporation, Shanghai
(49:197)

Chu-fang -- Editor, SHANSI HSIN MIN PAO, Tai-yuan,
North China (52:246)

CHINESE

Yang Chung-chien -- Prize Winner, North China Labor
Association (52:246)

Chung-fang -- Secretary, Examination Yuan, Nanking
(1943)

Chung-hua -- Officer with Nanking Army; Commander-
in-Chief, Kiangsu-Anhwei Border Pacification Army (OSS-Ms.)

En-hui -- Director, Sino-Japanese Cultural Association, Wu-ch'ang and Hankow Branch (1943)

En-wei -- Executive Inspector, East Asia League,
Hupeh Branch (1943)

Fa -- Commander, Peace Corps Unit, Hsinhsien
Peace Preservation Corps, Shansi (7/7/44)

Ho-ch'ing -- Member, Oil and Grain Special Committee, National Trade Control General
Association, Shanghai; member, Committee
on Grain Control; Director, Shanghai Chamber of Commerce (49:197)

Hsiao-tseng -- Head, Hua Chung City Bus Company,
Shanghai (49:197); Chairman, Board of Direc-
tors, Central China City Bus Stock Company,
Shanghai (1943)

Hsing-hua -- Director, General Affairs Department,
Ministry of Finance, Executive Yuan, Nanking
(OSS)

Hua -- Editor, CHIAO WU CHI KAU, a quarterly,
Nanking (IDC 2562)

Hui, Gen. -- Chief, Hupeh Provincial Government

Hui-lang -- Director, Shanghai Newspapermen's
Association (1943)

Hung-hsiao -- Chief Manager, Committee on Application of Constitution, Nanking (1943)

Hung-lieh -- Chief of Affairs, Ministry of Infor-
mation, Nanking (1943); member, National
History Editing Committee, Control Yuan,
Inspector, China-Japan Returned Students
Club; Director, China Educational Reconstruc-
tion Association; Director, China Writers
Club

Hwei-po -- Member, Education Committee, Municipal
Council, Shanghai (49:197)

Hsing-hua -- Director, Huai Nan Salt Industry
Stock Company, Shanghai (IDC 1943)

Kuang-cheng -- Director, Shanghai Magazines Asso-
ciation; Director, Sino-Japanese Cultural
Association, Shanghai Branch; Publisher,
KUO CHI LIANG CHOU PAO (49:197)

CHINESE

Yang K'uei-i (-yi; Yang Kwei-li) -- Member, Designated Committee, Central Political Council, Nanking (12/38); member, Central Executive Committee; Vice-Chief, General Staff, National Military Council (from 12/38); member, Central Political Council, Nanking Kuomintang (OSS-Ms.); member, Military Affairs Commission, Wang Ching-wei's regime (3/31/41; OSS-Ms.); Chief-of-Staff, Nanking puppet armies; went to Japan (6/3/42; OSS-Ms.); Commander, 21,600 puppet troops, Wuhan Area (5/20/43; OSS-Ms.); Governor, Hupeh (1943); member, China-Japan Returned Students Club; Inspector, China Office, East Asia League; Chief Director, East Asia League, Hupeh Branch; decorated by Japanese Emperor (3/23/44)

Kuei-itang -- Chief of Staff, Military Commission (0-62)

K'uei-yi -- Executive Director, China-Japan Returned Students Club (1943)

Kung-tso -- Inspector, Citizens Savings Movement Committee, Shanghai (49:197)

Kuung-ch'iu -- Candidate Director, China Educational Reconstruction Association, Anhwei Branch (1943)

Kya-chu (Col. Walter Yang) -- Member, Huang Tao Hui; arrested (9/38) (OSS-Ms.)

Lien-fu -- Executive Inspector, Social Welfare Committee, East Asia League, Canton Branch (51:254)

Lieng -- See Hsu Liang, Dr.

Lo-san -- Member, Flour Special Committee, National Trade Control General Association, Shanghai (49:198)

Lung-kuang -- Publisher, WU TE PAO, Peiping (1943) (52:246)

Miao-t'ing -- Councillor, Chinghsiang Administration, Hangchou Sector (IDC 6/8/43)

Pao-yi -- Commissioner of Reconstruction, Huaihai Province (1943); Chief of Construction, Administrative Office, Su-huai

Ping-chien -- Propaganda Head, Kuomintang First District Party Headquarters, Canton (51:254)

Po-kang -- Commander pro-Japanese troops; with Japanese Huang Hsieh Chun in Shanghai, commanding about 1,000 men (6/39; OSS-Ms.)

Po-ming -- Candidate Inspector, China Educational Reconstruction Association, Anhwei Branch (1943)

Shou-hao -- Councillor, Municipal Government, Hankow (IDC)

CHINESE

Yang Shou-mei -- Irrigation Commander, Wang Ching-wei's
National Government (3/22/40; OSS-Ms.);
State Councillor, Nanking (1943); Inspector,
China Office, East Asia League

Shu-cloh -- China Press Association (2/23/44; DIO)

Shu-ting -- Manager, Yung Ta Bank, Shanghai (IDC
7270 1943)

Ta-huang -- Member, Publication Committee, China
Writers Club (1943)

Te-jung -- Commander, pro-Japanese troops; with
pro-Japanese forces in area of southern
Shansi and Hopeh and northern Honan, commanding about 5,000 men (6/39; OSS-Ms.)

Ti -- Candidate Director, Shanghai Special Municipality Association (49:198)

Ting-hsun -- Chief of Police, Tai-shan Road District Office, Third Police Office, Shanghai
(49:198)

Tsun-jun -- Inspector, Shanghai Wharf Labor Union
(49:198)

Wei-ch'ang -- Director, North China Electrical
Communications Stock Company, Shanghai
(1943); member, Social Welfare Committee,
China Office, East Asia League

Wei-chen -- Vice-Minister of Education (1/43);
member, New Citizens Movement Promotion Committee

Wu-chang -- Head, Information Unit, Canton Bureau
of Police (51:254)

Yi-hsun -- Editor, TA TAO, a monthly, Chang-chou,
Kiangsu (49:198)

Yin-hua -- Head, General Affairs; member, Committee,
for Stopping the Breakage at Chung-mon of
Huang-ho, Nanking (1943)

Ying-huang -- Judge, and Chief, Nanking Province
(1943)

Ying-kun -- Vice-Minister of Legislative Administration (2/43)

Yu-cheun -- Commander-in-Chief, Provincial Peace
Preservation Corps, Shantung (3/2/45)
(52:246)

Yu-p'o -- Publisher, CHU YUNG SHENG PAO, Chu-yung,
Kwangsu (IDC 2562)

Yuan-chieh -- Manager, Chin Chang Bank, Peiping
Branch (1943) (52:246)

Yuan-ming, Capt. -- Surgeon, Chinese National Army,
reportedly gone over to Japanese side in
Anking (12/31/42; OSS-Ms.)

-194-

CHINESE

Yang Yun-hua -- Director, Shanghai Special Municipality
        Journalists Association (49:198)

    Yung-fang -- Chairman, Directors, Iron Plans and
            Porcelains Association, Shanghai (IDC 7264
            1943)

Yank K'nei-yi -- Ex-Chief of Staff (O-57)

Yao Chia-kuei -- Assistant Chief of Police, Bubbling
            Well Temple District Office, First Police
            Office, Shanghai (49:198)

    Chia-wa -- Assistant Chief, Ching-an-szu Branch,
            (#1), Shanghai Police (IDC 1943)

    Chiang -- Member, Publications Committee, China
            Writers Club (1943)

    Chun-wei -- Chairman, Directors, Advertisement
            Association, Shanghai (IDC 7264 1943)

    Keng -- Head, Kaifeng Pacification Corps (12/38)

    Hsi-chao -- Candidate Inspector, China Educational
            Reconstruction Association, Anhwei Branch
            (1943)

    Hsi-chiu, Lt. Gen. -- Vice-Chief of Staff, National
            Military Council, Nanking (1943)

    Ke -- Director, Sino-Japanese Cultural Association,
            Shanghai Branch (49:198)

    Lo-ch'uan -- Candidate Director, Shanghai Special
            Municipality Journalists Association (49:198)

    Nai-chang -- Manager, Tsung Te Hsien Farmers Bank,
            Chekiang (IDC 1943)

    Shun-po -- Secretary General, Judicial Yuan, Nan-
            king (1943)

    Tsun-chih -- Director, Citizens Savings Movement
            Committee, Shanghai (49:198)

    Wen-tao, Gen. -- Chinese General; presented 500
            yen to Hongkong Government (51:254)

    Wen-tsun -- Chairman, Directors, Standard Workshops,
            Shanghai (IDC 7264 1943)

Yean Chung, Lt. Gen. -- Member, Nanking mission to
            North China (52:246)

Yeh Chew-tung -- Counsellor, National Government,
            Nanking (1943); of Anhwei Provincial Gov-
            ernment; member, Pao-chia Promotion Committee

    Huan-ju -- Chief, General Affairs, Ministry of the
            Army, Nanking (1943)

    P'eng -- Minister, Ministry of the Army, Nanking
            (1943)

244   -195-

CHINESE

Yeh Ching-fong -- Publisher, TIEN HSIA, a monthly, Shanghai (49:198)

Fu-hsiao -- Director, Shanghai Labor and Business Social Union; Managing Supervisor, Shanghai Chamber of Commerce; Manager Director, Shanghai Citizens Welfare Union; Director, National Trade Control General Association, Shanghai; Manager, Shanghai Savings and Trust Department, Ta In Bank; (49:198); Commissioner, Public Utilities, Shanghai (1943); Chairman, Board of Directors, China Products Bank; Director, National Commercial Control Association

Fu-shu -- Member, Financial Consultation Committee, West Shanghai (12/42; 49:198)

Hsi-chin -- Candidate Director, China Educational Reconstruction Association, Hankow Branch (1943)

Hsia-sheng -- Counsellor, National Government, Nanking (1943)

Hsueh-sung -- Chief, Public Utilities, Shanghai; Director, East Asia League, Shanghai Branch; Advisor, Citizens Savings Movement Committee, Shanghai (49:198); Inspecting member, China Journalists Association; Director, Central Electrical Communications Corporation, Nanking

Hung-yu -- Director, China Educational Reconstruction Association, Chekiang Branch (49:198)

I-chou -- Editor-in-Chief, HSIANG KANG JIH PAO, Shanghai (1943) (IDC 7267)

K'e-chi -- Chief, Correspondence Office, Civil Affairs, National Government, Nanking (1943)

Lan-chuan -- Chairman, Chung Hua Factory and Trade Association, Shanghai; Director, Hongkong Chinese Residents Graveyards; Superintendent, Hongkong Hall of Confucious; member, China Representatives (Discursive) Association; Director, Commercial Institute, Hongkong

Ming-che -- Director, China Educational Reconstruction Association, Hankow Branch (1943)

P'eng, Gen. -- Member, Designated Committee, Central Political Council, Nanking (from 12/38); member, Central Executive Committee; member, China Military Mission to Japan (5/21/43); War Minister, Nanking Government (1943); member, National Military Council; Director, China Office, East Asia League; Honorary Adviser, Sino-Japanese Cultural Association, Wu-ch'ang and Hankow Branches; decorated by Japanese Emperor (3/23/44)

P'eng-chih -- Commander, 29th Division, Nanking Army (IDC 3/30/42)

-196-

CHINESE

Yeh Pung -- Department Head, Northwest China; attempted
       to revolt and join Japanese (10/27/42);
       Dean, Orthodox Kuomintang Military Academy
       (O-57); Puppet Army Minister,(Yennan 1/5/45)

   Shou-peng -- Head, Central Opium-curing Hospital,
       Department of Public Health, Nanking (OSS)

   Shueh-sung -- Chief, Bureau of Public Utilities,
       Shanghai (49:198)

   Te-ming -- Manager Director, Shanghai Magazines
       Association; Publisher, CHUNG KUO YU TUNG
       YA, a monthly (49:198)

   Yao-kong -- Manchukuo Consul General, Shanghai

   Yi-chih -- Candidate Director, China Educational
       Reconstruction Association, Chekiang Branch
       (49:198)

   Yu-ts'ai -- Head, Electrical Appliances Enterprise
       Trade Association, National Trade Control
       General Association, Shanghai (49:198)

   Yueh-fang -- Inspector, East Asia League, Hupeh
       Branch (1943)

Yei Ho-chiang -- Shanghai financial leader; established
       a land development company in collaboration
       with Dr. W. W. Yen (8/7/43) (49:198)

Yen Chang-ching -- Member, Central China News Agency;
       headed North China Press Corps on mission to
       Hsinking (8/16/43) (52:246)

   Ch'eng-k'un -- President, Hongkong Automobile Dis-
       tribution Center; member, China Discursive
       Association (51:254); member, Council,
       Chinese Representatives Association, Hong-
       kong (OSS)

   Ch'i-hsing -- Chief, Military Regulations, Ministry
       fo the Army, Nanking (1943)

   Ch'i-hsuan -- Chief, Bureau of Finance, Kiangsi
       Province (1943)

   Chi-yun -- Member, Committee on Grain Control,
       Shanghai (49:199)

   Chia-chih -- Political Vice-Minister, Minister of
       Finance, Wang Ching-wei's regime (3/41; OSS-
       Ms.); Inspector, Central Yuan, Nanking
       (1943)

   Chia-pao -- Inspector, Citizens Savings Movement
       Committee, Shanghai; Director, East Asia
       League, Shanghai Branch; Director, Shanghai
       Newspaper Association (49:199); Editor,
       CHUNG HUA JIH PAO; Chief, Planning Section,
       China Educational Reconstruction Associa-
       tion; Advisory member, Ministry of Informa-
       tion

-197-

CHINESE

Yen Ch'ing-hsiang -- Director, Citizens Savings Movement Committee, Shanghai (49:199)

Chueh-chih -- Secretary, Examination Yuan, Nanking (1943)

Chun-hui -- Professor, Peking University; delegate from North China to GEA Medical Conference (4/20/44) (52:246)

En-tso -- Member, Legislative Yuan (1943); Chairman, China Movie Association, Anhwei Office; member, Committee on Culture, China Office, East Asia League (1943); Assistant Chairman and Chief of General Affairs Section, China Educational Reconstruction Association

Hou-yi -- Executive Director, China Educational Reconstruction Association, Chekiang Branch (49:199)

Hsi-fan -- Manager, Kiangsu Bank, Shanghai (IDC 7270 1943)

Hu-chan -- Auditor, Ministry of Auditing, Nanking (1943)

Hui-ching -- See Yen, Dr. W. W.

Ling-tao -- See Jen Yuan-tao

Lung-yun -- Director, Citizens Savings Movement Committee, Shanghai (49:199)

O-sheng -- Director, Sino-Japanese Cultural Association, Shanghai Branch (49:199)

Pao-lien -- Accounting Office, Narcotic Prohibition Headquarters, Shanghai (49:199)

Shu-ho -- Manager, Shanghai Women's Commercial and Savings Bank (IDC 1943)

Siao-tan -- Member, ... Committee, Municipal Council, Shanghai (49:199)

Su-chou -- Commander, pro-Japanese troops; with Japanese Huang Hsieh Chun, Wuhing, commanding about 800 men (6/39; OSS-Ms.)

Su-tung -- Chief newsgatherer, SHUN PAO, Shanghai (49:199)

Te(h)-kuei -- Born, 1906, Wentang, Shantung; graduate, Central Political College, Kuomintang; Chief, Civil Affairs Section, Kiangning Self-Government Experimental Hsien, Kiangsu (1932-36); concurrently Chief, First Section, Office of Administrative High Commissioner, Kiangsu 10th District and High Commissioner, Kuomintang Headquarters, Kiangning, Kiangsu; Magistrate, Shucheng, Anhwei (1937); Magistrate, Nanan and Quemoy, Fukien (1938-40); Magistrate, Minhow (Foochow), Fukien (OSS-Ms.) Vice-Minister, Ministry of Personnel or Estimation, Executive Yuan, Nanking (1943)

-198-

CHINESE

Yen Teng -- Vice-President, Hsin Min Society; member, Art and Literature Council, Educational Administration, Peiping (52:246)

, Dr. W. W. -- Former Chungking Diplomat; with National Government of China; established a land development company (8/7/43); member, Shanghai Municipal Advisory Committee (1943)

Yan-tao -- Ministry of Navy, Nanking (O-56)

Yu-tan -- Member, Committee of Territories and Borders, Municipal Council, Shanghai (5/13/44) (49:199)

Yuai-fu -- Vice-Chief, Inspection party on Transportation, Northwest China (1/13/43)

Yung-hsiao -- Inspector, Citizens Savings Movement Committee, Shanghai (49:199)

Yeung Tsin-lei -- Chairman, East Asia Cultural Association, Asiatic Affairs Bureau, Hongkong (51:254)

Yun-tak -- Member, Executive Committee, Bankers Association, Hongkong (51:254)

Yi Chen-kuang -- Chief, Publicity Bureau, North China Political Affairs Commission (52:247)

Ch'uan-hsi -- Candidate Inspector, China Educational Reconstruction Association, Hankow Branch (1943)

Ho-fing -- Former ambulance driver, British Army; student engineer, Hongkong University; released prisoner (51:254)

Yung-ching -- Publisher, HSIN HSING JIH PAO, Hsinghua, Kiangsu (IDC 2562)

Yin Chih -- Vice-Chairman, Committee for Stopping the Breakage at Chung-mon of Huang-ho, Nanking (1943)

Ju-ken -- Interpreter with Japanese forces in Shanghai "war" (1932); Commissioner, East Hopeh Zone (1937); detained by Japanese military; in retirement (OSS-Ms.); member, National Economic Commission (1943); Chief, Chihli Canal Improvement Office, Central China (3/25/44); Chief, Toll Department, Chihli Canal (5/11/44)

Mei-po -- Publisher, FU NU JIH PAO, Tientsin '52:247)

Tsai-wei -- Head, Central Electrical Communciations Corporation, Wu-han, Hankow Branch (1943); Chief, Office of Propaganda, Hupeh Province; Candidate executive member, China Journalists Club

Tso-chien (-kan) -- Member, National Military Council (OSS)

CHINESE

Yin T'ung -- Studied in Japan; Director, Peiping-Liaoning Railway (OSS-Ms.); member, Standing Committee, North China; Head, Construction Bureau, North China (12/38); Superintendent, Reconstruction (52:247); Vice-President, Hsin Min Hui (6/3/41; OSS-Ms.)

Yi-hsuan -- Chief, Production Increase Administration, Ministry of Grains, Nanking (1943)

Ying Ch'ing-p'ing -- Chief, National Editing and Translation, Ministry of Education, Nanking (1943)

Ping-hsin -- Secretary, Ministry of Education, Nanking (1943)

Sheng-chung -- Director, China Educational Reconstruction Association (1943)

Tsung-chun -- Secretary, Ministry of Industries, Nanking (1943)

Tzu-t'ung -- Editor, HSIN TAN YANG PAO, Tan-yang, Kiangsu; Editor, paper in Chin-tan, Kiangsu (IDC 2562)

Yung -- Assistant Chief, Ministry of Social Welfare, Nanking (1943); member, Social Welfare Committee, China Office, East Asia League

Yip Kui-ying -- Member, Racing Committee, Hongkong Jockey Club (51:254)

Shien-chung -- Head, Yuimati Fishing Syndicate, Hongkong (51:254)

Yo Sho-ko -- Ambassador without portfolio; appointed Commissioner, Hankow (3/16/43)

You Ling, Lt. Gen. -- Appointed Chief of a "Koshi", Chengchow, strategic point of Peking-Hankow Railway (9/2/44)

Ysao Ching-feng -- Member, Education Committee, Municipal Council, Shanghai (49:199)

Yu Ah-huang -- Pirate leader who captured Pingtan Island (7/6/39); ousted by Chinese volunteers from mainland of Fukien coast (9/5/39); said to have escaped by sampan to Japanese gunboat (OSS-Ms.)

Chao-ling -- Inspecting member, Control Yuan, Nanking (1943)

Ch'en -- Inspector, Citizens Savings Movement Committee, Shanghai (49:199)

Cheng-fei -- Member, Publications Committee, China Writers Club (1943)

Cheng-wen -- See Yu Ching-wen

Chi -- Director, North China Salt Corporation, Tientsin Branch (1943) (52:247)

-200-

CHINESE

Yu Chi-fan -- Inspector, China Writers Club (1943)

Chi-hung -- Director, Committee for Airplane Donations, Peking (8/2/44) (52:247)

Chieh -- Counsellor, Directorate-General of Pacification, North China Political Commission (7/40;
OSS-Ms.)

Chien-chung -- Candidate Director, Shanghai Special
Municipality Journalists Association (49:199)

Chien-tang -- Commander, pro-Japanese troops; with
pro-Japanese forces in Honan, near Chiaotso,
commanding about 1,000 men (6/39; OSS-Ms.)

Chih -- Member, Legislative Yuan, Nanking (19430

Chin-ho -- Born, about 1888, Chekiang; graduate,
Tokyo Military Academy; long time member,
Cheng Hsueh Hui; Chief of Police, Tsingtao
(until 1933); transferred to Peiping (1933);
Mayor, Amoy (1935); Chief of Police and
Mayor, Peking (1937); member, North China
Political Commission (since 3/40) (Oss-Ms.)
Executive Committee member, All-China Econom-
ic Council (OSS)

Ching-fo -- Director, Reconstruction, Nanking;
present at inaugural meeting of New Communist
Eradication Committee (5/2/43)

Ching-ho -- Mayor, Peiping; member and Superinten-
dent of Construction, North China Political
Council (12/4/43); delegate to North China
Political Council; Chief of Internal Af-
fairs (2/43) (52:247); member, National
Economic Committee; Chairman, Committee
for Stopping Breakage at Chung-mon of
Huang-ho

Ching-tai -- Governor, Pingyang-fu (0-61)

Ching-wen (Yu Cheng-wen) -- Councillor, North China
Political Council; witness to revised by-
laws of National Government by North China
Political Council (52:247)

Ching-wu -- Director, Shanghai Education Committee;
Executive Director, China Educational Recon-
struction Association, Shanghai Branch;
Director, Sino-Japanese Cultural Association,
Shanghai Branch (49:199)

Ching-yuan -- Minister of People's Welfare (4/10/44)

Chu-lai -- Publisher, CHU CHIANG MIN KUO JIH PAO,
Yun-chou, South China (IDC 2562)

Chueh-yun -- Governor, Toishan Hsien (OSS)

Fen, Gen. -- Chief, Army Department, Military Council; sent on inspection trip to Japan
(4/23/43)

Han-mou -- Commanding General, Seventh War Zone
(51:254)

CHINESE

Yu Haueh-chung -- Mayor, Nanking (8/17/43)

Hsi-chieh (Yu Shi-chen) -- Vice-President, Hsin Min
    Society (5/13/43); Secretary General,
    Headquarters Society, Peiping; returned from
    Hakata and Tokyo, Japan (12/29/43);
    Chinese Delegate to Second Asiatic Youth
    Conference (10/10/44); Vice-Chairman, New
    Citizens Committee (52:247)

Hsiao-yen -- Chairman, Directors, Gramaphone and
    Record Dealers, Shanghai (IDC 7264 1943)

Hsing-pen -- Inspector, Citizens Savings Movement
    Committee, Shanghai (49:199); Chairman,
    Directors, Rubber Manafacturing Companies

Kuang-shi -- Judge and Chief, North China Supreme
    Court (1/17/43) (52:247)

Kung-chia -- Chief Prosecutor, North China Supreme
    Court (1/17/43) (52:247)

Mao-won -- Labor man, Hsinking; member, Labor
    Bureau, Peiping (8/26/43); made inspection
    tour in Manchukuo to discuss present and
    future labor problems (52:247)

Nai-liang -- Director, Shanghai Special Municipality
    Journalists Association (49:199)

, O.K. -- Vice-Minister of Finance (9/23/43 DIO)

Pan-k'uang -- Central Electrical Communications
    Corporation, Peng-pu Branch (1943); Execu-
    tive member, China Journalists Association;
    Executive Inspector, China Writers Club

Pao-hsuan -- Inspecting member, Control Yuan, Nan-
    king (1943)

Po-lu -- Finance Commissioner, Kiangsu Province
    (OSS)

Pu-ho -- Member, North China Political Commission
    (12/38) (52:247)

San-k'ai -- Propaganda Head, 1st District Party
    Headquarters, Kuomintang, Swatow (IDC)

Sei-su -- Professor of Literature

Shan-min, Maj. Gen. -- Told of new province formed:
    Hwai-hai (2/4/44)

Shao-i -- Appointed Manager, Central Bank of China
    (5/11/44)

Shao-ying -- Chief of Treasury, Ministry of Trea-
    sury, National Government, Nanking (1943)

Shi-chen -- Vice-President, Hsin Min Society,
    Nanking; see also Yu Hsi-chieh

Shi-keh -- Member, North China Political Council,
    Publishing Department (2/8/43) (52:247)

-202-

CHINESE

Yu Shih -- Publisher, HSIN SHEN PAO, Shanghai (OSS)

Shih-chieh -- Vice-Chairman, Hsin Min Association;
    Councillor, National Government (1/19/45)

Shou-ch'ien -- Member, Legislative Yuan, Nanking
    (1943)

T'ien-lin -- Member, National Economic Committee
    (1943)

Tzu-chieh -- Inspector, Shanghai Special Municipality
    Journalists Association (49:199)

Tsung-yao -- Manager, I Tung Pu Local Farmers Bank,
    Tung Yang, Chekiang (IDC 1943)

Wei-nan -- Secretary, 2nd District Party Headquarters,
    Kuomintang, Swatow (IDC)

Yu-hsiu -- Candidate Director, and Assistant in
    Planning Section, China Educational Recon-
    struction Association (1943)

Yu-jen -- President, Control Yuan (1/1/42) (DIO)

Yun-ch'iu -- Chairman, Production Education and Re-
    search Committee, China Educational Recon-
    struction Association (1943)

Yung-chuan -- Joined "Peace Camp" (3/9/44) (52:247)

Yuan Ch'ang -- Counsellor, National Government, Nanking
    (1943)

Chi-p'ing -- Manager Director, Shanghai Post Office
    Labor Union; Manager Director, Readjustment
    Committee, National Post Office Labor Union,
    Shanghai (49:199)

Ching-pang -- Chairman, Directors, Artificial Silk
    Stores, Shanghai (IDC 7264 1943)

Ch'u -- Special Administrative Emissary, 1st Dis-
    trict, Chekiang; Head, Civilian Defense,
    South District, Canton; attended 2nd
    Anniversary, Sino-Japanese Cultural Institute
    Nanking (19/42); Director, Central Electri-
    cal Communications Corporation; Chairman,
    Village Pacification Committee, Chen Chiang
    (51:254); see also (49:199); Chief, Bureau
    of Education, Kiangsu (1943); member, Com-
    mittee for Application of Constitution;
    Editor, CHENG CHIH YUEH K'AN, Shanghai;
    Director, China Office, East Asia League;
    member, New Citizens Movement Promotion Com-
    mittee

Chu-fan -- Director, Public Health, Shanghai Special
    Municipality; represented China at 3rd
    East Asia Medical Conference; Advisor,
    Citizens Savings Movement Committee, Shanghai
    (49:200)

252   -203-

CHINESE

Yuan Hou-chih -- Advisor, Citizens Savings Movement Committee, Shanghai; Chief, Bureau of Finance; Director, East Asia League, Shanghai Branch; Inspector, Sino-Japanese Cultural Association (49:200)

Kuei -- Chief, Peiping Public Police Bureau (52:247)

Li-teng -- Member, New Citizens Committee, North China Political Council;(52:247); member, New Citizens Movement Promotion Committee; Director, National Commercial Control Association; Manager Director, Shanghai Citizens Welfare Association; Chairman, Committee on Grain Control; Director, Shanghai Municipality Labor and Business Social Union; Inspector, Shanghai Education Committee; Chairman, Board of Directors, Shanghai Chamber of Commerce; Manager Director and Vice-Chairman, Citizens Savings Movement Committee; Director, National Trade Control General Association; Publisher, NING P'E KUNG PAO, Shanghai (49:200); Special Government Delegate and Chairman, Rice Control, Shanghai

Liang -- Born, 1883, Hangchow, Chekiang; Graduate, Waseda University, Tokyo; Commissioner of Public Safety, Kiangsi Province (1930); Mayor, Peiping (5/33); resigned (11/3/35) (OSS-Ms.)

Nai-knan -- Director, Central China Mining Stock Company, Shanghai (1943)

Shu -- Member, Central Executive Committee, Nanking (1943); member, New Citizens Movement Promotion Committee; Director, Standing Committee, Shanghai Press Association; President, HSIN CHUNG KUO PAO; Editor, CHENG CHIH YUEH PAO; Education Commissioner and Pacification Superintendent, 1st District, Kiangsu Province (1943); Director, Central Electrical Communications Corporation, Nanking

Tsao-sen -- Electric School, Peiping; on inspection tour (52:247)

Yi-tsung -- Member, ... Committee, Municipal Council, Shanghai (5/13/44) (49:200)

Yin-tsun -- Manager, Chu Hsing Cheng Bank, Shanghai (IDC 7270 1943)

Ying-chih -- Commander, Independent Fifth Regiment, Nanking Army (IDC 3/30/42)

Yu-chi -- Director, Salt Administration, Ministry of Finance, Executive Yuan, Nanking (OSS)

Yu-ch'uan -- Vice-Minister and Chief, Price Administration, Ministry of Industry (Interior?) (1943); member, Committee of Political Councillors, National Government, Nanking

CHINESE

Yuan Yu-hsu -- Minister of Interior; Ex-Vice-Minister, Commerce and Industry, Nanking (10/5/43)

Yu-t'ung -- Inspector, China-Japan Returned Students Club (1943)

Yung-lien -- Commissioner, North China Consolidated Tax Administration, Directorate-General of Finance, North China Political Commission (7/40; OSS-Ms.)

Yung-ting -- Chairman, Directors, Electrical Material Stores, Shanghai (IDC 1943)

Yuang Ho-shi -- Nanking President, ... Yuan

Yueh Ch'ao-yang -- Executive Inspector, China Educational Reconstruction Association, Chekiang Branch (49:200)

Ju-hua -- Member, Sugar Enterprise Special Committee, National Trade Control General Association, Shanghai (49:200)

K'ai-hsien -- Old-school military officer; graduated in Japan; Chinese M/A to Tokyo (1914-28); Director, Directorate-General of Industry, North China Political Commission (7/40; OSS-Ms.) Chief, Industries, North China Political Council (1943)

Sung-kuang -- Inspecting member, Control Yuan, Nanking (1943)

Yun Pao-hui -- Born, 1885, Wanping, Hopeh; Lt. Gen. of the Yellow Banner of the Chinese Manchu Army during first year of the Republic; Acting Mayor, Peiping (1926); member, People's Political Association (OSS-Ms.)

Tse-liao -- Commander, 110th Division (5/4/44) (DIO)

Yung Chia-chun -- Police student sent to Formosa for training; assigned to Police Branch Bureau, Sha-ho (Canton) as member of training division (51:254)

Ching-pin -- Member, Legislative Yuan, Nanking (1943)

Kwang Hsing-shang -- Councillor, North China Political Council; witness of revised by-laws of National Government by North China Political Council (52:247)

Ngai-sung -- Director, Census Bureau, Hongkong (51:255)

T'ien-hui -- Police student sent to Formosa for training; assigned to various bureaus in Tai-p'ing-ching and Hai T'ien-shou for additional training (51:255)

Tzu-heng -- Commander-in-Chief, South Shantung Army of Chuuking; surrendered (6/43)

254   -205-

CHINESE

ADDENDA

The following Puppets are included in the roster of employees of the Puppet Central Savings Bank, Nanking and Shanghai Branches:

Chen, Chih-shih	--	Stationery Committee
Chen, Chuen-hui	--	-do-
Ku, Pao-hun	--	Common Committee
Wu, Chi-yun	--	-do-
Yang, Shu-ping	--	-do-
Shao, Hung-chu	--	-do-
Lo, Chun-chiang	--	Supervisor Chairman
Chu, Fu-chuan	--	Advisor
Pei, Shao-hsiang	--	-do-
Chen, Hua-po	--	Assistant Business Manager
Tsai, Kan	--	-do-
Wang, Shu-mei	--	-do-
Wang, Chung-tao	--	-do-
Shao, Shu-hua	--	-do-
Shao, Hung-chiu	--	Register and Printing Manager
Mao, Jen-yu	--	Assistant Register and Printing Manager
Wang, Mao-chi	--	-do-
Yu, Shao-ying	--	Manager of the National Treasury
Huang, Tung	--	Assistant Manager of the National Treasury
Chien, Ta-kiu	--	Stabilization Manager
Chuang, Po-jung	--	Assistant Manager of the Stabilization Board
Li, Hsien-chih	--	General Secretary
Chen, Chu-chen	--	-do-
Hu, Chiu-luan	--	Inspecting Department
Yang, Ti-chung	--	-do-
Wu, Chi-yun	--	Investigating Department Head
Feng, Yu	--	Assistant Head of Investigating Department

JAPANESE

Abe, Kazuo -- Publisher of monthly magazine, "Shih-ch'ang", Shanghai (1943) (49:201)

Abe, Nobuyuki -- Honorary Chairman, Sino-Japanese Cultural Association (1943)

Abe, Tomoji -- Visitor of Japanese Literary Patriotic Society to Shanghai in exchange of literary men (10/5/43); Japanese representative to third conference of literary men of the GEA to be held in Nanking during the middle of November (9/15/44)

Abe, Bishop Yoshimuni -- Former Bishop of Japanese Methodist Church; President, Japanese Christian Council; aided the Chinese Christian churches (1/30/44); Pastor of Continental Church in Shanghai; asked Church of Christ in Japan to send capable assistant pastor (8/6/44) (49:201)

Aburadani, Kyoichi -- Director, Prosperity Corporation of Central China (IDC 4/5/43)

Adachi -- Detachment Commander, North China Expeditionary Force; reported Army considering problems of foodstuffs and price control (9/30/42) (52:248)

Adachi, Motonji -- Standing Director, North China Iron Works Corporation (8/5/43) (52:248)

Ajiyuya, Kyoichi -- Director, Labor and Business Social Union, Shanghai (1943) (49:201)

Akamatsu, Naoaki -- Director, Shanghai Newspaper Association (49:201); Editor, TA LU HSIN PAO (IDC 7266 1943)

Akinaga -- Bureau Chief of Cabinet Planning Board of Japan who attended Coordination Conference of North China, Mongolia, Manchukuo and Korea at Peiping (11/8/42) (52:248)

Akitoni, Kentano -- Director, North China Electrical Industry Company located in Peiping (8/5/43) (52:248)

Amakasu, Shro -- Director, Sino-Japanese Cultural Association, Shanghai Branch (1943) (49:201)

Amejima, Tatsuo -- President, North China Gold Mine Corporation, Peiping (1943) (52:248)

Ando -- Vice President, IRAA (North China) (52:248)

Ando, Heizo -- Director, North China Salt Corporation, Tientsin Branch (1943) (52:248)

Aoki -- Resigned as Economic Advisor to Nanking Government; Sotaro Ishiwata appointed to fill place (10/29/42)

Aoki, Eiichiro -- Director, Sino-Japanese Cultural Association, Wu-Ch'ang & Hankow Branch (1943)

Aoki, Kazuo -- Minister of GEA Affairs; visitor to Nanking (11/27/42); spoke at North China Development Committee meeting re Japan's relinquishment of rights in China (2/20/43); spoke re rehabilitation of flood sufferers (2/23/43); became member of Cabinet as Minister without Portfolio, "September, last year" (4/28/43); urged all-out cooperation with National Government of China (11/29/43)

JAPANESE

Aoki, Misao -- Director, Central China Water & Electric Stock
        Company, Shanghai (IDC 7262 1943)

Aoki, Satsu (Setsu) -- Vice Chairman, Hua Chung Hydro-Electric
        Corporation, Ltd., Shanghai (8/5/43); Managing Director,
        Shanghai Municipality Labor and Business Social Union
        (1943) (49:201)

Aomizu, Yonosuke -- Chief of Police at Hsin-Cha District Office of
        First Police Office, Shanghai (1943) (49:201)

Aota, Kanei -- Accompanied Japanese Ambassador to Nanking (5/14/43)

Arai, Kuroishi -- Chamberlain; dispatched to Kwangtung Army Head-
        quarters with gift (9/1/44) (51:256)

Arakawa, Dr. Bunroku -- President of Kyushu Imperial University;
        attended the 6th deliberative committee meeting of the
        East Asia Cultural Conference at Peiping University
        (8/31/42) (52:248)

Araki, Eikichi -- Supreme Adviser, Hsin Min Society (7/6/43); mem-
        ber, North China-Asia Development Association; Chief
        Economic Adviser, National Government; attended reorgani-
        zation meeting of All-China Commercial Control General
        Association (6/8/44) (52:248)

Araki, T. -- Vice President, Shanghai Railway Company (49:201)

Araki, Zuito -- Member, Sugar Enterprise Special Committee, National
        Trade Control General Association in Shanghai (49:201)
        (1943)

Ariki, Kingoro -- Member of Standing Committee; Vice President of
        Dai Nippon Aviation Company (2/29/43)

Arima, Count Raimei -- Appointed first President of Southern Japan
        Marine Products Control Corporation (2/8/44)

Arino, Manabu -- Japanese Consul-General in Tsinan, China (10/39)
        (52:248)

Arita (Arikas), Hachiro -- Former Foreign Minister, Tokyo; special
        mission to Nanking (9/8/42)

Arita, Toshiharu -- Chief of Police at Hui-Sze District Office of
        First Police Office, Shanghai (1943) (49:201)

Asahi, Teruo -- President of Tokyo Bank; visited China on Good Will
        Mission (6/19/44)

Asahina -- Chancellor, Japanese Consulate, Macao (51:256)

Asahina, Takashi -- Tokyo conductor and composer; visited Shanghai
        (11/25/43) (49:201)

Asahina, Tatsutaro (Sakutaro) -- Vice President, All Nippon Youth's
        Association (8/1/42); conducted studies with National
        Government re plans for training boys and young men
        (8/26/42); returned to Japan (9/8/42)

Asano, Kazuo -- Managing Director, Committee for Establishment of
        China's Broadcasting Business, Shanghai; connected with
        Kiyasei Studio; member, China Broadcasting Enterprise &
        Reconstruction Association (1943) (49:201)

-208-

JAPANESE

Azuma, Dr. Jiro -- Medical Department of Tokyo Imperial University; chosen as instructor for Doojinkai (Tungjen) Medical College, Shanghai (7/7/44; 9/11/44) (49:201)

Banda, Sosaku -- Inspector, Sino-Japanese Cultural Association, Wu-Ch'ang & Hankow Branch (1943)

Bekkuya -- Director, North China Development Company (2/2/44) (52:248)

Betsukoya -- Director, North China Development Company (3/43) (52:248)

Chasi, Madam Hiroko -- Nippon Women's University; invited to teach in Peiping (12/29/42) (52:248)

Chiba, Nario -- Director, Sino-Japanese Cultural Association, Shanghai Branch (1943) (49:201)

Chiba, Sotaro -- President of Meiji University; attended the 6th deliberative committee meeting of the East Asia Cultural Conference at Peiping University (8/31/42) (52:248)

Debuchi, Major Isamu -- Adviser, Shanghai Citizens' Savings Movement Committee (1943); Honorary Director, Sino-Japanese Cultural Association, Shanghai Branch (1943) (49:201)

Den, Makoto -- Ex-Vice Governor, Central China Transportation Company (0-41)

Den, Makoto -- Vice President of Central Railway Company in Central China (IDC 8/3/43); Director, Central China Railroad Stock Company, Shanghai (IDC 7262 1943)

Deshimaru, Sozo -- Supervisor, Manchuria Railroad Company, which owns more than half the shares in Shantung Mining Industrial Company, Ltd. (8/5/43); Supervisor, Shantung Mining Industrial Company (52:248)

Ebehara, Takenosuka -- Inspector, Sino-Japanese Cultural Association, Shanghai Branch (1943) (49:202)

Eguchi -- Chief, Army Press Section, Shanghai; attended conference (9/4/43) (49:202)

Endo, Sasuke -- Director, China Movie Association (1943)

Endo, Teijiro -- Councillor and Inspector, North China Communications Corporation (1944)

Endo, Yoshitoki -- Member of Menchiang Embassy Staff in Peiping (8/23/44) (52:248)

Eto, Toshihiko -- Publisher, HSIANG KANG JIH PAO, Hongkong, established February, 1930 (IDC 1943)

Foyuchi, Kanjo -- Japanese Minister, Shanghai; Central China Agricultural Promotion Association established by Shanghai Office of Japanese Embassy (2/6/43) (49:202)

Fujihara -- High ranking member, Japanese Army; associate member, Commodity Investigation Committee, Canton (51:256)

Fujii -- Nichiren Sect Priest in Nanking (10/6/44)

Fujii, K. -- Counselor, Japanese Embassy, Nanking (0-60)

258

JAPANESE

Fujimori, Kunshi -- Managing Director, Shantung Coal Production & Marketing Company (8/5/43) (52:248)

Fujino, Seitaro -- Managing Director, Shanghai Municipality Labor & Business Social Union (1943) (49:202)

Fujisawa, Chikao (Fujiwasa) -- President, Fujisawa Oriental Thought Research Institute; will open the Oriental International Thought Research Institute in North China (6/25/44) (52:248)

Fujisue, Kenzo -- Chief, Inspection Office, East Asia Communications Association, North China Branch (1943)

Fujiwara -- Chief, General Affairs Section, Peiping; requested by Ambassador Tani to attend meeting, apparently in Peiping, of 20 diplomats to consider Japan-China Mutual Alliance Pact, world situation, economic trend, etc. (11/28/43) (52:249)

Fujiwara, Yasuaki -- President, Central China (Telegraphic) Communications...(IDC 1/16/44)

Fukida, Major General Ryuzo -- Liaison Officer of East Asia Affairs Bureau at Amoy (DIO)

Fukinaga -- Chief, Division of Japanese Planning Office, North China (3/43) (52:249)

Fukuchi -- Member, Committee for Investigation of Resources & Materials, Shanghai (1943) (49:202)

Fukuda -- Councillor; North China Representative; attended 6th Continental Liaison Deliberative Conference (10/15/44) (52:249)

Fukuda, E. -- Japanese Consul in Peiping, China (10/39) (52:249)

Fukuda, Ko -- Chairman, Directors, Central China Electrical Communications Stock Company, Shanghai (IDC 7262 1943)

Fukuda, Minoru -- Head of Hua Chung Electric Communications Co., Ltd., Shanghai (8/5/43) (49:202)

Fukuda, Seku -- President, Central China Telegraph Communications Company (IDC 8/3/43)

Fukuda, Tatsuma -- Director & Manager, Shanghai Municipality Labor and Business Social Union (1943) (49:202)

Fukui, Yasumitsu -- Japanese Consul, Macao; assassinated February 2, 1945 (51:256)

Fukuishida, Teisaburo -- Honorary Adviser, Sino-Japanese Cultural Association, Wu-Ch'ang & Hankow Branch (1943)

Fukuma -- Vice Consul General; Adviser, Shanghai Citizens' Savings Movement Committee (1943) (49:202)

Fukunita, Capt. -- Naval Attache, Japanese Embassy, Canton; Associate Member, Commodity Investigation Committee, Canton (4/5/44) (51:256)

Fukushima -- President, North China Development Company; Vice President, East Asia IRAA (7/8/43) (52:249)

-210-

JAPANESE

Fukuta, Ko -- (See Fukuda, Ko) (0-67)

Fukuteno, Boku -- Chief, Office of Economics, Sino-Japanese Cultural
Association, Shanghai Branch (1943) (49:202)

Fukuyama, Yoshio -- Honorary Director, Sino-Japanese Cultural Association, Shanghai Branch (1943) (49:202)

Funabashi, Viscount -- House of Peers; attended North China Committee
Meeting (52:249)

Funatsu, Tatsuichiro -- Director, Shanghai Municipality Labor &
Business Social Union (1943); Adviser, Sino-Japanese
Cultural Association (1943); lectured under auspices of
Press Federation, Chamber of Commerce, etc. (10/30/44)
(49:202)

Furuta, Shunnosuke -- Secretary, North China Development Company
(7/1/44) (52:249)

Furuyama, Katsuo -- Supervisor, Shantung Mining Industrial Co., Ltd.;
Supervisor, Manchuria Railroad Co., which owns more than
half the shares in Shantung Mining Industrial Co. (8/5/43)
(52:249)

Fushima -- President, North China Development Company (7/6/42)
(52:249)

Fushimi, Prince -- Honorary President, Literature Association, which
sponsored 37th Festival of Confucius in Tokyo (4/25/43)

Fuwa, Suketoshi -- Executive Director, Sino-Japanese Cultural Association, Shanghai Branch (1943) (49:202)

Gobi -- General, Kwangtung Army; attended Manchukuo National Guber-
natorial Conference (1/20/44)

Goshima -- Chief of Office; Adviser, Shanghai Citizens' Savings
Movement (1943) (49:202)

Goto, Fumio -- Vice Governor of IRAA; Vice President, Cultural Data
Translation Office of Sino-Japanese Cultural Association;
Professor of Tungwen University (6/7/44) (52:249)

Goto, Major Shigeru -- Bureau Head, International Settlement,
Shanghai (2/22/42) (49:202)

Goto, Teiji -- Vice President, North China Communications Corporation
(1944)

Hachisei, Masayuke -- Owner, Kyowa Drug Manufacturing Company,
Tientsin, etc. (1943) (52:249)

Haga, Shiota -- Connected with North China Railway Company; commented
on Japanese activities in China making a trunk railway
linking Fusan and Singapore possible in near future (7/6/44)
(52:249)

Hakane, Katuki -- Head Branch, Japanese Embassy, Canton; arrived in
Canton to assume post of first head of new branch office of
Japanese Embassy (8/9/43) (51:256)

Hamada, Kiichi -- Superintendent of Schools in Hupeh Province; headed
group of 50 Chinese students selected from Hupeh schools
for higher and technical education in Japan (8/19/42)

JAPANESE

Hamada, Yukio -- Hongkong Civil Court; appointed head of newly established local Justice Department (9/10/43) (51:256)

Hanamizu -- Chief of Finance, Japanese Embassy, Shanghai (2/43)
(49:203)

Hanayama, Chikayoshi -- Ministry Secretary; Councillor, Japanese
Embassy in China; concurrently Consul-General in Peiping
(5/31/44) (52:249)

Hanga, Takao -- Inspector, Domei-Tsuskin Sha (IDC 7/1/43)

Hantano, Rinichi -- Director, Central China Silk Stock Company
(IDC 7262 1943)

Hara, Kumakichi -- Standing Director, North China Transportation
Corporation in Peiping (8/5/43) (52:249)

Hara, Zenichiro -- Director, Sino-Japanese Cultural Association,
Shanghai Branch (1943) (49:203)

Harada -- Chief, Monopoly Bureau Chiefs' Conference

Harada, Lt. General Kumakichi -- Decorated by China National Government for meritorious services (4/16/44)

Harada, R. -- 3rd Secretary, Japanese Embassy, Nanking (0-60)

Harada, Major General Seichi -- Commander whole force, one battalion,
guarding Amoy; promoted to Lt. General (7/17/44) (49:203)

Haranuma -- Special Japanese Envoy to China (IDC 1/9/43)

Harnada, Kiichi -- Superintendent of Schools, Hupeh Province
(Assem. 17)

Hasebe, Dr. Gunji -- Professor of Anthropology; excavated at Shuko-
ten, Hupeh Province

Hasegawa -- Head of Commerce and Industry Section, GEA Ministry;
attended Coordination Conference, North China, Mongolia,
Korea, and Manchukuo at Peiping (11/8/42) (52:249)

Hasegawa, M. -- Japanese Consul in Shanghai, China (DIO 10/39)

Hasegawa, Mitsuo -- Director, Sino-Japanese Cultural Association,
Shanghai Branch (1943) (49:203)

Hashida -- Ex-Minister of Public Education, North China (52:249)

Hashida, Yoshiyuki -- Chairman, Financial Dept., Japanese Embassy,
Kalgan (9/27/43) (52:249)

Hashimoto, Sajiaro -- Chief, General Affairs Department, East Asia
Communications Association (1943)

Hata, Vice Admiral Hikosabur -- Vice-Chief of Naval General Staff;
decorated by China National Government for meritorious
services (4/16/44)

Hata, General Shunroku (Shenroku), (Shunruhu) -- Field Marshal;
Commander in Chief, Japanese forces in China (11/24/42 -
12/6/44); model village established in Kiangsu Province
commemorating historic meeting of Hata and...at the canal
zone northwest of Suchow (1/22/43); tendered dinner party

-212-

JAPANESE

in Nanking in honor of Subhas Chandra Bose, head of
Provisional Government of Free India (11/19/43); member,
Board of Marshals and Fleet Admirals

Hattori, H. -- Attache, Japanese Embassy, Nanking (0-60)

Hayashi, Colonel -- On inspection tour, Menchiang and North China
(1944) (52:249)

Hayashi, A. S. -- High Priest of Japanese-China Buddhist Research
Association, Nanking (5/10/44)

Hayashi, K. -- 3rd Secretary, Japanese Embassy, Nanking (0-60)

Hayashi, S. -- Attache, Japanese Embassy, Nanking (0-60)

Hayashi, Shinsaku -- Supervisor, Shantung Mining Industrial Company
(8/5/43) (52:250)

Hayashida, K. -- 1st Secretary, Japanese Embassy, Nanking (0-60)

Hemia, Kiamatsu -- Director, North China Development Company (2/16/43)
(52:250)

Hidaka, Kiyomasa -- Director, Sino-Japanese Cultural Association,
Shanghai Branch (1943); Editor-in-Chief, HSIN-SHEN-PAO,
Shanghai, and of HSIN-SHE-PAO-WAN-PAO (49:203)

Hidaka, Kosaburo -- Inspector, Shantung Mining Industrial Company
(8/5/43) (52:250)

Hidaka, Seimasa -- Director, Shanghai Newspaper Association (49:203);
Editor, HSIN SHEN PAO (IDC 7266 1943)

Hidaka, Shinrokuyo -- Japanese Military Attache in Nanking; returned
to Nanking from Tokyo where he made an interim report to the
Foreign Office (8/25/42); Director, Sino-Japanese Cultural
Association, Nanking (49:132)

Higashi, Kaneki -- Chief of Staff, China Sea Fleet (9/1/43)

Higashimori, Shinichi -- Managing Director, North China Electric
Wire Corporation (2/17/44) (52:250)

Hirada, Doctor -- Professor of Ancient History, Tokyo Imperial University; to do excavation work at Hufo, Shantung Province,
North China (8/23/42) (52:250)

Hirai, Atsuke -- Japanese Consul, Kaifeng, Honan

Hiranaga, Onshu -- Cultural Goodwill Party to China (Party Head)
(5/3/43) (51:256)

Hiranuma, Ryozo -- Cultural Goodwill Party to China (5/3/43) (51:256)

Hiranuma, Baron Tiicho (Kiichiro) -- President of Privy Council; to
be dispatched to China on special mission (8/28/42);
Ex-Premier; attended dinner in Tokyo for revival of Confucianism among Chinese (11/28/42)

Hirao -- Councillor of Hsin Min Society; member, North China Development Association (7/6/43) (52:250)

Hirasawa, Kanamo -- Vice President, Prosperity Corporation of Central
China (IDC 4/5/43)

262   -213-

JAPANESE

Hirai, Tsukumatsu (Kikumatsu) -- Director, North China Railway
        Corporation; made Vice President, Southern Manchuria Rail-
        way (3/25/44) (52:250); Director, North China Communica-
        tions Corporation (1944)

Hirata, Komaichiro -- Chief, Transportation & Automobile Bureaus,
        North China Transportation Corporation (1944)

Hirata, Kozo -- Director, Central China Electrical Communications
        Stock Company, Shanghai (IDC 7262 1943)

Hirata, Seiichiro -- Director, North China Communications Corp.
        (1944)

Hirayama, Ko -- Chairman, Board of Directors, East Asia Communica-
        tions Association (1943)

Hiroma, Junichi -- Member, Committee on Grain Control, Shanghai
        (1943) (49:203)

Hirota, Yoji -- Chief, Press Section, Japanese Embassy Office,
        Shanghai; Chief of Information; Adviser, Shanghai Citi-
        zens' Savings Movement Committee (1943); attended Shanghai
        Co-Prosperity Round Table Conference (9/4/43); Honorary
        Director, Sino-Japanese Cultural Association (1943)
        (49:203)

Hirozawa -- Chairman, China Affairs Board; reported to Hupeh Co-
        ordinating Council (8/13/42) (52:250)

Hishida, Itsuji -- Director, Shanghai Municipality Labor & Business
        Social Union (1943) (49:203); Director, Shanghai Realty
        Stock Company (IDC 7262 1943)

Hishimura, Dr. Eibo -- North China Japanese Expeditionary Force
        (Medicine and Fever) (5/4/43) (52:250)

Hitaka -- Former Minister to China; appointed Japanese Ambassador to
        Italy (IDC 10/42)

Hoga, Chiyota -- Chief, Railroad Bureau, Peking Office, North China
        Communications Corporation (1944)

Honda -- Japanese Vice Consul, Amoy (1/18/44) (49:203)

Honda, Kishidi -- Director, Patriotic Labor Service Bureau, North
        China (6/21/44) (52:250)

Honda, Kumataro -- E. E. & M. P., Japanese Embassy, Nanking (O-60)

Hori, T. -- 1st Secretary, Japanese Embassy, Nanking

Horiba, Kyoshi -- Executive Member, Oil and Grain Special Committee,
        National Trade Control General Association in Shanghai
        (1943) (49:203)

Horie, Katsumi -- Director, Central China Water & Electric Stock
        Company, Shanghai (IDC 7262 1943)

Horio, Toyokuma -- Director, Central China Railroad Stock Company,
        Shanghai (IDC 7262 1943)

Horiuchi, Kanjo -- Member, Committee on Return of Concessions,
        Nanking; member, Committee on Abolition of Extraterritor-
        iality (IDC 2/43)

-214-

JAPANESE

Horiuchi, Takechi (Horiguchi, Hideki) -- Appointed Japanese Minister
to Nanking (11/27/42); attended conference re retrocession
of concessions in China (3/14/43); Minister; spoke to Material Control Deliberative Council at Shanghai (4/1/43);
exchanged official memo with Cho Fu Hai re agricultural
cooperatives (7/29/43); Vice Minister of Education (10/21/43);
presence requested by Ambassador Tani at meeting of 20 diplomats in Peiping, apparently, to consider significance of
signing of Japan-China Mutual Alliance Pact, future policies
of diplomatic corps, present world situation, economic
trend (11/28/43) (52:250)

Hosaka, Yasutaro -- Central China Prosperity Insurance Association,
Hisan Fire Insurance Company

Hoshino, Yoshiki -- Resident of Shanghai area. Presented letter of
commendation from Japanese Embassy at Nanking for services
as lecturer to Chinese language students; presentation
made by Ambassador Tani (3/5/44) (49:204)

Hosu, Retto -- Member of Literature Association; recited Shinto pray-
er at 37th Festival of Confucius at Nishima Temple in
Tokyo, acting for Honorary President of Association
(4/25/43)

Hyun, Kito -- Obtained license to operate mines in Nankang and Wayao,
Kwangtung (1942) (51:256)

Ibi, Shinzo -- Member, Flour Special Committee, National Trade Control General Association in Shanghai (1943) (49:204)

Ichigawa, Lt. General -- Governor-General, Hongkong (4/23/43) (51:256)

Ichihashi, Hikoji -- Director, Shanghai Municipality Labor & Business
Social Union (1943) (49:204)

Ichikawa, Hoju -- Assistant Chief of Police at Lo-Yang Road District
Office of Third Police Office, Shanghai (1943) (49:204)

Ichikawa, Kenkichi -- Director, North China Communications Corporation (1944)

Ichiki -- Chief, Civil Administration Department, Hongkong Government (10/25/42) (51:256)

Ichiwata, Soto -- Financial Adviser to National Government at Nanking
(11/2/42)

Iguchi, Sadao -- Board of Information spokesman (8/28/44)

Iida, Hiroshi -- Japanese representative to the 3rd conference of
literary men in GEA to be held in Nanking during the middle
of November (9/15/44)

Ikeda -- Director, Bureau of Rights, Justice Ministry; called to
meeting in Nanking by Embassy to discuss Japan's extraterritoriality rights (4/23/43)

Ikeda, Chushi -- Civil Administrator, Hainan Island (4/12/42); conducted entering ceremony for pioneers arriving at Settlement Farm (7/31/42); Commissioner General, Hainan Island
(2/19/43); Inspector General, Hainan Island (12/29/43);
visited Japan (12/31/43, 7/12/44)
See Ikeda, Kiyoshi (Idda, Kiyoshi) (51:256)

-215-

JAPANESE

Ikegami, Terasu -- Director, Central China Silk Stock Company
(IDC 7262 1943)

Ikei, Keiuji -- Inspector, North China Communications Corporation
(1944)

Ikko -- Appointed President of newly formed China Newspaper Association; President of Shanghai...Newspaper (9/20/44) (49:204)

Ikoma, Minoru -- Director, Shanghai Municipality Labor & Business
Social Union (1943) (49:204)

Imoto, Itsuo -- Director, Sino-Japanese Cultural Association,
Shanghai Branch (1943) (49:204)

Inagaki (Inakaki) -- Member, Committee for Investigation of Resources
& Materials, Shanghai (1943) (49:204)

Inagawa, Saburo -- A director, North China Electric Wire Corporation
(2/17/44) (52:250)

Inoue -- Unit Commander; Committee on Commodity Prices

Inoue, Otohike (Inouye) -- President, North China Telephone &
Telegraph Corporation, Peiping (9/23/43) (52:250)

Inouye -- Acting Japanese Consul, Anshan-Tatung (0-61, 0-62) (52:250)

Inouye, Madam Hideko -- Principal, Nippon Women's University; invited
to teach in Peiping (12/29/42) (52:250)

Inouye, Yasutada -- Assistant Chairman, Flour Special Committee of
National Trade Control General Association in Shanghai
(1943) (49:204)

Irisawa, Fumiaki -- Chief, Culture Department, East Asia Communications Association (1943)

Ishi (Ichi) -- Counselor, Nanking, China

Ishiba, Goro -- Auditor, North China Electric Wire Corporation
(2/17/44) (52:250)

Ishida -- Railway Inspector, Transportation & Communications Ministry;
on tour of inspection - Menchiang area and North China
(1944) (52:250)

Ishida (Ochida) -- Consul-General, Hankow (6/26/44)

Ishigura, S. -- 3rd Secretary and Consul, Japanese Embassy, Nanking
(0-60)

Ishigurokawa -- President, Chung Chiang Industrial Bank, Hankow,
Hupeh (IDC 7270 1943)

Ishihashi, Toyoo -- Managing Director, Shantung Mining Industrial
Company (more than half the shares of company owned by
Manchuria Railroad Co.); Trustee, Lu-ta Mining Industrial
Company (over half capital of this company owned by Shan-
tung Mining Industrial Co.); Inspector, Lu-ta Mining In-
dustrial Company; Inspector, Shantung Coal Production and
Marketing Company (8/5/43) (52:250)

Ishii -- Charge d'Affaires, Japanese Embassy in Nanking; Chief,
Economic Department, Japanese Embassy, Nanking (8/23/43);

-216-

JAPANESE

Member, Material Investigation Council of Nanking (5/13/43)

Ishii -- Member, Committee for Investigation of Resources & Materials, Shanghai (1943) (49:204)

Ishikawa, Lieutenant -- Member of Volunteer Production Corps to work mine in Honan Province (7/25/44) (52:251)

Ishikawa, Akisa -- Assistant Chief of Police, Tai-Shan Road District Office of Third Police Office, Shanghai (1943) (49:204)

Ishikawa, Hoju -- Head, Lo-Yang Branch (#3), Shanghai Police (IDC 2973 1943)

Ishikawa, Minoru (Viniro) -- Japanese Consul, Canton (Consul-General); received Governor-General of Macao (4/18/43) (51:256)

Ishiwata, Sotaro (Ishiwatari) -- President, East Asia Economic Conference (10/1/42); as Supreme Military Adviser to Nanking Government, visited Tokyo; returned to Nanking, conferred with Ambassador Shigemitsu and Premier of Nanking, Wang Ching Wei, possibly re future management of economic plan of Nanking Government (1/6/43); former Minister of Finance, Nanking (4/15/43); Supreme Economic and Financial Adviser to Nanking Government from 4/15/43 to 3/7/44; met with Ambassador Tani and others in Shanghai (6/22/43); wrote "The Decisive Battle of GEA and New Economic Policy of China" (8/7/43); released as highest Economic Adviser to National Government of China (3/1/44)

Ishuin -- Deputy Manager, Peiping Branch, Yokohama (Nishi) Bank (52:251)

Isono, Y. -- 3rd Secretary, Japanese Embassy, Nanking (O-60)

Isoroku -- Nanking educator (8/16/42)

Isoya, Kozun -- Chairman, Board of Directors, Hua Chung Mining Corporation, Shanghai (8/5/43) (49:204)

Isugai (Isogai), Lt. General Rensi -- Former Chief of General Staff of Kwangtung Army and authority on foreign affairs; appointed Governor-General of Hongkong (1/18/42); present, as Governor-General of Hongkong, at unveiling of memorial to brave warriors on 1st anniversary of GEA war, Hongkong (12/8/42); decorated for meritorious services by National Government (4/16/44); (51:256)

Itabashi, Shigeo -- Publisher, WEI HAI WEI HSIN MIN PAO, Wei-hai-wei, North China (1943) (52:251)

Itagaki, General Seishiro -- Commander in Chief, Korean Army; Governor-General of Hongkong (51:257)

Itami, Hidehiko (Mitani, Mizuhiko) -- New Minister to Shanghai (3/29/44) (49:204)

Itamoto, Teinen -- Editor in Chief, YUNG PAO, Tientsin (1943) (52:251)

Itaya, Taro -- Editor, HSIN SHEN PAO, Shanghai (IDC 7266 1943)

Ito, Hidezo -- Honorary Director, Sino-Japanese Cultural Association, Shanghai Branch (1943) (49:204)

JAPANESE

Ito, Ken -- Ex-Superintendent of Education, Anhwei Province; President, Anhwei Branch of Chinese-Japanese Cultural Society (Assem. 17)

Ito, Kenmoto -- Head, Shanghai Patriotic Association of Arts (IDC 7265 1943)

Ito, Kenyuki -- Director, Sino-Japanese Cultural Association, Shanghai Branch (1943) (49:204)

Ito, Ryuji -- Chief, Bureau of Literature, Japanese Embassy, Shanghai; head of emergency office for investigation of East Asia historical materials within former Royal Asiatic Society, the former Museum of Natural History in the International Settlement (12/4/42); Counsellor to Japanese Embassy in Nanking; appointed as Counsellor, Portugal (5/10/44) (49:204)

Ito, Taro -- Chief, General Affairs Bureau, North China Communications Corporation (1944)

Ito, Yasushi -- Central China Prosperity Insurance Association, Honorary Marine Insurance Company

Iwai, Hideichi -- Secretary, (Japanese Embassy, Shanghai?); Adviser, Shanghai Citizens' Savings Movement Committee; Director, Sino-Japanese Cultural Association (1943) (49:205)

Iwamoto, Kiyoshi -- Executive Director, Sino-Japanese Cultural Association, Shanghai Branch (1943); publisher, HSIN SHEN PAO, which was established in Oct., 1937; publisher, HSIN SHEN PAO WAN PAO, which was established in Dec., 1941 (1943) (49:205)

Iwamura -- Minister of Justice (China); spoke at Conference of All-Japan Judicial Officers (5/3/43)

Iwane -- Recently assumed post of Supreme Adviser of the Hsin Min (Kai) (1/4/44) (52:251)

Iwaru, General Yotijiro -- Commander in Chief, Kwangtung Army (51:257)

Iwasaki -- Head, Information General Affairs Department, China (1943) (Assem. 17)

Iwasaki, Harushige -- Noted as being Chief of Army Press in China (DIO 5/22/42)

Iwasaki, Kentaro -- Director of former Chamber of Commerce, Hankow; made Director of Japan Industrial Economic Association at Hankow (10/10/44)

Iwata, Ryojo -- Member, Sugar Enterprise Special Committee of National Trade Control General Association in Shanghai (1943) (49:205)

Izubuchi, Lt. Colonel Isao -- Chief, Press Bureau of Japanese Army in Shanghai (12/2/44) (49:205)

Isogaya, Kokyo -- Chairman, Directors, Central China Mining Stock Company, Shanghai (1943)

-218-

JAPANESE

Jissoji, Tadahiko -- Inspector, Shantung Mining Industrial Company;
Trustee, Lu-ta Mining Industrial Company (8/5/43) (52:251)

Jitsugatashiro, Jurokuro -- Head, Hsiao-tungmen Branch (#3), Shanghai
Police (IDC 2973 1943)

Junshi, Katsuo -- Member, Shanghai Newspaper Association (49:205)

Kabayama -- President, Peking Branch, IRAA (10/19/44) (52:251)

Kada, Dr. Tetaji -- Economic expert speaking in China on conditions
in Japan (4/11/45)

Kadoaki, Colonel -- Chief, Transportation Coordination Committee,
Chinese Affairs Board (8/19/42)

Kadono, Masaji -- Supervisor, Shantung Mining Industrial Company
(8/5/43) (52:251)

Kagayama, Hajime -- Vice President, Sumitomo North China Mining
Company; Chief, Non-ferrous Metal Bureau, Munitions
Ministry (1943) (52:251)

Kagawa, Dr. Toyohiko -- Missionary for Protestant Church in Japan;
visitor to churches in China (1/7/45) (52:251)

Kagesa, (Major (?) General) Sadaki -- In charge of committee studying matter of taking over French concessions in Shanghai
with Hsu Liane, Foreign Minister, Wang Ching Wei Government (Conf. Far Eastern Agent) stationed at Nanking
(DIO 8/41) (49:205)

Kahoshi -- Non-official Staff Member, Adviser, Shanghai Citizens'
Savings Movement Committee (1943) (49:205)

Kajiki, Hirao -- Member, Sugar Enterprise Special Committee, National
Trade Control General Association in Shanghai (1943)
(49:205)

(Kajiwara), Dr. Takehei -- Chief of the Central Meteorological Ob-
servatory, Japan; attended the 6th deliberative committee
meeting of the East Asia Cultural Conference at Peiping
University (8/31/42) (52:251)

Kakinuma, Dr. Ensaku -- Tokyo Imperial University; lecturer, Chinese
Medical Association (10/23/43)

Kamagaryo, Kyosei -- Secretary, Paochia Office, First Police Office,
Shanghai (49:205)

Kambayashi, Ichitaro -- Vice Governor, Central China Transportation
Company (O-41)

Kamibayashi, Ichitaro -- Director, Central China Railroad Stock
Company, Shanghai (IDC 7262 1943)

Kamiya, Haruo -- Special Director, Huai Nan Coal Mine Corporation,
Shanghai (8/5/43) (49:205)

Kamiyatani, Kiyomatsu -- Director, North China Iron Works Corporation
(8/5/43) (52:251)

Kanda -- Professor, Taihoku Imperial University; invited to come to
Hongkong to collect valuable books (9/29/44) (51:257)

JAPANESE

Kaneyama, Kuniomi -- Economic Adviser, Japanese Consulate, Canton
        (1/44); General Counsellor, Commodity Investigation Com-
        mittee (51:257)

Kanki, Shoichi -- Governor of Chientao Province (O-41)

Kao, Serai -- Japanese Consul, Kaigung, Honan; former Chief, Shita
        Branch, North China; Liaison Office, Chinese Affairs
        Board of Japan (52:251)

Karasawa, Nobuo -- Publisher, KUANG TUNG HSUN PAO, Canton (1943)
        (51:257)

Karui, Vice Admiral Minoru -- Chief of Staff, China Seas Fleet;
        relieved of duties (9/1/43)

Katabira, Katsuo -- Editor, TA LU HSIN PAO, Shanghai (IDC 7266 1943)

Katase, Tadao -- Director, Sino-Japanese Cultural Association,
        Shanghai Branch (1943) (49:205)

Kataoka, Harutaka (Kataoda) -- Chief, Business Dept. and General
        Affairs Dept., East Asia Communications Association,
        North China Branch (1943)

Katayama, Katsuzo -- Executive Director, Central China Tel. Co.,
        Shanghai (O-67); Director, Central China Electrical
        Communications Stock Company (IDC 7262 1943)

Kato -- Japanese naval officer in North China, 1944; attended North
        China Political Council meeting at Peiping (5/22/44)
        (52:251)

Kato, Ekuya -- Chief, Travel Department, East Asia Communications
        Association (1943)

Kato, Nakaji -- Director, North China Communications Corporation
        (1944)

Kato, Naosaburo -- Member, Committee on Grain Control, Shanghai
        (1943) (49:205)

Kato, Shinkichi -- Manager, Business Investigation Committee,
        North China Communications Corporation (1944)

Katsushiro, Lt. General Sumida -- Reached Hunan-Hopeh border and
        is stationed in Pai-Lo-Shih, according to information
        dated 6/5/44; (OSS note states that he was Commanding
        General, 39th Division, but it is believed that he was
        relieved in 1943 -- name was given as Sumida Raishiro)
        (8/2/44) (52:251)

Katsuyama, Kunimitsu -- Embassy (Commercial) Secretary, (Finland);
        relieved of post at his request; appointed Director, Japan
        Economic Assistance Association in Nanking (10/30/44)

Kawabe, Lt. General -- Chief, General Staff, Japanese Expeditionary
        Force in China; transferred to another post (2/17/43)

Kawaguchi, Kenichi -- Director & Treasurer, Shanghai Municipality
        Labor & Business Social Union (1943) (49:206)

Kawahayashi, Nishiro -- Director, Shanghai Municipality Labor &
        Business Social Union (1943) (49:206)

-220-

JAPANESE

Kawai -- Director, Sino-Japanese Cultural Association, Shanghai Branch (1943) (49:206)

Kawakita, Nagamasa -- Honorary Director, Sino-Japanese Cultural Association, Shanghai Branch (1943) (49:206)

Kawamura, Mothoiro -- Managing Director, Shantung Mining Industrial Company; Trustee, Lu-ta Mining Industrial Company (8/5/43) (52:251)

Kawamura, Nishiro -- Manager, Shanghai Branch, Yokohama Specie Bank (3/10/42) (49:206)

Kawasaki, Masao -- Director, Sino-Japanese Cultural Association, Shanghai Branch (1943) (49:206)

Kawasaki, T. -- 2nd Secretary and Interpreter, Japanese Embassy, Nanking (0-60)

Kawauguchi -- Chief, Judicial Bureau, Communications Corporation (1944)

Kaya, Okinori -- President, North China Development Company (1941) (52:251)

Kelambi, D. W. S. -- Editor and Publisher of "Buddhist China" (5/10/44)

Kiamatsu, Hemia -- Director, North China Development Company, Peiping (2/16/43) (52:251)

Kikuchi, Dr. Masutaro -- Publisher, SHANSI HSIN MIN PAO, T'ai-yuan, North China, established Dec., 1937 (1943) (52:251)

Kimura, Dr. Masutaro -- Economic Adviser, Japanese Embassy (11/12/42); Adviser, Central Reserve Bank in Nanking (4/6/44) (0-60)

Kimura, S. -- 3rd Secretary, Nanking, China

Kinoshita, Major General -- Attended raising of new flag of Socialist Italian Republic at Shanghai (9/13/44) (49:206)

Kinoshita, Nirosaburo -- Member, Committee on Grain Control, Shanghai (1943) (49:206)

Kishi -- Minister, Commerce & Industry; spoke re problem of price control (2/15/43)

Kishi, Iichi (Ischi) -- Counselor, Japanese Embassy, Nanking; Chairman, Press Section, Japanese Embassy, Nanking (10/6/43); Chairman, Press Section, Japanese Embassy, Shanghai (9/26/44) (49:206)

Kishima, Genshi -- President, North China Development Company (11/15/42) (52:252)

Kita, Nagao -- Japanese Consul, Tsingtao; ex-Consul General in Honolulu (52:252)

Kita, Takino -- Japanese Consul, Hankow (0-60)

Kitakawa, Hideji -- Assistant Chairman, Oil and Grain Special Committee, National Trade Control General Association in Shanghai (1943) (49:206)

270

JAPANESE

Kitana -- Assistant Chief, Hongkong Branch, Nishi Nippon Company; Director, Hongkong Trade Syndicate; transferred to head office in Tokyo (7/29/44) (51:257)

Kitamura, Daisuke -- Former Director, Central China Salt Industry Company, Shanghai (11/25/43) (49:206)

Kitamura, Dr. Tsutsuhiko -- Nagasaki Medical University; one of the discoverers of cause of Yangtze rheumatism (10/27/44) (49:206)

Kitamura, Ukeichi -- Member, Sugar Enterprise Special Committee, National Trade Control General Association in Shanghai (1943) (49:206)

Kitanishi, Isaku -- Vice Chairman, Huai Nan Salt Industry Stock Company, Shanghai (IDC 7262 1943)

Kitano, Eiichi -- Inspector, Sino-Japanese Cultural Association, Shanghai Branch (1943) (49:206)

Kitazawa -- Consul General; President, Peking IRAA (3/20/43) (52:252)

Kito, Hyun -- Requested permit to operate all mines in Nankang and Wayao in P'anyu-hsien (IDC 5/29/42)

Kiyama, Shigeru -- President, Hongkong Loss Insurance Company Association (51:257)

Kiyomizu, Taro -- Special Director, Tungyang Paper Industry Corporation, North China (8/5/43) (52:252)

Kiyozawa -- Minister; attended Nippon Chamber of Commerce & Industry meeting in North China at Peiping (2/15/43) (52:252)

Klimenko, N. S. -- Head, Su-lien-hu-sheng Broadcasting Station, Shanghai (1943)

Kobayashi, Hideo -- Member, Japanese Literary Patriotic Society; visitor to Shanghai in exchange of literary men (10/5/43) (49:206)

Kobayashi, Mamoru -- Director, Central China Silk Stock Company, Shanghai (IDC 7262 1943)

Kobetto, Sozo -- Honorary Director, Sino-Japanese Cultural Association, Shanghai Branch (1943) (49:206)

Kochu -- Took over Northwest Lime Builders at Taiyuan (52:252)

Kodama -- Vice President, China Transportation Company, Peiping (52:252)

Kodama, Kenji -- President, Central China Development Company (retired 3/8/43); Chief Manager, Prosperity Corporation of Central China (1/43); Chairman, Central China Industrial Production Co-Prosperity Association, established in Shanghai (1/43); President, Prosperity Corporation of Central China (4/5/43); Vice President, China Transportation Company (9/23/43); Honorary Director, Sino-Japanese Cultural Association, Nanking Branch (1943) (49:207)

Koga, Admiral Meinichi -- Ex-Commander in Chief, Japanese Fleet in China; member, Supreme War Council, Nanking; naval funeral honoring the late Fleet-Admiral Mineichi Koga, May 12, Shanghai (5/12/44) (Assem. 17)

-222-

JAPANESE

Kohiyama -- President, South Manchuria Railway Company; made inspection tour in North China (1943) (52:252)

Koida, Kohei -- Peers School; invited to teach in Peiping (12/29/42) (52:252)

Kojima, Hiroshi -- Editor, TA LU HSIN PAO, Shanghai (IDC 7266 1943)

Komaya, Dr. Ginji -- Head of Komaya Hospital, Shanghai; one of the discoverers of cause of Yangtze rheumatism (10/27/44) (49:207)

Komiya, Dr. Yoshitaka -- Director, Shanghai Natural Science Research Institute; one of the discoverers of cause of Yangtze rheumatism (10/27/44) (49:207)

Komori, Akira -- Director, Sino-Japanese Cultural Association, Shanghai Branch (1943) (49:207)

Komuchi, Tsunetaka -- Vice President, North China Development Co. (1941) (52:252)

Komura, Hoshitaro -- Director, Huai Nan Coal Mine Stock Company, Shanghai (IDC 7262 1943)

Komura, Kenda -- Manager, Mitsui Company, Shanghai (49:207)

Komura, Sentaro -- Supervisor, Shantung Mining Industrial Company (8/5/43) (52:252)

Kondo, Admiral Nobutake -- Supreme War Council; Commander-in-Chief, China Waters Fleet (DIO-139, 215)

Kondo, Tetsuji -- President, Shantung Electric Corporation, Tsingtao (1943) (52:252)

Kondo, Yasuichiro -- Adviser, Sino-Japanese Cultural Association, (1943) (49:207)   Shanghai Branch

Kono, Kuro -- Standing Director, Board of Directors, North China Transportation Corporation in Peking (8/5/43) (52:252)

Korenaga, Akiko (Miss) -- Resident of Chookakoo area; presented letter of commendation from Japanese Embassy at Nanking for services in education of Chinese girls. Presentation was made by Ambassador Tani (DIO 3/5/44)

Koroda -- Pastor, Japanese church (Protestant), Nanking; assisted in conducting service at union celebration of Lord's Supper of Protestant churches in Nanking (4/30/44)

Koshima, Hiroshi -- Member, Shanghai Newspaper Association; Director, Sino-Japanese Cultural Association, Shanghai Branch (1943) (49:207)

Kotabe, Masurao -- Director, Sino-Japanese Cultural Association, Shanghai Branch (1943) (49:207)

Kotaka, Chosaburo -- Of Chiba Prefecture; spoke before North China Development Committee, House of Representatives (1/31/44) (52:252)

Koto, Fumio -- Professor of Tungwen University; Vice President, "Cultural Data Translation Office", Shanghai Publishing Institution (6/7/44)

JAPANESE

(Kovaki, Reverend Michio) -- Sent to China and Manchukuo (for three
        months) as representative of Christian Council and Church
        of Christ of Japan (5/21/44)

Koyama, Dr. Matsushi -- Professor Emeritus, Peiping University
        (8/13/42) (52:252)

Koyama, Naishin -- Auditor, Kako Commercial Bank, Shanghai (49:207)

Kozaka, Masayasu -- Japanese representative at 2nd East Asiatic
        Youth Conference held in Nanking (10/10/44)

Kozaki, Naganichi -- Vice President, Japanese Christian Council;
        visited China

Kubota -- Naval Attache at Peiping (11/8/42, 7/8/43) (52:252)

Kubota, Santaro (Mantaro) -- Playwright and critic; toured China
        (2/2/44); selected by Japanese Literary Patriotic Society
        to go to Shanghai in exchange of literary men (10/5/43);
        delegate of Japan Writers National Service Association to
        China on inspection tour (3/1/44) (49:207)

Kuda, Timosaki -- President, Japanese Residents Association, Shanghai
        (49:207) (Assem. 17)

Kuichi, Lieutenant General Tanaka -- Commander, 23rd Army Corps,
        "South Kwangtung Branch Units" (7/29/44) (51:257)

Kukita, Shigemichi -- Member, Sugar Enterprise Special Committee,
        National Trade Control General Association, Shanghai
        (1943) (49:207)

Kumizu, Tadazo -- Candidate Director, Sino-Japanese Cultural Associ-
        ation, Nanking (1943) (49:132)

Kurashi -- Vice President, Nippon Buddhist Association (10/5/44)

Kurihara, Akira -- Supervisor, Shantung Mining Industrial Company
        (8/5/43) (52:252)

Kuriki, Toroji -- Member, Oil and Grain Special Committee, National
        Trade Control General Association in Shanghai (1943)
        (49:207)

Kurimoto, Toraji -- Director and Manager, Shanghai Municipality
        Labor and Business Social Union   (1943) (49:207)

Kuroda, Count Kiyoshi -- Managing Director, Society for International
        Cultural Relations, Shanghai (3/14/44) (49:207)

Kusumoto, Lt. General Sanetaka (Tanetaka) -- Decorated by China
        National Government for meritorious services (4/16/44);
        Envoy Extraordinary, Minister Plenipotentiary to China
        (10/26/44); former Vice Chief of Central China Liaison
        Section of Asia Promotion Board (52:252)

Kuwahara, Juemon -- Former Director, Central China Salt Industry
        Company, Shanghai (11/25/43) (49:208)

Kuwahara, Shigeishiemore -- Director, Huai Nan Salt Industry Stock
        Company, Shanghai (IDC 7262 1943)

Mafuna, Yutaka -- Japanese Literary Patriotic Society; visitor to
        Peking in exchange of literary men (10/5/43) (52:252)

-224-

JAPANESE

Makasa, Prince Takahito -- Staff Officer, China Expeditionary Forces;
promoted to Military General Staff of Imperial Headquarters;
returned to Tokyo (1/14/44)

Makayama, Mesiro -- Member of Parliament; sent to China and Manchukuo
as representative of Japan's Christian Council and Church
of Christ in Japan (5/21/44)

Manao (?) -- One of staff of Tokyo Asahi Shimbun Agency who came to
Hongkong to take charge of a newspaper (51:257)

Manjo, Oda -- Chairman, Board of Directors, Tungyang Paper Industry
Corporation (1943) (52:252) (See Oda, Manjo)

Marimoto, Kangaburo -- President, Takeda Drug Company, North China
(1943) (52:253)

Marita, Shiganin -- Japanese Head of Hua Chung City Bus Company,
Shanghai (8/5/43) (49:208)

Maruyama -- Chief, General Affairs Bureau of IRAA, North China
(52:253)

Maruyama, Masao -- Inspector, Sino-Japanese Cultural Association,
Shanghai Branch (1943) (49:208)

Masadokoro, Kisumi -- Chief Ritualist of Hongkong Shrine (51:257)

Matsuda -- Chief, General Affairs Bureau, Finance Ministry; made
inspection tour of Mengchiang area, North China (52:253)

Matsuda, Lt. Morito -- Assistant Japanese Interpreter for prisoners,
Shanghai (2/12/42) (49:208)

Matsudaira -- Chief, Information Dept., Japanese Embassy in Nanking;
received Chinese correspondents (IDC 3/9/44)

Matsugata, Yoshisaburo -- Director, China Broadcasting Enterprise
& Reconstruction Association, Shanghai (IDC 7268 1943)

Matsuhara, Hisashi -- Candidate Director, Sino-Japanese Cultural
Association, Wu-Ch'ang & Hankow Branch (1943)

Matsui -- Appointed Chief of Staff, Japan's Expeditionary Forces
in China (IDC 3/43)

Matsui -- Assistant Head of Department of News Guidance of Japanese
Occupation Government in Hongkong (8/30/43) (51:257)

Matsui, General Iwanao (Iwane) -- Vice President, Japan Asia Development League (6/24/43); Vice President, East Asiatic League;
guest of honor at round-table conference held by Shanghai
East Asia Society, where he spoke (11/28/42) (49:208)

Matsui, Tetsugan -- Resident of Chookakoo area; presented letter of
commendation from Japanese Embassy at Nanking for work on
relief and protection of indigent Chinese and for contribution to agricultural development; presentation made by
Ambassador Tani (DIO 3/5/44)

Matsukata, Matagoro -- Director, Sino-Japanese Cultural Association,
Nanking (1943) (49:132)

Matsukata, Yoshisaburo -- Director, Committee for Establishment of
China's Broadcasting Business, Shanghai (1943) (49:208);
Substitute Director, Central Electrical Communications

JAPANESE

Corporation (IDC-2562)

Matsuma, Kazutate -- Chief, First Department, Paochia Office, First
Police Office; Assistant Chairman, Paochia Office, Third
Police Office, Shanghai (1943) (49:208)

Matsumoto, Shinta -- President, Board of Directors, North China
Electric Wire Corporation (2/17/44) (52:253)

Matsumura, Susumu -- Councillor for GEA Ministry; concurrently
Professor at Chiba Medical College (10/30/43) (O-60);
Counselor, Japanese Embassy, Nanking (8/27/44)

Matsunaga, Tatsunan -- Candidate Director, Sino-Japanese Cultural
Association, Wu-Ch'ang & Hankow Branch (1943)

Matsunaga, Yasuzaemon -- Director, North China Electrical Industry
Company located in Peiping (8/5/43) (52:253)

Matsuo (?) -- One of staff of Tokyo Asahi Shimbun Agency who came
to Hongkong to take charge of a newspaper (51:257)

Matsushima, Colonel -- Adviser, Shanghai Citizens' Savings Movement
Committee (1943) (49:208)

Matsushima, Captain Keizo -- Appointed Chief of Press Section of the
Japanese Fleet in China waters (9/2/43); spoke at rally
commemorating annihilation of American bases in China
(12/2/44); Honorary Director, Sino-Japanese Cultural Assoc.,
Shanghai Branch (1943); appointed Chief of Office of Information (9/43) (49:208)

Matsutani, Hideo -- 1st Secretary, Japanese Embassy, Peiping (52:253)

Matsuura, Kenkichi -- Exporter; donated money for aircraft, Shanghai
(3/9/44) (49:208)

Matsuyama, Adaji -- Supervisor, North China Iron Works Corporation
(8/5/43) (52:253)

Matsuyo, Keiji -- Author, "Industrial Development of the North China
Development Co." (8/5/43) (52:253)

Matsuyoshi -- Japanese prisoner of war, announced shipping loss from
war (3/4/44)

Matsuzaki -- Chief, Special Affairs Organization Meeting of Peiping
IRAA (3/20/43) (52:253)

Mihara -- Office Director of Headquarters, North China-Asia Development Assistance Association; selected as North China representative to attend round-table conference in Japan on
national movement organizations (8/25/43) (52:253)

Mikageike, Tatsuo -- Inspector, North China Communications Corporation
(1944)

Mikami, Yasuyoshi -- Managing Director, Shantung Mining Industrial
Company; Managing Director, Shantung Coal Production &
Marketing Company (8/5/43) (52:253)

Mimura -- Vice President, Reclamation Insurance Association

Mimura, Kii (Kiichi) -- Adviser to Japanese Embassy, Nanking (9/25/44);
has held directorships in Sumitomo Copper and Steel Tubing

-226-

JAPANESE

Company, Besshi Mining Company, and Sumitomo Machinery Manufacturing Company (9/25/44); member, Board of Directors of Sumitomo Company, sent to North China and Inner Mongolia to promote new industries and accelerate old (10/1/44); President, Sumitomo Mining Company (52:253)

Minakawa (Minagawa) -- Chief, Iron Ore Bureau, Ministry of Munitions, on inspection tour of Mengchiang area, North China (52:253)

Mineshita, Koki -- Head, Loo-cha Branch (#1), Shanghai Police (IDC 2973)

Misawa, Mototsura -- Resident of Peiping area; presented letter of commendation from Japanese Embassy, Nanking, for establishment of Peiping Welfare Medical School and his popularization of medical treatment among rural residents of Peiping area; presentation made by Ambassador Tani (52:253)

Mishina, Lt. General (Lt. Colonel) -- Chief, Information Bureau, Japanese Expeditionary Force in China (6/12/43); represented Debuchi, Chief of Army Press Section, at inaugural meeting of new China Newspaper Association (9/26/44) (Assem. 17)

Mitamura, Takeo -- Wartime Criminal Law Committee of House of Peers (52:254)

Mitani, Mizuhiko -- Minister Extraordinary & Plenipotentiary to China Republic (3/15/44); President, Hopeh Transportation Co. (4/14/44); made statement re materials to be sent to China this year (5/7/43); Chief, Chinese Bureau of GEA Ministry (52:254) (Same as Itami, Hidehiko?)

Mitini -- Minister (?); Director, headquarters for supervision of increase in industry in Central China (8/30/44) (49:209)

Mitsukoijii, Tomiatsu -- Japanese writer; visits China; Head, 2nd Writers' Conference in China (4/4/43)

Mitsushima -- Chief, Shanghai Police (12/29/44) (49:209)

Miura, Dr. Ihachiro -- Professor of Agriculture & Forestry, Tokyo Imperial University; directing development of agriculture and forestry on Hainan (51:257)

Miura, Shichiro -- Chief, Technological Section, China Affairs Board, North China (8/6/42); Director, North China Communications Corporation (1944) (52:254)

Miura, Takemi -- Manchukuo Minister, Nanking (O-61)

Miura, Tamon -- Central China Prosperity Insurance Association; Vice Chairman, Taisho Marine Insurance Company

Miura, Y. -- Counselor, Japanese Embassy, Nanking (O-60)

Miwata, Mitsuo -- Of House of Peers; Chief Director, Japan Asia Development Federation, Shanghai (11/4/42) (49:209)

Miyakawa, Shinsaburo -- Honorary Director, Sino-Japanese Cultural Association, Wu-Ch'ang & Hankow Branch (1943)

Miyakawa, Dr. Yoneji -- Tokyo Imperial University; lecturer, Chinese Medical Association (10/23/43)

JAPANESE

Miyake, Masatro -- Director, Sino-Japanese Cultural Association,
Shanghai Branch (1943) (49:209)

Miyake, Shotaro -- Vice Chief Justice, Supreme Court, North China
(7/4/43) (52:254)

Miyasawa, Koreshige -- Chairman, Shantung Mining Industrial Company;
Assistant Manager, Lu-ta Mining Industrial Company; Chief
Director, Shantung Coal Production & Marketing Company;
representative of Ryokuka Mining Industrial Company, also
of Kuan-chuang Mining Industrial Company (8/5/43) (52:254)

Miyazaki -- Minister representing Mongolia in Coordination Conference,
Peiping (11/8/42) (52:254)

Miyoshi, Gosaburo -- Former Director, Chamber of Commerce at Takaoka;
made Vice Director of Japan Industrial Economic Association,
Hankow (10/10/44)

Miyoshi, Seisaburo -- Member, Financial Consultation Committee,
W. Shanghai (12/42) (49:209)

Miyoshi, Toshiro -- Director, Red Cross, Kwangtung Branch (1/9/45)
(51:257)

Mizutani, Senchuma -- Inspector, North China Aluminite Mining Industrial Company, Ltd. (8/5/43) (52:254)

Momoi -- Chief, Japanese Army Surgical Department, National Government, Nanking (2/4/44)

Mori -- Section Chief of Cabinet Planning Board, Peiping (52:254)

Mori, Shinji -- Director, North China Salt Corporation, Tientsin
Branch (1943) (52:254)

Mori, Takashi -- Director, Sino-Japanese Cultural Association,
Nanking (1943) (49:132)

Mori, Usaku -- Director, North China Electrical Industry Company,
Peiping (8/5/43) (52:254)

Morie, Hosoki (Hosoki, Morie?) -- Director, Central China Mining
Stock Company, Shanghai (1943)

Morimoto, Shotaro -- Member, Financial Consultation Committee,
W. Shanghai (12/42) (49:209)

Morita, Ichimatsu -- Director, Huai Nan Salt Industry Stock Company,
Shanghai (IDC 7262 1943)

Morita, Shigenobu -- Vice Chairman, Central China City Bus Stock
Company, Shanghai (IDC 7262 1943)

Morito, Kiyoshi -- Director of Manchukuo 10th Anniversary Felicitation Athletic Meet (8/1/42); member, Cultural Goodwill
Party to China (5/3/43) (51:258)

Moriyama, Takashi -- Managing Director, Shanghai Newspaper Association (49:209); Editor, HSIN SHEN PAO (IDC 7266 1943)

Muroki, Ryusaburo -- Director, Central China Mining Stock Company,
Shanghai (1943)

Moroto, Suematsu -- Author, "The Story of Communications in East Asia"
(IDC 8/43)

-228-

JAPANESE

Motono, Kyozo -- Executive Director, Sino-Japanese Cultural Associa-
    tion, Shanghai Branch; Consul-General, Hangchow (10/31/44)
    (49:209)

Movinaga, Fujio -- Standing Director, Board of Directors, North China
    Transportation Corporation in Peiping (8/5/43) (52:254)

Mukai, Tadaharu -- Chairman, Board of Directors, Mitsui Controlling
    Group (Somotokata); resigned after assuming responsibility
    for Shansi Incident (12/10/43, 1/14/44) (52:254)

Munesuku, Terasua -- Author, "The Great East Asia War" and "The Es-
    tablishment of Industry in North China" (8/5/43) (52:254)

Murado, Sonosuke -- Head, Yang-shu-pu Branch (#1), Shanghai Police
    (IDC 2973 1943)

Muragami, Kagashi -- Publisher of semi-monthly magazine, WEN-YU,
    Shanghai (1943) (49:209)

Murakami, Ho -- Managing Director, Shanghai Magazine Association
    (49:209)

Murakami, Yoshiichi -- Director, Central China Railroad Stock Company,
    Shanghai (IDC 7262 1943)

Murata, Sonosuki -- (See Murado, Sonosuke) (49:209)

Murikone, Reverend Otamura -- Superintendent, Japan Mission, North
    China (1944) (52:254)

Muro, Kimio (Kimio, Muro?) -- Director, Central China Mining Stock
    Company, Shanghai (1943)

Mushakoji, Saneyeshi -- Member, Cultural Goodwill Party to China
    (5/3/43) (51:258)

Nabeshima, Kimon -- Trustee, North China Aluminite Mining Industrial
    Company, Ltd. (8/5/43) (52:254)

Nabeshima, Ryoichi -- Director, Sino-Japanese Cultural Association,
    Shanghai Branch (1943) (49:209)

Nagai -- Japanese Special Envoy, spoke on inter-dependence of Japan
    and China (Sept., 1942); Committee for Investigation of
    Resources and Materials, Shanghai; Professor, Tokyo Imper-
    ial University, on inspection tour of Menchiang area,
    North China (49:209; 52:254)

Nagai, Ryutare -- Member, House of Representatives, Tokyo; special
    mission to Nanking (8/28/42)

Nagakawa, Kubo -- In Peiping Office, Central China Railway Company
    (1944) (52:254)

Nagamatsu, Shuichi -- Standing Director, Tungyang Paper Industry
    Corporation, North China (8/5/43) (52:254)

Nagano -- Instructor, University of Peiping; will be appointed to
    the foundation resulting from the reorganization of the
    Nippon Cultural Association in China (8/4/44) (52:255)

Nagaoka, Tetsuji -- Managing Director, Japan Raw Silk Association;
    appointed Vice President, Central China Raw Silk Company
    (Shanghai, 49:209)

JAPANESE

Nagata, Hiroshi -- Executive Member, Flour Special Committee, National Trade Control General Association, Shanghai (1943) (49:209)

Nagata, Hisajiro -- Chief, Enterprise Bureau, North China Communications Corporation (1944)

Nagatsu, Lieutenant General Sahiju -- Commander, 13th Army, Shanghai (8/17/44) (49:209)

Nagayo, Yoshiro -- Author, "Japanese Culture", to be published by Cultural Data Translation Office of Sino-Japanese Cultural Association, Shanghai Branch (6/7/44) (49:209)

Nagi -- Member of special mission to Nanking (9/8/42)

Naito -- Vice President, Industrial Association, North China (9/23/43) (52:255)

Naito, Kuisoburo -- Director, Central China Sea Products Stock Co., Shanghai (IDC 7262 1943)

Naito, Tatsuin -- Inspector, Sino-Japanese Cultural Association, Wu-Ch'ang & Hankow Branch (1943)

Nakabe, Etsuyoshi -- Director, Central China Sea Products Stock Co., Shanghai (IDC 7262 1943)

Nakada, Shinpai -- Chief, Business Department, East Asia Communications Association (1943)

Nakada, Suehiro -- Member, Executive Committee, China Broadcasting Enterprise & Reconstruction Association, Shanghai (1943)

Nakagari, Konosuki -- Honorary Director, Committee for Establishment of China's Broadcasting Business, Shanghai (1943) (49:210)

Nakagawa -- Mouthpiece of Japanese Army in Shanghai (12/14/43) (49:210)

Nakagawa, Toru -- Member, Japanese Council, Shanghai (49:210)

Nakahara, Yashio -- Chief of Police, Cheng-tu Road District Office, First Police Office, Shanghai (1943) (49:210)

Nakamori -- Chief, General Affairs Section, Japanese Embassy, Peiping (1/30/44) (52:255)

Nakamura, Goshichi -- Director, Huai Nan Coal Mine Stock Company, Shanghai (IDC 7262 1943)

Nakamura, Dr. Koya -- Ex-Professor, Tokyo Imperial University; Chairman, Japanese Culture, Central State University, Nanking (Assem. 17; 10/25/42)

Nakamura, M. -- Attache, Japanese Embassy, Nanking (O-60); Councillor, Japanese Embassy, Nanking; spoke regarding Japanese retrocession in China (4/15/43)

Nakamura, Michizo -- Special Trustee, Lu-ta Mining Industrial Company; Managing Director, Shantung Coal Production and Marketing Company (8/5/43) (52:255)

Nakamura, Takeo -- Japanese Vice-Consul, Shanghai (49:210)

-230-

JAPANESE

Nakamura, Tameo -- Manager, North China Takeda Drug Company (1943)
(52:255)

Nakamura, Toyoichi (Toyohiko) -- Japanese Consul, Canton (1937);
attended conference re retrocession of concessions in
China (3/14/43); Councillor to Japanese Embassy, Nanking;
Minister Plenipotentiary to Finland (4/28/43); expects to
visit China with Yuki, GEA Adviser (10/2/44); relieved of
post in Finland; temporarily assigned to duties in Foreign
Office (10/30/44); member, Committees on Return of Concessions and Abolition of Extraterritoriality (2/43) (51:258)

Nakamura, Toyokazu -- Member, Japanese Embassy, Nanking (0-60)

Nakan, Masaharu -- President, Japanese Chamber of Commerce, Peiping
(8/11/44) (52:255)

Nakane, Naosuke -- Japanese Consul, Pengfu, Anhwei (0-60)

Nakane, Shinsuke -- Candidate Director, Sino-Japanese Cultural Association (1943) (49:132)

Nakanishi -- Unit Commander, Japanese Forces in North China (1943-44)
(52:255)

Nakano -- Councillor of Canton; requested by Ambassador Tani to
attend meeting of 20 diplomats at Peking, apparently, to
consider significance of Japan-China Mutual Alliance Pact,
world situation, economic trend, etc. (11/28/43) (51:258)

Nakano, Masanaga (Masaharu) -- Head, Japanese Chamber of Commerce,
Peiping; Resident Director at Peking Bank of Chosen
(5/23/44); established Increased Promotion Council
(8/11/44) (52:255)

Nakata, Suechiro -- Managing Director, Committee for Establishment
of China's Broadcasting Business, Shanghai (49:210)

Nakata, T. -- 2nd Secretary and Interpreter, Japanese Embassy,
Nanking (0-60)

Nakatax, Toyochiyo -- Executive Director, Sino-Japanese Cultural
Association, Shanghai Branch (1943) (49:210)

Nakayama, Shinpei -- Chief Secretary, Southern Region Music Committee
(11/10/42)

Nanba, Hiroshi -- Director, Sino-Japanese Cultural Association,
Shanghai Branch (1943) (49:210)

Nango, Haruo -- President, Trade Control Association; visited China
on Goodwill Mission (6/19/43)

Nanjo, Kaneo -- Superintendent, Prosperity Corporation of Central
China (IDC 4/5/43)

Narasaki, Dr. Asataro -- Dean of Education, Tokyo University of
Literature and Science; invited to lecture at National
Central University in Nanking (10/18/43)

Nasu, Dr. -- Employed by National Government of China to aid in increase of agricultural output (4/1/44)

Nehakugo -- Chief, Traffic Department, Peking Office, Japanese Embassy; appointed Head of Chamber for Promoting Production

JAPANESE

Increase of Wrought Iron and Alumina (12/6/44) (52:255)

Niazaki, Major General Shigeru (Miazaki) -- Chief, Japanese Army
Special Service Station, Shanghai; attended discussions
of Asiatic Problems Research Institute in Shanghai (8/8/42)
(49:210)

Nishida, Shoichi -- Vice President, Peiping IRAA (3/20/43); Auditor,
North China Electric Wire Corporation (2/17/44) (52:255)

Nishikawa -- Director, Shanghai Municipality Labor & Business Social
Union (1943) (49:210)

Nishikawa -- Chief, Technical Research Department of Southern Manchuria Railway; made Director of North China Railway
Corporation (3/28/44) (52:255)

Nishikawa --- Head, Department of News Guidance of Japanese Occupation Government, Hongkong (8/30/43) (51:258)

Nishimoto, Kazuo -- Auditor, North China Electric Wire Corporation
(2/17/44) (52:255)

Nishimura -- Commander in Army, North China (2/15/43) (52:255)

Nishio, Hisai -- Chief, Tokyo Railway Bureau, retired; appointed
Director of...in Central China (6/28/44)

Nishiyama -- Representative of Japan at Economic Round-Table Conference

Niyiki -- Head Councillor, National Government, Canton (51:258)

Noda, Yoichi -- Inspector, Sino-Japanese Cultural Association,
Shanghai Branch (1943); Managing Director, Shanghai Hemp
Company (organized by Tooyoo Hemp Co. and Shanghai Cotton
Dyeing Works) (2/21/44) (49:210; 50:147; 51:258)

Noda, Yutaka -- Head, Shanghai Economic Research Institute (IDC
7265 1943)

Nomura -- Head, Co-Prosperity School, Amoy (1/18/44) (49:210)

Nomura, Ichijiro -- Director, Sino-Japanese Cultural Association,
Shanghai Branch (1943) (49:210)

Nono, Yamashige -- Director, Sino-Japanese Cultural Association,
Shanghai Branch (1943) (49:210)

Nozaki, Yuzuru -- Member, Oil and Grain Special Committee, National
Trade Control General Association in Shanghai (1943)
(49:211)

Nukii, Mitsuzo -- 1st Secretary, Japanese Embassy, Peiping; Chief,
Department of Economics, Japanese Consulate, Canton;
member, Commodity Investigation Committee (4/5/44)
(51:258)

Nukii, Terushiro -- Chief, Water Transportation Bureau, North China
Communications Corporation (1944)

JAPANESE

Oba -- Chief, Special Service Facilities (Assem. 17); attended
ceremony for formation of Anhwei Province Branch of
China-Japan Cultural Society (10/4/42)

Obayashi, Sotaro -- Head, Tii-lin Road Branch (#1), Shanghai Police
(IDC 2973 1943)

Obikawa, Genshichi -- Author of book, "Chinese Resources" (IDC
4/5/43)

Ochiai -- Military Attache, Japanese Embassy, Nanking (O-60)

Ochiai, Genko -- Director, North China Electric Industry Company
(52:255)

Ochiai, Jinkuro -- Honorary Adviser, Sino-Japanese Cultural Association, Wu-Ch'ang & Hankow Branch (1943)

Ochiai, Minoru -- Member, Shanghai Newspaper Association (1943)
(49:211); Editor, TA LU HSIN PAO (IDC 7266 1943)

Ochida (Ishida) -- Japanese Consul-General, Hankow (6/24/44)

Oda, Manjo -- Chairman, Board of Directors, Tungyang Paper Industry
Corporation, North China; concurrently Deputy Director of
Asahi (Ashai) Industry (8/5/43) (52:255)

Oda, Takeo -- Japanese Literary Patriotic Society; visitor of
Shanghai in exchange of literary men (10/5/43) (49:211)

Ogami, Yoshio -- Publisher, TSINGTO TA MIN HSIN PAO, Tsingtao, established April, 1938 (1943) (52:255)

Ogawa -- Chief, Investigation Department, Japanese Embassy, Nanking
(8/23/43); member, Studies & Documentation Section (8/1/44)

Ogawa, Shizuhiko -- Editor, SHANTUNG HSIN PAO, Tsinan, North China
(1943) (52:255)

Oguchi, Kienyu -- Head, Oguchi Financial Corporation, Tientsin (1942)
(52:256)

Ogura -- Councillor, National Government, Canton (51:258)

Ogura, Chiyozo -- Standing Director, China Ship Company Corporation,
Ltd., Shanghai (8/5/43) (49:211)

Ogura, Matsatsune -- President, East Asia Economic Round Table Conference; President, Wartime Financial Bank; visited China
on Goodwill Mission (6/19/43); former Finance Minister;
member of Japanese Economic Mission to Central China
(7/8/43); leader, Nippon-China Goodwill Economic Party
convening with Chinese economists, Shanghai (7/11/43);
In press interview, he stated he will do his utmost to
cement Japan-China relations in economic field (3/2/44);
appointed Supreme Economic Adviser to National Government
in March, 1944; attended reorganization meeting of All-China
Commercial Control General Association (6/8/44); visited
Japan for consultation (7/3/44)

Ogura, Takuzo -- Vice Chairman, Trustees, North China Aluminite
Mining Industrial Company (1943) (52:256)

Ohashi, Chuichi (?) -- Adviser to Peace Preservation Army, Peiping;
attended a regular conference of P.P.A. at Peiping (9/12/43);

-233-

JAPANESE

Supreme Adviser, Mengchiang Government; attended 5th anniversary of Federated Autonomous Government of Mongolia in Tokyo (9/2/44) (52:256)

Ohata, Shigero -- Assistant Chief of Police, Chung-yang District Office, Third Police Office, Shanghai (1943) (49:211)

Ohayashi, Sotaro --- Chief of Police, Yu-ling District, First Police Office, Shanghai (1943) (49:211)

Ohshima, A. -- Attache, Japanese Embassy, Nanking (0-60)

Ohta -- Secretary to Japanese Ambassador to Nanking, Masayuki Tani; accompanied Tani to Peiping on tour of inspection (5/28/43) (52:256)

Ohta -- Chief, Political Affairs Department, Nanking (8/23/43)

Ohta, Tomotsune -- Japanese Consul-General at Tientsin; present at ceremony transferring Italian Concession to National Government of China (8/17/44) (52:256)

Oita, (Yoich) -- Director, Standing Committee, Shanghai Press Association; President, Hsin Shen Pao (IDC 7266 1943)

Okabe -- Education Minister; present at 37th Festival of Confucius held in Tokyo under auspices of Literature Association (4/25/43)

Okabe, Viscount Nagakage -- Attended 6th deliberative committee meeting of the East Asia Cultural Conference at Peiping University (8/31/42) (52:256)

Okabe, General Naosaburo --- Supreme Commander, Japanese Forces in North China; invited Chinese officials to confer on various problems at his official residence, Peiping; ex-Military Commander in Java (9/7/44) (52:256)

Okada, Reverend -- In charge of religious activities in Government-General's Office in Hongkong (51:258)

Okada -- Member, Committee for Investigation of Resources & Materials, Shanghai (1943) (49:211)

Okada, General Kenichi -- Vice President, Board of China Affairs; Japanese Army Unit Commander, Shanghai (7/9/42) (49:211)

Okahori -- Japanese Consul-General to Chinese Mayor of Amoy (7/30/43) (49:211)

Okamoto -- Chief, Gendarmes, Soochow; delivered speech at transfer of 560 items (including land and buildings of former Chungking assets) to Governor of Kiangsu Province (2/10/44) (49:211)

Okamura, General Yasuji -- Supreme Commander, Japanese Expeditionary Forces in North China (1943-44) (52:256)

Okano -- Leader of Anti-Military struggle and Japanese Emancipation League in Yenan (9/27/44) (52:256)

Okayama, Kiroshi -- Supervisor, North China Iron Works Corporation (8/5/43) (52:256)

-234-

JAPANESE

Okawa, Hayahira (Rimpei) -- Chief of Police, Chung-yang District
Office, First Police Office, Shanghai (1943) (49:211)

Okawa, Reverend Sho (Hakaai) -- Japanese Christian leader; advisory
member, Protestant Ministers' Council of Amoy , S.E.C.
(11/21/43) (49:211)

Okawa, Shumei -- Doctor of Literature; envoy to Central China
as Adviser of East Asia General Headquarters (12/3/43);
leader of the Nationalist Movement; inspected the New
Asia Movement in China (1/7/44)

Okazaki, Kaheita (Kieta) -- Chief of General Affairs (1943); Adviser,
Shanghai Citizens' Savings Movement Committee (1943);
Executive Director, Sino-Japanese Cultural Association,
Shanghai Branch (1943); Director, Keko Commercial Bank,
Shanghai (0-67); member, Special Commission concerning
Retrocession of International Concessions in Shanghai;
Counselor, Japanese Embassy, Shanghai (5/30/44); Chief,
new Economic Division, Japanese Embassy, Shanghai (6/14/44);
Vice Director, Industrial Headquarters, Central China
(8/30/44) (49:211; 51:258)

Okemuri, Juro -- Head, Chung-yang Branch (#3), Shanghai Police
(IDC 2973 1943)

Oki, Noboru -- Acting Japanese Consul, Anshan and Tatung; Vice
Consul, Tangshan (52:256)

Okinachi -- Chief, Economic...Affairs Department, Peiping Office,
Japanese Embassy; appointed Head, Chamber for Promoting
Production Increase of Wrought Iron and Alumina (12/6/44)
(52:256)

Okubo -- Ex-Mayor of Tokyo; appointed Mayor of Shanghai (8/13/43)
(49:211)

Okuma, W. -- 3rd Secretary, Japanese Embassy, Nanking (0-60)

Okumara, Fuji -- Authority in Education Research (5/5/44)

Okumura -- Supreme Commander of Japanese Forces in North China (1944)
(52:256)

Okumura, Katsuzo -- Honorary Director, Sino-Japanese Cultural Association, Shanghai Branch (1943) (49:212)

Okumura, Shinji -- Standing Director, North China Iron Works Corporation (8/5/43) (52:256)

Okura, Kimmochi -- President, East Asia Communications Association
(1943)

Okura, Takuji -- President, North China Alumina Mine Corporation,
Peiping (1943) (52:256)

Omori, Professor Shigeki -- Kyoto Imperial University; lecturer,
Chinese Medical Association (10/23/43)

Omura, Masatsune -- President, East Asia Round Table Conference (0-58)

Omuri, Saburo -- Teacher, Protestant Theological Seminary, Shantung
Province (1944) (52:256)

Omuro, Tatsuo -- Manager, Mitsui Products Co., Shanghai (8/3/43)
(49:212)

JAPANESE

Ono, Katsumi -- 1st Secretary, Embassy, Nanking; Secretary, GEA
          Ministry; Director, General Affairs Section, China Affairs
          Bureau (12/19/44)

Onta -- Secretary to Japanese Ambassador, Nanking (0-60)

Ookido -- Associated Branch Director, Japanese Homeland's Ex-Service-
          men's Association (9/6/44) (52:256)

Ookodo -- Commander of a North China Army Unit (5/26/44) (52:256)

Oong, Wenaho -- Minister of Economics (DIO 1941)

Oqura, Takuzo -- Vice Chairman of Trustees, North China Aluminite
          Mining Industrial Co., Ltd., and shareholder (8/5/43)
          (52:257)

Osato, Jinsaburo -- Councillor & Inspector, North China Communica-
          tions Corporation (1944)

Osawa -- Administrative official, GEA Ministry, occupying post in
          China; called to meeting in Nanking by Embassy to delib-
          erate relinquishing of Japanese rights to Nanking Govern-
          ment (4/23/43)

Oshiei -- Military Attache; accompanied Ambassador Masayuki Tani to
          Peking on inspection tour (5/28/43) (52:257)

Ota -- Japanese Consul-General, Peiping (52:257)

Ota -- Councillor, Japanese Embassy, Nanking (9/15/43)

Ota, Shukuzui -- Manager, North China Takeda Drug Company (1943)
          (52:257)

Ota, Unosuke -- Economic Adviser, Soochow (49:212)

Otamura, Murikona -- Superintendent, Japanese Christian Mission,
          North China (12/31/44) (52:257)

Otani, Kanemo -- Head, Shanghai Cultural Thought Research Institute
          (IDC 7265)

Otani, Kozui -- Noted Buddhist Scholar; represents Japan in GEA
          Buddhist Association, Shanghai; Buddhist High Priest and
          Scholar Abbot (of Japan) (11/2/43) (49:212)

Owayegi, Eoi -- Consul at Japanese Consulate in Hankow, Central China;
          communicated with Japan Catholic Church concerning fine
          condition of Roman Catholic Church in Hankow (6/11/44)

Oya, Nobuniko -- Publisher, YUNG PAO, Tientsin, established June,
          1926 (1943)(52:257)

Oyama, Sekinan -- Director, Shanghai Municipality Labor & Business
          Social Union (1943) (49:212)

Oyoshima -- President, North China Development Company (3/27/44)
          (52:257)

Ozaka, Koichi (Yoichi) -- Managing Director, Shanghai Newspaper
          Association (1943); executive, Sino-Japanese Cultural
          Association (1943) (49:212)

Ozawa, Shigeichi -- Japanese Consul-General, Canton (1/44) (51:259)

-236-

JAPANESE

Ozawa, Shoeichi -- Retired as Adviser to First District Administration of former International Settlement, Shanghai (9/11/43) (49:212)

Rinko, (O.) -- Associate Professor, College of Medicine, Taiwan Imperial University; invited to lecture at National Central University, Nanking (10/18/43)

Riroku, Kyo -- Representative of Chinese daily newspaper; states he is determined to exert all his efforts to attaining aims of (war) (DIO Nov., 1943)

Rishi -- Chief, Information Section, Japanese Embassy (9/26/44)

Sadanaga, Chino (Nobuo) -- Chief of Police, Chia-hsing District Office, First Police Office, Shanghai (1943) (49:212)

Sahara, Kenji -- Chief, North China Branch, East Asia Communications Association (1944)

Saiki, (Dr. Yoshiro) -- Produced two volumes on Christianity in China; considered an authority on (Nestorian) movement in China (10/1/44)

Saito, Noburo -- Central China Prosperity Insurance Association, Taihoku Fire Insurance Company

Saito, Shigeru -- Candidate Inspector, Sino-Japanese Cultural Association, Wu-Ch'ang & Hankow Branch (1943)

Saito, Sho -- Japanese Literary Envoy, Chinese Cultural Society (3/31/43); member, Cultural Goodwill Party to China (5/3/43)

Saito, (Soichi) -- General Secretary, Japan Y.M.C.A. Council; made 2-month trip to China on policy of Japan Y.M.C.A. Council in reconstructing Y.M.C.A. work in GEA region (7/2/44) (Shanghai, 49:212)

Saito, Takeo -- Ex-Vice President, Dai Nippon Aviation Company (2/29/43)

Saito, Yozo -- Assistant Chief of Police, Mai-lan District Office, Third Police Office, Shanghai (1943) (49:212)

Saito, Yu -- Publisher, LU TUNG JIH PAO, Yen-t'ai, North China, established Oct., 1938 (1943) (52:257)

Saka -- Adviser to North China Industrial Bank (1944) (52:257)

Sakado, Katsuya -- Member, Shanghai Newspaper Association (49:212)

Sakaguchi -- Adviser at Headquarters, East Asia IRAA, North China (52:257)

Sakahara -- Japanese representative, 3rd conference of literary men in GEA to be held in Nanking during the middle of November (9/15/44)

Sakai, Lt. General -- Commander, Expeditionary Forces, Hongkong; attended unveiling ceremony of memorial to warriors on first anniversary of GEA war in Hongkong (12/8/42) (51:259)

Sakai, Count Tadamasa -- Attended the 6th deliberative committee meeting of the East Asia Cultural Conference, Peiping University (7/13/42) (52:257)

286

-237-

JAPANESE

Sakamoto -- Chinese mission to Switzerland; Minister to Switzerland; reported Swiss intention of relinquishing special rights in China (4/8/43)

Sakamoto, Kazutoshi -- Editor-in-Chief, YUNG PAO, Tientsin, June, 1926 (52:257)

Sakamoto, Lieutenant Tesuo -- Spokesman for Japanese Army Press Section, Shanghai (5/23/44) (49:212)

Sakata, Sumio -- Councillor, Japanese Embassy, Shanghai; Assistant Chief, New Economic Division, Shanghai Embassy (49:212)

Sakatami -- Adviser, Political Commission, Peiping (9/23/43) (52:257)

Sakatani, Kiichi -- Adviser, Federal Reserve Bank of China and North China Industrial Bank (10/3/44) (52:257)

Sakatani, Taro -- Member, Shanghai Newspaper Association (49:212)

Sakato, Katsumi -- Editor, HSIN SHEN PAO, Shanghai (IDC 7266 1943)

Sakeyori, Hatsugoro -- Assistant Chairman, Sugar Enterprise Special Committee, National Trade Control General Association, Shanghai (1943) (49:212)

Sakon, Major General Watari -- Commander-in-Chief, Luichow Peninsula Forces (IDC 7/29/44)

Sakuguchi -- Divisional Commander; Adviser, East Asia IRAA (7/8/43)

Sakura -- Vice Minister, Communications

Sakurai, Haruo -- Member, Flour Special Committee, National Trade Control General Association, Shanghai (1943) (49:212)

Salada, Renzo -- Ex-Ambassador to Rumania; on Chinese inspection tour (6/7/43)

Samejima, Tatsuo -- Director, North China Electric Wire Corporation (2/17/44) (52:257)

(Samijima), Reverend -- To lead prayers at 5-day Christian Revival Meeting, sponsored by Hongkong Chinese Christian Association, at Wan Tsai Church in Hongkong and Hillwood Road Church in Kowloon; to give service for Kowloon on meaning of love, service, hope, faith, worship on Sabbath (8/15/44) (51:259)

Sanekata, Shirojurokuro -- Assistant Chief of Police, Hsiao-tung-men District Office, Third Police Office, Shanghai (1943) (49:213)

Sangosian -- Inspector, Judicial Section, Shanghai Police Department; member of mission to visit police departments in Japan, Manchukuo and North China (4/18/44) (49:213)

Sanho, Takeo -- Vice Chairman, Shanghai Municipality Labor & Business Social Union (1943) (49:213)

Sarji, Kenyo -- Investigator, Asia Development Board; attended sessions of Asiatic Problems Research Institute, Shanghai (8/8/42) (49:213)

Sasaki, Kenji -- Head, Chung-hua-she, North China Electrical Communications Company, established 1940 (52:257)

-238-

JAPANESE

Sasaki, Kintaro -- Chief, Archives & Documents Section, Cabinet
Secretariat (GEA Ministry); Councillor, 2nd Class, of
Japanese Embassy, Nanking (7/29/44)

Sasaki, Kunizo -- President, North China Cotton Corporation, Tientsin
(1943) (52:257)

Sasaoka, Kikuo -- Chosen Vice President, Hankow Japanese Industrial
Economic Association (10/11/44)

Sato -- President, Hopeh Alumina Company, China (8/3/44) (52:257)

Sato -- Chief, Japanese Defense Corps, Amoy; attended inauguration
ceremony of corps at Amoy (9/12/43) (49:213)

Sato, Chusaburo -- Chief, Railroad Bureau, Kaifeng; North China
Communications Corporation (1944)

Sato, Hideichi -- Member, Flour Special Committee, National Trade
Control General Association, Shanghai (1943) (49:213)

Sato, Hidezo -- Honorary Director, Sino-Japanese Cultural Association,
Shanghai Branch (1943) (49:213); Head, National Science
Research Institute (IDC 7265 1943)

Sato, Kenji -- Director, North China Communications Corporation,
T'ai-yuan Office (1944)

Sato, S. -- 2nd Secretary and Consul, Japanese Embassy, Nanking (0-60)

Sato, Saburo -- Adviser, North China Political Council (1942) (52:257)

Sato, Seitaro -- Trustee, North China Aluminite Mining Industrial
Comany, Ltd. (8/5/43) (52:257)

Sato, Takao -- Member, Cultural Goodwill Party to China (5/3/43)
(51:259)

Sawamiya, Shigeo -- President, Shantung Mining Corporation, Tsingtao
(52:257)

Sedizawa, Akira -- President, Japanese Resident Club; Assistant
Manager, Yokohama Specie Bank, Shanghai (49:213)

Segawa, Shigeo -- Chief of Police, Chiang-ning Road District Office,
First Police Office, Shanghai (1943) (49:213)

Seiki, Colonel -- Japanese Staff Headquarters, Shanghai (7/24/44)
(49:213)

Sekawa, Shigeo -- Head, Chiang-ning Road (#1), Shanghai Police
(IDC 2973 1943)

Sekijuji -- Chief, Administrative...Bureau of Special Municipality
and concurrently Commander of...; appointed Vice Commander
of Tsingtao Special Municipality Peace Preservation Corps,
Vice Ba Unyei resigned (8/15/44) (52:257)

Senjo, Takeiuchi -- Standing Director, Tungyang Paper Industry Corporation (1943) (52:258)

Serai, Kao -- 1st Japanese Consul to Kaifeng, Honan Province; ex-
Chief, Shita Branch of North China Liaison Office of China
Affairs Board (2/14/43) (52:258)

288

JAPANESE

Seto, Naoshi -- Candidate Director, Sino-Japanese Cultural Association, Wu-Ch'ang & Hankow Branch (1943)

Shemotzu -- Secretary, Japanese Embassy, Nanking; arrived in Nanking with Japanese Ambassador, Masayuki Tani, and Kanei Aota (5/14/43)

Shiano, Lt. Colonel Hitoshi -- Chief, Press Section, Publicity Dept., Kwangtung Headquarters (8/9/43)

Shibata, Hotaro -- Economic Adviser, Nanking Government (DIO July, 1943)

Shibata, Shiji -- Member, Committee on Grain Control, Shanghai (1943) (49:213)

Shibayama, Lt. General -- Nanking Army; attended 6th entrance ceremony of Army Officers Training Association of the National Army of China in Nanking (8/18/43)

Shida -- Chief, General Affairs Department, Japanese Embassy, Peiping (1/30/44) (52:258)

Shien, Ku -- Hongkong delegate, Nippon Press Association of GEA Conference

Shiga, Shigeyoshi -- Noted authority on Chinese finance (7/10/44)

Shigefuji -- Commander, Japanese Gendarmere Detachment; Associate member, Commodity Investigation Committee, Canton (4/5/44) (51:259)

Shigemitsu, Mamoru (Shigametsu, Minuro - Mamaro - Mamura) -- Appointed Japanese Ambassador to China - Nanking, Dec., 1941 (11/27/43); host at 2nd anniversary party of Tri-Partite Pact in Shanghai (9/27/42); presented decorations on behalf of Japanese Emperor (5/14/43); Foreign Secretary and Minister of GEA Affairs; attended 5th anniversary celebration of Federated Autonomous Government of Mongolia in Tokyo (9/2/44); Minister of GEA Affairs (9/13/44)

Shigemoto, Aki -- President, Shanghai Hemp Co. (2/21/44) (49:213, 51:259)

Shigeta -- Assistant Chief of Office; Adviser, Shanghai Citizens' Savings Movement Committee (1943); Assistant Chief, Paochia Office, First Police Station (1943) (49:213)

Shiina -- Chief, General Affairs Bureau, Munitions Ministry; on inspection tour of Mengchiang area, North China (52:258)

Shiki, Koo -- Former member of Standing Directors, Nanking General Office, Central Reserve Bank; appointed President, Souchow Branch Office (2/17/44) (49:213)

Shima, Ichiro -- Chief, Tokyo Branch, North China Communications Corporation (1944)

Shimada, Professor -- To supervise Hongkong University library; arrived in Hongkong from Taiwan (3/25/44) (51:259)

Shimada, S. -- Commercial Secretary, Japanese Embassy, Nanking (O-60)

Shimada, T. -- 3rd Secretary, Nanking, China

-240-

JAPANESE

Shimizu, Mrs. Ikiku -- Japanese Christian educator of Peiping
visiting Japan; wife of famous Japanese Christian edu-
cator in China (Rev. Yatsuzo Shimizu); graduate of Tokyo
Women's Higher Normal School; studied at Oberlin and Boston
University; taught at girls' school of Aoyama Gakui College,
Tokyo (10/18/43) (52:258)

Shimizu, Junji -- Inspector, Committee for Establishment of China's
Broadcast Business, Shanghai (49:213); Supervisor, China
Broadcasting Enterprise & Reconstruction Association (IDC
7268 1943)

Shimizu, Kiku -- Resident of Peiping area; presented letter of commendation from Japanese Embassy, Nanking, for contribution
to general Chinese education; presentation made by Ambassador Tani (3/5/44) (52:258)

Shimizu, Shin -- Meiji University of Japan; alumnus of Literary Department; to Peiping to study (10/5/43) (52:258)

Shimizu, Shunji -- Hsin-cha Branch (#1), Shanghai Police (IDC 2973
1943)

Shimizu, Reverend Yatsuzo -- Founder of a Christian Girls' School
in Peiping (10/18/43) (52:258)

Shimomura, Major General Sadashi -- Named Military Supreme Commander
in Shanghai by the Japanese military authorities in Central
China (11/42) (49:214)

Shimoro -- Assistant Secretary of Tokyo Y.M.C.A.; largely responsible
for transfer of Nanking hospital, of which he was first
in charge, to Tokyo Y.M.C.A. (9/3/44)

Shimotsu, Harugoro -- Director, East Asia Communications Association
(1943)

Shimuzu, T. -- 3rd Secretary, Japanese Embassy, Nanking (0-60)

Shinoda, Ichiji -- Head of China Cotton Spinning Association, Shanghai
(8/3/43) (49:214)

Shioda, Lieutenant -- Adviser, Shanghai Citizens' Savings Movement
Committee (1943) (49:214)

Shionoya, Dr. -- Japanese Literary Envoy, All-China Cultural Society
(3/31/43)

Shiosawa, Kiyo-Nori -- Member, Committee on Return of Concessions,
Nanking, and Committee on Abolition of Extraterritoriality
(IDC 2/43)

Shiozawa, Major General Yanago (Kiyonobu) -- Japanese Minister to
North China, Peiping (1942, 43, 44); attended 6th deliberative committee meeting of East Asia Cultural Conference
at Peiping University (8/31/42); represented North China
at Coordination Conference at Peiping (11/8/42); Chief,
Hopeh Coordination Dept., China Affairs Board; President,
East Asia IRAA (7/8/43); attended 4th Continental Liaison
Conference (10/6/43); presence requested by Ambassador Tani
at meeting of 20 diplomats in Peiping, apparently, to consider general situation, trend, future policies, etc.
(11/28/43); President, North China Asia Developing Assistance
Headquarters (1/15/44); attended North China Political
Council meeting at Peiping (5/22/44) (52:258)

JAPANESE

Shirai, Kiichi -- Vice Chairman, Board of Directors, North China
Transportation Corporation, Peiping (8/5/43) (52:258)

Shiraishi, Kozaburo -- President, Spinning and Weaving Industry
Association in North China (3/24/44) (52:258)

Shiraka -- Section Head, Cultural Relations, Japanese Consulate
in Amoy (1/18/44) (49:214)

Shiraki, Yoshimoto -- Director, Central China Water & Electric
Stock Company, Shanghai (IDC 7262 1943)

Shirakura, Suekichi -- Director, (Greater) Shanghai Gas Stock Co.
(IDC 7262 1943)

Shirawada -- Counsel, Japanese Ambassadorial Office, Peiping; ex-
plained new government wartime policy (9/24/43) (52:258)

Shironogi, Dr. Sugi -- Leader of Confucianism; urged China's return
to time-honored spirit of Confucianism - Nanking (4/1/43)

Shirozawi, Major General Shigenori -- Commander of Japanese forces
in North China; attended ceremony returning to the National
Government of China the administration of former British
Concession in Tientsin, North China, taken over by Japanese at outbreak of GEA war (3/28/42) (52:258)

Shiyma, Major General -- Chief Military Adviser (0-57)

Sho, Igaku -- Military leader, Felicitation Party to Manchukuo;
Special Mayor of Nanking

Shokin -- Counselor, Nanking Embassy in Japan; invested with order
of Third Order of Merit with small Cordon of Rising Sun
(5/4/43)

Shoo, Sobu -- President, Cotton and Woolen Fabrics Purchasing Agency,
China; appointed Chief, Cotton and Wool Supervisory Office
in nationwide Industrial Control Association (11/11/43)

Shuichi, Nagamatsu -- Standing Director, Tungyang Paper Industry
Corporation (1943) (52:259)

Shunzoi (?) -- Vice Chief, Bureau of Provisions Department, Kiangsu
Provincial Administration; to be tried on charges of food
conspiracy (3/12/44)

Shuyogawa, Brigadier General -- Japanese Minister in North China
(5/4/43) (52:259)

Sikim, Juiichi -- President, North China Development Company (1/43)
(52:259)

So, Dr. Masao -- Professor of Agriculture, Tokyo Imperial University;
lecturer in Nanking National Central University (10/18/43)

Sonoda, Saburo -- Director, Prosperity Corporation of Central China
(4/5/43); Director, Central China Railroad Stock Company,
Shanghai (IDC 7262 1943)

Sonoda, Captain (Shoichi) -- Ex-Press Section Chief of China Water
Fleet; ordered to return home 8/31/43 (9/2/43)

Soyejima, Reverend Muritaka --. Sent to South China by Japanese
Church of Christ to assist churches there (3/19/44)

-242-

JAPANESE

Suga, Kenjiro -- Chief, Railroad Bureau, Tsinan Office, North China
     Communications Corporation (1944)

Sugai, Lt. General Rensugi -- Governor-General of Hongkong; spoke
     at inaugural meeting of Hongkong Foreign Trade Association
     (10/9/42) (51:259)

Suganuma, Shoji (Shosi) -- Chief Economic Secretary, Japanese Embassy,
     Peiping (52:259)

Sugihara, A. -- 1st Secretary, Japanese Embassy, Nanking (0-60)

Sugiku, Taro -- Vice Chairman, Board of Directors, Shanghai River
     Boat Corporation (8/5/43) (49:214)

Sugili, Ryuichi -- Publisher, YUEH TUNG PAO, South China, Swatow,
     established July, 1940 (51:259) (1943)

Sugimoto -- Patriotic song composer; composed song expressing sublime
     feelings of men engaged in volunteer labor service in con-
     struction of war memorial, Hongkong (5/17/44) (51:259)

Sugimoto, Hisataro -- Director, Shanghai Inland Steamship Stock
     Company (IDC 7262 1943)

Sugisaki, Toshimitzu -- Chief of Police, Bubbling Well Temple Dis-
     trict Office, First Police Office, Shanghai (1943) (49:214)

Sumita, Sakujiro -- Director, Tsingtao Putou Corporation, Tsingtao
     (1943) (52:259)

Suzuki -- Chief Adviser, New People's Movement; on way to Tokyo
     for consultation with leaders of IRAA (9/20/42)

Suzuki, Gozaburo -- Former Director, Chamber of Commerce at Takaoka;
     appointed Vice Director of Japan Industrial Economic
     Association, Hankow (10/10/44)

Suzuki, Kabusaburo -- Standing Director, Hua Chung Silk Corporation,
     Ltd., Shanghai (49:214); Director, Central China Silk
     Stock Company (IDC 7262 1943)

Suzuki, Kiyomiki -- Author, "Natural Resources and Industries in
     North China" (1942) (52:259)

Suzuki, Lt. General Soosaku -- Decorated by China National Government
     for meritorious services (4/16/44)

Suzuki, Lt. General Yoshinichi -- Chief, Taxation Bureau, Central
     Government; Supreme Adviser, Headquarters, Hsin Min Society,
     Peiping; decorated by National Government; attended meeting
     of Supervisors of Taxation Bureaus in Manchukuo (2/4/44);
     left for Japan, Jan., 1944 (52:259)

Taguchi, Chejiro -- Director, Central China Sea Products Stock Co.,
     Shanghai (IDC 7262 1943)

Tai, General -- Chief Adviser of Hopei Province (52:259)

Tajima, Akira -- Consul General, Shanghai, China (49:214)

Tajiri, Aimata -- Adviser, Sino-Japanese Cultural Association, Shanghai
     Branch (1943) (49:214)

JAPANESE

Tajiri, Akiyoshi (Aiyoshi) -- Adviser, Shanghai Citizens' Savings
Movement Committee (1943); member, Committee for Return of
Concessions and Committee for Abolition of Extraterritoriality
(IDC 2/43); met with Ambassador Tani and others in Shanghai
(6/22/43); Minister in Charge of Japanese Embassy, Shanghai
(7/10/43) (49:214)

Tajiri, Shogo (Seizo) -- Head, North China Iron Works; President,
North China Iron Works, Peiping (12/2/43) (52:259)

Tajiro, Kiyoshi -- Represented Japan in conference with officials of
National Government of China on return of foreign concessions (3/14/43) (Shanghai, 49:214)

Tajivi (probably Tajiri) -- Member, Committee for Investigation of
Resources & Materials, Shanghai (1943) (49:214)

Takada, Hiroshi -- Special Director, East Asia Communications Association (1943)

Takagaki, Katsutaro -- Manager, Mitsubishi Shoji Company, Ltd.,
Shanghai (8/3/43) (49:214)

Takagaki, Shotaro -- Manager, Mitsubishi Company, Shanghai (49:214)

Takagi, Shin -- Japanese representative to 3rd conference of literary
men in GEA held in Nanking during middle of November (9/15/44)

Takahara, Susumu -- Director, North China Electrical Industry Company,
Peiping (8/5/43) (52:259)

Takahashi -- Japanese Consul, Shanghai (49:214)

Takahashi, Dr. Akira -- Tokyo Imperial University; lecturer, Chinese
Medical Association (10/23/43)

Takahashi, Kuraji -- Manager, Planning Office, East Asia Communications
Association (1943)

Takahashi, Ryozo -- Director and Chief of Office of Enterprise, Sino-
Japanese Cultural Association, Shanghai Branch (1943)
(49:214)

Takahashi, Admiral Sankichi -- Adviser, East Asia General Central
Headquarters; visiting in Peking (12/8/43); Envoy representing the GEA Affairs Headquarters of the IRAA to the
Nanking Government (1/6/44); former Commander-in-Chief
of the Japanese combined fleet (1/7/44)

Takahashi, Toyoichi -- Chief, Railroad Bureau, Chang-chia-k'ou Office,
North China Communications Corporation (1944)

Takamatsu -- Communications Minister; spoke re shipyards at press conference at Chinese Reporters' Club (IDC 1/18/43)

Takamitsu, Tadao -- Director, Sino-Japanese Cultural Association,
Shanghai Branch (1943) (49:215)

Takanawa, Kenzo -- Ex-President, Dai Nippon Aviation Company (1/29/43)

Takano, Dr. Rokuro -- Proposed establishment of Central Anti-Epidemic
Research Institute during group discussion in Shanghai;
former Director, Prevention Bureau, Welfare Ministry of
Japan (4/27/44) (49:215)

-244-

JAPANESE

Takao, Isoichi -- Vice Chairman, Board of Directors, Hua Hsing Commercial Bank, Shanghai (8/5/43) (49:215)

Takao, Kiichi -- Vice Chairman, Board of Directors, Kako Commercial Bank, Shanghai (49:215)

Takasaki -- President, Manchuria Industrial Development Company; visitor to Peiping (1944) (52:259)

Takase, Shinichi -- Member, Committee on Abolition of Extraterritoriality (2/43); Councillor, Japanese Embassy, Nanking (4/28/43); relieved of post in Hainan (10/30/43); Japanese Consul-General, Tientsin (O-63)

Takashima, Kikujiro (Fukujoro) -- Formerly of Oji Paper Company; selected as successor to Kenji Kodama as President of Central China Development Company (3/8/43); Adviser, Sino-Japanese Cultural Association, Shanghai Branch (1943); President, Central China Bank (7/26/43); President, Central China Development Company (9/21/44) (49:215)

Takasu, Shunichi -- Chief, Central China Branch, East Asia Communications Association (1943)

Takatani -- Adviser, National Federal Reserve Bank of China (52:259)

Takatsu, Tomio -- Japanese Consul in Hankow (IDC)

Takauchi -- Chief, Supervisory Bureau, Home Affairs Ministry

Takebe, Nagakane -- President, Society for the Promotion of International Cultural Relations (5/3/43); attended assembly of Cultural Goodwill Party which went to China and heard reports on conditions in progressive China (5/3/43) (51:259)

Takeda, Heiseburo -- Inspector, North China Electrical Industry Company, Peiping (8/5/43) (52:259)

Takeda, Jyukichi -- Acting Superintendent, Shanghai Branch, Yokohama Specie Bank; Adviser, Central Reserve Bank Branch, Canton (9/30/42) (49:215)

Takeda, Nanyo -- Publisher, HSIN MIN PAO, Peiping (1943); Chief, Press Section, North China Forces (1944) (52:259)

Takeiuchi, Senjo -- Standing Director, Tungyang Paper Industry Corporation, North China (8/5/44) (52:259)

Takemoto, Katsuyoshi -- Adviser, North China Political Affairs Commission; to become president of the foundation resulting from a reorganization of the Nippon Cultural Association of China (8/4/44) (52:259)

Takeuchi -- Secretary, General Affairs, GEA Ministry; on tour in North China (1944) (52:259)

Takeuchi -- Secretary, Mining Development Council

Takeuchi, Yoshisuke -- Assistant Chief, Central China Branch, East Asia Communications Association (1943)

Takohigan, Tomizo -- Director, Sino-Japanese Cultural Association, Wu-Ch'ang & Hankow Branch (1943)

JAPANESE

Tamakoto -- Vice President, Central China Railroad Company, Shanghai

Tanaka -- Consul-General, Nanking; Chief, Tungjen Epidemic Prevention Bureau (1944)

Tanaka -- Acting Consul-General, Peiping; Chairman, Public Cooperative Farmers Association (3/7/44) (52:259)

Tanaka, Hikozo -- Honorary Chairman, Directors, Sino-Japanese Cultural Association, Wu-Ch'ang & Hankow Branch (1943)

Tanaka, Lieutenant General Hisakazu -- Commander, 23rd Army, (Canton) (8/17/44) (51:259)

Tanba, Yuji -- Director, Central China City Bus Stock Company, Shanghai (IDC 7262 1943)

Tani -- Chief, Press Section, North China Political Commission; sponsored round-table conference for returned students from tour of rice cultivation areas (8/8/44) (52:259)

Tani, Masayuki -- Naval Attache for Japan at transfer of property from Naval Attaches' Office to Navy Department of Nanking Government (2/6/43); Ex-Foreign Minister of Japan; appointed Japanese Ambassador to Nanking, April, 1943 (5/16/43, 3/8/44); concluded relinquishment of Extraterritoriality Pact (8/1/43); presented decorations (3/7/44); conference with Chinese officials in Nanking (5/3/44); conferred with municipal authorities in Shanghai (1/15/45)

Tanigawa, Tokuzo -- Member, Cultural Goodwill Party to China (5/3/43) (51:260)

Taniguchi, Kuranosuke -- Head, Grain & Animal Products Research Association, Shanghai (IDC 7265 1943)

Taniguchi, Tadashi -- Member, Shanghai Newspaper Association (49:215); Editor, HSIN SHEN PAO (IDC 7266 1943)

Taro, Kiyomizu -- Special Director, Tungyang Paper Industry Corporation (1943) (52:260)

Tashiro, Shigenori -- Minister of Japan to China, Canton; formerly Minister to French Indo-China (11/19/44) (51:260)

Tasima, Akira -- Japan Consul-General, Shanghai (49:215)

Tatake, Yoshishige -- Head, Li-yang Road Branch (#1), Shanghai Police (IDC 2973 1943)

Tasiri, Akiyoshi -- Minister, Shanghai, China (49:215)

Taskiro -- Vice Chairman, Board of Directors, Hua Chung Railroad Corporation, Ltd., Shanghai (8/5/43) (49:215)

Tazawa, Lieutenant General Kiyonobu -- Japanese Minister Plenipotentiary stationed in Peiping (3/5/44) (52:260)

Teado, Irisho -- Director, Bureau of Criminal Affairs, Nanking; attended meeting re relinquishment of extraterritoriality rights of Japan (4/23/43)

Tenkyo, Yurikan -- Resident of Peiping area; presented letter of commendation from Japanese Embassy, Nanking, for his promotion of Chinese relief; presentation made by Ambassador Tani (3/5/44) (52:260)

-246-

JAPANESE

Teraoka, Rear Admiral -- Adviser to Chinese Navy (6/10/43) (Shanghai, 49:215)

Teraoka, Kohei -- Assigned a new post in Japanese Embassy in Italy (IDC 12/42)

Terasaki, H. -- 2nd Secretary, Japanese Embassy, Nanking (O-60)

Teruo, Asahi -- President, Tokyo Bank

Tinga, Masataro -- Adviser, Central Reserve Bank of China (11/11/42)

Tisiokawa -- President, Hsikkado Agricultural Development Company

Toda, Nacharu -- Chairman, Board of Directors, North China Transportation Corporation, Peiping (8/5/43) (52:260)

Togucki, Chojiro -- Standing Director, Hua Chung Fishing Corporation, Ltd., Shanghai (8/5/43) (49:215)

Tohei, M. -- Japanese Adviser, North China Political Council (1942) (52:260)

Tokugawa, Dr. -- Attended meeting of Central Public Health Association, Nanking (2/4/44)

Tokunaga -- Commander, Japanese forces in North China; attended meeting of North China Political Council at Peiping (5/22/44) (52:260)

Tomimiya, Kan -- Resident of Shanghai area; presented letter of commendation from Japanese Embassy, Nanking, for work in medicine and sanitation thru trade; presentation made by Ambassador Tani (3/5/44) (49:215)

Tomomo -- Director, Central China Development Company (5/21/44)

Tomono, Makoto -- Director, Prosperity Corporation of Central China (IDC 4/5/43)

Torigoe, Shinichi -- Civil Administrator, Hainan Island (1943) (51:260)

Toshihiko, Eto (Eito) -- Formerly connected with newspaper in Hongkong, supported by Government of Formosa (51:260)

Toyoda, Kaoru -- Foreign Office Inspector; appointed Consul-General and concurrently Embassy Councillor at Shanghai (12/21/44) (49:215)

Tsoushahedo, Viscount -- Member of Japanese Scientific Investigation Mission, surveyor of resources of Wutow Mountains in Shansi Province (4/21/42)

Tsuchia, Yutaka -- Assumed post at Ambassadorial Office, Shanghai, November 19 (11/27/44) (49:216)

Tsuchida, Yutaka -- Chief, General Affairs Bureau (7/15/44); Minister to Peiping (12/16/44); 1st Secretary, Japanese Embassy, Nanking (52:260)

Tsuchiya, Dr. -- Attended meeting of Central Public Health Association, Nanking (2/4/44)

296

-247-

JAPANESE

Tsuchiya, Bungo -- Japanese representative to 3rd conference of literary men of GEA to be held in Nanking during middle of November (9/15/44)

Tsuda -- Well-known industrialist; appointed in charge of ship-building at Hongkong (1/18/43) (51:260)

Tsuda, Goro -- Chief of Police, P'u-t'o Road District Office, First Police Office, Shanghai (1943) (49:216)

Tsuda, Shingo -- Chairman, Board of Directors, Chung Yuan Kung Ta Industry Corporation (8/5/43) (Shanghai, 49:216)

Tsuda, Shizue -- Honorary Director, Sino-Japanese Cultural Association, Nanking Branch (IDC 1943)

Tsukamoto -- Commander, unit of Japanese forces in North China (7/15/44) (52:260)

Tsukasa, Tsuruhara -- Head, Administrative Section, Japanese Consulate, Canton; Associate member, Commodity Investigation Committee (4/5/44) (51:260)

Tsukikawa, Samon -- Head, Alien Internment Camp, Nanking; Ex-Vice Consul of Japan, Honolulu

Tsurumi, K. -- 1st Secretary to Counselor, Japanese Embassy, Nanking (0-60)

Tsushima, Juichi (Tushima, Juichi?) -- President, North China Development Company (1/23/43, 12/22/43, 3/24/44 and 4/4/44); Honorary President, North China Development Corporation (1/15/44); Vice President, North China Asia Development Assistance Headquarters (1/15/44); Chairman, first Electric Power Liaison Conference among Manchukuo, China and Menchiang (3/12/44); President, Inner China Development Corporation (52:260)

Tsutsuki, Dr. Masao -- Professor, Tokyo Imperial University; to be adviser to Tungjen Medical College in Shanghai (9/11/44) (49:216)

Tsutsumi, Takashi -- Managing Director, Shanghai Municipality Labor & Business Social Union (1943) (49:216)

(Tudanani), Shoji -- China Affairs Board (9/6/42)

Uchida -- Councillor, Japanese Embassy, Peiping (8/29/43) (52:260)

Uchida -- Chief, Finance Department, Japanese Embassy; attended Shanghai meeting on rice control (10/20/43) (49:216)

Uchica, Dr. Ginzo -- Author, "A History...Restoration of Modern Japan," published by Cultural Data Translation Office of Sino-Japanese Cultural Association, Shanghai Branch (6/7/44) (49:216)

Uchida, Keizo -- President, North China Salt Industrial Corporation, Peiping (1943) (52:260)

Uchida, Sawakichi -- Director, Sino-Japanese Cultural Association, Wu-Ch'ang & Hankow Branch (1943)

Uchida, Shozo -- Professor, Tokyo Imperial University; Honorary Vice President, GEA Deliberative Association, Peiping (11/27/43) (52:260)

-248-

JAPANESE

Uchifuchi, Noki -- Vice President, North China Electrical Industry
        Company, Peiping (8/5/43) (52:260)

Uchiyama, Lieutenant General Hidetaro -- Commander, 12th Army
        (Tsinan, North China) (8/17/44) (52:260)

Uchiyama, Kanzo -- Resident of Shanghai area; presented letter of
        commendation from Japanese Embassy, Nanking, for exchange
        of ideas thru publications and lectures; presentation was
        made by Ambassador Tani (3/5/44) (49:216)

Ueba, Tetsuzo -- Honorary Director, Sino-Japanese Cultural Associa-
        tion, Shanghai Branch (1943) (49:216)

Uebayashi, Ichitaro -- Honorary Director, Sino-Japanese Cultural
        Association, Shanghai Branch (1943) (49:216)

Ueda, Kenjiro -- Member, Committee on Grain Control, Shanghai (1943);
        Vice Director, Industrial Headquarters, Central China
        (8/30/44) (49:216)

Ueda, Tetsuzo (See Ueba, Tetsuzo) -- Vice Director, headquarters
        for supervision of increase in industry in Central China
        (8/30/44); appointed Vice President, Central China De-
        velopment Company (3/12/43)

Uehara, Hinosuke -- Supervisor, North China Salt Corporation,
        Tientsin Branch (1943) (52:260)

Uehori, Sotaro -- Chief, General Affairs Section, China Movie
        Association (1943)

Uemura, Kimio -- Director, Huai Nan Coal Mine Stock Company, Shanghai
        (IDC 7262 1943)

Ugaki, Rear Admiral Kanji -- Chief of Staff, China Sea; Vice Admiral,
        appointed Chief of Staff, Japanese Fleet in China (IDC
        9/43)

Umesawa, Manjiro (Gujiro) -- Member, Flour Special Committee, National
        Trade Control General Association, Shanghai; member, Com-
        mittee on Grain Control, Shanghai (49:216) (1943)

Umikohara, Takenosuke -- Director, Kako Commercial Bank, Shanghai
        (49:216)

Umishida -- Counselor, Japanese Embassy

Urakami, Shuo -- Publisher, SHANTUNG HSIN MIN PAO, Tsinan, estab-
        lished Aug., 1916 (1943) (52:260)

Usami, Kanji -- President, North China Communications Corporation,
        Peiping (1943); Director, China Affairs Bureau, GEA Min-
        istry; called to meeting in Nanking by Embassy regarding
        Japan's extraterritoriality rights (4/23/43); GEA Ministry,
        North and Central China; President, North China Transpor-
        tation Company (9/23/43) (52:260)

Usami, Uzukiko (Uzuhiko) -- Director, China Affairs Bureau, GEA
        Affairs Ministry; appointed Minister Plenipotentiary of
        China; represented Japan on Commission for Abolition of
        Extraterritorial Rights (4/23/43); attended opening of
        Shanghai Institute for training Indian National Army vol-
        unteers (7/9/44); Minister in charge of Shanghai Office of
        Japanese Embassy (6/30/44); attended ceremony of raising

JAPANESE

new flag of Socialist Italian Republic at Shanghai
(9/13/44) (49:216)

Ushiroku, Lieutenant General Jun -- Chief, General Staff, Chinese
Expeditionary Forces; Commander, Central Headquarters
(2/10/43)

Wachi, Major General Yoji -- Chief of Staff, Army; had undertaken
intelligence work and command duties in Hongkong and
South China areas (8/3/44) (Yoji, Major General Wachi?)
(51:260)

Washida, Kunihiko -- Ex-Education Minister, Tokyo; inspected educational conditions throughout North China (12/14/43)
(52:261)

Washio, Isoichi -- Vice Chairman, Board of Directors, Chinese Commercial Bank (Shanghai, 8/3/43) (49:217)

Watanabe -- Chairman, (Patriotic Association in Shanghai?); gave
address at mass meeting of the total national mobilization movement (7/21/44) (49:217)

Watanabe, Gisuke -- Chairman, Board of Directors, North China Iron
Works, Inc. (8/5/43) (52:261)

Watanabe, Dr. Hiroshi -- President, Nippon Tanko (Coal Mining)
Company; leading authority on mining research; made geo-
logical survey for boring tunnel under Yangtze River
(7/30/44); President, Geophysical Prospecting Company of
Japan (1/14/45)

Watanabe, Jukichi -- Vice Chairman, Central China Steamship Stock
Company, Shanghai (IDC 7262 1943)

Watanabe, Kanae -- Chief of Police, Hung-k'ou District Office, First
Police Office, Shanghai (1943) (49:217)

Watanabe, Nobuo -- Japanese Consul-General in Chanchiakou (DIO 10/39);
Honorary Director, Sino-Japanese Cultural Association,
Shanghai Branch (1943) (49:217)

Watari -- Peace Preservation Officer, Shanghai International Settlement (9/20/42) (49:217)

Watashi -- Assistant Chief of Office; Adviser, Shanghai Citizens'
Savings Movement Committee (1943) (49:217)

Yabe, Masanobu -- Author, "Shanghai Foreign Trade in General" (4/5/43)
(49:217)

Yada, Hichitaro -- Member, Financial Consultation Committee, West
Shanghai (Dec., 1942); Honorary Director, Sino-Japanese
Cultural Association, Shanghai Branch (1943) (49:217)

Yada, Sukado -- President, (Tungwing) University, Shanghai; chosen
President of the GEA Friendship and Sports Carnival to be
held in Shanghai, November 11 (10/25/44) (49:217)

Yagi, Dr. Hidetsugu -- President, Tokyo Technical University; attended
the 6th deliberative committee meeting of the East Asia
Cultural Conference at Peiping University (8/31/42) (52:261)

Yajima, Yasuzo -- Manager, Nippon Yusen Kaisha in Shanghai (8/3/43)
(49:217)

JAPANESE

Yamada, Colonel -- Chief, Liaison Department, Canton; Associate
        member, Commodity Investigation Committee (51:260)

Yamada -- President, Headquarters, IRAYA, North China (52:261)

Yamada -- GEA representative of the Economic Bureau; attended 6th
        Continental Liaison Deliberative Conference (10/15/44)

Yamada, Kosaku -- Vice President, Southern Region Music Committee;
        entertained Japanese soldiers in Manchukuo, Central China
        and Mongolia (11/10/42)

Yamada, Fukuda -- Director, Sino-Japanese Cultural Association,
        Shanghai Branch (1943) (49:217)

Yamada, Junsaburo (Jinzaburo) -- Resident of Shanghai area; presented
        letter of commendation from Japanese Embassy at Nanking
        for services rendered Japan and China during revolutionary
        period preceding establishment of Republic by Dr. Sun Yat-
        sen; presentation was made by Ambassador Tani (3/5/44);
        leader of plan to construct memorial for those who have
        sacrificed lives for development of present-day China
        (June, 1941) (49:217)

Yamada, Takaoi -- Chief of Police, Lao-cha District Office, First
        Police Office, Shanghai (1943) (49:218)

Yamaguchi -- Chief, Coal Department (1944); on inspection tour of
        Mengchiang area, North China (52:261)

Yamaguchi, Hideo -- Chairman - Inspector, Flour Special Committee,
        National Trade Control General Association in Shanghai
        (1943) (49:218)

Yamaguchi, Jusuke -- Councillor, North China Communications Corpora-
        tion (1944)

Yamaguchi, Keizo -- Director, Central China Steamship Company,
        Shanghai (IDC 7262 1943)

Yamami, Kashiro -- Supervisor of ship repairing at Hongkong (51:260)

Yamamoto, Jikau -- Vice Minister of GEA; gave report on coal mines
        in North China (1944) (52:261)

Yamamoto, Kumaichi -- Vice Minister, GEA Ministry (2/4/44); inspected
        industries in China and Mongolia (4/22/44); requested by
        Ambassador Tani to attend meeting in Peiping, apparently,
        of 20 diplomats to consider Japan-China Mutual Alliance
        Pact, world situation, economic trend, etc. (11/28/43)
        (52:261)

Yamamoto, Nobuo -- President, North China Coal Sales Corporation,
        Peiping (1943) (52:261)

Yamamoto, Tokuichi -- Director, Shanghai Inland Steamship Stock
        Company (IDC 7262 1943)

Yamamoto, Yutaka -- 1st Secretary, Japanese Embassy, Nanking; Secretary,
        3rd Class, Ministry of GEA Affairs; concurrently Chief, Agri-
        culture & Forestry Section, China Affairs Bureau (5/10/44)

Yamamuro, Hikaru -- Resident of Peiping area; presented letter of com-
        mendation from Japanese Embassy, Nanking, for contribution
        to general education of Chinese youth; presentation made by
        Ambassador Tani (DIO 3/5/44) 52:261)

300
-251-

JAPANESE

Yamanaka -- Investigating Officer from GEA Ministry to Coordination Conference of Mongolia, Korea, North China, Manchukuo at Peiping (11/8/42) (52:261)

Yamanaka, Kiichi -- Director, Shanghai Municipality Labor & Business Social Union (1943) (49:218); Director, Shanghai Inland Steamship Stock Company and Central China Steamship Stock Company (IDC 7262 1943)

Yamanaka, Ryoki -- Chief, Engineering and other Bureaus, North China Communications Corporation (1944)

Yamanishi, Tsunero -- Vice President, North China Development Company (DIO 1941); Director, Hsing-chung Corporation, Peiping (1943) (52:261)

Yamaoka, Mannosuke -- Ex-Chief Director, Japan Asia Development Federation (11/4/42) (Shanghai, 49:218)

Yamaota, S. -- Chief Inspector, Police Department, Shanghai; in charge Police Precautional Affairs Section; member of mission to visit police departments in Japan, Manchukuo and North China (4/18/44) (49:218)

Yamasaki -- Member, Committee on Investigation of Resources & Materials, Shanghai (1943) (49:218)

Yamasaki, Seiichiro -- Honorary Director, Sino-Japanese Cultural Association, Wu-Ch'ang & Hankow Branch (1943)

Yamazake, Lt. Colonel Takuo -- Head, Information Board, South China (6/27/43)

Yamazaki, Shojun -- Member, Cultural Goodwill Party to China (5/3/43) (51:260)

Yamori, Sadakichi -- Director, Shanghai Realty Stock Company (IDC 7262 1943)

Yanagimachi, Sei -- Chief Adviser, Minister of Publicity, National Government of China; died (8/24/44 DIO)

Yanago, Shiozawa -- Represented Japan in conference with officials of National Government of China on return of foreign concessions (3/14/43) (Shanghai, 49:218)

Yano, Ninki -- Adviser, Sino-Japanese Cultural Association, Shanghai Branch (1943) (49:218)

Yano, Shoki (Seigi - Seiki) -- Japanese Consul-General, Shanghai (7/10/43); spoke, as Consul-General, re excellent attitude of Chinese people in Shanghai (3/3/43); Adviser, Committee on Resources and Material Control, Shanghai (1943); Adviser, Committee for Shanghai Citizens' Savings Movement (1943); President, Patriotic Association (7/21/44) (Shanghai, 49:218)

Yashima, Auzo -- Manager, Nippon Yusen Company, Shanghai (49:218)

Yasuda, Juzo -- Chief of Police, Hui-shan District Office, First Police Office, Shanghai (1943) (49:218)

Yatsuneri, Tomomichi -- Appointed to represent Japan on Commission for Abolition of Extraterritorial Rights (8/26/44)

Yohada, Shigata -- Doctor, Japanese Church in Suichow (12/3/44)

JAPANESE

Yoji, Hirota -- 1st Secretary, Embassy, Shanghai; 3rd Secretary,
GEA Ministry; concurrently Chief, Training Dept., General
Affairs Bureau (4/6/44) (49:218)

Yokohama, Hideichi -- Executive member, Oil and Grain Special Committee, National Trade Control General Association,
Shanghai (1943) (49:218)

Yokota -- Military officer; guest of Association of Teachers in
Amoy (1/18/44) (49:218)

Yokota, Eiji -- Director, Tangku Transportation Corporation, Tientsin
(1943) (52:261)

Yokota, Masao -- Chief, Office of Economics, Sino-Japanese Cultural
Association, Shanghai Branch (1943) (49:218)

Yokoyama, Lt. Colonel Hikozane (Hikozo?) -- Japanese Army Press
Bureau, Shanghai; "devoted Catholic"; Chief, General
Affairs Department, Peking; named regimental commander
in Manchuria (12/42) (49:219)

Yokoyama, Lieutenant General Isamu -- Commander, 11th Army (Hankow)
(8/17/44)

Yokoyama, Yaro -- Made contribution for education of Chinese youths,
Kowloon (51:260)

(Yomiuri) -- Reported on developments in East Asia since the war
(9/23/42)

Yonegaki -- Chief, Administration Section, Japanese Embassy, Peiping
(1/30/44) (52:261)

Yorozutani, Hisaemon -- Maritime transportation business man who
donated a naval communications vessel at Shanghai (2/22/44)
(49:219)

Yosano, S. -- 2nd Secretary, Japanese Embassy, Nanking (0-60)

Yoshida, Masaji -- Director, Mitsubishi Bank, Nanking; gave press
interview re policy of keeping price and currency under
complete central control (7/17/43)

Yoshida, Admiral Zengo -- Named Commander-in-Chief of Japanese Fleet
in China waters (2/6/43) (Shanghai, 49:219)

Yoshii -- North China representative to meeting of National Federation
of Total Mobilization (52:261)

Yoshihara, Michi -- Director, Greater Shanghai Gas Stock Company
(IDC 7262 1943)

Yoshikara, Uzuru -- Standing Director, Greater Shanghai Gas Corporation,
Ltd. (8/5/43) (49:219)

Yoshikawa, Chiemaru -- Vice Counselor, Shanghai Branch, Chung Yang
Savings and Reserve Bank (8/5/43) (49:219)

Yoshikawa, Seishichi -- Inspector, Shantung Mining Industrial Company
(8/5/43) (52:261)

Yoshioka, Hedio -- Director, Sino-Japanese Cultural Association,
Wu-Ch'ang & Hankow Branch (1943)

JAPANESE

Yoshitomi, Masaharu (Masayuki - Masao - Nagaumi) -- Head, Information
Board, Japanese Embassy, Nanking (8/3/42); spokesman for
Japanese Embassy, Nanking, at meeting to rally support
for Indian Independence Movement held in Nanking (3/1/43)

Yoshiya, Nobuko -- Japanese Literary Patriotic Society; visitor to
Peiping in exchange of literary men (10/5/43) (52:261)

Yukimura, Oba -- Japanese Technician, Central Public Health Association, Nanking (2/4/44)

Zuranuma, Baron -- Special mission to Nanking (9/8/42)

Reproduced from the Unclassified / Declassified Holdings of the National Archives

BURMESE

Oke, Tun -- Burmese Ambassador, Nanking (0-59)

FILIPINOS

Kalambical, Dr. Jakudo (Dalambaical, Dr. Getudo) -- Head, Philippine
Association, Shanghai (49:220)

Lee -- Representative of Philippine Association at round-table conference of Shanghai East Asia Society, where he spoke
(11/28/42) (49:220)

Uy, Conrado A. -- Active member of the Filipino Association; spoke
before Filipino Association in Shanghai (9/23/44) (49:220)

THAILANDERS

Batha -- Thailand Embassy, Commercial Attache (0-61)

Chalermatibaed, Dr. -- Director, Public Health Department, Public
Health Ministry; member, Thai Delegation to 3rd GEA
Medical Conference, Shanghai (4/25/44)

Lekmenaruji, Dr. -- Selected as representative to GEA Medical Conference in Shanghai previous to being replaced by
Dr. Manoh Somboon as representative (4/25/44)

Muang-Maen, Dr. Pin -- Superintendent, Siraj Hospital; head, Thai
Delegation to 3rd GEA Medical Conference, Shanghai
(4/25/44)

Somboon, Dr. Manoh -- Public Health Ministry; member, Thai Delegation to 3rd GEA Medical Conference, Shanghai (4/25/44)

Ten Sen -- Thai Commercial Attache, Shanghai (3/20/44) (49:220)

Tharami, Major General -- Thailand Military Attache, Nanking (0-61)

INDIANS

Arculli -- Noted Indian lawyer, Hongkong, "detained" by Japanese
(51:260)

Boonsaw, A. R. -- Businessman in Canton; starting newspaper,
KUNGCHENPAO, to be under guidance of Japanese military
authorities as well as provincial government (51:261)

Chang, Nanak -- Chairman, Shanghai Chapter, Indian Independence
League (6/20/44) (49:220)

Cor, Aji -- Elected head of a committee of Indian women in Hongkong;
to lecture for education of Indian women (8/19/44) (51:260)

Eh, B. Bobby Chied Fot -- Liaison Division, Shanghai Branch, Indian
Independence League (4/12/44) (49:220)

Everin -- President, New Branch Indian Association, Tientsin
(12/16/44) (52:262)

Jarlemarn -- Managing Director, Shanghai Chapter, Indian Independence

DECLASSIFIED
Authority NND853154

INDIANS

League; spoke at round-table conference of Shanghai East
Asia Society (11/28/42) (49:220)

Jee, Rutten -- Wine merchant, Hongkong; "detained" by Japanese
(51:260)

Khan, Abbas -- Formerly under government contract, Hongkong;
"detained" by Japanese (51:260)

Khan, Dr. D. Nader -- Former Indian dispatch clerk, Medical Department; Chairman, Indian Independence League, Hongkong
(1942) (51:261)

Krisha, (T. V.) -- Chairman, Indian Independence League, Hongkong
(7/3/44) (51:261)

Malayan, Colonel (Narayan?) -- Sent to Shanghai by the Indian
National Army in Rangoon; recall demanded on account of
bad conduct (6/22/44) (49:220)

Naidu, Dr. Deja (Nai Ding, Dr.?) -- Chief, Hongkong Branch, Indian
Independence League (8/11/43); spoke at celebration of
4th Provisional Government Day in Hongkong; chairman of
the meeting (5/22/44) (51:261)

Narain, Captain Bee -- Commandant, Azad Hing Fauj Training Camp,
Shanghai (6/20/44) (49:220)

Noga Nadan, Lt. Colonel -- Representative, Indian Independence
League, China (9/20/43)

Paglar, C. J. -- President, Eurasian Association (0-58)

Rahman, J. -- Secretary-General, Shanghai Chapter, Indian Independence League (5/22/44) (49:220)

Singh, Jamedar Jagat -- Indian singer of national song at ceremony
at Hongkong (3/24/44) (51:261)

Soon, Chet -- President, Shanghai Chapter, Indian Independence
League (7/26/43) (49:220)

FRENCH

Alad (Aladoshi) -- French Consul-General, Nanking (2/23/43)

Azonin, Father -- Representative of Holy See at Peiping; liaison
officer between Church and Nanking Government (52:262)

Beaumarchais, Jack George -- French Consulate General, Shanghai;
1st Consul, Taihoko, Taiwan (49:220)

Beauroy, H. -- French Consul, Nanking (0-59)

Blondeau, R. -- French Consul, Hankow (49:220)

Boisson, Robert de -- Counselor, French Embassy, Nanking; 1st Secretary, Peiping Embassy (52:262)

Briouvol, J. -- French Consul, Shanghai (49:220)

(Buffin), M. -- Former Counselor, French Embassy, Tokyo; took over
Consul-Generalship of France at Shanghai, replacing

-256-

FRENCH

M. (de Marguerite), presently French Charge d'Affaires, Peiping (9/29/44) (49:220)

Busient, Rev. John (Rusiet) -- Vicar of Tientsin (pro-Japanese); Catholic University of Peiping (52:262)

Cadol, A. -- French Consul, Pakhoi (0-59)

Chihel, (Father) -- Conducted ceremony at memorial rite in honor of Japanese and Nanking heroes in French Concession (10/21/42) (49:220) (Shanghai)

Cosme, Henri (Cozme, Cardin) -- French Ambassador to Nanking; returned to Nanking from Shanghai (2/20/43); conferred with Ambassador Tani of Japan and Foreign Minister Chu of Nanking on transfer of French Settlement to Nanking (7/21/43); having been Ambassador to China since 1939, named Ambassador to Tokyo (6/25/44) (49:221)

Crepin, M. P. -- French Consul, Kuenginine (0-59)

Dubosc, P. -- 2nd Secretary and Interpreter, French Embassy, Peiping (52:262)

Eguard -- French Consul, Canton (51:261)

La Ferte, Senectere (Commander de) -- French Embassy, Air Attache, Nanking (0-59)

Lipissier, Charles -- French Consul, Tientsin (52:262)

Lodovia, Charles -- Vichy Consul, Shanghai (49:221)

Margerie, Roland de (same as M.(de Marguerite)?) -- Consul-General of Vichy, Shanghai; arrived in Shanghai with Ambassador Cosme for conferences (7/6/43); took charge of French Embassy in Peiping as Charge d'Affaires at time of Ambassador Cosme's departure for Tokyo to assume duties there (6/25/44); replaced as Consul-General of France at Shanghai by M. (Buffin) (9/29/44) (49:221)

Rhein, D. -- French Consul, Nanking

Roy, F. -- French Consul, Amoy (49:221)

Segrander, Mrs. Earl -- Professional Artist, Nanking

Simon, Ph. -- French Consul, Longteheou and Nanking (0-59)

Stable, Colonel L. -- Chief of Police, French Concession, cooperating with Japanese, Shanghai (9/2/42) (49:221)

GERMANS

Altenburg, Dr. F. -- Counselor, German Embassy, Peiping (52:262)

Bohlurg, Dr. H. -- German Attache, Nanking (0-60)

Bracklo, Dr. E. -- German Consul-General, Hankow (49:221)

Cordt, F. -- German Press Attache, Nanking (0-60)

Doltze, Dr. F. -- Counselor, German Embassy, Nanking (0-59)

GERMANS

Drake -- Leader, German Community, Shanghai (1942-43) (49:221)

Erlewein -- Secretary, German Embassy, Nanking (O-59)

Fisher, M. (Fischer) -- German Consul-General, Shanghai (9/13/44)
(49:221)

Flicksteger, C. -- In German Broadcasting Station, Shanghai (1943)

Gipperich -- German Consul-General, Nanking (O-60)

Grothe -- German speaker in Shanghai commemoration of German war
dead (3/31/43) (49:221)

Hollingworth -- One of Chiefs, German Broadcasting Station, Shanghai
(1943)

Hoops, Dr. -- Secretary, German Embassy, Peiping (52:262)

Hornemann, F. -- Secretary, German Embassy, Peiping (52:262)

Kordt, Dr. Erich -- German M.P. Charge d'Affaires, Nanking; attended
luncheon given by Ambassador Woermann for members of
Shanghai office of Japanese Embassy (5/30/44) (49:221)

Ley, Dr. Horst -- Director of Ostatischer Lloyd, German Language
School; addressed meeting at opening ceremony of Azad Hind
Fauj Training Camp, Shanghai (6/20/44) (49:221)

Mehnert, Dr. Klaus -- Editor, "Twentieth Century" Magazine; formerly
Professor of History at Universities of California and
Hawaii; broadcasting in Shanghai on the Soviet Revolutio.
(9/17/44) (49:221)

Moy, Herbert -- One of Chiefs, German Broadcasting Station, Shanghai
(1943)

Rosenberg (Rosenbruch) -- Director, German East Asiatic Bank; visited China on inspection trip (11/16/43)

Stahlmernew, Dr. Heinrich (Stahlmer) -- German Ambassador to China
(1/19/42); succeeded by Ambassador Woermann (6/8/43)

Steger, C. Flick -- One of Chiefs, German Broadcasting Station,
Shanghai (1943)

Stoller, Dr. W. -- German Consul-General in charge of Embassy
Office, Shanghai (49:221)

Tapold, A. F. -- Vice President, German Residents' Association,
Hongkong (6/23/44) (51:262)

Vegh, Nicolas de -- German E.E. & M.P., Nanking (O-60)

Von Randow -- German Consul (Counselor in Embassy), Shanghai
(49:221)

Von Saucken, Dr. H. -- German Consul, Tsingtao (52:262) (O-63)

Walcott, Dr. Vincent -- Chief, German Economic Mission

Wiedemann, Dr. -- German Consul-General, Tientsin (52:262)

Woermann, Dr. Ernst (Woehrmen, Ernest) -- Arrived Nanking; greeted
by officials of National Government (8/3/43); presented

-258-

GERMANS

credentials to Premier Wang; expressed views on relation-
ship between Germany and Japan (8/5/43); German Ambassador
to China (11/16/43); gave luncheon in Shanghai for staff
members of Japanese Embassy, Shanghai (5/30/44)

Wolthat, Dr. Helmuth -- Head, German Economic Mission to Nanking
(11/16/43)

ITALIANS

Brigidi, Guiseppi -- Italian Consul, Tientsin; present at ceremony
transferring Italian Concession to National Government of
China (8/17/44) (52:262)

Brugnioni, Isolina -- Roman Catholic rescued from Chinese internment
by Japanese at Chengchow (10/18/44)

Calligaro, Adadio -- Roman Catholic rescued from Chinese internment
by Japanese at Chengchow (10/18/44)

Calzer, Luigi -- Roman Catholic rescued from Chinese internment by
Japanese at Chengchow (10/18/44)

Cocconcelli, Gisberto -- Roman Catholic rescued from Chinese internment by Japanese at Chengchow (10/18/44)

Danieli, Romano -- Roman Catholic rescued from Chinese internment
by Japanese at Chengchow (10/18/44)

Ferrajolo, R. -- 1st Secretary and Interpreter, Italian Embassy,
Nanking (0-60)

Fratti, Emilio -- Roman Catholic rescued from Chinese internment
by Japanese at Chengchow (10/18/44)

Grimolti, Giuseppina -- Roman Catholic rescued from Chinese internment by Japanese at Chengchow (10/18/44)

Mantiogneze, Tetta -- Roman Catholic rescued from Chinese internment
by Japanese at Chengchow (10/18/44)

Melito, Capt. Pagano de -- Italian Consul-General, Shanghai (49:221)

(Notchez, Francisco Maria Coliente) -- Italian Ambassador to China
(1/19/42)

Piazzini, Maria -- Roman Catholic rescued from Chinese internment
by Japanese at Chengchow (10/18/44)

Pinelli -- Italian Charge d'Affaires to China; returned to Shanghai;
reported on progress in foreign policy matters (6/18/44)
(49:222)

Principe, Colonel Omero -- Military Attache, Italian Embassy, Nanking
(0-60)

Prunas, Nob. P. -- 2nd Secretary, Italian Embassy, Nanking (0-60)

Rape, Dr. Raffael -- Judge; head of local Italians, Shanghai (4/4/44)
(49:222)

Ros, Guesse -- Italian Consular General, Canton; well-known authority
on customs and geography in Southwest China (2/28/44)
(51:262)

-259-

ITALIANS

Rossi, Guissopp -- Former Consul-General, reappointed as first Consul-General after Badaglio's betrayal; assumed post in Canton (7/11/44) (51:262)

Sansoni, Amedio -- Roman Catholic rescued from Chinese internment by Japanese at Chengchow (10/18/44)

Santa Maria, Father Alberto -- Head, Dominican Monastery, Hongkong (51:262)

Sartelli, Inesca -- Roman Catholic rescued from Chinese internment by Japanese at Chengchow (10/18/44)

Sironi, Maria -- Roman Catholic rescued from Chinese internment by Japanese at Chengchow (10/18/44)

Spinelli, P. P. (Same as Pinelli?) -- 1st Secretary, Italian Embassy, Nanking (O-60); newly appointed Italian Charge d'Affaires to China; arrived Nanking (6/25/44)

Stefennelli, F. -- Italian Consul, Tientsin (52:262)

Straneo, Nob. C. A. -- Counselor, Italian Embassy, Nanking (O-60)

Taliani -- Italian Ambassador to Nanking; signed document for transfer of International Settlement at Shanghai to Nanking Government (7/23/43)

Valentine, Father -- Roman Catholic rescued from Chinese internment by Japanese at Chengchow (10/18/44)

Von Winterfeld, S. R. -- German Commercial Attache, Nanking (O-60)

Zinbaldi, Emiglia -- Roman Catholic rescued from Chinese internment by Japanese at Chengchow (10/18/44)

PORTUGUESE

Das Chagas, J. F. -- Secretary - Interpreter, Portuguese Legation, Shanghai (49:222)

Lebre E Lima, Dr. Joao de -- Portuguese E.E. & M.P., Shanghai (49:222)

Litz Branquinho, Dr. A. C. de -- Secretary, Portuguese Legation, Shanghai (49:222)

Malo, J. A. Ribeiro de -- Portuguese Consul-General, Shanghai (49:222)

Monteiro, A. Sacramento -- Portuguese Consul, Canton (51:261)

Pripp, Malte J. H. -- 1st Secretary and 1st Vice Consul of Portugal, Shanghai (49:222)

Teikera, Commander Gabriel Maurice -- Source of report in HONGKONG NEWS that Portuguese-Japanese relations are cordial (6/30/44) (51:261)

Teixera, J. F. (Teixeira) -- Portuguese Assistant Consul, Shanghai (49:222)

Teixeira, Madame J. F. (Teixera) -- (Wife of Governor, Portuguese Consul?); participated in function for Macao Portuguese Red Cross Society to distribute clothing (6/10/44) (51:261)

-260-

PORTUGUESE

Testera (Teixeira), (Tesera) -- Governor-General of Macao; visited
        Canton to confer with leaders of Japan and China (4/18/43);
        host to members of Foreign Diplomatic Corps on Portugal's
        National Day, October 5, in Macao (10/15/44) (51:261)

RUSSIANS

Bitner -- USSR Consul-General, Tientsin (52:262)

Kilmenko, N. S. -- In Russian Broadcasting Station, Shanghai (1943)

OTHER EUROPEANS

Bagulesco, G. -- Rumanian Envoy, Nanking (0-61)

Borne, Major K. M. -- Resigned as Commissioner of Police, Shanghai
        (2/21/42) (49:222)

Bosselmand, A. -- Swedish Consul, Nanking (0-61)

Duvais, Nicholas -- Hungarian Minister to Japan; will also serve as
        Minister to Nanking (DIO 4/1/42)

Eckford, Vyvyan R. H. -- Swedish Consul, Tehefu (0-61)

Engstrom, Ralph -- Swedish Consul, Tientsin (52:262)

Feyeff -- Bulgarian Minister to Nanking (6/8/43)

Fontanel, Emick -- Swiss Charge d'Affaires to Consul-General, Shanghai
        (49:222)

Gerede, Husrev -- Turkish Minister, Nanking (0-61)

Graham, Dr. David C. -- Professor of Ethnology, Southwestern Federated
        Universities; reported, after tour thru interior, many
        people facing starvation (12/2/42)

(Heidel, J.) -- Spoke on behalf of Afghanistan at round-table confer-
        ence of Shanghai East Asia Society (11/28/42) (49:222)

Hoffmeister, C. August -- Swiss Consul, Canton (51:261)

Hollingworth, R. -- In German Broadcasting Station, Shanghai (1943)
        (See GERMANS - Hollingworth)

Kappeler, Gaston -- Chancellor, Swiss Legation, Shanghai (49:222)

Kruper, Georg Henrik -- Finnish Consul, Tehefu

Kunger, Professor -- From Taiwan to supervise Hongkong Library (51:261)

Lester, David -- Pro-Japanese announcer from Shanghai Station (4/42)
        (49:222)

Lundh, Gustaf H. -- 1st Chancellor, Swedish Legation, Shanghai (49:222)

MacIntosh, Allan -- Radio Commentator (DIO 5/31/44)

Maedonado, Alvaro (same as Maldonado?) -- Spanish Minister, Nanking
        (0-61)

OTHER EUROPEANS

Maldonado, Alvaro (same as Maedonado?) -- Spanish Ambassador to
China - Shanghai; announced transfer of Spanish Embassy
in Peking to Nanking (8/6/43)

Mar -- Czech expert on rubber; long connected with Toko Bata Company
in India

Matali, Fato -- Deputy Commissioner of Police; appointed Commissioner
of Police, Shanghai (2/21/42) (49:222)

Moy, Herbert -- In German Broadcasting Station, Shanghai (1943)
(See GERMANS - Moy, Herbert)

Perry, Bishop James Joseph -- Work praised by Bishop Rakawa (8/23/44)

Peyeff, Vango -- Bulgarian Minister, Nanking (0-59)

Piers -- Bulgarian Minister to China - Nanking

Schilling, W. -- Swiss Vice Consul, Shanghai (49:222)

Schubert, Armin -- Finnish Consul, Canton (51:262)

Schuette, Johan Gottfried -- Finnish Consul, Tsingtao (52:262)

See, William -- President, French (John) University; appointed
secretary-general of the new athletic association of
Shanghai (11/27/42) (49:222)

Siebert, Dr. F. -- Finnish Consul-General, Canton (51:262)

Stiner, S. K. -- Swiss Vice Consul, Shanghai (49:222)

Weaver, Frederick (Wheel, Frederick) -- News commentator: "What
Every American Should Know" (DIO 7/24/44)

Will, Eduard -- Finnish Consul, Tientsin (52:262)

Zanin, Archbishop M. -- Apostolic Administrator, Peiping (52:262)

Zulauf, Erich -- Honorary Chancellor, Swiss Consulate, Canton (51:262)

欠落頁（256 〜 262）があります。
恐れ入りますが、奥付の前に差し込んでください。

おうちょうめいせいけんじんめいろく
汪兆銘政権人名録 ―OSS（米諜報機関）1944 年作成―

発　　　行	2019 年 5 月 31 日　初版第 1 刷

編集・解題	三 輪 宗 弘
発 行 者	川 角 功 成
発 行 所	有限会社 クロスカルチャー出版
	〒 101-0064　東京都千代田区神田猿楽町 2-7-6
	TEL 03〈5577〉6707　　　FAX 03〈5577〉6708
印刷・製本	モリモト印刷株式会社

ISBN 978-4-908823-52-7　C0522（全 1 巻）
2019 Printed in Japan